Captain America
and the American Journey,
1940–2022

ALSO OF INTEREST
AND FROM MCFARLAND

We Are Gotham: *Finding American Society
in the Television Series*
(Richard A. Hall, Maria Antonieta Reyes
and Josh Plock, 2022)

Captain America and the American Journey, 1940–2022

Richard A. Hall

McFarland & Company, Inc., Publishers
Jefferson, North Carolina

LIBRARY OF CONGRESS CATALOGUING-IN-PUBLICATION DATA

Names: Hall, Richard A., 1969– author.
Title: Captain America and the American journey, 1940–2022 / Richard A. Hall.
Description: Jefferson, North Carolina : McFarland & Company, Inc., Publishers, 2024. | Includes bibliographical references and index.
Identifiers: LCCN 2023059558 | ISBN 9781476688749 (paperback : acid free paper) ∞ ISBN 9781476651361 (ebook)
Subjects: LCSH: Captain America (Fictitious character) | National characteristics, American, in comics. | National characteristics, American, in motion pictures. | Superheroes. | Patriotism. | BISAC: LITERARY CRITICISM / Comics & Graphic Novels | HISTORY / United States / General | LCGFT: Comics criticism. | Film criticism.
Classification: LCC PN6728.C35 H35 2024 | DDC 741.5/973—dc23/eng/20240102
LC record available at https://lccn.loc.gov/2023059558

BRITISH LIBRARY CATALOGUING DATA ARE AVAILABLE

ISBN (print) 978-1-4766-8874-9
ISBN (ebook) 978-1-4766-5136-1

© 2024 Richard A. Hall. All rights reserved

No part of this book may be reproduced or transmitted in any form or by any means, electronic or mechanical, including photocopying or recording, or by any information storage and retrieval system, without permission in writing from the publisher.

Front cover images © 2024 Digital Vision/Shutterstock

Printed in the United States of America

McFarland & Company, Inc., Publishers
  Box 611, Jefferson, North Carolina 28640
    www.mcfarlandpub.com

*For Joe Simon and Jack Kirby ...
and Future Generations of Americans*

Table of Contents

Preface: My Journey with Cap   1

Introduction: "I can do this all day!"   5

CHAPTER 1. Sentinel of Liberty:
    1940s America and the Birth of Captain America   21

CHAPTER 2. Commie Smasher!
    Captain America in the Age of Consensus, the 1950s   46

CHAPTER 3. Man Out of Time:
    Captain America and a Society in Transition, the 1960s   69

CHAPTER 4. Man Without a Country:
    Captain America and a Nation in Crisis, the 1970s   90

CHAPTER 5. *Captain America No More* (Again):
    Captain America in the Age of Reagan, the 1980s   115

CHAPTER 6. *Heroes Reborn*:
    Captain America, the 1990s, and a New World Order   140

CHAPTER 7. *Civil War* and *The Death of Captain America*:
    America in the 2000s   164

CHAPTER 8. From *Two Americas* to "Hail Hydra!":
    Captain America and a Divided Nation in the 2010s
    and Beyond   192

CHAPTER 9. The Star-Spangled Man with a Plan:
    Steve Rogers and the Marvel Cinematic Universe   216

CHAPTER 10. The Legacy of the Shield:
    Truth, *The Falcon and the Winter Soldier*, and Race
    in Captain America Comics   232

Conclusion: "We Can Do Better!"	239
Chapter Notes	243
Bibliography	255
Index	263

Preface
My Journey with Cap

First, full disclosure, this isn't exactly a book "about" Captain America ... except when it is. Instead, it is the story of America as it progressed through the decades of Captain America's existence, from the late 1930s to the early 2020s, and how Cap both reflected and influenced that progress. It just happens that this story coincides with the lifetime of the comic book superhero Captain America, cemented in the 21st-century American zeitgeist in the physical form of actor Chris Evans (who is so eerily dead-on perfect as Cap that it seems like the comic book has come to life). Since just before American involvement in World War II, Captain America has traveled the decades of history with us, the writers and artists behind his many adventures literally living history as it unfolds. This history comes alive to us in the present through the window of Captain America comic books, cartoons, and movies. That is the story this book attempts to tell. Having said that....

In the spring of 2007, I found myself in quite the quandary. I had just passed my written and oral exams for my PhD in history at Auburn University, and I had no idea what I would focus my dissertation on (something most grad students have established long before that point). After my orals, my major professor took me across the street for a celebratory drink. Over the bar, CNN was playing, reporting on the recent announcement that Marvel Comics was going to kill off long-running superhero Captain America. The company had decided that the star-spangled hero of World War II was no longer representative of the 21st century, post–9/11, George W. Bush America. He would be replaced with the Winter Soldier, a former Soviet/Hydra assassin who was, in fact, Captain America's old World War II sidekick, Bucky Barnes. As my conversation with my professor had reached an awkward silence, I brought up the breaking news event. Only vaguely familiar with Captain America (and comic books in general), my professor expressed surprise that such a complex social commentary would be presented in a children's medium. I then pointed out that comic books had not been "just for kids" for many decades, and that superhero comics (especially Captain America comics) had covered topical social commentary almost since the very beginning. He looked at me and said something that would forever change my life: "I think you just found your dissertation topic."

I was not big into comics as a kid. Of the couple dozen comic books I owned, most were "funny books" (Bugs Bunny, Richie Rich, Woody Woodpecker, etc.) or *Star Wars* (my childhood obsession); only a handful were superheroes (a couple of Spider-Mans, a Hulk, a Superman, and a couple of Batmans). It wouldn't be until 1988, just after I graduated high school, that a friend of mine who was in the army reintroduced me to the medium. After my best friend and I poked fun at him for being a grown man and soldier reading "kiddy books," he challenged us to read a couple issues of *Uncanny X-Men*. Once read, our collective response was "You got any more?" We were hooked! We became part of the historic collectors' bubble of the late 1980s/early '90s, amassing a joint collection of over a thousand comics in just a five-year period. Aside from Batman, I had no interest in DC Comics. I loved Marvel! My comics of preference were the solo titles: Spider-Man, Hulk, Iron Man, Daredevil, and Captain America.

By 1994, as a divorced soldier, I could no longer afford my weekly doses of comic book adventures, and by the end of the decade, I was a remarried father of five (so, still unable to afford comics). When I took on the challenge of writing about Cap for my dissertation, I had no idea how I was going to find the necessary primary documents (the comics themselves) from World War II to 9/11. Luckily, right around that same time, Marvel had released full digital copies of all the Cap comics from 1964 to that year on a very affordable CD-ROM. Then a colleague of mine, a university librarian, was able to find a European nonprofit that had been working diligently to collect and preserve Golden Age comics digitally. When my friend contacted them, they were able to provide us with a CD-ROM of all Cap issues from 1940 to 1953. I now had every single issue of Cap's main title at my fingertips (something far easier today with apps such as Marvel Unlimited). Over the next four years I became one of very few people in the world to have read every single issue of *Captain America* ever published. The Star-Spangled Avenger became very much a part of me.

In 2011, just a month after I defended my dissertation (and nearly a month before graduation), Marvel Studios released *Captain America: The First Avenger*. Though it was not as big a box office hit as the two prior *Iron Man* films, most comics experts agreed: they got Cap right. I left the theater with a different thought: *I* got it right! The first accurate live-action depiction of Captain America (and Steve Rogers) portrayed the hero *exactly* as I had interpreted him from the printed page. My major professor viewed the film (being a newly minted Cap expert himself), and conveyed to me that, assuming the filmmakers got the material right, it was clear that I had accurately interpreted and analyzed comics' "Sentinel of Liberty." I could now face graduation—and my impending career as an academic—with confidence in my analytical and writing skills. If anyone had ever told me I could get a PhD in comic book superheroes, I likely wouldn't have waited decades to get my degree. A lifetime of absorbing, analyzing, and discussing popular culture had actually paid off. Pop culture studies are actually very important. A study of popular culture can bring about a clearer understanding of American society at any given point in time; the better we understand ourselves, the easier we can find consensus and begin to solve society's big problems.

In the years since, I have published, presented, and taught courses on various media of popular culture (including comics). Now here I am, back with Cap again. I am honored that McFarland has allowed me to tell Cap's tale, from his origins in World War II to the present, on the page and on the screen. As Cap frequently states, he does not represent America as it is. He represents the *ideal* of what America can and should aspire to be. Like America, Cap's adventures are not without their flaws, often expressing prejudices and prevalent attitudes of each respective period. The writers behind Cap have been people of their times, and it is *their* experiences in the America of their respective eras that come through on the page, making Captain America comics a valuable primary source for historical analysis of America since World War II: the good, the bad, and the all-too-often ugly. Captain America holds a mirror up to American society over the decades, forcing us to see ourselves and constantly reminding us, "We can do better!" Today, more than perhaps ever before, it is vitally important that we go back and examine our pop culture icons within the overall context of the history that produced them, if for no other reason than to better understand that history. Americans' biggest problem when it comes to our history—as I'm sure many before me have stated—is how we remember it.

Introduction

"I can do this all day!"

Over the last few decades, many comic book historians and enthusiasts have pointed out that superheroes are our modern-day mythology. As the ancient Greeks had Zeus and Hercules, so people of the modern world have Superman and Batman. Through these four-color tales of heroism, audiences are exposed to noble examples that all may aspire to (along with action-packed stories of over-the-top supervillains out to take over the world). Since 1938, superheroes have grown up alongside the country that has devoured their adventures since day one. Through them, we can see ourselves. Through them we see who we have been, who we are, and who we hope to be. This book seeks to explore the American experience from 1941 to 2021—its political, social, and cultural history; the evolution of the comic book industry; and the first eighty years of the Sentinel of Liberty—through the prism of Captain America in comic books, on television, and in feature films. It is as much a primer for modern U.S. history as it is a beginner's guide to examining the cultural icon that is Captain America.

Why Captain America?

Though present in the superhero comic book medium since 1941, more or less, Captain America has really only recently become a larger part of the American zeitgeist, due entirely to the brilliant performance of actor Chris Evans in the wildly popular films of the Marvel Cinematic Universe, from his debut in *Captain America: The First Avenger* in 2011 to his "final" (or, as many fans hope, only his most recent) appearance in *Avengers: Endgame* in 2019. Prior to that, many Americans still had only a vague awareness of who Captain America was (i.e., red, white, and blue costume, shield, "A" on his forehead), due to some exposure to the character as a child, either through a comic book or some appearance in Saturday morning cartoons featuring other Marvel characters. However, a closer examination of the character's history shows that he has always been at the center of one primary argument: does this representation of the "American Ideal" support liberalism or conservatism? The truth, as with all art, lies mostly in the eyes of the beholder.

Creative teams over the decades have, of course, possessed their own perspectives, promoting their own versions of the American ideal, but much of the interpretation lies with the reader (as will be discussed later). Overall, Cap represents the best of American ideals, the ones that both ends of the political spectrum claim to revere: patriotism (not to be confused with nationalism, which is a darker, racist, xenophobic extreme of "love of country"); a belief in freedom for *all* life-forms; the ability to live up to one's potential and seek out one's own destiny; and being a symbol for such beliefs to the rest of the world (and, in the case of Marvel Comics, the entire multiverse). Like the superhero genre itself, Cap was a product of the World War II era, a time when America itself was viewed by the rest of the world as a potential superhero. With the massive sociopolitical divides in 21st-century America, there has never been a more important time to give Captain America a proper extensive examination, allowing the character to do what such characters do best, provide us with a reflection of ourselves: who we are, who we aspire to be, and who we fear to become.

Birth of the Superhero

As America entered the 1940s, with the Great Depression nearing its end, a new children's entertainment medium had been born: comic books. Originally simply reprinted collections of newspaper comic strips, by the mid–1930s, original material began to emerge. In 1938, a new genre was introduced: superheroes. *Action Comics* #1 introduced Superman, created by Jerry Siegel and Joe Shuster. The massive popularity of this new phenomenon soon led to the creation of equally iconic heroes: Batman, created by Bill Finger and Bob Kane, and Captain Marvel (better known today as "Shazam"), created by C.C. Beck and Bill Parker. By that time, World War II raged in both Europe and the Pacific. Originally, America did their best to stay out of the growing conflicts, with most Americans still remembering the more than 100,000 American boys that had been lost in the last European war (World War I) just 20 years earlier. However, as the massive economic—and potential military—might of the U.S. remained on the sidelines, fascism—and particularly the Nazi menace and their leader, Adolf Hitler—posed a serious threat to freedom around the world.

Introduction

In December 1940, then, burgeoning comics publisher Timely Comics produced their own addition to the new superhero craze. Captain America was the brainchild of writer Joe Simon and legendary artist Jack Kirby. Debuting in *Captain America Comics* #1 (the first superhero to debut in a comic bearing the character's name as the title), this red-white-and-blue Sentinel of Liberty was introduced to the world by slugging Adolf Hitler himself in the jaw. The previous year, a Superman comic strip had portrayed the Man of Steel delivering Hitler and Soviet leader Josef Stalin to the League of Nations to answer for their alleged crimes against humanity, but otherwise, comic book superheroes had yet to address unfolding events in the real world. Initially controversial for its obvious support for American involvement in the war, *Captain America Comics* quickly became Timely's best-selling book.

Die-hard comics enthusiasts may note that *Captain America Comics* #1 had a cover date of March 1941, not December 1940. This brings up an important issue concerning the dating of Golden and Silver Age comic books. While comics today have a cover date consistent with the date of publication, that was not always the case. Originally, comic books were sold on street corner newsstands (wooden booths frequently found on most big city street corners offering the most recent offerings of newspapers, magazines, and comics). When newsstands received comic books, they were supposed to keep the issues on their stands for a period of roughly three months. The "cover date," then, was the date on which newsstand proprietors could remove that particular issue from their shelves. As a result, determining the actual publication date of comic books from the 1930s, '40s, '50s, '60s, and even into the 1970s can be problematic. The first issue of *Captain America*, however, first hit newsstands on December 20, 1940, nearly a year before the Japanese attack on Pearl Harbor, Hawaii, which would finally draw the United States into World War II.

Who Is Captain America?

Though a handful of characters have worn the mantle of Captain America over the decades—later chapters will look at the tenures of John Walker, Isaiah Bradley, Bucky Barnes, Sam Wilson, and Peggy Carter (technically "Captain Carter" rather than "Captain America")—the person most people think of when they hear "Captain America" is Steve Rogers, a scrawny but fiercely patriotic young white man who desperately wanted to serve his country against the Nazis, Italians, and Japanese in World War II. Designated "4-F" (or physically unfit for military service), Rogers agrees to take part in the government's top-secret "Super Soldier" program, which involves being given an experimental serum. Though successful, the serum's creator is assassinated shortly after Rogers's transformation, making him the only recipient of the perfected formula. Rogers then dons the mantle of "Captain America" to fight America's enemies at home and abroad.[1] It is important to note, however, that although Captain America was meant to embody American values, he actually embodied what the majority of white Americans at the time believed those values to be, despite what the harsh reality of 1940s America truly embodied for non-white Americans. Ironically, with his (scientifically altered) perfect physique, blond hair and blue eyes, Steve Rogers became the very embodiment of Nietzsche's *ubermensch* ("superman"), which was the Nazi ideal.

Though popular during and shortly after World War II, *Captain America Comics* fell due to rapidly declining superhero comics sales by 1950. Briefly returning in 1953 as "Captain America: Commie Smasher," the hero returned for good in 1964, becoming a staple of the burgeoning Marvel Universe of comic book superheroes. Though never as big a seller as fellow Golden Age heroes such as Superman or Batman, or fellow Marvel hero titles *The Amazing Spider-Man* or *The Uncanny X-Men*, the monthly adventures of Captain America have appeared consistently since his 1960s return. Largely considered a "B-list" hero in the Marvel pantheon over the decades, his introduction into the Marvel Cinematic Universe with the 2011 film *Captain America: The First Avenger* once more made the Star-Spangled Avenger a household name. His modern incarnation being a product of the turbulent 1960s, this hero who claims to stand for the "American ideal" has often been questioned as to his political leanings. Is Cap a representative of the political left or the right? The answer is complex, debatable and, ultimately, unimportant.

What Are Captain America's Powers?

According to *The Official Handbook of the Marvel Universe, Master Edition*, Captain America's powers include "peak human" intelligence, strength, speed, stamina, durability, agility, and reflexes; "mastery of hand-to-hand combat, various martial arts"; "combat strategy, survival skills, acrobatic skills, military strategy, piloting, demolitions"; and *no* "superhuman physical powers."[2] This, of course, was written before Steve Rogers received "new" or "reborn" bodies (several times) over the course of the decades that followed. It would be challenging at this point to determine how much (if any) of Steve Rogers's body in the 21st century resembles his original body from World War II. If, however, one assumes that the source of his power remains the original Super Soldier Serum, then its effects on whatever body he inhabits remain the same.

This is probably the most controversial issue concerning Captain America. Some point to the above-given official description that the Super Soldier Serum simply raised Steve Rogers to the peak of theoretically possible human strength, speed, stamina, and agility. Others say that his abilities exceed what is possible for the human body, essentially giving him *super* strength, speed, stamina, and agility (though, admittedly, not as "super" as that of, say, Spider-Man). The comics have shown repeatedly over the decades that Cap's physical abilities are greater than those of Daredevil or Punisher (heroes that, like Cap, are not "super"), but not greater than Spider-Man or Ghost Rider (both of whom have abilities tied to nonhuman entities). Grab any two Cap experts and each will probably argue the opposite of the other regarding the level of Captain America's abilities. The truth is quite simple, but not exactly satisfying: his physical abilities are exactly what the writer at the time needs them to be.

Cap's Shield

The one thing that makes Captain America stand out among other heroes is his weapon of choice: his shield. The iconic circular shield bears a white star on a blue field at its center, surrounded by three rings: red, white, and red. It is aerodynamically perfect for throwing as a disc, but—as pointed out by Spider-Man in the 2016 MCU film *Captain America: Civil War*—it utterly defies the laws of physics (though it is fair to point out that it defies the *established* laws of physics…). Though the shield works as a defensive implement (and is certainly meant to symbolize protection over aggression), Cap has frequently used it as an offensive weapon. While his original, badge-shaped shield introduced in *Captain America Comics* #1 (March 1941) has been established as simply a standard metal shield, the more iconic circular shield has been suggested as being made of either vibranium, adamantium, or a vibranium/adamantium alloy (in the MCU it is established as vibranium in 2011's *Captain America: The First Avenger*). No matter which is accurate, one thing is clear: it is (mostly) indestructible.

Captain America: Conservative, Liberal, or Moderate?

Decades before the internet, chatrooms, or social media, fans of superhero comic books had one primary method of communication: the letters pages of monthly magazines. Letters to the editors of comic books were published at the end of each month's issue. Most letters consisted of either praise or criticism for each respective title. In the pages of *Captain America*, some of these letters actually became ongoing arguments between readers with differing opinions on Cap's political leanings. Liberal readers who disliked Cap's actions viewed him as conservative; those who agreed with his actions viewed him as liberal (and vice versa). In real time, a reader might have to wait months to see a response from other readers to their letters. With the digital preservation of these older issues, researchers can read each month's letters and following responses much as they would an online discussion (making it quite a surreal experience when realizing the actual time that would pass between comment and response).

The answer to the question is actually ... that there is no clear answer. Since Captain America (whether Rogers, Bradley, Walker, Barnes, Wilson, or Carter) is a fictional character, written by a constantly revolving door of writers over a span of decades, Cap's actions and utterances are coming from whoever is writing the title that month. However, since Cap is an ongoing commercial product, writers who sign on to continue the adventure are somewhat bound to keeping the character as much in line with who he has been before. The personal politics of any particular writer may be conveyed exactly on the page, or slightly muted, or not at all. From the overall run of the character, however, some consistent characteristics have become clear:

- Captain America (no matter who is wearing the uniform) is *patriotic*—not to be confused with *nationalistic* (the difference will be discussed in an upcoming chapter)—with a firm belief in the general American principles of liberty and freedom for all. While each fringe of the political spectrum considers themselves patriotic, they differ wildly on what those principles mean.
- Captain America is unfailingly brave, honest, and dependable (no real political affiliation there).
- Captain America believes that the United States is part of the larger global community, possessing certain responsibilities due to their "superpower" status (in the 21st century, globalism has become an increasingly liberal ideal).
- Captain America believes in maintaining a strong defensive posture against potential threats (for decades, this has been an area of policy most embraced by conservatives).
- In the MCU, Cap has been frequently portrayed as being opposed to foul language and believing in only one God (these

are characteristics most closely associated with evangelical conservative Christians).
- Captain America is strongly opposed to prejudice and bigotry toward anyone, being respectful of moral/ethical relativism (considered a largely liberal trait).

Taking these aspects of the character into consideration, it is safe to conclude that Captain America is apolitical, eschewing any dedication to any one political outlook or philosophy (so, in the real world, he would likely be considered moderate, though most analyses of the character more commonly identify him as left of center). As the character himself has frequently repeated over the decades, Captain America does not stand for any particular political party or philosophy, but rather for the "American ideal."

What Is the "American Ideal"?

Ask any random 100 Americans to define the American ideal, one will likely receive 100 different answers, "ideal" being a completely subjective term. What does it mean, then, as regards the character of Captain America? Though a product of World War II, much of what has come to define Captain America was developed during the Cold War (c. 1947–1992). This nearly half century of political and economic struggle between the capitalist United States and the communist Union of Soviet Socialist Republics kept the world on the brink of nuclear annihilation for decades.

The U.S. viewed itself as the hero of the Cold War story: the valiant defender of freedom, liberty, and democracy in the world (including its role as a stalwart of capitalism). Even the iconic 1950s television program *The Adventures of Superman* changed its titular hero's tagline from its original stand for "truth and justice" to the more pro–American "truth, justice, *and the American way.*" Though kept purposely vague over the decades, Captain America's "American ideal" essentially consists of these Cold War ideas of what America *should* stand for: freedom, liberty, truth, justice, morality, and standing up to bullies, autocrats, and those who would suppress the rights of others.

Since his reintroduction in 1964, in the early years of the Marvel superhero comics, Cap has repeatedly been held up by other heroes (and villains) as the moral center of the Marvel Universe, a standard by which all other characters judge themselves. He has long been considered the de facto leader of the Avengers (even though he was not one of the original organizers of the team). This is, of course, partially due to his tactical genius and his leadership skills, but it is also due largely to the high regard in which he is held by all the other Marvel heroes. Cap's honesty and integrity are unquestionable, unbending, and incorruptible (until they aren't, but that's a longer story for a later chapter). As such, when Captain America refers to representing the American ideal, he is referring largely to this long-held image that America has had of itself and has attempted to portray to the world (called an ideal because America has frequently fallen short of living up to these goals, and—considering how high a bar those ideals are—likely always will). For much of the character's history, he was primarily a comic book-only character (a black-and-white movie serial, some cartoons, and two made-for-TV movies being his only forays beyond the four-color page). That would change and bring the character more into the overall American (and global) zeitgeist with the rise of Marvel Studios and the Marvel Cinematic Universe.

The MCU and the Physical Embodiment of Captain America

Since the 2011 film *Captain America: The First Avenger*, audiences around the world have equated Captain America with the actor who has portrayed Steve Rogers on film: Chris Evans. Over seven films from 2011 to 2019, Evans masterfully walked the political tightrope in his performance, embracing all of the above-mentioned characteristics, giving physical form to a hero that all Americans can take pride in supporting. Though his initial cinematic outing was not as successful as the two previous *Iron Man* films, Evans's Cap would play a significant role in making Marvel's *The Avengers* (2012) the most successful film of all time (to that date). Throughout the 2010s, Evans's Captain America would become a symbol of all that is best in America, and an admonition against all that is worst.

The first live-action portrayal of Captain America was in the fifteen-chapter movie serial released by Republic Pictures in 1944 (during World War II). While the costume remained loyal to the comic book source material, the similarities ended there. Instead of wannabe soldier Steve Rogers, Cap was District Attorney Grant Gardner (Dick Purcell). Instead of a shield, Cap carried a pistol; trusty sidekick Bucky Barnes is nowhere to be seen. Fans of the comic book were likely disappointed by these changes, and fans of the serial inspired to buy the comic were equally likely disappointed. Republic Pictures frequently made significant changes to source material when translating them to the big screen, much to the irritation of the parent companies, creators, and fans.

Cap would not be seen in live action again until 1979, when CBS aired two made-for-television movies starring Reb Brown as Steve Rogers/Captain America and produced by Universal Television. In this incarnation, however, Steve Rogers is a (roughly) thirty-year-old former U.S. Marine whose father was a career spy dubbed "Captain America" by his coworkers due to his patriotic fervor (though it is not explained, the reference intended by the nickname as the comic book superhero does not exist in this fictional reality). Steve is given a similar Super Soldier Serum as his comic book counterpart, a similar costume (with motorcycle helmet replacing his traditional cowl), a motorcycle, and—this time—an indestructible shield (though limited special effects technology result in its being little more than an inflatable Frisbee). If it had been picked up as a series, Cap would then travel the country fighting bad guys he encountered (very similar in structure to the following decade's *Knight Rider*). With the considerable small screen success of superheroes Wonder Woman and the Incredible Hulk, Cap was considered a safe gamble, but met with low ratings. A second film was broadcast that same year, *Captain America II: Death Too Soon*, but it had even lower ratings and the project was canceled at that point.

A *Captain America* feature film was set to be released in 1990. Much closer to the source material than either previous project, Steve Rogers/Captain America was played by Matt Salinger. The massive success of the previous year's *Batman* by Tim Burton suggested that superhero movies were once more a good gamble. Though this latest Cap project was consistent in both style and accuracy with similar superhero films of the period, the movie was never released theatrically, eventually being aired on cable television and released on home video in 1992. When two superhero films—*Spawn* and *Batman & Robin*—both performed disastrously in 1997, it appeared as if the days of comic book superheroes on the big screen might be over. That low point, however, would not last long.

When Marvel Enterprises declared bankruptcy in late 1996, the company was forced to sell off screen rights to some of their catalog of characters just to stay afloat. In 1998, New Line Cinema released *Blade*, starring Wesley Snipes and based on the Marvel Comics vampire hunter. The movie was a massive success, spawning two sequels. This trilogy would be followed by two even more successful big-budget superhero trilogies based on Marvel properties: *X-Men* by 20th Century–Fox, and *Spider-Man* from Sony Pictures. Throughout the early 2000s, other Marvel characters would make their big screen debuts: Hulk, Daredevil, Elektra, Ghost Rider, and the Fantastic Four (all to varying degrees of moderate success). Regardless of how successful these Marvel films were, however, die-hard comic book fans had one universal complaint: their digression from the source material. It was at that point that Marvel Enterprises concluded that the best people to produce Marvel superhero films were at Marvel itself, and Marvel Studios was born.

When it was announced that Chris Evans would be playing the Star-Spangled Avenger on the big screen, many fans were skeptical (much as they had been when Michael Keaton was announced as the big screen's first Batman two decades earlier). Evans had recently portrayed another Marvel character, Johnny Storm/Human Torch, in the feature film *Fantastic Four* (2005) and its sequel *Fantastic Four: Rise of the Silver Surfer* (2007), both from 20th Century–Fox. Though Evans's portrayal of the Torch was seen by many to be the highlight of both films, the character was such a stark (pun intended) contrast from Steve Rogers that many fans doubted Evans's acting ability could stretch so much (after all, he wasn't Mister Fantastic!). As with Keaton in 1989, fans' fears were allayed when *Captain America: The First Avenger* was released in July 2011. More than a decade later, true Marvel fans cannot fathom anyone else ever doing the character justice. In 2021, the MCU officially passed the mantle of Captain America to Sam Wilson/the Falcon, played by Anthony Mackie, in the Disney+ series *The Falcon and the Winter Soldier*. Though this transfer had been made in the comics back in 2015, seeing a Black man wearing the stars and stripes and bearing Cap's shield in live action elicited some negative responses, once more bringing the issue of race into the world of Captain America, as it had consistently done in the comics going all the way back to the magazine's beginnings.[3]

Cap's Crew

Unlike most comic book superheroes, Captain America comics do not have regularly occurring "normal" characters. Superman has his parents, Lois Lane, and the employees of *The Daily Planet*. Spider-Man has his Aunt May, best friend Norman Osborn, and girlfriend/wife Mary Jane. Even Batman has his butler Alfred, tech support Lucius Fox, and ally Police Commissioner Gordon. Cap—while occasionally having interactions with normal people for a few issues at a time—is surrounded by *other heroes* as his supporting cast. Those that will appear repeatedly throughout our tour of Captain America over the decades include:

- Bucky Barnes—Cap's World War II sidekick and later enemy-turned-ally, the Winter Soldier
- Sam Wilson/the Falcon—Cap's partner beginning in the late 1960s who later dons the mantle of Captain America
- Sharon Carter/Agent 13—Agent of SHIELD and longtime romantic interest

- Nick Fury—Director of SHIELD
- The Avengers—Earth's mightiest heroes, the team Cap has led since the 1960s with a revolving door of fellow superheroes that frequently includes Iron Man, Thor, Black Widow, Hawkeye, Vision, Scarlet Witch, the Wasp, and She-Hulk

This difference from most superheroes is due mostly to the fact that Steve Rogers is *always* Captain America (even when others officially carry the title). He has no private life or alter ego to maintain. This is a fairly common trope among Marvel heroes, particularly among members of the Avengers.

Captain America and Race

Race in America has been a recurring theme in the pages of *Captain America* since its World War II beginnings. After the Japanese attack on the U.S. naval base at Pearl Harbor, Hawaii, on December 7, 1941, the Japanese were frequently portrayed in both war propaganda and American popular culture in extremely racist ways. In the pages of *Captain America Comics*, the Japanese were usually shown with either buck teeth or fangs, yellow skin, and cartoonishly slanted eyes. Though this can be explained, to a degree, by the fact that the Japanese were our enemy and viewed as a monstrous threat to the world, depictions of Black Americans were similarly racist, featuring thick lips, wide eyes, broken, uneducated English, and usually being portrayed as cowardly. This was not, of course, limited to the pages of *Captain America*, as all comic books of the period were portraying these groups in similar fashion (the sole exception being the short-lived *All-Negro Comics*, the brainchild of distinguished Black journalist Orrin Evans, to be discussed later).

In 1953, Atlas Comics—the new name for the previous Timely Comics—attempted to bring back their superhero line of comics (namely the original Human Torch, Sub-Mariner, and Captain America). Though cut off after only a few appearances, the brief return of Captain America saw the Sentinel of Liberty aggressively fighting Communists around the world (the Cold War with the Soviet Union having begun just a few years earlier). In these issues, Asian allies, namely Japan and South Korea, were portrayed "normally," with no negative stereotypes or racist tropes (other than their skin color being a deep yellow, but this was more an aspect of the difficulty in portraying different skin tones within the very limited confines of the four-color medium). However, enemy Asians—North Koreans, communist Vietnamese, and Chinese—still had racially stereotypical villainous appearances.

In 1969, in the pages of *Captain America* #117, readers were introduced to Sam Wilson, aka the Falcon, the first Black *American* superhero (comics' first *Black* superhero being Black Panther, the African King T'Challa, introduced in *Fantastic Four* #52 three years earlier). Falcon soon became Cap's partner, even sharing the title of the monthly comic throughout most of the 1970s. During that decade and into the next, the comics focused on the issues facing Black Americans in the wake of the civil rights movement of the two previous decades, specifically issues of continued prejudice and the economic plight of the inner cities. An early 1970s storyline by writer Steve Englehart retconned the 1950s "Commie Smasher" Cap as a fake, designed by the government to hide the fact that the original Captain America had been missing since falling into the ice in the waning days of World War II. ("Retcon" is short for "retroactive continuity.") This 1950s Cap reflected the racist conformity of his times, reacting violently to this Black superhero (the Falcon) when awakened from his government-induced suspended animation after 20 years. Later, an early 1980s storyline by J.M. DeMatteis saw the Red Skull pointing to Cap's respect for diversity and inclusion as liberal weakness. In the mid-1980s, the villainous Watchdogs were introduced in the comics, pitting a new Captain America and his own Black partner against a radical violent racist organization.

In 2003, Marvel published the miniseries *Truth: Red, White, and Black* by the creative team of writer Robert Morales and artist Kyle Baker. In this story, readers see that in the wake of Captain America's disappearance during World War II, the government sought to recreate the Super Soldier Serum that had given Cap his enhanced powers. They chose to use Black soldiers as guinea pigs, knowing that many—and possibly all—would die due to the untried experimental serum. This was meant to be an analogy of the infamous Tuskegee experiments of the 1930s, where Southern Black men were used to experiment with the long-term effects of syphilis. In the book, the one surviving participant—Isaiah Bradley—was then hidden from the public by the government and allowed to suffer long-term effects of the serum on his own, aware that the country would not embrace a Black Captain America.

Captain America in the 21st Century

While the Captain America comic has consistently addressed political issues since its inception in December 1940, the book has been particularly focused on the increasing divide in American political culture in the first two decades of the 21st century. In the wake of the 9/11 terrorist attacks of 2001, the book could have followed a "go get 'em!" format, but instead focused on the ideas of what terrorism is, and how one man's terrorist is another's hero. The *Civil War* storyline of 2006–2007 examined the arguments over government oversight versus personal liberty, culminating with the death of Steve Rogers/Captain America, the World War II icon seemingly inconsistent with post–9/11 America. Rogers's successor to the shield, Bucky Barnes/the Winter Soldier, faced the growing issue of "two Americas" in 2010, presaging the massive political divides that would increasingly split the nation over the decade that followed. In 2015, Sam Wilson/the Falcon became the first (official) Black Captain America, to considerable racist response (as he would be again when the story was repeated in the MCU in 2021), and in 2017, controversy arose again when Marvel Comics suggested that Steve Rogers (and therefore Captain America) had secretly been a fascist Hydra agent from the very beginning, exploring the danger of America's deadliest enemy coming from within our own ranks.

The Star-Spangled Avenger: Who We Are and Who We Could Be

These issues and many more will be explored in this decade-by-decade analysis of Captain America and his place in the unfolding drama of American history since World War II. Chapter 1 will examine the origins of Captain America as the country emerges from the Great Depression and dives into the maelstrom of World War II, where Captain America is introduced as a Sentinel of Liberty against global fascism, underscoring the fine line between patriotism and nationalism. Chapter 2 enters the Cold War and Cap's attempt at being a "Commie Smasher" during the height of McCarthyism in America. Chapter 3 delves into the turbulent 1960s as Steve Rogers experiences being a "man out of time," emerging from 20 years in the ice to see a deeply divided America. Chapter 4 examines the 1970s, seeing Captain America as Nomad, the Man Without a Country in the wake of the Watergate crisis that some mark as the beginning of America's current political divide. Chapter 5 looks at the Reagan Era of the 1980s, when during a period of rampant patriotism, Captain America finds himself replaced with someone more in line with the conservative agenda of the iconic president. Chapter 6 examines Cap's place in the post–Cold War 1990s, when both the comics and the country asked the question, "In a world with no more enemies, what do heroes do?" Chapter 7 examines the confusing early 2000s, when the unification through fear after 9/11 fades into the deep political divides of the decade to follow.

Chapter 8 looks closely at the 2010s, when America has two presidents who each in their own way further divide the nation, and Steve Rogers passes the shield on to Sam Wilson, America's first Black Cap serving under America's first Black president. Chapter 9 focuses on Captain America in live action from 1943 to 2019, examining in detail the big and small screen representations of Cap briefly mentioned above. Chapter 10 focuses on the legacy of race in the print and film projects of Captain America in the 21st century, from *Truth* to *The Falcon and the Winter Soldier*. Finally, in conclusion, an overall review of Captain America will remind us that, in this divided and troubled country, we can do better.

As to sources used, to include every appearance of Captain America in Timely/Atlas/Marvel Comics would require a book three times this size. Even including *The Avengers*—where Cap has spent most of that title's run as its de facto leader—requires too much space and time. As such, this book will focus on the regularly produced *Captain America* title from its inception during World War II to the present. As Cap takes a more prominent role among the Marvel hierarchy in the 21st century, that will expand to include the standalone *Truth* graphic novel mentioned earlier, some tie-ins to the overall *Civil War* event, and, of course, the films over the decades. That, I believe, provides ample fodder for presenting how Captain America has both reflected and attempted to influence events in the real world since the end of the Great Depression.

Returning to the question of "Why Captain America?," Cap is perhaps the most relatable of the popular comic book superheroes. He is not an omnipotent alien like Superman. He is not a gadget-laden billionaire like Batman or Iron Man. He is not a god like Thor or Wonder Woman. He is not the result of mutation like Spider-Man or the X-Men. Captain America is one of us. He is a simple American citizen who just wants to serve. Yes, Steve Rogers receives physical enhancements from the Super Soldier Serum, but later Cap Sam Wilson (who possesses no physical enhancements) proves that anyone with the heart and dedication can serve as Captain America. Throughout America's turbulent history since its rise as a superpower after World War II, popular culture has often been used as a mirror, reflecting back to us who we are and who we could be. Captain America has been one such example.

Loving and serving one's country does not entail blind obedience to one political party, ideology, or politician. America is, has always been, and was always meant to be a melting pot of diversity: respecting diverse races and ethnicities, diverse religions, diverse genders, diverse abilities, and diverse *ideas*. Particularly over the last century, diversity has been America's primary strength, and at a time when both sides of the political spectrum seek to ostracize and silence one or more "others," the *United*

States has never needed Captain America more. While many have been driven to throwing up their hands and exasperatedly shouting, "I give up on America!" Captain America never gives up. He never gives in to popular pressure or fads. He never disrespects or disparages. He never accepts defeat. He consistently promotes the American ideal of liberty and justice for *all*. To paraphrase the hero himself, Captain America can do this all day![4]

CHAPTER 1

Sentinel of Liberty

1940s America and the Birth of Captain America

World War II was a turning point for America and the world, setting the stage for the modern era, and establishing the United States as the world's premier superpower. It required the citizens of every country to show their full devotion to their governments and armies, often blurring the line between patriotism and a more jingoistic nationalism. As America initially remained on the sidelines of the conflict, the burgeoning industry of superhero comic books introduced yet another member to their already booming cadre of brightly clad superpowered protagonists: Captain America. Though all of the superheroes would soon take up the cause of America's war against fascism, Superman, Batman, and Captain Marvel (the original male "SHAZAM!" Captain Marvel, not the female Captain of 21st-century MCU fame) initially made little to no reference to the overseas conflict until America herself joined the fray. Captain America was different. Cap was introduced to the world in December 1940—nearly a year before Pearl Harbor—punching out German Fuhrer Adolf Hitler right across the jaw! While many Americans still strongly opposed entry into the war, Captain America (and his creators) already understood the need for the United States to become a Sentinel of Liberty.

From War to Depression

World War I had been devastating for Europe and, by proxy, the rest of the world. For the United States, however, it had been a mixed bag. On the one hand, America lost more than 115,000 young men in its roughly 18-month involvement in the conflict. On the other hand, it emerged from the war and entered the 1920s as perhaps the strongest economy left standing in the world. As business boomed and three million boys returned home, the country shifted from a wartime to peacetime economy. Young women with recently codified political freedoms and young men who had seen the horrors of war and the fragility of life came together, intent on enjoying every moment life had to offer. This led to the youth of America being dubbed "the Lost Generation," seemingly more concerned with partying than with planning for the future.

Back-to-back (to back) conservative Republican presidential administrations emphasized a laissez-faire approach, essentially allowing businesses to conduct their affairs—and Wall Street—unchecked by unwanted government oversight. Americans trusted entrepreneurs such as Henry Ford, who revolutionized production by applying the assembly line method to automobile manufacturing and paying his workers a heretofore unheard-of $5 a day (as opposed to the standard $1 a day found in most factories at the time). Cars were more affordable, giving the average American feelings of wealth they had never experienced before, and they liked it. The extension of credit gave many access to more money than they actually had, or that many would ever be able to pay back. Over the course of the Roaring Twenties, the overextension of credit, the overproduction of goods, and the overvaluation of corporate stocks created a snowball effect that came crashing down in the fall of 1929, ushering in the Great Depression.

By 1932, unemployment in the United States had reached 25 percent. Among racial/ethnic minorities, those numbers rose to as high as 50 percent. This was felt most throughout America's burgeoning urban regions, as over the previous generation, more and more Americans had abandoned rural life in favor of opportunities in the big city. This meant that the self-sufficiency consistent with rural life was no longer an option. Instead of owning your home and land, you now rented smaller accommodations. Food and milk had to be purchased rather than grown.

These factors—exacerbated by increasing unemployment—led to a massive increase in poverty and therefore crime. The increased crime required increased police resources, requiring increased local taxes, adding still more to the burden of the urban poor. As an urban America was a relatively new phenomenon, few experts knew how to deal with the ever-increasing challenges. The failure of President Herbert Hoover to address the ever-declining economy led to an easy political victory in 1932 for his Democrat opponent, Franklin Delano Roosevelt. During the decade of the 1930s, more than at any other point in their history, Americans needed some form of release, some escape from the worries and stresses of Depression life. This need would be met by what we have come to call "popular culture."

American Popular Culture

Popular culture has had many varied definitions over the years, but an overall consensus defines it as cultural recreations and entertainments that appeal to the masses. Previously, cultural respites had fallen into two major categories: high culture and low culture (or, more derisively, high-brow and low-brow). High culture—generally enjoyed by the upper classes—consisted of things like the theater, opera, golf, tennis, and other distractions still associated largely with the wealthier classes. Low culture, therefore, was usually those entertainments enjoyed by the lower classes. These would primarily consist of activities associated with local bars (drinking games, mass sing-alongs, etc.) or sports of a more physical variety (such as the fairly new sports of football and baseball). Popular culture became a sort of melding of the two, with entertainments that were enjoyed by people across the socioeconomic spectrum.

Throughout the 1920s, movies had become such a medium of mass appeal. Americans became enthralled with the new phenomenon of "movie stars" like Charlie Chaplin and Gloria Swanson. In 1928, the recently formed Walt Disney Studios released the animated short film "Steamboat Willie," featuring its new star, Mickey Mouse. Coming into the 1930s, the movie industry—finally finding its home in Hollywood, California—entered a golden age, producing films that remain classics well into the 21st century: the Universal "Monster" films such as *Dracula*, *Frankenstein*, and arguably the greatest example of the genre, *The Bride of Frankenstein*; the madcap comedies of the Marx Brothers, Groucho, Harpo, and Chico, which kept audiences laughing through the country's darkest hours; the collected films of the young Shirley Temple, her adorable youthful exuberance a welcome distraction from the harsh realities outside the theater; and two of the most beloved and classic films in movie history, *Gone with the Wind* and *The Wizard of Oz*.

Jazz music—growing primarily out of New Orleans and the New York City borough of Harlem—spread beyond its African American roots to become the most popular form of music across the racial/ethnic spectrum, becoming, in essence, the soundtrack of the decade. The famous jazz cornetist Louis Armstrong became one of America's most beloved musicians. The Black origins of jazz represented just one part of what became known as the Harlem Renaissance, a cultural explosion of music, art, and literature stemming from the Black communities of the larger cities and embraced by Americans of all races and ethnicities. The poetry and prose of Langston Hughes became a mouthpiece for the Black experience in America. While only a few Americans at this time had access to phonographs (record players), most Americans could enjoy jazz as well as other types of music and entertainments through the medium of radio. Most Americans had access to a radio, which provided hours of various entertainments for free (minus, of course, the cost of the radio) and gave advertisers quick and easy access to American hearts and minds.

Advertising became another area of business that helped define the 1920s and beyond. The art of manipulation as applied on a societal scale, advertising convinced American consumers that they needed specific products.[1] Rather than simply going to the grocery store for a box of cereal, Americans were convinced to seek out specific brands of cereal, and to stay loyal to that brand. This would soon be applied to everything from corn flakes to Cracker Jacks, from cars to toasters, and from candy to comic books. During the worst of the Depression, advertising would be even more important as businesses had to work harder than ever for their share of Americans' dwindling consumer dollars. What made advertising even more important was the fact that, due to the already widespread global economic depression, the American economy shifted from a "producer" economy (dependent on what one country sells to other countries) to a "consumer" economy (primarily dependent on what consumers at home spend within the national economy). American businesses, more than ever before, became reliant on American dollars. Beginning in the 1940s—and expanding over the following decades—a key sales demographic for American products would be children.

For children oblivious to how the country had changed in the last few years, a new medium emerged to capture their young hearts, minds, and dimes: the comic book. Originating in 1933 as essentially reprints of previously published newspaper comic strips, by 1935 the burgeoning industry was seeking out original material to satisfy their growing numbers of dedicated customers.[2] In 1938, National Allied Publications—the leading comic book seller of the day and the future "DC Comics"—paid roughly $130 to the creative team of Jerry Siegel and Joe Shuster for their unique idea: a human-looking alien from another planet who was faster than a speeding bullet, more powerful than a locomotive, and able to leap tall buildings in a single bound. Superman, the world's first "superhero."[3] With his blue circus-strongman tights, flowing red cape, red boots, and red underwear (for some reason on the outside of his clothes, and held up by a yellow belt), and a shield symbol emblazoned with an "S" on his chest, Superman was like nothing Americans had ever seen before. Appearing in the first issue of *Action Comics*, Superman quickly became modern pop culture's first true phenomenon, on a par with what Mickey Mouse, Elvis, and *Star Wars* would become over succeeding decades.

Comic book superheroes immediately captured the imaginations of American children, and as success breeds imitation, a flood of spandex-clad demigods soon followed the Man of Steel to compete for their market share. Batman, the gadget-armed billionaire vigilante avenging the murders of his parents (a nightmare scenario with which any young child could sympathize); the original Captain Marvel, the young boy who by simply uttering the word "SHAZAM!" could transform into a powerful adult superhero (a fantasy that any young child could imagine with delight); the original Human Torch, an android whose body could burst into flames, making him lighter than air, giving him flight (mixing the superhero genre with the simultaneously burgeoning science fiction craze); and the Sub-Mariner, the half-human/half–Atlantean aquatic superhero (appealing to all those children whose most dreaded words from their mothers were "get out of the pool"). The latter two debuted in *Marvel Comics* #1, published by National Allied competitor Timely Comics.

Timely Comics was a division of the larger Timely Magazine Publications, owned by Martin Goodman. Like other publishers at the time, Goodman sought to cash in on these cheap novelty magazines for children. No one at the time could have ever imagined or even dreamed that 80 years later a 10-cent issue of *Action Comics* #1 would be valued at over $3.2 million. At the time, comic books were mere trinkets, sold cheaply to children, to be consumed and discarded much like the candies kids would buy alongside their favorite superhero mags. As far as anyone knew at the time, superheroes were a fad that would come and go like later such fads as the hula hoop, pet rocks, and the Rubik's Cube. Such prognostications, however, would prove very wrong. The comic book superhero was here to stay.

From Depression to War

America was not the only country struggling financially in the 1930s. As one of the instigators of World War I, Germany's defeat would leave them even more financially devastated. Hit with massive reparations to the war's victors—Great Britain, France, and, to a lesser degree, Italy—the German economy was completely devastated, with many Germans resorting to burning cash, as the currency was more valuable for fueling the family fire than as a medium of exchange for goods and services. With national morale as low as the national economy, and little faith in the new Weimar Republic government of the new President Von Hindenburg, a significant portion of German people turned to the new National Socialist German Workers Party. Though the party's name appeared to be in line with many socialist/communist movements and parties emerging during the period, the NSGWP—or "Nazis"—were neither socialist nor communist. They were fascist, and their leader, the charismatic Adolf Hitler, promised that supporting the Nazis would not only bring about a resurgence of the German economy, but would also take Germany on to global domination. While most Germans were more concerned with feeding their families than world conquest, the message still resonated.

By the time the Nazis began their push to take over the German government in 1933, on the other side of the world Japan was already beginning its own war of conquest in the Pacific and East Asia, invading neighboring China in 1931. Both were preceded in the 1920s by Italy's own fascist dictator, Benito Mussolini, beginning his own aggressive campaigns in the Balkans and Ethiopia. Autocracy was on the march around the world, and the vast majority of Americans did not care. The economic hardships of the Depression and the memory of losing more than 100,000 boys in the last global conflict left most Americans in a very isolationist mood. Groups like the America First Committee, supported by such celebrities as Henry Ford and the pilot Charles Lindbergh, pressured political officials—particularly President Franklin Roosevelt—to steer the country clear of global disputes, focusing instead on getting America and Americans back on their feet. Roosevelt, however, in constant contact with British prime minister Winston Churchill, understood that if America did not help defeat Hitler and his ilk "over there," then, sooner or later, she would be forced to deal with them "over here."

Once Hitler took firm control of Germany in 1935, one of the largest groups adversely affected by the new Nazi regime was the German Jewish population. Though only making up a small percentage of the overall German population, German Jews made up a considerably larger percentage of the German wealthy class. Add to that the fact that most of the German delegation who agreed to the Versailles Peace Treaty that ended World War I and, essentially, rang the death knell of the German economy were Germans of Jewish descent, and it was not difficult for the Nazis to promote and gain support for a racist agenda targeting German (and overall European) Jews as the primary cause of the nation's woes. Hitler and his SS rounded up members of the Jewish community, confiscating their wealth and belongings (no matter how much or little they actually had), confining them first to "ghettos" and later to labor and concentration camps throughout Europe.

Beginning with the 1938 annexation of neighboring Austria and the apparent appeasement by England and France (seemingly sold on Germany's argument that their only goal was to place all German peoples under one flag), Hitler was emboldened to continue with his conquest of Europe and eventually the world. By 1940, having formed an Axis alliance with Mussolini's Italy—and nonaggression pacts with the communist Soviet

Chapter 1. Sentinel of Liberty

Union and fellow-fascist Francisco Franco's Spain—Hitler was well on his way to fortifying his "Fortress Europa" under German rule. With France quickly overrun and the Soviets voluntarily sidelined, Great Britain stood as the last stalwart of democracy meeting the fascist threat in Europe, while in the Pacific, Japan continued its aggression with no serious threat to its ambitions, and even supported largely by American oil and steel purchased by Emperor Hirohito's government, further expanding their considerable naval and air forces.

As large numbers of European Jews sought escape from the Nazification of Europe, their desired destination was the United States, the so-called land of opportunity. They would soon discover that America was no more welcoming than Nazi Germany. While most of America's race history is often portrayed as black and white (literally), many races, ethnicities, and nationalities have suffered systemic and societal racism throughout U.S. history: American Indians, peoples of Hispanic origin, and even white European groups like the Irish. Among these mistreated and alienated groups throughout the country's history were people of Jewish descent. Even in 1945, long after Americans had been made aware of the atrocities against Jews at the hands of the Nazis, the newly crowned Miss America, Jewish American Bess Meyerson, faced such hatred and vitriol that her regular duties as Miss America were dramatically reduced to keep her out of the public eye.

One area where Jewish Americans flourished in the 1930s and '40s, however, was the burgeoning comic book industry. Viewed as a joke and sub-standard by many publishers, writers, and artists, comic book companies desperately needed talent to produce their cheap but profitable fare. As such, comic books became fresh ground for talented Jewish American writers and artists not only to find work, but ultimately to become American icons. Two such gentlemen worked for the new Timely Comics: Joe Simon and Jack Kirby. Up-and-coming writer Simon met his legendary creative partner Kirby (born Jacob Kurtzberg) while the former was working as editor-in-chief at Fox Publications, where Kirby was working as an artist. Simon soon dragooned Kirby to come work for Simon's other employer, Martin Goodman's Timely Comics.[4] It was there that these two young men would become pop culture legends.

In the first summer of the European war, Great Britain was on the ropes, constantly bombarded by Germany's air force, the Luftwaffe. While President Roosevelt had committed the United States to a policy of "neutrality"—refusing to officially take a side in the conflict, leaving the door open for American businesses to profit from war supplies to both sides—by June 1940, it was clear to FDR that continuing this policy could spell certain doom for Britain and eventually the world. With American popular support for the war still a good eighteen months away, Roosevelt took a politically slicker approach: changing America's official policy from "neutral" to "non-belligerent" (taking a side, but still refusing to fight). That year, Roosevelt ran for a third term as president (still constitutionally allowed at that point). Until 1940, only two other U.S. presidents had ever run for a third term: Ulysses S. Grant in 1880 (failing even to regain the Republican nomination), and FDR's own distant relative, Teddy Roosevelt, in 1912 (running as a third-party candidate, finishing an impressive second in the national election). Franklin Roosevelt would make history by winning a third term (and later a fourth before his death in 1945) with an incredible 449 (out of a possible 531) electoral votes and 55 percent of the popular vote.[5]

After winning his landslide reelection, FDR was no longer bound by political polls (certain his third term would be his last). On December 29, 1940, in one of his famous "Fireside Chats" (radio addresses in which he spoke directly to the American people), Roosevelt called for America to push forward with a massive rearmament campaign to assist the British, declaring that "We must be the great arsenal of democracy."[6] Just nine days prior, on December 20, the children of America had already been introduced to a new superhero, promoting just such a policy by boldly punching out the German autocrat Hitler on the cover of his own self-titled comic book: *Captain America Comics* #1.[7]

In his memoirs of his decades in comics, Joe Simon said of creating Cap: "Even though the United States wasn't in the war, we read the newspapers. We knew what was happening in Europe, and we were outraged by the Nazis—totally outraged. [Kirby and I] thought it was a good time for a patriotic hero."[8]

This obvious pro-war propaganda, however, led to massive backlash from American isolationist organizations such as the America First Committee and pro–Nazi organizations such as the German American Bund, going so far as to threaten Simon and Kirby personally for their pro-war messages.[9]

In the year following Cap's debut, a series of events would push the United States onto an inevitable course toward war. With the U.S. Congress increasingly disinclined to extend credit to the financially weak Great Britain, President Roosevelt signed the Lend-Lease Act, allowing him, as commander in chief of the U.S. military, to "loan" much-needed military supplies to Britain. He sold this idea to Congress and the American people with the analogy that if your neighbor's house is on fire and he has no hose with which to fight it, you would loan your own to prevent the fire from spreading to your own house.[10] Soon after, Germany invaded the Soviet Union, bringing the communist power into the war on the side of the capitalist countries. In the Pacific, Japan invaded the small country of Vietnam, leading the U.S. to cut off future oil and steel sales in response to the empire's continued aggression (thus leading the island nation to consider military retaliation on the sleeping giant that was the United States).

America's sideline activities would come to a halt after the events of December 7, 1941. On that clear Sunday morning, in three waves of attack over the span of about an hour, Japanese planes repeatedly bombed the U.S. naval port of Pearl Harbor, Hawaii. As a result of the attack, 2,403 Americans lost their lives, and 19 ships and roughly 150 planes were destroyed. Americans were no longer isolationist. On December 8, President Roosevelt asked for and quickly received a declaration of war on Japan. On December 10, Japan invaded Hong Kong (a British possession), giving the already beleaguered United Kingdom a second front on which to fight. Finally, on December 11, the Axis powers of Germany and Italy (by this time allied with Japan) declared war on the United States, truly making these hitherto separate conflicts a world war.

The U.S. military that went to fight World War II was still a racially segregated institution (as it had been since Black soldiers were first allowed to serve during the Civil War of 80 years earlier). This war, however, would be the first American war to see the commission of Black officers, due largely to the growing number of Black men attending and graduating from college in the decades since World War I. The most famous of these would be the Tuskegee Airmen, pilots trained at the segregated Tuskegee Army Airfield in Alabama. The 332nd Fighter Group of these Black pilots proved to be the only fighter group of any military in the war to never lose a bomber under their protection. The importance of Black soldiers and officers in the war would be a major factor in postwar President Harry S Truman's decision to put together the President's Commission on Civil Rights and, in 1948, finally desegregate the U.S. military. As has always been the case concerning progress for Americans of African descent, there would be considerable white backlash.

Race in the 1940s

At the beginning of the decade, as Europe and the Pacific were consumed by war, Americans at home enjoyed the 1940 World's Fair in New York City. While comic books opened the festivities with "Superman Day" celebrating America's new icon, much of the focus of the fair was on America's racial and ethnic diversity. The final week of the war was dubbed Negro Week, featuring the unveiling of sculptor Augusta Savage's statue *Lift Every Voice and Sing*, which portrayed a harp, the strings of which were Black men and women singing; in front of the harp was a kneeling Black man holding a bar with musical notes showing on it. The Fair closed with a speech by civil rights legend Dr. W.E.B. Du Bois, the first Black man to graduate from Harvard University with a PhD in history. These public displays, however, did little to solve or salve the continuing problem of deeply embedded systemic and social racism throughout the country.

While most Americans today associate the civil rights movement for Black Americans with the 1950s and '60s under the leadership of Dr. Martin Luther King, Jr., there had been a long and consistent struggle for Black rights going all the way back to Emancipation in 1865. In 1940, civil rights icon A. Philip Randolph planned a civil rights march on Washington, D.C. (similar to the iconic march in 1963 culminating with King's "I Have a Dream" speech, a march where Randolph was also present). He was asked to postpone the march by President Franklin D. Roosevelt, aware that the coming storm of war was going to require national solidarity and not wanting to rock the boat with the kind of division a public discussion of racism would definitely promote. Roosevelt promised to address racism from his own position of power once American involvement in the war became inevitable. Randolph conceded, going on to help promote the "Double-V" campaign throughout the war: promoting victory against fascism abroad and racism at home.

Roosevelt kept his promise, signing Executive Order 8802 in June 1941 (six months before America entered the war). This EO made it illegal to practice racial discrimination in the workplace for any companies holding government contracts (this would be particularly powerful once America entered the war, with nearly every company from automakers and radio makers to comic book and bubble gum companies holding government contracts). Roosevelt's record on race was not completely good, however, as he also signed Executive Order 9066 in February 1942, rounding up Japanese Americans (both naturalized and natural born) and placing them in internment camps for the duration of the war. This was done in the wake of the fear that Japanese Americans might have worked as spies to assist Japan in their attack on Pearl Harbor (there were a handful of such cases, but hardly enough to justify such a widespread policy). These citizens— nisei (natural born Americans of Japanese descent) and issei (immigrants from Japan who had become U.S. citizens)—had their personal finances, homes, and business confiscated by the government, most of which would never be returned. An issue of the comic book *Four Favorites* showed a scene where a Japanese American issei father is explaining to his nisei son why they are being detained:

> The country that your mother and I came from is at war with America. And we must stay here [in an internment camp] in order that we may help America

to win! ... And if you're a good American, you'll stay here and not go home....
There are bad Japanese who want to harm America.... That's why we've been
sent here, to keep us away from bad Japanese, so we can help America win the
war!"[11]

The artwork depicting this Japanese American family is devoid of the usual racial stereotypes, portraying them instead as very human (no doubt attempting to explain to their young readers the complex issue they had doubtless heard adults talking about over the previous holidays).

Popular culture would be slower to respond than the Roosevelt and Truman administrations. Though Jackie Robinson became the first Black player in Major League Baseball in 1947, Black representation across other media of pop culture remained much as it had been before the war. Even the comic book industry resisted change. In 1947, Orrin Cromwell Evans, a Black journalist known historically for being the first Black reporter for mainstream white publications, came up with the idea to publish a comic book *by* Black creators and distributed primarily *for* a Black audience. The anthology comic *All-Negro Comics* #1 featured original characters such as detective Ace Harlem and the superhero Lion Man by creators including editor Bill Driscoll and writers/artists John Terrell and George Evans, Jr. (Orrin's brother). The first—and only—issue was immediately met with racist resistance, with Evans's newsprint provider suddenly and miraculously unable to provide paper for any future issues (despite paper rations having been over for two years). It would be nearly 20 years before Black Americans would be able to see themselves in mainstream comic books to any respectable degree.

Patriotism vs. Nationalism

French president Charles de Gaulle said, "Patriotism is when love of your own people comes first; nationalism, when hate for people other than your own comes first."[12] While a bit oversimplified, the interpretation does not fall far from reality. At their cores, the terms "patriotism" and "nationalism" can be best defined as "I love my country" and "My country is the *best* country," respectively. Since the early 20th century, however, nationalism has taken on a darker connotation. Due to his American-flag-based costume motif and red, white, and blue shield, a word often associated with Captain America is patriotism. Over the course of the last century—and at an increasing rate in recent years—this term has frequently been confused with or intermixed with the term nationalism. Though both terms do, essentially, express a love of country, their connotations within real-world politics have been dramatically altered by groups choosing to use them for their own political benefit. Considering that Cap, perhaps more so than any popular superhero in comic book history, exhibits the ideals of patriotism and love of country, it is important to note the distinctions in the way the terms are used, particularly in 21st-century American politics, to better understand the character, and for audiences of Captain America in various media to know more clearly what it is that the character stands for.

In his essay, "In Defense of a Reasonable Patriotism," William A. Galston, the Ezra K. Zilkha Chair and Senior Fellow of Governance Studies at the Brookings Institute, defined patriotism as "a special attachment to a particular political community, although not necessarily to its existing form of government." He defines nationalism as "the fusion, actual or aspirational, between shared ethnicity and state sovereignty.... The nation-state, then, is a community [in] which an ethnic group is politically dominant and sets the terms of communal life."[13] These definitions are more in line with how the two terms are widely used in political forums across the United States in the 2020s. Though both exhibit a love of country, they have come to do so from dramatically different political perspectives.

White supremacist groups frequently use the term "white nationalism," specifically identifying a goal for a country run specifically by Americans of white/European descent and fundamentalist Protestant evangelical Christian ideology (the "fusion ... between shared ethnicity and state sovereignty" defined above[14]). Some conservative politicians in the 2022 election cycle even embraced the term "Christian nationalism" (likely to avoid any racist overtones, yet leaving the initial intent/message of the movement unchanged). During World War II—the time of Captain America's creation—Germany's Adolf Hitler promoted just such a version of love of country, pushing for Aryan (i.e., white/Germanic) political domination of not only Germany, but the world. This fact, on its own, is evidence enough that Captain America is not, in any way, a nationalist hero.

The term that perhaps best describes Captain America, then, is Galston's definition of patriotism. This is supported by every creative team behind Captain America comic books and films since 1940. Captain America does love the United States of America, but he has frequently pointed out the nation's many flaws and shortcomings and has on numerous occasions disagreed with its current government. Cap firmly stands for liberty and justice for *all*, not just for those who look like him, believe like him, and support him. For decades following World War II, this was the standing definition of patriotism, whereas nationalism frequently stood for the idea of "My country, right or wrong" (with no clear intention, definition, or desire to change what was wrong). Geographer Jason Dittmer, however, does point out that "Captain America ... was written as a

Chapter 1. Sentinel of Liberty

super-soldier created by the U.S. government and later sees himself as the living embodiment of the American Dream."[15]

Cap is definitely a symbol of national identity (hard to wear the stars and stripes and not be), and from an academic standpoint and definition of nationalist that is certainly true, and there is a great deal to explore from that perspective. The modern, more popularly recognized connotation of the term nationalist, however, is definitely a stark contrast to all that Captain America has come to represent.

This is not to say that Americans who identify as nationalist are inherently racist or Nazi. Many who utilize the word are truly unaware of the negative connotations it has accumulated over decades of misuse by nefarious groups and politicians. Most who use the word, in fact, would argue that nationalism *is* patriotism (though it is important to note that many who make that argument are doing so to further their own agendas rather than defend their position). Indeed, on its surface, nationalism *feels* like a patriotic word. Like many words in every language, original definition or intent can be dramatically altered through repeated misuse. Particularly in the 21st century, numerous politicians and voters have used the word to promote and/or support policies that negatively target racial and ethnic minorities, the LGBTQ+ community, immigrants (both documented and undocumented), and non–Christians. This exclusivity regarding political and economic power and basic rights goes against the very principles that the United States claims as its foundation. The Declaration of Independence—considered by most to be the de facto birth certificate of the country—proposes that "*all* [people] are created equal" [emphasis added] with equal rights to "life, liberty, and the pursuit of happiness."

In his 1976 work *The Captain America Complex*, theologian Robert Jewett discussed the concept of nationalism, utilizing Cap as an example of America's more destructive policies, both foreign and domestic. In the wake of the 9/11 attacks, Jewett returned to this thesis alongside co-author and philosophy professor John Shelton Lawrence in their book *Captain America and the Crusade Against Evil: The Dilemma of Zealous Nationalism*. In that work, they suggest—using Cap as an analogy for America itself—that U.S. policy and ideals promoted the concept that America was both a "city set upon a hill," acting as an example to the rest of the world, and also utilizing its economic and military might to force its own ideals on those who resisted the lessons of our example.[16] While their criticisms of America's "war on terror" have considerable validity, the connection of their theories to Captain America falls somewhat short, focusing almost entirely on Cap's World War II adventures (and one issue from 1999). To anyone who had read Cap's many criticisms of such policies since 1964, the analogy quickly falls flat. The two scholars make much stronger arguments in their other work, *The Myth of the American Superhero*, where they expand the analogy to the larger zeitgeist including such fictional icons as *Star Trek*'s Captain Kirk and Clint Eastwood's cowboy, the Man with No Name.

More recently, philosophy professor Mark D. White has suggested that Cap's patriotism is in no way nationalist. According to White, Captain America "embodies an inclusive and cosmopolitan patriotism that balances idealism with clear-eyed pragmatism ... [and that he] stresses principles over politics, opposing his government when it does not live up to the same standards to which he holds himself," even going so far as to hand over the mantle of Captain America to others when he is unable to support a certain administration's policies.[17] This perspective is far more reflective of the overall continuity of Captain America, particularly since 1964, and the one most embodied in the live-action portrayals in the MCU since 2011. While America has certainly had its periods of zealous nationalism, those ideals have become much more tied to the far right (which, as a straight, white male, Steve Rogers could easily be pigeonholed into despite his numerous examples of promoting more diverse perspectives).

Since his return to comics in 1964, Captain America has frequently and consistently presented support for inclusivity in the United States. As will be further discussed in later chapters, one of Cap's most trusted partners is Sam Wilson/the Falcon, the first African American superhero in comics; in the early 1980s, Arnie Roth—a childhood friend of Steve Rogers—is introduced as the first gay character in American superhero comics. When the U.S. government has supported policies that oppose Cap's basic ideals, he has resisted those policies (in the 1980s when the government declares that "Captain America" belongs to the government, and in the early 2000s in defiance of the Superhuman Registration Act). His is not a "my country, right or wrong" type of love of country. Captain America clearly sees his nation's flaws, ever hopeful that its founding principles will someday overcome them.

Despite this more politically liberal slant since the 1960s, it is important to note that Captain America is a fictional character, whose adventures have been written for over three-quarters of a century by an ever-changing group of multiple creators across several generations. As such, this dedication to patriotism is very much defined by the times in which his adventures were written, and the personal experiences of the writers and artists who have been behind those adventures. Perhaps the best way in which Captain America reflects his audience throughout his history is in the fact that, as he is (and has been) written by real, flawed, imperfect people, the character himself has fallen short of his own ideals from time to time. The original adventures of Captain America in the 1940s were very much a reflection of their times, with all the political and social ideals—and shortcomings—that period and its people possessed.

Captain America in the 1940s

The patriotic fervor that took the country by storm after Pearl Harbor became heavily reflected in the burgeoning superhero industry. Most Americans in the 21st century are well aware of the two most famous, Captain America and Wonder Woman, but the Golden Age produced many more: AC Comics produced Captain Freedom and Miss Victory; Crestwood Publications had Yank & Doodle; comics legend Will Eisner transformed the army poster recruiter Uncle Sam into a superhero for Quality Comics; and Archie Comics published Captain Flag and the first of the World War II patriotic heroes, the Shield (originally under MLJ Comics). Created by Harry Shorten and Irv Novick and appearing in *Pep Comics* #1, the Shield was FBI agent Joe Higgins, a chemist who utilizes his dead brother's secret serum to give himself enhanced strength and invulnerability. Added to this is his costume, the torso of which is a literal shield.[18] If this sounds familiar, that is no mistake; recently hired on as editorial/artistic director at Timely Comics, Joe Simon used the Shield as a template for his own patriot hero.[19]

Cap's initial adventures were, of course, originally produced by writer Simon and artist Kirby. However, by 1942, Simon and Kirby had left Timely (Kirby eventually enlisting to serve in the war), and Stan Lee—who had contributed some stories to the comic by that point—took over writing duties. When Lee, too, left to serve, no writer is documented (Al Avison, Syd Shore, and others are credited as the artists for the wartime issues, but it is unclear if Avison or some uncredited person did the actual writing). After the war, Avison, Shore and others continue to be credited with art for *Captain America Comics*, while Lee is credited only as "editor," but it is highly likely that—as would be the case in the 1950s and '60s—Lee was the primary writer for all postwar issues.[20]

Though the initial sketch of Captain America was Simon's, artist Jack Kirby soon added his own style and dash to the comic (including changing Cap's shield from badge-shaped to its iconic circular form). In his first adventure, "Case No. 1: Meet Captain America," the U.S. military, fearful of growing "fifth column" spies as the conflicts in Europe and the Pacific rage on, express their concerns to President Franklin Roosevelt. The president refers them to FBI director "J. Arthur Grover" (a clear allusion to real-world FBI director J. Edgar Hoover, who was directly named in the Shield comics) and his top-secret project to create a Super Soldier. Their volunteer is a scrawny Steve Rogers, who submits to the test of Dr. Reinstein's (a play on "Einstein") formula, which turns him into Captain America, the very peak of human physical perfection. When a Nazi spy kills Reinstein and takes a beating from the new Captain America, he stumbles into a pile of electrical equipment, meeting a shocking death. With Reinstein dead, the secret formula is lost, and Cap becomes the one and only American Super Soldier. When the "camp mascot" (it is not at all clear what this is), young teen Bucky Barnes, discovers Steve changing into his Captain America costume, Cap makes the boy his partner (part of a new wave of child sidekicks originating with Robin the Boy Wonder in *Batman* #1), who, for unexplained reasons, goes by his actual name despite wearing a mask.[21]

It is clear that although Americans were still largely opposed to becoming involved in the war, it was obvious to many that Adolf Hitler was a threat. As previously stated, the cover of *Captain America Comics* #1 saw Cap punching out Hitler. The dictator appeared again on the cover of the following issue, showing Cap pushing Hitler over as Bucky kneeled behind the Fuhrer (a common way of making people fall on playgrounds, an image that doubtless made many Cap readers giggle with joy). Hitler appears again on the cover of issue #36 (March 1944), with Cap, hanging from a low-flying plane, pulling Hitler out of the backseat of a car.[22] The message to Cap's readers was clear: Adolf Hitler is a clear and present danger to the American people, and he is a threat that America must stop. On a side note, in 2022, an original copy of *Captain America Comics* #1 sold for $3.12 million, making it (to date) the fifth most valuable American superhero comic book, following a copy of *Amazing Fantasy* #15 (first appearance of Spider-Man) at $3.6 million and three copies of *Action Comics* #1 (first appearance of Superman) at $3.25 million, $3.2 million, and $3.18 million.[23]

Even though the country was still a year away from being pulled into the war, *Captain America Comics* was a huge success, soon becoming Timely's best-selling title. Joe Simon would later recount, "The Nazis were a menace ... maybe [Cap] was our way of lashing out against the Nazi menace. Evidently, Captain America symbolized ... the American people's sentiments. When [Jack Kirby and I] were producing Captain America [throughout 1941], we were outselling Batman, Superman, and all the others."[24] It is more than a little ironic that this Jewish-created blond-haired white example of physical perfection should become an American symbol against the Nazis, who promoted physically perfect blond-haired white people as the "master race." On the surface, Steve Rogers/Captain America appears to support this idea of the *ubermensch* (the Aryan "superman"). However, Simcha Weinstein, author of *Up, Up, and OyVey!: How Jewish History, Culture, and Values Shaped the Comic Book Superhero*, proposes that Cap does the opposite, arguing that Cap actually subverts the racist ideal, standing as he does against the concept of racial superiority (his physical perfection coming from science rather than genetics).[25]

On the ethical questions regarding such human experimentation, Major Todd A. Burkhardt, a professor at the U.S. Military Academy at West Point, suggests that, in reality, experimenting to create a Super Soldier such as Captain America would only be ethically sound if it met two key parameters: "if the enemy we oppose can be easily recognized as *evil objectified in the world which negates our right to autonomy*"; and "if the situation must be considered a *supreme emergency*" [emphasis added].[26] In the case of the Nazi menace during World War II, both of these situations were clearly well established. One clear area of discussion and/or concern, however, would be the hypothetical question: What if the serum had not been destroyed after this initial test? How many "super soldiers" would the U.S. create if it had the ability? What degree of "programming" would be involved in training them for combat? What would be done with them once the war was over? In a real-world situation, the concept of a Captain America is a frightening one, to say the least.

In the year leading up to Pearl Harbor, Cap and Bucky would primarily fight this aforementioned fifth column of mostly pro–German spies within America's borders. That first issue of *Captain America Comics* also introduced another character that has become synonymous with the hero: the archvillain Red Skull. In this first appearance, however, he was not the Red Skull fans have come to know since 1941. The original Skull was a man in a mask: George Maxon, head of the American company Maxon Aircraft, conspiring to sabotage America's military through his own aircrafts. Like many 1940s Cap villains, Maxon meets a deadly end.[27] As the concept of "supervillains" took off during the early 1940s, the Red Skull was too terrifying a visage to simply kill off. He would return in a more permanent capacity just a few stories later (as his permanent identity of "Johann Schmidt") and continue on with Cap through the decades, becoming the proverbial Joker to Cap's Batman.

Like Superman before him, Captain America was an immediate smash hit, soon reaching Superman's record of one million copies of each issue sold. National Allied Publications (by this time more commonly known as DC Comics, Superman's publisher) had spearheaded the idea of fan clubs with the Supermen of America club, through which members received a tin ring bearing the image of the Man of Steel. Timely and Cap followed suit with the Sentinels of Liberty. For ten cents, members would receive the following: an enamel badge bearing an eagle, Cap's face and name, and "Sentinels of Liberty" along the bottom; a membership card stating Cap's and the club's principles ("1. In God We Trust; 2. Allegiance to the flag and the Constitution of the United States of America; 3. To make myself a better citizen and defend my government forever"... that last one feeling more than a tad nationalist).[28] Throughout the war, Sentinels would be called on to collect glass, paper, and scrap iron, as well as being vigilant against air strikes (which, of course would never come) and spies at home.

The first issue published after the Japanese attack on Pearl Harbor on December 7, 1941, was #13 (no month is identified, but it would have been the first issue published in 1942). A logo was added to the cover reading "Remember Pearl Harbor," accompanied by a graphic of Captain America punching a Japanese general and proclaiming, "You started it! Now—We'll Finish It!"[29] This staunch patriotism would be evident in superhero comics across the board, with America's children's favorite heroes strongly supporting the war effort, encouraging their readers to do the same by collecting paper and scrap for local drives and buying war bonds. In issue #15, Cap warns a group of people (and his readers), "Now that we've licked this Nazi fifth column plot, folks, you can see how important it is not to believe planted rumors, fake reports and terror propaganda!" (Advice people in the 21st century would do well to embrace.)[30]

That same issue included an ad showing Captain America informing his readers that their ten cents would be better spent on "Captain America's War Fund" than on their favorite pulp pastime. Timely Comics vowed to match every dime donated, sending the funds to the Treasury Department for the war effort. To underscore the fact that every cent matters, a chart was added to show how much various war supplies cost (in dimes):

485 dimes = 1 M-1903 rifle
35 dimes = 1 haversack
25 dimes = 1 hand grenade
70 dimes = 100 bullets
55 dimes = feeding 10 soldiers for one day
350 dimes = 10 bayonettes[31]

In another ad a few months later titled "Your Life Depends on It: A Special Captain America Feature," Cap eerily predicts the future, showing an American bomb from a fleet of bomber planes, bearing the caption "Paid for by your war bonds," being dropped on the Japanese and Nazi flags, with the added statement: "This is the way the war will end!"[32] Considering that three years later the war would end with the dropping of two atomic bombs on Japan, this ad is nothing short of prophetic.

While this "Golden Age" of Cap adventures is most important for its introductions of Cap, Bucky, and Red Skull, little else stands out in the overall history of the character other than his direct connection to real-world events during the war years. On the whole, however, the adventures are rather cookie-cutter, constantly repeating tropes and storylines (i.e., bad guy poses threat, Cap and Bucky learn of threat, Cap and Bucky stop threat, bad guy often "accidentally" dies). Perhaps the biggest standout story comes near the end of the 1940s run. In issue number 66 (April 1948), Bucky is shot by the villainess Lavender, taking the boy hero out of commission for the remainder of Cap's Golden Age run. Bucky would be replaced as Cap's sidekick with Golden Girl (whose real name is Betsy Ross—it was the '40s).[33] This would all be retconned in later decades as Captain America being frozen in ice and Bucky apparently dying at the end of World War II necessitated other men posing as Cap and Bucky after the war. According to the official online Marvel Database, this means that, in this story, Cap was really a man named Jeff Mace and young "Bucky" was actually Fred Davis, Jr.[34]

Aside from Joe Simon and Jack Kirby, another comics legend associated with Cap's 1940s run is Marvel Comics icon Stan Lee. Stanley Martin Lieber, the seventeen-year-old cousin of Jean Goodman, wife of Martin Goodman, owner of Timely Comics, was an aspiring writer. His mother helped get him the job with Timely. At first, Stanley was mainly a gofer, refilling ink wells, delivering office mail, picking up lunch, making coffee, etc. However, in order for comic books to receive cheaper magazine postal rates, at least one story in the issue needed to be completely text (i.e., no pictures). For *Captain America Comics* #3 (May 1941), Simon assigned the task of writing the text story to the new young hire. Aware that comic books were a derided medium in the literary world and wanting to keep his options open for the future, Stanley created a pen name, cutting his first name in half: "Stan Lee."[35] This first story, "Captain America Foils the Traitor's Revenge," where Cap and Bucky prevent a dishonorably discharged soldier from murdering his former commander,[36] would launch perhaps the most legendary career in comic book history. After World War II—where he served in the Training Film Division of the army, writing training manuals and pamphlets—Lee would return to Timely as head writer and editor of the comics division while still in his mid-twenties.

Cap in the Golden Age was very much a product of his time. As stated earlier, he was a straight, white male, as all heroes in American pop culture—film, radio, and literature—were then. Portrayals of race in these 1940s comics are a general example of the worst of racism in pop culture at that time. The Japanese antagonists were portrayed as the "yellow peril," with dramatically slanted eyes and either fangs or buck teeth (to be fair, they were the enemy then; Germans were likewise often portrayed as animalistic beasts). Though these racist/beastly portrayals of World War II's antagonists were common in *Captain America Comics* from the very beginning, by 1944, the U.S. government's Writers' War Board (WWB) was officially strongly encouraging American comic book publishers to illustrate America's enemies as being as racist and beastly as possible.[37] After 1944, the WWB felt that enemy atrocities spoke for themselves, and racist portrayals would no longer be necessary.[38]

Portrayals of Black Americans are not so easily explained: with thick lips, wide eyes, pidgin English (suggesting they are illiterate and/or not "real" Americans), and almost always shown to be cowardly. Perhaps the worst example of this comes from the Timely comic *Young Allies*, where Bucky has adventures alongside a team of other children. One member of the team was "Whitewash" Jones, a young Black kid with overtly racist features, occasionally dressed in a Cab Calloway–style suit and wide-brimmed hat (odd clothing choices for a child). Even in the very first issue of *Young Allies*, Whitewash is introduced in a racist manner. After being complimented as being able to "make a harmonica talk," Whitewash responds, "Yeah man! I is also good on de watermelon!"[39] Though Whitewash did occasionally save the day, it was mostly due to accidents occurring due to his cowardice (not dissimilar to Shaggy and Scooby-Doo decades later). Race in Cap comics will be discussed in more detail later, but it is difficult to comprehend how comic book artists, the majority of whom were Jewish Americans well aware of the horrors of racism, could contribute so overtly to this problem. It does show, however, how deeply embedded racism and racist ideas were in the American zeitgeist (also a topic of deeper discussion in a later chapter).

Modern Takes on Cap's Golden Age

Prior to the 21st century, superhero studies were primarily a fringe area of academics. The topic has become far more popular since the 9/11 attacks of 2001, when the idea of heroes became much more a part of the American popular discussion. Though not as closely studied as, say, Superman, Batman, or Wonder Woman, some significant studies of Captain America have appeared over the years. As mentioned earlier, Robert Jewett took some interest in the character in his analysis of American "zealous nationalism." His *Captain America Complex* suggests that:

> Captain America's approach to peacemaking, so to speak, derives from a pervasive tradition and its power is manifest even in the ways that many who oppose current militarization visualize the problem. The American sense of mission influences both the supporters of militant rearmament and the advocates of a nuclear freeze. Yet to a substantial degree this influence is invisible. The public is largely unaware of the origins of its convictions about peacemaking or how they are conveyed.[40]

Chapter 1. Sentinel of Liberty

The book was originally published in 1973, as U.S. involvement in Vietnam was coming to a close. The second edition (from which the above quote is derived) was published in 1984, as the Cold War between the United States and the Soviet Union was once more heating up. While Jewett's analogies regarding Captain America in no way reflected the comics of the times, for anyone who connected America's continuous military excursions of the previous decades with her involvement in World War II, Captain America would be a logical figure with which to associate it. Cap's militant approach against America's enemies in his Golden Age adventures would certainly seem relevant.

In his groundbreaking seminal work on superheroes, Richard Reynolds outlined a definition of what constitutes a "superhero":

1. "The hero is marked out from society," often without any relationship with his/her parents (no mention of Cap's parents is given for many decades, later shown he was an orphan by World War II).

2. Most will have godlike powers (while not godlike, Cap is the physical peak of possible human perfection, so at least demi-godlike).

3. "The hero's devotion to justice overrides his devotion to the law" (most villains in Cap's Golden Age adventures meet a deadly end, with no due process or protection of their rights).

4. The superhero will stand out as extraordinary compared to his surroundings (this is true of Cap).

5. The superhero's alter ego will be the hero's exact opposite (like Clark Kent, Bruce Wayne, and Steve Rogers).

6. Superheroes are patriotic and "loyal to the state, though not necessarily to the letter of its laws" (superheroes—including Cap—are, in essence, vigilantes).

7. "The stories are mythical," interweaving "science and magic" (this certainly describes Cap's Super Soldier Serum).[41]

Though at this point Captain America needs no justification to be called a superhero, this template by one of the founders of superhero studies does set the stage for all analysis of the character that follows over the following decades.

Geographer Jason Dittmer has written several articles on the various ages of Captain America, culminating in his *Captain America and the Nationalist Superhero* (Dittmer's definition of nationalist being more associated with national identity than the negative connotation of domestic politics described earlier). In that work, Dittmer states:

> Captain America's small role in the shifting of the United States toward an interventionist attitude is but one manifestation of how superheroes, and

especially their nationalist variant, can be understood as geopolitical. Superheroes are not reflections of, but are instead (along with many other elements) co-constitutive of, the discourse popularly known as American exceptionalism.[42]

Of the tendency for Cap's enemies in his Golden Age adventures to ultimately die for their misdeeds (specifically the aforementioned first Red Skull), Dittmer says, "This rather harsh ending to a story read by millions of children is indicative of the America that Simon and Kirby wanted to promote. Their desired national identity was of an America engaged in the world's conflict, idealistic but with a dose of gritty realism."[43]

There is a bit of poetic irony to the fact that the country that invented superheroes would itself become the very embodiment of superheroism to a world dangerously close to falling to the boot of global fascism. As Dittmer points out, Captain America is what Simon and Kirby wanted America to be, and ultimately, it is how the country and its citizens came to view themselves in the decades that followed (though that ideal would inevitably become a delusion).

In what is perhaps the most comprehensive study of Captain America to date, media studies professor J. Richard Stevens concludes his 2015 analysis of Golden Age Cap, *Captain America, Masculinity, and Violence*, as follows:

> The 1940s Captain America was not the liberal bastion of gender and racial equality that he would eventually become. [He] does not seem particularly interested in challenging traditional conceptions of social norms. Characters in his comics seldom prove to be more than the labels that define them ... [Cap] does not spend much time questioning the role his patriotism has in shaping his worldview.[44]

This analysis of Golden Age Captain America is consistent with Jewett's interpretation of the character, and is certainly backed up by the original source material. Unlike today, there was no thought given to social messages in comic books. They were considered cheap throwaway children's novelty items. They were primarily commercial in nature, and "commercial" during World War II meant zealously patriotic. Captain America in these early adventures is Simon's and Kirby's idea of what America needed to be: a stalwart protector of freedom and liberty, both at home and around the world. This would, of course, be exactly how America—and a significant portion of Americans—viewed the United States in the decades to come.

Approaching American involvement in the war, President Roosevelt felt that in order to face the massive threat of global fascism, America needed to put aside any domestic problems and internal strife that might exist and become united as a force for a greater good (in 1940, FDR would encourage Black civil rights leader A. Philip Randolph to postpone a planned civil rights march in Washington, D.C., in order to avoid any social division over the topic of race). Cap's lack of focus (for lack of a better phrase) on the many social issues facing the U.S. in the early 1940s has much more to do with this idea of presenting a united front against a common foe than a disregard for those issues (though the racist portrayals evident in all popular comics of the period clearly show a lack of concern by the creators). Simon and Kirby, being of Jewish descent, were undoubtedly well aware of the systemic racism in America, but they viewed the threat posed by Nazi victory in Europe as a problem that, left undealt with, could make addressing all other more domestic problems moot.

Not the Cap You Thought He Was: The Need for Retconning Golden Age Cap

Continuity in fiction, like history in reality, is relative. Just as historians are constantly rewriting history as new evidence on any particular topic comes to light, so too do the creators of popular fiction occasionally rewrite a character's past. When Stan Lee and Jack Kirby brought Captain America into the burgeoning Marvel Comics Universe in 1964, rather than recreate the character or create a new incarnation, as Julius Schwartz had recently done with Flash and Green Lantern over at DC Comics, they chose to bring the actual original Steve Rogers from World War II to the present. To do so, they had the Captain found frozen in a block of ice and delivered to the newly formed superhero team, the Avengers. Readers soon learned that Cap had fallen into the ice following a mission near the end of World War II, leaving him frozen, essentially in suspended animation, for 20 years.[45]

While an excellent way of bringing the World War II hero into the turbulent 1960s, Lee and Kirby likely did not consider that there might be older readers out there who remembered that Captain America had many adventures in the years following the war, including an infamous run in the early 1950s as a "Commie Smasher"; but remember some did. As a result, over the following decades, it would be up to succeeding generations of creative teams to retcon Cap's post–World War II history, ultimately proclaiming that a series of gentlemen took up the shield and the mantle of Captain America from 1944 to 1954, even going so far as to assume the identity of "Steve Rogers" as well. When part of Cap's 1960s return story included the presumed death of young Bucky during the same mission that sent Cap into the ice, Bucky also required the retcon of other

"Buckys" after the war (hence the earlier mentioned retcon that the Bucky that was shot in the late 1940s was not, in fact, the original). Ultimately, the original Bucky's "death" would also be retconned when he also returned, in the early 21st century, as the mysterious Winter Soldier (to be discussed in *much* more detail later).

The problem with fictional characters that are also valuable commercial properties is that they can (1) never die, (2) never age, and (3) never experience significant growth that might alter in any way the character's initial personality and/or worldview. When someone who read Captain America as a child then recommends the comics to their child or grandchild, there is an expectation that the character remains much the same as in the initial reading. Some characters have experienced more change over the decades than others. Considering the rather conservative nature of Captain America in the Golden Age, it is remarkable how the character in the 21st century is still very much the same while at the same time being completely different. Cap remains Cap, regardless of writer, decade, or history.

Captain America and 1940s America

When Joe Simon and Jack Kirby created Captain America in 1940, the country was predominantly opposed to entry into the growing conflicts in Europe and the Pacific. American families had lost nearly 117,000 young men in just over a year of actual combat in World War I (or the Great War, as it was originally called). Organizations such as America First saw no profit in supporting foreign countries while America herself was still limping its way out of the Great Depression. President Franklin Roosevelt, while publicly supporting isolationism, privately knew that without American involvement, Germany and Japan would conquer the world—and eventually come knocking on our doors as well. The plight of European Jews was not unknown to Americans as thousands came to the U.S. seeking refuge, only to be refused entry (most European Jews ended up finding sanctuary in Mexico, the true "land of the free," it would seem).

Simon and Kirby, both Jewish Americans (as were a significant majority of comic book creators in the 1930s and '40s due to the aforementioned systemic racism denying them employment elsewhere), knew well what President Roosevelt felt unable to proclaim. Hitler must be stopped. Though not the first patriotic hero of the era, Captain America soon became the most popular. Once America found herself pulled into the global conflict, Cap became a superhero who symbolized the American philosophy: victory against fascism at all costs. When people in the present look back on what has become identified as the Greatest Generation (i.e., those Americans who survived the Great Depression, won World War II, and created the modern American economy), the mental image they conjure could be best described as "Captain America."

Though the hero and his comic adventures ignored the many problems facing America at the time—continuing sexism, racism, and homophobia, to state only the most obvious—it is important to note that the majority of Americans at the time did too. It was almost as if the thinking of the day was "ignore the problem and there is no problem." That perception of American society would change—as indeed would Captain America—in the decades to come. Problems would be put front and center. If change was needed, change was demanded, and Captain America would join that call. Until that time, though, America had one more dark period to endure as America transitioned from the World War II of the 1940s to a new type of war in the 1950s. American politicians like Joe McCarthy would begin to conduct witch hunts based on political philosophy, targeting private American citizens of a more liberal bent. After a brief retirement, comics would once more call upon the service of Captain America, but this time, to smash some commies as Americans began to live under the constant threat of the Cold War and the daily possibility of all-out nuclear war.

CHAPTER 2

Commie Smasher!

Captain America in the Age of Consensus, the 1950s

Many Americans today look back on the 1950s very nostalgically. It appears to us through the veil of history as a simpler time, a more honest time, when opportunities for economic advancement seemed more abundant. The U.S. emerged from World War II as a military, economic, and political superpower, cementing itself as the leader of the free world. Furthermore, when twelve million boys came home from World War II with the benefits provided by the revolutionary G.I. Bill, providing money for higher education, help in receiving home loans, and numerous job opportunities for veterans, the overnight creation of a vibrant middle class—for really the first time in the country's history—was the immediate result. The American Century continued to boom. That was America on the surface, and the surface is all most consider when remembering history.

The decade, however, was not without many significant flaws. At home, the continued economic prosperity coincided with some of the largest individual income tax rates in the country's history. Women, who had gained considerable political and economic opportunities over the previous thirty years, were now sent back into the kitchen. Women attended college to a considerable degree in order to ultimately gain their "MRS degree" (a common term used to mean finding a suitable husband to support them and give them children). Systemic racism—particularly in the Southern states—continued unabated, with the Ku Klux Klan and their ilk enforcing 90-year-old Jim Crow laws with threats of beatings, lynchings, and home burnings. The LGBTQ+ community—historically marginalized but largely ignored to date—suddenly became enemies of the state, their lifestyle deemed a threat to national security, and their "condition" considered a mental disease.

With World War II decidedly over, and the fascist threat to the world quashed, a new type of conflict emerged: the Cold War. America's newfound superpower status was challenged by a former ally: the communist superpower, the Soviet Union. In the years following the war, the globe divided between the pro-capitalist and pro-communist worlds. By 1950, both the U.S. and the U.S.S.R. possessed atomic weapons technology, with an active weapons program built on it. The emerging arms race increasingly placed the planet on the verge of mutually assured destruction, and newly prosperous Americans began building bomb shelters in their back yards in lieu of swimming pools. With both nations sitting as permanent members of the U.N. Security Council, the new international organization would become the primary arbiter of peace between the two competing superpowers.

Across America, politics became weaponized. With communism being a leftist political philosophy (as opposed to fascism's more rightist stance), any sign of "liberalism" at home would lead to accusations of disloyalty to the American way. Neighbor reported on neighbor and family members turned on each other based on political ideology. In Washington, Republican senator Joe McCarthy of Wisconsin made anti-Communism his personal crusade to such an extent that the ensuing communist "witch hunts" led to the phenomenon being named after him: McCarthyism. Everyone with liberal ideas was considered a Communist. Anyone seeking racial equality? Communist! Better opportunities for women? Communist! Being LGBTQ+? Absolutely Communist! America's first superhero, Superman—having expanded from the printed page to the radio and movie serials throughout the previous decade—now made the transition to the TV screen, changing his tagline from standing for "Truth and Justice" to "Truth, Justice, and the *American Way!*"

Across the board, American pop culture—more and more a mainstay of American society since the Great Depression—continued to boom. Science fiction played an increasing role in Hollywood productions. The beatnik culture proved a precursor to the following decade's youth culture movements. Television—a rarity prior to 1950—became as much a staple in American households as radios had been in the decades prior. A new musical genre, rock and roll, became the soundtrack to a new and powerful sales demographic: the American teenager. Comic books—still a popular children's pastime—came under attack, accused of promoting everything from juvenile delinquency to homosexuality by American adults. By 1955, it seemed the comic book industry would not survive the decade. Superheroes became all but nonexistent in the four-color medium, with Superman and to a much lesser extent Batman and Wonder Woman the only superheroes to remain in publication throughout the decade. Captain America would make a brief return before mid-decade, not to fight Nazis, but to smash "Commies."

A Cold War Emerges

With the Nazis and Japan defeated in 1945, and the world once more thrown into economic uncertainty where it came to rebuilding, it was clear that the "Big Three"—the U.S., U.K., and U.S.S.R.—would be largely responsible for getting the nations of a battle-weary Europe back on their feet, economically and politically. Unlike World War I, where all the fighting nations essentially went home once the fighting stopped, leaving each respective government to clean up its own mess, the Big Three would divide responsibility for cleaning up the aftermath of World War II. At the Yalta Conference in February 1945, Soviet leader Josef Stalin demanded that the U.S.S.R. take responsibility for rebuilding the nations of Eastern Europe, the nations along the Soviet Union's western borders. Great Britain and the U.S. were uneasy with allowing Soviet influence anywhere in postwar Europe, but they had little room to argue as the Soviets had done the bulk of the fighting—and dying—that had led to Hitler's defeat.

By 1947, it was clear that the Soviets were creating communist puppet states along their border, building what British prime minister Winston Churchill dubbed an Iron Curtain, behind which the western allies could not see what the Russian Communists might be up to (with spy satellites and even effective spy agencies still years away). When the Soviets declared in 1949 that they had achieved a working atomic bomb, the next threat to the world seemed clear to the British–American coalition: global Communism. By that time, U.S. president Harry S Truman had issued his Truman Doctrine, dedicating the U.S. to using all its resources—economic, political, and military—to stopping the spread of Communism throughout the world (which, of course, the Soviets read as an outright declaration of war on their entire way of life). Since a war between these two new superpowers would now mean an exchange of atomic weaponry, an official declaration of hostilities was unwise. Instead, the two nations would spend the next 45 years in a tense struggle of will they/won't they, with the future of the human race hanging in the balance (which, in hindsight, sounds a lot like a comic book storyline).

At home, a fear of Communism dipping its toe into the American political landscape turned into outright hysteria. When President Truman made civil rights for Black Americans an official platform of his administration (going so far as to desegregate the U.S. military), this new liberal agenda coming out of the White House gave the opposition Republican Party fodder for a new political warfare. In the late 1940s, the U.S. House of Representatives took over the House Un-American Activities Committee to investigate the private lives of American citizens in order to weed out any potential Communist infestation. The committee was headed by

Chapter 2. Commie Smasher! 49

future vice president and eventual president Richard M. Nixon, then a Republican congressman from California.

However, the character that emerged as the center of this anti–Communist crusade was the abovementioned Senator Joe McCarthy. In his study of McCarthyism, Richard M. Fried defined the period thusly:

> Beset by Cold War anxieties, Americans developed an obsession with domestic communism that outran the actual threat and gnawed at the tissue of civil liberties. For some politicians, hunting Reds became a passport to fame—or notoriety.... A new vocabulary entered political discourse. "Are you now or have you ever been a member of the Communist Party?" "I refuse to answer on grounds that the answer may tend to incriminate me." "Fifth-Amendment Communist!" "Soft on communism..." "Witch-hunt!" "McCarthyism!" In the barrage of accusations that rumbled through the late 1940s and early 1950s, reputations were made or ruined, careers blasted or created, lives and families shattered.[1]

While this summation was published in 1990, with just over a year left in the Cold War, some of the phraseology may sound disturbingly familiar to readers in the 21st century, as much of the tactics and demagoguery that arose from this "Red Scare" are once more being heavily utilized in the American political sphere.

In 1950, Senator McCarthy—his own goal of reelection seeming unlikely—picked up the issue of anti–Communism, going so far as to suggest that he had personal information that Communists had infiltrated the federal government and even the U.S. military (he never had anything resembling actual evidence). He proclaimed that year:

> The real, basic difference, however, lies in the religion of immoralism—invented by Marx, preached feverishly by Lenin, and carried to unimaginable extremes by Stalin. This religion of immoralism, if the Red half of the world wins—and well it may—this religion of immoralism will more deeply wound and damage mankind than any conceivable economic or political system.[2]

Gay men were targeted as being Communist (which begs the question, were they "mentally disturbed" or "politically leftist"?). Iconic television actress Lucille Ball was accused, as was Dr. J. Robert Oppenheimer, head scientist on the Manhattan Project, which had developed the atomic bomb that ended World War II (he now opposed the use of such weapons, which doubtless led to the accusations). For the next three years, Americans lived in constant fear that some aspect of their behavior might be viewed as nonconformist and leftist enough to be accused of being a Communist. While these investigations had no real prosecutorial power, the mere public allegations were enough to destroy careers and lives (and they did). This dread fear of Communism at home came from the apparent global spread "over there."

In his analysis of Marvel Comics in the Cold War, political scientist Matthew J. Costello defined American Cold War consensus regarding American philosophy and policy thusly:

> Drawing on the major elements that have always defined the American identity, the Cold War American was viewed as an individual who lived in the most virtuous political system in the world, as evidenced by American prosperity, and whose divine mission was to extend the benefits of that prosperity to all American citizens and promote the virtue of its governmental system around the world by defending against the evil forces of totalitarianism.[3]

Like the fight against the threats of World War I and World War II, if America is to be victorious against the new threat of international communism, then Americans must all be on the same page. Defiance against Communism must be a national effort, and that effort must be supported through a general consensus that America is in the right. In reality, however, the push to protect democracy and Christianity was less important than the push to protect the global capitalist market (and American hegemony in that market). While the Soviet Union was deemed the primary threat, domino theory suggested that Communism would spread, causing nation after nation to "fall" (like a proverbial domino) ... and the evidence suggested that this was, in fact, the case.

Aside from Soviet puppetry of the Eastern European countries making up the Iron Curtain, the victory of Mao Zedong's Chinese communists establishing the People's Republic of China, and the conflict in French Indochina with Ho Chi Minh and his nationalist communist movement, on June 25, 1950, North Korean dictator Kim Il Sung ordered his military forces to invade South Korea, quickly taking most of the peninsula. After World War II, the Soviet Union—having been invaded twice in just over 20 years—wanted to secure their borders by having friendly nations along their borders as a sort of protective barrier. For their assistance in the final stages of the Pacific war, the small Asian peninsula nation of Korea was cut in half. The northern half (located on a small section of the Soviet eastern border) created a communist government under Kim, while the southern half created a more democratic/capitalistic regime. Kim's invasion led the new United Nations to respond with an international military force led by American General Douglas MacArthur. The conflict lasted for three years, ending in a stalemate with neither side really gaining or losing any ground. The U.S. committed 1.8 million soldiers to the "police action," losing more than 36,000 lives. This first "hot" conflict of the Cold War showed the American people that, unlike the threat of Adolf Hitler, the communist threat was not going away any time soon and would not be defeated easily. Americans must be vigilant.

Communism/Socialism vs. Authoritarianism/Fascism

During the Cold War, the words "communism" and "socialism" became synonymous with each other, and that confusion continues to the present day. In the American dialogue, they simply *feel* like they mean the same thing. It is vitally important to know that this is simply not true. While all communist systems may be socialist, not all socialist systems are communist. All of the world's leading capitalist countries practice a considerable degree of socialism. In the U.S., public education, unemployment benefits, food stamps, G.I. Bill benefits, Medicare, and Social Security are all socialist programs. Few Americans would wish to part with any of those.

Distinguishing arguments on the differences between the two philosophies are myriad. According to the online educational reference source *ThoughtCo*: "The main difference is that under communism, most property and economic resources are owned and controlled by the state (rather than individual citizens); under socialism, all citizens share equally in economic resources as allocated by a democratically-elected government."[4]

It is important to note that during the Cold War, members of the Soviet legislature were popularly elected, but elected officials swore loyalty to the Communist Party, not to their constituents (though, in the 2020s, the same could be argued for elected officials from the Democratic and Republican parties in the U.S.).

Western democracies have attempted to soften the word "socialism" by rebranding it "democratic socialism," but few voters on either side of the political divide understand the distinction. In truth, however, everything from the EPA to the FDA could be argued as being socialist, utilizing tax dollars to perform functions that are for the betterment of the overall populace. Communism, on the other hand, has become synonymous with the authoritarian regimes that have claimed it as their banner: the Soviet Union, China (the People's Republic of China [PRC]), North Korea, and Cuba specifically. These, however, are merely dictatorships that have hijacked the word and redefined it on a global scale. True communism as outlined by Karl Marx in the mid–1800s has never truly been implemented.

Here is where the similarities lie between leftist communism/socialism and World War II's rightist authoritarian fascism. Though communism and fascism as ideologies are polar opposites on the political spectrum, where they ring similar in the American mindset is the lack of personal freedom for those living under the respective regimes. To the everyday joe, there is no difference between Adolf Hitler and Josef Stalin (and his successors in the U.S.S.R.). At the time of fascism's rise in Europe, both America and Great Britain were primarily conservative countries, so the conservative aspects of fascism were never commented upon. With communism declaring itself a leftist philosophy, conservative politicians in the U.S. (and throughout the western democracies) could bring political leaning into the argument for their own political gain. Despite any benefits that communism (or socialism) may contain, the fact that they were "evil" made essentially any leftist policy, philosophy, or teaching vilified by association.

In 1950s America, communism was understood as (1) a total lack of freedom, and (2) a total renouncement of religion. These two ideals were in direct contrast to everything that most Americans believed that the United States stood for (even though there were many Americans—particularly racial/ethnic minorities, women, and the LGBTQ+ communities—who not only were denied basic civil liberties, but also lived in constant fear, not unlike peoples in actual communist countries). As such, it was vitally important for overall political morale that a true dedication to Americanism was loudly and frequently proclaimed. It important not only for Superman to declare his dedication to the American way, but also everyday regular Americans as well. On June 14, 1954, the words "under God" were added to the Pledge of Allegiance, and in 1957, "In God We Trust" was first inscribed on U.S. currency, both to underscore the country's dedication to Judeo-Christian values and opposing any system that did not. Superman's declaration, however, particularly underscores one area where American adults were especially concerned: the potential corruption of their youth by the growing influence of popular culture.

American Society, Consensus, and Pop Culture Collide: Uniting and Dividing

A key aspect of American society that developed due to the Cold War and the ensuing communist witch hunts was the idea of consensus. Consensus had been a key factor in American victories in both world wars, the idea that we were all in this together uniting American hearts and minds toward a central cause. By 1950, however, consensus played an additional role: proving to others that you were not a communist. Consensus, then, evolved into conformity. We must all look, act, and think alike to prove that we are not communist (a rather ironic notion, as those are exactly the ideals that communism promotes). This societal demand to oppose communism—enhanced, no doubt, by the ever-

Chapter 2. Commie Smasher! 53

escalating threat of possible nuclear war—drove millions of Americans back to church. Religious revivalism became a vital part of a normal American life.

A key factor that drove both political consensus and religious revivalism was fear. Socially, there was the fear of being labeled a communist, putting your job and perhaps even your basic freedoms at risk. Mentally and physically, however, there was the fear of a possible nuclear war. The very science that had saved us from fascism now threatened the very future of the human race. This new fear of science was frequently portrayed in American films of the time, from 1954's *Godzilla* and *Them!* to 1958's *The Fly* and *The Blob*. A fear of communism infiltrating American society was manifest on the big screen through the concept of alien invasion, with *The Day the Earth Stood Still* (1951), *The War of the Worlds* (1953), and *Invasion of the Body Snatchers* (1956) key among them. Consensus, then, seemed the most logical and effective weapon against these perceived threats.

Consensus, however, led to a reversal of fortunes for minorities and American women. Racial minorities—who had seen some advances in a burgeoning push for civil rights immediately after World War II—would see consensus as accepting the status quo and, with it, systemic racism. For women, having gained political freedoms in 1920 and increased economic opportunities during World War II, the rise of a more conservative/traditionalist and religious interpretation of a "proper" life meant that millions of women were expected to return to their roles of housewife and mother. This was emphasized as "good" and "proper" through such popular television programs as *Ozzie and Harriet*, *Leave It to Beaver*, and *Father Knows Best* (images from which are still constants in many people's minds when remembering the 1950s). In her groundbreaking analysis of family and home life during the Cold War, Elaine Tyler May pointed out:

> For women, the rewards offered by marriage, compared to the limited opportunities in the public world, made the homemaker role an appealing choice. So women donned their domestic harnesses. But in their efforts to live according to the codes of domestic *containment* [emphasis added], they were bound to encounter difficulty. Only later did they discover how uncomfortable those harnesses could be.[5]

May's use of "containment" is particularly important. Containment was the primary government policy regarding international communism, suggested in the so-called "long telegram" sent by George Kennan recommending the policy to keep communism from spreading, and solidified as policy in the 1947 Truman Doctrine.

The drive for consensus would take its first major gut punch in 1956, when a popular new song—"Rock Around the Clock" by Bill Haley and the Comets—became a national sensation, creating a new genre of American music: rock and roll. This new musical artform was an amalgamation of traditional "country/western" white music and Black rhythm and blues. This cross-culturalization of music might have been stamped out easily by the powers that be, had it not been for the simultaneous explosion of a new rock artist: Elvis Presley. The son of Mississippi sharecroppers, the 21-year-old Presley, with his slick black hair, captivating voice, and sexually suggestive onstage moves while singing, swept the nation—particularly young women, one of the groups hardest hit in the push for consensus—and became an overnight sensation. Providing a white face to what many white adults were damning as "black music" broke down an important wall in American pop culture entertainment and spearheaded the rebelliousness for which the '50s generation of American youth would become infamous.

While containing communism to its current boundaries was deemed important on the global scale, here at home containment was just as important. People must contain their passions as well and accept the status quo if we were to prevent communism here at home. A lack of such personal containment meant danger to society as a whole. When Elvis Presley blew onto the American music scene in 1956, there was a fear that his gyrating hips and uncommonly good looks might cause American girls to lose containment of their own sexual passions, leading to a crisis (a crisis of what was never exactly made clear). Children, likewise, must contain their own energies, focusing them toward more positive ends. Otherwise, the country would be beset by an epidemic of juvenile delinquency! The 1950s did see a rise in such delinquency. While it was blamed largely on rock and roll music and the films of actors such as James Dean and Marlon Brando, delinquency by children was largely blamed on once source: comic books.

Who were these juvenile delinquents? Mostly, they were the rising Baby Boomers, that generation of Americans born to the Greatest Generation that had come of age during the Great Depression and World War II. Largely born in the immediate aftermath of the war, the Baby Boomers would be the first generation of young Americans to ultimately work less during their formative years. Their parents having seen depression and global war, the Baby Boomers benefited from parents who—having experienced lives of constant struggle and sacrifice—sought to provide their children with childhoods of happy memories and the enjoyment of youth. That freedom, ultimately, would lead this generation to have the time to focus on systemic inequities in American society, becoming a driving force for social change in the decades to come.

Wertham's Crusade

In the realm of comic book history, one name that has become synonymous with this McCarthy-esque conservative crusade in favor of censorship is that of German-born psychiatrist Fredric Wertham. In recent years, however, deeper research into the man and his own research has provided a more complex and sympathetic view. For example, Wertham was a staunch anti-segregationist, opening clinics for Black residents of New York City who were often denied or could not afford treatment at white clinics.[6] He is better known for his crusade against the comic book industry, which he blamed for inciting violence and juvenile delinquency in American youth. To be fair, the horror and crime comics of the day (such as *Tales from the Crypt*, *The Vault of Horror*, *Crime SuspenStories*, and *Shock SuspenStories*, all published by EC Comics) were both particularly graphically violent and wildly popular, having pushed traditional superhero comics almost entirely off the racks by the mid–1950.

Wertham had spent the bulk of the 1940s and early '50s writing his opinions against comic books. However, though he may have had a valid point in many cases, he had no actual research to support his claims, instead making educated guesses based on small samples of interactions with young people.[7] Not all academics agreed at the time. Professor of education Frederic Thrasher wrote:

> Wertham's dark picture of the influence of comics is more forensic than scientific and illustrates a dangerous habit of projecting our social frustrations upon some specific trait of our culture, which becomes a sort of "whipping boy" for our failure to control the whole gamut of social breakdown ... it may be said that no acceptable evidence has been produced by Wertham or anyone else for the conclusion that reading comic magazines has, or has not a significant relation to delinquent behavior.[8]

Though the bulk of Wertham's arguments were aimed at the horror and crime genres, he did have some complaints regarding superheroes. He coined the term "Superman Complex" to describe young people getting a thrill from seeing people repeatedly physically punished. Likewise, he argued that Batman and Robin promoted a homosexual lifestyle.[9] This latter charge prompted DC Comics (publisher of the Batman titles) to give Batman and Robin girlfriends (Batwoman and the first Batgirl) and a dog (presuming, one supposes, that gay couples would not have a dog?).

As stated earlier, due to conformity and consensus, what was considered "normal" in American society came primarily from the dictates of the U.S. government and conservative interpretations of the Christian Bible. As such, in 1952, in the first edition of the *Diagnostic and Statistical Manual of Mental Disorders*, compiled by the American Medical Association, homosexuality was listed as a mental disorder (a definition that would not be removed for over 20 years, and largely still accepted as such throughout American society for much longer). Just the year prior, in 1951, Christine Jorgensen (born George Jorgensen, a veteran of World War II) became the first public transgender case in the United States. Though initially desiring a quiet life, Jorgensen took her historic role seriously, becoming a public advocate for transgender rights until her death in 1989.

Overall, Wertham's arguments were very popular with parents', religious, and teachers' organizations, frequently leading to bonfires that burned thousands of Golden Age comics (which, in hindsight, significantly added to the scarcity of those comics, leading to their considerable monetary value in the 21st century). When Wertham took his arguments to the floor of the U.S. Senate, the Subcommittee on Juvenile Delinquency published their own report, concluding:

> First, there was a growing concern in many countries over the rising popularity of American crime and horror comic books.... Second, violent comic books exposed foreign readers to "a hardened version of killing, robbery and sadism which is not only an undesirable pattern to emulate but is also a negative version of the American way of life." Third, uncensored American comic books additionally created particular problems in countries with non–White citizens. Finally, the committee found substantial evidence that Soviet propagandists used comics as prime examples of depraved American culture.[10]

A frightened comic book industry soon reacted by creating the Comics Code Authority, a self-regulating censorship board that would place a stranglehold on the industry's creativity for the next two decades. Some of the rules of this new code included:

1. Criminals could not be portrayed as sympathetic or in the right
2. Details on how to commit crimes must never be included
3. Police and government officials could never be portrayed negatively
4. "Good" must always triumph and criminals always punished
5. No use of words "horror" or "terror" and limited use of "crime" in titles
6. No blood, gore, or graphic violence
7. No vampires, werewolves, or zombies
8. Good grammar wherever possible
9. No portrayals of sex, "perversion," divorce or any disrespectful representation of parents or the "moral code"
10. "Ridicule or attack on any religious or racial group is never permissible."[11]

Comic book historian Mark Evanier has pointed out that although Wertham's "science" as described in his book *Seduction of the Innocent* was flawed, some of his conclusions were not entirely off the mark, and that many critics over the decades have been as irresponsible in their presentation of Wertham's work as Wertham was in his science.[12]

As the anti-comic book crusade was at its fever pitch, however, over at the recently renamed Atlas Comics (after the publishing/printing company recently purchased by Timely Comics owner Martin Goodman, a company which would not survive the decade), writer/editor Stan Lee was bringing back the company's own Golden Age superheroes, this time aiming their attentions not at Nazis, but at communists.

Captain America has a smaller presence in the 1950s than the previous decade or literally any decade since. In 1953, the 1944 movie serial was rereleased, changing its title to *Return of Captain America*. This coincided with the character's brief return in comic books. Running for just a few issues of *Young Men* and *Men's Adventures* and his own revived title, the hero of World War II was called into action once more. Though superheroes had been out of vogue since 1950, the continuing popularity of Superman—both on television in *The Adventures of Superman* starring George Reeves in his iconic run as the character and on the printed page in nine titles at DC Comics—suggested to Stan Lee that a comeback for the Sentinel of Liberty might be ... timely. With no more Nazis to fight, however, and with the American political climate being what it was in 1953, this time Captain America would become a "Commie Smasher!"

"Captain America: Commie Smasher!": Cap in the 1950s

The short run of 1950s Captain America adventures were drawn primarily by another comic book legend, John Romita (Sr). The online Marvel Database identifies the writer of the "Commie Smasher" stories as Don Rico, but other sources identify Rico as an artist for Timely/Atlas. The *Official Index to the Marvel Universe*, by contrast, references no writers for these issues, and does not mention Rico at all.[13] As Stan Lee was the editor of all Atlas Comics at the time, and is historically recognized as writing all of the comics being published in the 1950s, Lee was the likely author of Cap's tales. Romita had worked as an artist for Timely for about a year before being drafted into military service in 1951, and was an active-duty corporal in the army while working on the Captain America run. With cover dates of *Young Men* and *Captain America* running from December 1953 to September 1954, these stories would have run from just after

McCarthy's political downfall through the Senate subcommittee hearings on comics and the ultimate success of Wertham's crusade.

Timely (now Atlas) Comics was a very different place in the 1950s. Captain America creators Simon and Kirby had left Timely prior to the war over the controversial decision of Timely owner Martin Goodman in regard to their royalties for *Captain America Comics*. The agreement was that the two creators would receive a 25 percent royalty on profits from that magazine. From Simon's and Kirby's perspective, that meant 25 percent of what the magazine made minus production costs. From Goodman's perspective, however, it meant 25 percent of what each Cap issue made minus *all* corporate costs (production of all magazines, creator pay, staff pay, rent, utilities, etc.). Simon referred to this as "Hollywood accounting." When Goodman discovered that the two were secretly doing freelance work for his competitors, they parted ways with Goodman, Timely, and Captain America.[14]

With Stan Lee performing essentially all writing duties for the comics magazines, a dramatic downturn in overall comics sales—due in no small part to Wertham's crusade—forced Lee to dismiss all of his artists, keeping on as many as he could in a freelance capacity, often paying them for work that he ultimately kept stored in a closet (due to his freelancers providing more product than he could publish but not wanting to leave them empty-handed).[15] As Superman comics were still selling well (made all the more popular by the television program), Goodman ordered Lee to revive Timely's own trio of superheroes: the Human Torch, the Sub-Mariner, and Captain America.[16] Cap had only been gone for around three years, his last appearance being in *Captain America's Weird Tales* #74 (the title changed for the last two issues of its initial run), where the hero was brought to hell when the Red Skull (consigned there after his death) writes Cap's name in the "Book of the Damned." When the Master Judge (Satan, one presumes) is informed this is a mistake, he pits the two foes in combat to determine Cap's fate. His "final" victory over Red Skull frees him and he is returned to Earth.[17]

Captain America's initial return (along with the returns of the other two heroes) was presented in *Young Men* #24 (cover dated December 1953). In the story "Back from the Dead!" the Red Skull returns (inexplicably released from hell?) and has created an international crime syndicate to help the "Reds" (i.e., the Communists) in their murder and sabotage efforts across the globe. Red Skull only proceeds with this plan due to the fact that he believes Captain America to be dead. Cap, of course, comes out of retirement to save the day. Steve Rogers is now a schoolteacher and Bucky is one of his students (though Bucky should now be in his early twenties at least).[18] What makes this particular story stand out is that once Steve

Rogers is later revived from the ice in 1964, it will be discovered that he was, indeed, thought dead at the end of World War II. That will require a retcon for these 1950s storylines (to be discussed later). Cap would appear in four more issues of *Young Men* and two issues of *Men's Adventures* along with the three issues of his own revived comic throughout 1954.

For decades, these 1950s issues of *Captain America* were difficult to come by (as recently as 2011, it required a global search and considerable travel expense). Only a handful of libraries throughout the U.S. and anonymous European collectors possessed any copies, and some of those were in such states of disrepair that the text was illegible. Thankfully, due to reprints from Marvel (as well as digital copies available on the Marvel Unlimited app), these issues can be examined more closely and by a wider audience than at any point since their initial publication.

When *Captain America* returns with issue #76 (*Captain America's Weird Tales* #75, cover dated February 1950, had not actually featured Cap either on the cover or within its pages), though he had been established months earlier as a school teacher, he's now back in the army, and Betsy Ross—who had served as an FBI agent and eventually as Cap's second partner, Golden Girl, during the initial 1940s run—is now a Lois Lane-styled reporter, in love with Captain America but seeing Steve Rogers as an "All-American Flop."[19] In that issue's second story, Private Steve Rogers (who has somehow made it through all four years of World War II without a single promotion) works undercover to expose a communist plot in a non-aligned central European country (never named). Once he does so, Captain America appears to beat the bad guys into submission.[20] In the final Cap story from this issue, Captain America and Bucky head to Vietnam—where, at this time, the occupying French were fighting communist/nationalist Vietnamese under Ho Chi Minh—to investigate broadcasts from American citizens calling for America to cease its struggle against international communism.[21] The final panel clearly and boldly states: "Beware, commies, spies, traitors and foreign agents! Captain America, with all loyal, free men behind him, is looking for YOU [emphasis in the original], ready to fight until the last one of you is exposed for the yellow scum that you are!"[22]

It is important to note—considering comics' history of racist language—that the term "yellow" here is using the color to denote cowardice, though its use in a story with an Asian villain is noticeable. It is also worth noting that Romita's artistic portrayal of the Asian antagonist is much less stereotypical and racist than the Asian portrayals during World War II. Though using pale yellows for the skin tones, the eye slants are far less pronounced and more realistically lifelike.

In the next issue's first story, Cap and Bucky help a blind child whose father is being threatened by communist spies to steal a new atomic engine device or he and the boy will be killed (though eavesdropping on the spies indicates, naturally, that they will be killed no matter what).[23] In the next story, Captain America visits "Chinatown" (though it is not clear in which American city this particular Chinatown exists), where he meets a loyal Chinese American named Wing, who is being threatened by Chinese communist loyalists. The primary villain—the mysterious "Man with No Face"—is actually Wing's twin brother. This leads Cap to lament, "So Wing's own brother was ready to kill him for the cause! Another example of the brutal, twisted thinking of the Reds … when brother can be turned against brother!"[24]

Romita's artwork for the Chinese protagonist and antagonist are indistinguishable from the earlier Vietnam story. Cap's conclusion regarding the communist tendency to turn brother against brother is ironic, as this was exactly what McCarthy and his ilk were doing in their propaganda war against the Communists. The final story from this issue, titled simply "Captain America" (the previous story had been a Human Torch adventure), has Cap delivering a desperately needed drug to treat North Korean POWs being held by America, presumably in South Korea (or somewhere else in the region). It turns out that communist spies were poisoning their own men in order to use it as negative propaganda against the U.S. When Cap does arrive, however, the prisoners are so frightened by Americans—their minds presumably warped by communist propaganda—that they fight Cap until they see their comrades regain health.[25]

The final "Commie Smasher" issue from the 1950s was issue #78. In this issue's opening story, Cap finally faces off against the Soviets (the primary antagonists of the Cold War and its corresponding Red Scare). To battle America's Super Soldier, the Communists have created a monster called Electro (not to be confused with the Spider-Man villain of the same name a decade later).[26] In the next story, Cap visits the People's Republic of China to fight a giant dragon robot. While it may seem odd from a modern perspective that so many of Captain America's anti-communist enemies should be Asian, it is important to remember that at the time of these stories, the Korean War had just ended in a stalemate, and the French war in Indochina was just a year away from evolving into America's Vietnam War.[27]

Cap's final 1950s adventure would be in the story "The Hour of Doom!" In this story, Cap and Bucky face a homegrown threat in the form of television personality Chuck Blayne. Through his on-air charisma, Blayne has won the total devotion of America's young boys. He utilizes their devotion to turn them against the United Nations, warning that America's strength is weakened by "world cooperation," and promising to blow up the United

Nations at a designated hour. Cap successfully stops the bomb while also exposing Blayne's true cowardice live on television, destroying his hold on America's youth. Cap points out to Bucky that Blayne reminded him of Hitler: "Same words. 'Strong minds in strong bodies' and 'play to win'! Americans play not to win, necessarily, but for the sake of good sportsmanship and fair play … which Nazis and Reds know nothing about at all."[28]

While these "Commie Smasher" stories do promote the type of unquestioning loyalty and conformity that made the period so nightmarish for many and gave such power to the likes of Joe McCarthy, they do so more by painting the communist powers as dangers to personal liberty, which, of course, they were.

The Blayne story, however, also points out the dangers of demagogues at home. His "America First" message was very much reflective of McCarthy's own televised speeches. Coming as it did roughly a year after McCarthy's political downfall, it appears to show evidence that some, at least, had learned the lesson that McCarthyism taught. Overall, Captain America's conformity and pro–American/anti-communist stance appears much more in line with mainstream Americans at the time, rather than the radical McCarthyist fringe. Despite McCarthy's and Nixon's political abuse of the issue, the Soviet Union and the nations in their sphere of influence were, in fact, a threat to America and the world. Though the stories do not touch upon the many sociopolitical problems of the period, it is important to note that comic books were really not the venue for such commentary. Though the label "Commie Smasher" has negative connotations in the 21st century, it is very much emblematic of the mainstream thinking of the period.

Simon and Kirby's *Fighting American*

Joe Simon and Jack Kirby were naturally not thrilled at Captain America's return at their former employer. Now working at the smaller Prize Comics, Joe and Jack decided to show their former employer how it should be done. Their new—and last—joint creation would be *Fighting American*.[29] The premise: nerdy weakling Nelson Flagg is the intelligent younger brother of Johnny Flagg, a charismatic, once-athletic war hero, now crippled from service (whether from World War II or the recently ended Korean War is not made clear). Johnny is now a television personality speaking out on the dangers of communism with Nelson as his copywriter. When communist spies kill Johnny, Nelson swears to do whatever he can to continue his brother's quest against the communists. A general then approaches

Nelson with an idea. Johnny's body will be treated with a revitalization formula that will return it to its once-athletic form (though why this was not offered to Johnny as a de facto Super Soldier Serum while alive is unclear), and Nelson's mind will be transferred into his brother's body (yes, it sounds creepy). Nelson will then fight the communist threat as Fighting American, with a teenage sidekick named Speedboy, the Wonder Kid.[30]

The original run had only seven issues before being canceled, not much shorter than Captain America's return (though at one year—April/May 1954 through April/May 1955—a longer period of time than Cap's ten-month run). The first couple of issues were basic action/adventure stories, but Simon and Kirby soon took a campier approach which, in hindsight, appears to almost poke fun at the Cold War. In the final issue of the initial run, Fighting American faces off against an alien from another planet, here to observe the U.S./U.S.S.R. conflict. Once he shows that he is no threat to America, the alien tells the Fighting American, "After studying Earth people, I've found that those who practice *democracy* are closer than all others to a *better way of life* [emphasis in the original]."[31]

Simon would enlist Kirby again years later (presumably behind the backs of Stan Lee and the new Marvel Comics) to bring the Fighting American and Speedboy back for two brief issues under Harvey Comics in 1966. Two years earlier, Kirby had worked with Stan Lee at Marvel to bring Captain America back and into the burgeoning Marvel Comics Universe. That story (to be discussed in more detail later) will create the previously mentioned continuity error that those familiar with the hero's earlier run will remember. If Captain America was frozen in ice near the end of World War II, then who was this mysterious "Commie Smasher" posing as Cap?

Retcons to the "Commie Smasher"

When Stan Lee and Jack Kirby launched the Marvel superhero universe in 1961, the industry presumption was still that comics were primarily read by 8- to 12-year-old children who would eventually grow out of the medium and move on to other entertainments. It soon became clear, however, that some readers of these new Marvel adventures were older, some remembering the Golden Age comics (or were at least aware of them through conversations with adults). This became clear after the return of Captain America in *The Avengers* #4, explaining that Cap had disappeared near the end of World War II and had been frozen in ice for the last 20 years.[32] Readers sent in letters questioning this storyline, considering that Captain America had appeared in numerous comics for a decade after this alleged accident.

Steve Englehart would be the first Marvel writer to address this incongruity with what would become the first of many retcons to Captain America's (and Steve Rogers's) story in a 1972 issue of the recently renamed *Captain America and the Falcon*. After seeing Steve Rogers off on a long-overdue vacation, the Falcon (Harlem social worker Sam Wilson) discovers "Captain America" beating up a Black man in a New York alley, a man Falcon knows to be a good person, undeserving of such an attack by the Sentinel of Liberty. Unmasking the presumed imposter after a hard-fought battle, Falcon sees the face of... Steve Rogers! "Steve" is then seen to be in the company of Cap's presumed-dead World War II sidekick, Bucky Barnes (inexplicably still a young man nearly thirty years after he had supposedly died). The two claim to be "the REAL Captain America and Bucky! [emphasis in the original]."[33] This retcon will be examined in greater detail in a later chapter.

As the brief run of 1950s Captain America comics were so difficult to access for so many decades, much of what the comic book community in general "remembered" of the "Commie Smasher" Cap run has been tainted by this retconned interpretation. As this chapter has hopefully shown, however, the actual 1954 anti-communist stories of Captain America were far less radical than much of the anti-communist movement in American politics was at the time (due largely, no doubt, to Stan Lee's personal politics, which were far more liberal than the politicians of the day). In his analysis of the 1972 retcon, Jason Dittmer stated:

> The retcon that created [the different 1950s Cap] (as a separate entity from the "real" Captain America) was intended to establish the continuity of American national identity from the wartime righteousness of the 1940s directly to the liberal idealism of the 1960s, excising the red baiting McCarthyism of the 1950s ... linking the 1950s red baiting with the anti-integration movement of the 1970s and enabling the "real" Captain America to champion the cause of a multicultural America.[34]

This forced separation, making Captain America be distinctly "liberal" in his politics, more so than simply "patriotic" toward the nation's defense, has been an aspect of the character—and overall American identity—that scholars have had to keep in mind in their analyses.

Modern Takes on the "Commie Smasher"

Before examining what modern scholars have ascertained from the 1950s Cap stories, it is important to keep in mind the aforementioned difficulty in accessing complete and legible copies of these comics until very recently (and more so at the time that these analyses were originally published). In 2010, there were five libraries—four university libraries and the Library of Congress—that possessed some or all of the 1950s Cap issues, some of them so old and worn that the text was no longer legible. Now, with reprints from Marvel—such as *Decades: Marvel in the '50s* and *Captain America Strikes!* (2018)—and copies uploaded to the Marvel Unlimited digital comics reader app, researching these early eras of Timely/Atlas superhero comics is easier than ever.[35]

In his analysis of masculinity and violence in Captain America, J. Richard Stevens points out that the "Commie Smasher" stories paint the international communist threat as a danger equal to the Nazis in almost every way (approaching each philosophy as if they were identical). As stated earlier, this was primarily due to the fact that, in the eyes of the American government and a significant portion of the American people, they *were*. This was due to the two common threads evident in both Nazis and communists: the denial of personal liberties and enforced dedication to the state. Stevens writes,

> Captain America recasts Soviets as Nazis and uses the justification from a previous conflict with a previous opponent to support a new conflict. But the jingoism that was so successful in the early 1940s failed to capture the attention and imagination of the readership in the 1950s.... Apart from the lack of ideological engagement with an enemy that Cap often demonized, the violence leveled at such an unknown opponent appeared to have little appeal for the readers of comic books.[36]

Presenting this new Cold War as a threat as dangerous—or more so—than World War II would not be easy in regard to America's youth. From their perspective, how could it be? During the war, every child likely knew or knew of someone who was off fighting the war. Rationing, working mothers, and air raid sirens were a constant reminder of how dangerous the situation was. Other than the relatively small contingent of American soldiers sent to Korea (children being unaware of how much smaller a theater of war Korea was), and no real ramifications on daily American life (other than the new nuclear attack drills in school, which were not connected to the Korean conflict), as well as the daily escapism of television, the Cold War just did not seem as much of a threat, so how could the communists be? In his seminal work on comic book superhero history, Bradford W. Wright said of the "Commie Smasher" Captain America adventures,

> In [World War II], Captain America and Bucky had defended the American home front against Nazi and Japanese spies and saboteurs. Now they reprised that role against Communist agents, striking at "the betrayers" who hid behind the privileges of a free society in order to subvert American

institutions. The series offered no further discussion of Cold War issues beyond the message that Communists were evil, overweight, and poor dressers.... Times had changed since 1945, but these anticommunist superheroes had not changed with them.[37]

Indeed, times, and children, had changed considerably. The children reading Captain America adventures in the early 1940s had been born into the Great Depression, struggling families, hunger and want. The postwar children of a decade later had—to a much larger degree—known no such want, many thriving in middle-class families that enjoyed vacation time, allowances, television, and toys galore. The adults creating these comics could see the similarities in the threats of Nazism and communism because they were the same people. Their readers, however, were a new breed of American.

While it is true that the approach to Cap stories in World War II and the early Cold War were very similar in structure and dynamic, and the complexities of this new kind of warfare against a foe that very recently was our ally would be difficult to attempt to explain within the confines of a superhero comic book of the time, diluting the nuances of each conflict, it is also important to point out that these "Commie Smasher" adventures were not the red-baiting propaganda that many remember them as being. They essentially conveyed the same message that comic book readers were likely being fed every day in school: "Communists are bad people!"; "They want to destroy our way of life!"; and, perhaps most importantly, "If you see someone you suspect of being a communist, you should report it to your parents, your teacher, or the police!" Once atomic weaponry was added to the conflict—a matter of fact by 1954—the line between being vigilant against potential threat and blowing things out of proportion was a fine one indeed (as McCarthy's many victims could attest). The initial lesson taken from the failure of the "Commie Smasher" Captain America—and his fellow Timely/Atlas superheroes, Human Torch and Sub-Mariner—was that the day of the superhero might well be done. Though Superman was still wildly popular—as were, to a far lesser extent, Batman and Wonder Woman—it seemed that this new era of America no longer needed superheroes.

But just a couple of years after Captain America was re-cancelled, a new age of superheroes emerged. They would bring in the dawn of the Silver Age.

Birth of the Silver Age of Comics

Going into the 1950s, the superhero genre of comic books appeared to have seen its days pass away. Superman survived due to the popularity of his radio and, later, television programs. Batman survived primarily to his connection to Superman (Batman had appeared on the *Adventures of Superman* radio program when the *Superman* cast needed a break from their weekly grind and due to the heroes' shared comic title, *World's Finest Comics*). Wonder Woman survived due to a caveat in creator William Moulton Marston's contract with National Allied that stated if the company failed to publish at least four Wonder Woman comics in a twelve-month period, all rights to the character would revert to the Marston family, and the company did not want to lose the property. DC heroes Aquaman and Green Arrow also continued as stories in the Superman and Batman titles. Other than those, superheroes were all but gone. Timely/Atlas Comics' brief attempt to revive their own Golden Age heroes lasted no more than a year. Once the Comics Code was instituted by mid-decade, the entire comics industry appeared to be living on borrowed time. That would change in 1956, when the superhero genre would see a sudden resurgence and the industry would be changed forever.

Throughout the '50s, science fiction stories had become wildly popular. Science had won World War II with the discovery of atomic weaponry, and that same weaponry now threatened to destroy the world with mutually assured destruction (MAD) if the two new superpowers went to war with each other. This real-world scenario was like a story ripped right from the pages of science fiction magazines or movies. As such, in 1956, DC Comics editor Julius Schwartz decided to revive the Golden Age superheroes, but do so by giving them updated, science-fiction twists. Instead of simply bringing back the old heroes as Timely/Atlas had done, Schwartz took the hero name Flash and gave the character a new secret identity and a new sci-fi-influenced origin story. With the character's new appearance in DC's *Showcase* #4 (October 1956), the Silver Age of comics had begun. The massive success of the new Flash led Schwartz to do the same with other 1940s heroes Green Lantern, Atom, and Hawkman, eventually teaming them all up with Superman, Batman, Wonder Woman, Aquaman, and Green Arrow to form the Justice League of America in 1960.[38]

What follows is comic book history legend. As the story goes (and much of what follows is based on personal accounts, as no documentation exists to prove or disprove them), the success of DC's *Justice League of America* led Timely/Atlas owner Martin Goodman to order his comics editor Stan Lee to create a similar team of superheroes to compete. Lee, hoping to quit the industry entirely, was encouraged by his wife to do what was being asked of him, but to do so in his own style rather than following the genre norms. What resulted was Lee collaborating with his lead artist—the now-returned Jack Kirby—to create the Fantastic Four. The Marvel Age of Comics was born. From 1961 to 1963, Lee, Kirby, and artist Steve

Ditko would then create the core base of the Marvel Comics Universe: the Fantastic Four; the Incredible Hulk; the Mighty Thor; the Amazing Spider-Man; the Invincible Iron Man; Ant-Man and the Wasp; the Avengers; Daredevil, the Man Without Fear; Doctor Strange; and the X-Men. The market-shaking success of this new, interconnected superhero universe would soon be joined by the hero of World War II: Captain America.[39] By that time, the decade—and era—of "The Fifties" was over. America was undergoing rapid and volatile change.

Consensus Cracks: Setting up the 1960s

In 1956, President Dwight Eisenhower signed the Interstate Highway Act. With the growing threat of a possible attack by the Soviet Union, the president (as commander-in-chief of the armed forces) saw the necessity of keeping the military on high alert for fast movement anywhere in the country at any time. America's roadways were in dire need of repair, not to mention they were not wide enough for a massive military force to move quickly. The interstate highway system would create a network of interconnected multi-lane highways crisscrossing the country. Luckily, no invasion came, and the huge military project ultimately created something entirely new. The highway system created an infrastructure that would revolutionize transportation of goods and personal travel. This would have a ripple effect, creating the need for frequent gas stations, fast food restaurants, hotels, and attractions to help American drivers on their long journeys across the country.[40]

In 1957, the Cold War would open into a new battlefield: space. When the Soviet Union successfully launched the first manmade satellite into space—*Sputnik 1*—the United States was caught off guard. President Eisenhower requested and achieved a new American space agency: the National Aeronautics and Space Administration (NASA), which would quickly launch its Mercury program to not only catch up to the Soviets, but hopefully to beat them in the new space race. Prior to World War II, the widespread production of military supplies tended to end after the conflict had ended, but with the continuing threat of international communism—and the quest to beat them into space—the need for a nonstop, continuous military industrial machine was necessary. This would result in a military-industrial complex that would come to wield tremendous political and economic power in the country from this point forward.[41]

The push for civil rights for Black Americans (stalled during World War II in favor of a united war effort, as discussed in the last chapter) was revived with the 1954 Supreme Court case *Brown v. Board of Education of Topeka, Kansas*. The court-ordered desegregation of public schools—

followed the next summer by the highly publicized murder of 14-year-old Emmett Till in Mississippi by local white supremacists—gave impetus to an organized movement, led by groups such as the National Association for the Advancement of Colored People (NAACP) and the Southern Christian Leadership Conference (SCLC) with its charismatic leader, the Reverend Dr. Martin Luther King, Jr. This would be followed by other legendary events in the civil rights movement: the Montgomery bus boycott of 1955–1956, and government intervention to protect the "Little Rock Nine," Black students allowed to desegregate the all-white Central High School of Little Rock, Arkansas.[42] Widespread press coverage of these events played a large role in the successes that the movement would enjoy through the next decade. The new medium of television became a valuable tool for bringing the horrors evident in the American South into living rooms across the country and the world.

The new, thriving middle class meant that a new generation of teen-aged Americans no longer had to quit school to help support their families. These young people could focus on their high school educations and enjoy the full high school experience (sports, dances, socializing, etc.). Rock and roll became their soundtrack, and fast food joints became their after-school hangouts. Soon the teenager became its own distinct demographic, and a quest to find their identity through rebellion emerged as well. Younger children, too, had it easier than their parents or grandparents had. A widely expanding toy industry made children a key sales demographic as well, and these children would have the example of their older siblings to become their own brand of teenager in the decade to come. As various minority groups—and eventually women and the LGBTQ+ community as well—made it clear that they would not be silenced, America's youth would follow their example.

The consensus that had seemed so important at the beginning of the decade in order to prove a family's or individual's loyalty to the United States against its communist foes was cracking. Democracy and capitalism were not working for all Americans, and those long persecuted were prepared to pay whatever cost to change that for their children. If the American Way was to truly stand for "Truth and Justice," then changes needed to be made. As 1960 approached, few could know that the next decade would become the most turbulent, violent, and chaotic since the Civil War a century earlier. Multiple social movements, an increasingly unpopular war overseas, and heartrending assassinations would bring American society to the brink of apparent collapse. Luckily for those young people growing up surrounded by the unfolding drama of a society in distress, the superheroes were back to ease their concerns. Captain America would return just when he was needed most.

CHAPTER 3

Man Out of Time

Captain America and a Society in Transition, the 1960s

America exited the 1950s as a nation whose society was on the brink, though few could have seen it at the time. The warning signs were there. A razor-thin margin of victory in the 1960 presidential election showed the deep political divides that were building. The push for civil rights for Black Americans in the South was gaining national support through the strategic use of the media, particularly the country's new obsession: television. Rock and roll and hot-rod culture, spurred on by such celebrities as singer/actor Elvis Presley and actor James Dean, exhibited a rebellious streak in America's youth the likes of which had never been seen before. Within a few years, a book would be published that would cause American women to begin questioning their own place in society, a place that was no longer conducive to the proper housewife and mother presented on popular television sitcoms of the day.

Overseas, the Cold War continued. Five years earlier, America had quietly inserted herself into the ongoing civil conflict in the Southeast Asian country of Vietnam, which would soon explode into a quagmire of conflict and death. At the end of 1958, the small island nation of Cuba—just 90 miles off the Florida coast—fell to communism, bringing the threat of the Cold War to America's literal doorstep. Tensions with the Soviet Union went from bad to worse as the leadership vacuum left by the death of Josef Stalin was finally filled by Nikita Khrushchev, a man much more dedicated to globalizing communism than his predecessor had been. The new young American president, John F. Kennedy, would find himself leading America to the brink of utter destruction on more than one occasion.

After a chaotic decade that nearly saw the industry collapse entirely, the comic book business saw a considerable rebound, due primarily to the renewed popularity of superheroes and the burgeoning Silver Age of comics. Over at the newly minted Marvel Comics, Stan Lee and his bullpen of artistic masters were devising a new take on the 20-year-old concept: heroes with *problems*. When the country found itself reeling from the horrific events in Dallas, Texas, on November 22, 1963, Lee and original creator Jack Kirby would bring Captain America back. The Star-Spangled Avenger who had been there for America's children in the wake of Pearl Harbor more than two decades earlier would be there again for the nation's next darkest hour. But this time, rather than simply resorting to fisticuffs with Nazis or Commies, Cap would find himself a "man out of time," a modern-day Rip Van Winkle, symbolizing how different America had become since its Golden Age of World War II. He would also become the de facto leader of a new team of heroes, a team that would become a repository of reformed criminals seeking redemption, just as America sought redemption for the crimes of her past.

The Movement Builds Momentum: The Civil Rights Movement in the South

The stain of slavery, woven into the United States at its inception, had proven more complex an issue than simply a facet of the past like muskets or tri-corner hats. American slavery had been *race* based. Between 1619 and 1807, nearly half a million people had been stolen from their homes in Africa and forced into lifelong bondage in the United States. The number of slaves would grow to four million by 1865, and while many likely believed that the Civil War had settled the matter once and for all, the inherent racism that accompanied this race-based bondage would continue to have ripple effects on American society as decades turned into a century, and then beyond. Small victories here and there had given hope to Black Americans since the Civil War, but a century later, those victories were still too few, too small, and too far apart.

The South was the most blatant example of this ongoing racism. White supremacists, still disgruntled from losing their free labor a century earlier, had created a Southern society where Black citizens must "know their place" or face horrifying consequences, causing them to live lifetimes in fear and hopelessness. In the 1950s, the rallying leadership of Dr. Martin Luther King, Jr., gave Southern Blacks their greatest hope for change, and Southern whites their greatest fear of an integrated and amalgamated society. A violent clash between these competing ideas for the country's future was inevitable, but few Americans outside of the South could have fathomed just how violent that could be. As Americans en masse became more and more divided over the issue of the Vietnam War, the country's racism would become evident once again.

Chapter 3. Man Out of Time

Although Americans of African descent represented only about 17 percent of the overall population of the country, they represented roughly 30 percent of American boys drafted into military service in Vietnam. Other than physical deferments (for any malady that made military service impossible), the only way to avoid the draft (legally) was through college attendance. As few Black Americans had opportunities to attend college, more of their young men were available for the draft. This was just one of many, many societal flaws that Dr. King and his fellow activists sought to change (to a significant degree, they succeeded). The issue of racism would not end with the 1960s—though there were many Americans at the time who believed that it would—but by 1970, Black Americans had considerably more opportunities than in any decade prior. The sacrifices of the '50s and '60s did that.

Events in Birmingham, Alabama, in the spring of 1963 caught national attention when Black children marching in protest were attacked by city police and fire forces—led by the local head of public "safety," Eugene "Bull" Connor—with police dogs attacking the children and high-powered fire hoses aimed at them as well. Playing out on the evening news on television, President Kennedy responded by calling on Congress to pass a civil rights bill. This hopeful turn of events led Dr. King and his SCLC along with the Student Non-Violent Coordinating Committee (SNCC), the Congress for Racial Equality (CORE) and the NAACP to organize a march on Washington, D.C., in support of the president's new bill (essentially the march that A. Philip Randolph had planned in 1940). On August 28, 1963, Dr. King delivered his iconic "I Have a Dream" speech on the steps of the Lincoln Memorial. In the wake of this high point in the struggle, however, four young Black girls were killed just two weeks later when white supremacists set off a bomb at the 16th Street Baptist Church (the starting point of the children's march earlier that year).

After the assassination of President Kennedy that November, his successor, Lyndon B. Johnson, took up the late president's crusade, using a mixture of popular support, backroom deals, and outright political bullying to get Congress to pass the Civil Rights Act—eliminating laws on racial segregation in public places and establishing protections for equal opportunity—into law on July 2, 1964. A year later, in the wake of continued violence against Black protesters in Selma, Alabama, President Johnson signed the Voting Rights Act—tearing down the barriers preventing racial/ethnic minorities from voting (the actual *right* to vote already established in the 15th and 19th amendments to the Constitution)—on August 6, 1965. With legal protections now in place against segregation and voter suppression, Dr. King and the abovementioned groups next focused on economic opportunities for Blacks. It was while doing so in Memphis,

Tennessee, on April 4, 1968, that Dr. King was assassinated as well, standing outside of his hotel room. While this did not end the struggle for Black civil rights, the loss of Dr. King's rallying influence was a major setback to the organized effort. By that time, however, the movement had expanded, including several similarly persecuted groups across America.

The Movement Expands

In 1965, Filipino and Hispanic agriculture workers in California began their own struggle for better pay and an end to discriminatory practices, largely under the leadership of Cesar Chavez and Dolores Huerta. In Minnesota in 1968, the American Indian Movement (AIM) was formed under the leadership of Dennis Banks, Clyde Bellecourt, and George Mitchell to demand justice for American Indians, a group whose history with the United States was as tragic and horrific in its own way as that of Black Americans. From late 1969 to mid–1971, an offshoot of AIM led by Richard Oakes and LaNada Means organized an occupation of the abandoned island prison of Alcatraz in California, utilizing wording of the U.S. government's 1868 Treaty of Fort Laramie with the Sioux nations as justification for taking the island.

In 1960, college students in New York founded the Students for a Democratic Society (SDS). In 1962, SDS member Tom Hayden oversaw creation of a declaratory document, the Port Huron Statement, which essentially argued that continued racism and economic disparity in America was in direct opposition to the principles of the Founding Fathers. At first focusing primarily on civil rights, the outbreak of military operations in Vietnam in 1965 led the group to focus entirely on an anti-war agenda, launching a protest in Washington, D.C., that would last until the conflict's conclusion in early 1973. Originally a group of conservatively dressed and well-behaved young people, by '65 a stronger dedication to nonconformity (as well as the introduction of a considerable amount of illegal drugs) led the SDS members to take on the more traditionally recognized hippie persona of long hair and casual dress (and questionable personal hygiene).

Another long-persecuted group in America at the time was women. Though women had gained the right to vote nationally in 1919, experienced a breakdown of many social restrictions in the decade that followed, and come out in massive numbers to fill in gaps in the country's industrial machine during World War II, the onset of the Cold War had pushed women back into the kitchens and back into their "traditional" roles. In 1963, author Betty Friedan published her groundbreaking book

The Feminine Mystique, outlining what she called "the problem that has no name," this indescribable feeling felt by many—largely white middle-class—women that their lives were in some way unfulfilled. This would lead to the creation of the National Organization for Women in 1966, with Friedan named the group's first president. The ensuing women's movement would see considerable successes throughout the 1970s, permanently changing the social landscape for women going forward.

Another movement that picked up steam just as the decade drew to a close was the gay rights movement, more popularly known today as the LGBTQ+ movement. In the early hours of June 28, 1969, a police raid of a known gay bar at the Stonewall Inn in Greenwich Village, New York, led to a violent clash between police and patrons of the bar. Long ostracized from society (and even more so in the fundamentalist conservative fight against communism during the Cold War), the gay community had had enough. From that day to this, June 28 has been celebrated as Pride Day throughout the U.S., and the riots at Stonewall that day inspired a national movement that would be as significant in the 1970s as the women's movement.

The gay rights movement, the women's movement, and the Black movement in the South in the '60s: popular culture in the 1970s would stand firmly behind all of them.

While all of these movements were a long time in coming, their timing, coinciding as they did with the high point of the Cold War, both helped and hindered the collective movement. Some saw it as an opportunity for America to live up to its claims of liberty and freedom against the oppression of communism, while others viewed the movements as examples of the leftist philosophies of America's enemies. It is impossible to accurately argue one point or the other, as America itself was somewhat sketchy on living up to the principles it claimed to defend. This is something that the long-sleeping Captain America will discover in his own hero's journey.

The Cold War Heats Up

For most of the 1950s, the Cold War was very cold, with leadership of the Soviet Union essentially a vacuum from 1953 to 1957, but the launching of the "space race" and the appointment of Nikita Khrushchev as the new premier of the Soviet government reignited the conflict, making the Cold War much hotter in the decade that followed. In April 1961, President Kennedy approved an ill-conceived attempted insurrection by American-backed agents in Cuba's Bay of Pigs that ultimately humiliated the new young president. Just a few months later, Khrushchev ordered construction of a wall dividing the occupied city of Berlin, Germany, sealing off the free, capitalist, western part of the city from the rest of communist East Germany. At the end of World War II, the nation of Germany and city of Berlin were divided among the four "winners" of the European war: the U.S., the U.K., France, and the U.S.S.R. As the Cold War developed in the ashes of World War II, Berlin became a ground zero for the conflict, being the one point in the world where American and Soviet forces were most closely physically situated. The erection of the wall was a clear symbol to the world that the conflict between these two nuclear superpowers was growing and hardening.

In the wake of the American attempt on his government, Cuban dictator Fidel Castro turned to his Soviet allies for defensive weapons against possible future American incursions. The Soviets responded by providing the communist island nation with medium-range and intermediate-range ballistic missiles, with nuclear warheads capable of wiping out most of the United States with only minutes' warning. American discovery of these weapons led to a tense two-week crisis in October 1962, the Cuban Missile Crisis. While publicly it appeared that the Soviets backed down to President Kennedy, secretly an agreement between the two superpower leaders brought the crisis to an end with a whimper rather than the dreaded bang. Coming so close to mutually assured destruction, the Cold War between the superpowers would cool considerably for the remainder of the decade, paving the way for a policy in the 1970s that appeared to permanently end the conflict.

For the remainder of the '60s, America's struggle against international communism would be focused primarily on the small country of Vietnam, which had been divided in 1955 into the communist North under Ho Chi Minh and the "democratic" (for lack of a more accurate word) South under President Ngo Dinh Diem. America had been providing military training and assistance to the south ever since. An alleged attack on a U.S. naval vessel in 1964 led President Johnson to take a much more directly militant approach. In response to this alleged attack, Congress passed the Tonkin Resolution, essentially a blank check for President Johnson to use whatever means necessary to stop the communist North Vietnam. While support for the war was originally high among mainstream Americans, a large, well-coordinated strike against U.S. forces by communist sympathizers in South Vietnam on the Chinese New Year of Tet in 1968 led the news media (and, therefore, the populace at large) to turn against the war, making it a divisive political issue and a key factor in the presidential election of that year.

Comic book publishers understood that the Cold War and the conflict in Vietnam were far more complex than the traditional good vs.

Chapter 3. Man Out of Time

evil conflict of World War II, and, as such, few mentions appeared in the superhero adventures of the decade. While the origin stories of the Fantastic Four and Iron Man were both tied to the overall Cold War, Captain America—a symbol of American power and the hero of World War II—would make only one brief visit to Vietnam, and would face no confrontations with the Soviet Union, China, or Cuba (the lesson of the "Commie Smasher" failure no doubt still fresh in Lee's mind). The struggle against communism abroad and for civil rights at home had a massive body count in the 1960s. Bloodshed in Vietnam and here at home, along with the assassinations of civil rights leaders Malcolm X and Dr. King were bookended by two other political assassinations: two brothers, two popular leaders, two symbols of hope literally shot down in their prime.... John and Bobby Kennedy.

Two Brothers, Two Deaths

President John F. Kennedy was assassinated while traveling in a motorcade through the streets of Dallas, Texas, on November 22, 1963. His recent push for passage of a civil rights bill had severely divided the Democratic Party, the southern wing of which had been dominated by conservative white supremacists since its inception in 1826, the same southern wing which had been the core of the Confederate secession that led to the Civil War and implementation of the racist Jim Crow policies of the South in the century since. With his reelection bid just a year away, Kennedy visited the key Southern states of Florida and Texas in an attempt to bring the party together before the upcoming election year. Though unpopular with the conservative wing of his own party—and despite the well-documented history of violence from Southern white supremacists—the alleged assassin was, in fact, a leftist, pro–Marxist, former U.S. Marine, former Soviet defector named Lee Harvey Oswald.

The young president's brother—and attorney general—Robert F. "Bobby" Kennedy was elected U.S. senator from New York the year following the president's death. Deeply committed to civil rights for all Americans here at home and against the escalating war in Vietnam abroad—and with the sitting President Johnson deciding not to seek reelection—Bobby ran for the Democratic nomination for president in 1968. On June 6 of that year, immediately after being named the winner of the Democratic primary in California, Bobby was also shot and killed. Though, like his brother, unpopular with radical conservatives across the country, the alleged assassin was Palestinian/Jordanian immigrant Sirhan Sirhan. Though the official accounts of Oswald's and Sirhan's guilt remain the standard lines of the news media in general, extremely suspicious facets of both assassinations have led to multiple conspiracy theories in both cases, with the documented facts of the crimes inconsistent with the official stories.

The assassinations of the Kennedy brothers—and Dr. King just months before Bobby—and the questionable facts surrounding the cases (as well as the government's role in keeping certain facts from the public and promoting official conclusions that a growing percentage of the public doubted) created a distrust between the people and Washington that would become much larger in the decades to come. Prior to 1963, the vast majority of Americans trusted the office of the president, whether they liked the sitting president or not; but after 1963, that trust would begin to dwindle to the point of total *distrust*. For the time being, however, just as Captain America was there in the wake of the national heartbreak of Pearl Harbor, just weeks after the national heartbreak of President Kennedy's death, Captain America would return.

Pop Culture in a Time of Chaos

Like society itself, American pop culture also experienced a decade of considerable change. Television—by now the primary source of entertainment in the country—saw drastically different programming between 1960 and 1970. Traditional family sitcoms such as *Father Knows Best*, *Ozzie and Harriet*, and *Leave It to Beaver* were replaced with far sillier nonconformist family sitcoms such as *The Addams Family*, *The Beverly Hillbillies*, and *Bewitched*. Crime dramas like the straightlaced *Dragnet* was replaced with the more youth-oriented *The Mod Squad*. Comedy/variety programs such as *The Jack Benny Program* and *The Burns and Allen Show* were replaced with the far more liberal and socially critical *Rowan and Martin's Laugh-In* and *The Smothers Brothers Comedy Hour*. In the area of science fiction, the O.-Henry-esque, in-your-face social commentary of *The Twilight Zone* was replaced with the more subtle—but equally powerful—social commentary of *Star Trek*. As America's future appeared more and more uncertain, daily escapism for most Americans became more important than at any time since the Great Depression.

On the big screen, the massive success of Cecil B. DeMille's *The Ten Commandments* in 1956 inspired Hollywood studios to invest massive budgets in a succession of similar hours-long epics such as *Cleopatra*, *Lawrence of Arabia*, and *The Greatest Story Ever Told* (budgets that would come close to bankrupting the studios going into the 1970s). The cowboy western—a popular movie trope since the medium's inception—saw its swan song with the Italian-made Clint Eastwood "Man with No Name" trilogy and the beginning of the end of the long cowboy career of John Wayne. Science fiction films transitioned from the over-the-top silly horror of 1950s classics like *Godzilla* and *The Fly* to the more esoteric and socially conscious *2001: A Space Odyssey* and *Planet of the Apes*.

Thanks to the Silver Age of comics launched by DC's Julius Schwartz, comic books saw a new and unexpected resurgence in the 1960s. The frightening events unfolding at home and abroad being very likely as unnerving to observant youth as they had been in the 1940s, the comfort provided by the protective aspects of superheroes provided a much-needed balm. As mentioned in the previous chapter, Timely/Atlas Comics would change their name once again, as Stan Lee and his team of artists put their own twist on the Silver Age with the advent of the Marvel superhero universe. While still symbols of protection from dangerous threats, these Marvel heroes were different. They had problems. They were psychologically complex, and the problems they confronted, while steering clear of actual real-world events, closely reflected the world that young—and now older—readers would recognize and associate with. The superhero had evolved, and Captain America would evolve with them.

Marvel Comics

When it became clear to Timely/Atlas Comics owner Martin Goodman that superheroes were making a popular return to the medium, he instructed his editor/head writer Stan Lee to follow DC's example of *Justice League of America* with their own team of superheroes. Although Lee was tired of comics and considering leaving the industry altogether, his wife Joanie—as Lee recounted numerous times over the decades—suggested that he do as Goodman was asking, but in a way that Lee would prefer (worst-case scenario being that he was fired, and he wanted to quit anyway). That advice would change her husband's life, the future of Goodman's company, the comic book industry, and American popular culture forever. While Lee's and Kirby's concept of the Fantastic Four took shape, moving from concept to page throughout the spring and summer of 1961, in the real world the Soviet Union was launching cosmonaut Yuri Gagarin, the first human to go into space, and the issue hit newsstands the same week that the Soviets began construction on the Berlin Wall. As such, *Fantastic Four* #1's origin story—the four adventurers taking an experimental flight into space in order to beat the Soviets—proved … timely.[1]

Fantastic Four #1—under the company's new banner of "Marvel Comics"—was an instant hit, and as success breeds imitation, Goodman soon asked for more of the same. As it turned out, Lee and Kirby were on a creative roll. Over the next two years, Mister Fantastic, the Invisible Girl, the Human Torch, and the Thing would gain a lot of company as they became part of a much bigger universe; they just didn't know it yet (to paraphrase Nick Fury). Soon Lee and Kirby would introduce the world to the Incredible Hulk, the brutish monster that came about when physicist Dr. Bruce Banner was exposed to lethal amounts of gamma radiation. At first the Hulk was gray, his changes brought on by the setting of the sun.[2] By decade's end, the character's green appearance and rage-driven change would become the core of the Hulk's story. The following month, Lee introduced the mythical Norse god of thunder as a modern-day superhero: the Mighty Thor. When handicapped physician Dr. Donald Blake found himself trapped in a cave without his cane, he discovered a wooden staff that would suffice, only to realize that when he struck the stick on the ground, he transformed into the ancient god of thunder, and the stick became his magical hammer, Mjolnir.[3]

These future teammates would soon be followed by Iron Man, Ant-Man, and the Wasp, before bringing all five together to form the Avengers. When Thor's half-brother (stepbrother? adopted brother? It changes over time) Loki threatens the Earth, Thor rallies "Earth's Mightiest Heroes" to help him stop the threat (Hulk ally Rick Jones attempted to gain help from the Fantastic Four, but they were busy).[4] In the meantime, Lee and artist Steve Ditko had created the superhero that would come to be the face of Marvel Comics: the Amazing Spider-Man. When high school student Peter Parker is bitten by a radioactive spider, he gains the proportional strength and stamina of a spider, as well as the ability to stick to walls, but when his apathy toward helping a policeman capture a running criminal leads to tragedy, Parker learns the hard way that "with great power there must also come—great responsibility!"[5] Over the following year, Ditko would assist Lee in creating Doctor Strange, Master of the Mystic Arts, while Kirby would assist in creating the blind lawyer/vigilante Daredevil: the Man Without Fear, as well as the merry band of mutants known as the X-Men.

These heroes were unlike any the genre had known before. The Thing and the Hulk were monsters that neither man wanted to be. Peter Parker needed to help his elderly aunt financially along with all of the daily problems that all teenagers faced (while also stopping the villainous intents of the Green Goblin, Electro, Sandman, the Lizard, and more). Tony Stark (Iron Man) and Matt Murdock (Daredevil) had physical disabilities that they had to work around. The X-Men (young people born with a mutated "x-gene" that gave some of them fantastic powers) were sworn to defend a world that hated and feared them. The romantic relationship between Reed

Richard (Mister Fantastic) and Sue Storm (Invisible Girl) would prove far more complex, complicated, and realistic than the decades-long relationship between Superman and Lois Lane.

The Marvel heroes were ones that any reader could sympathize with and understand. This facet of Marvel characters (including those yet to come) was a key factor in Marvel slowly growing to dominate the industry for decades (and eventually Hollywood as well).

Over the course of two years, Marvel Comics built a universe of heroes that rivaled, in number and popularity, DC's accumulated universe of heroes built over nearly a quarter of a century. In addition to this new, modern take on superheroes, Lee also broke down the barrier between creators and audience. Marvel fans would not address letters to "Dear Editor." Lee built his own bullpen of artists and assistant writers into their own distinct personalities, making the readers feel as if they knew the men behind their new favorite heroes.[6] With the fact that so many of the Marvel heroes—the Fantastic Four, Hulk, Spider-Man, Daredevil, and possibly the X-Men (as the original source of human mutation)—were the result of radiation, the stories played into common social anxieties of the day regarding the dangers that the Cold War and atomic experimentation had introduced into daily life.[7] America had changed considerably since becoming a superpower in World War II. The very weapons that helped save the world then now threatened the world's future. Little could Americans know at the time that the unexpected death of President Kennedy in November 1963 would start a decade of chaos that threatened the very fabric of American society.

Luckily, just when he was needed most, Captain America returned.

Cap in the 1960s

In 1957, Timely/Atlas owner Martin Goodman was in desperate need of a new source for printing and distributing his magazines and comic books. He ultimately signed with Independent News. Unfortunately for his comics division, Independent was owned by his rival, DC Comics. Timely/Atlas's comic book output was reduced to eight titles per month. The resulting massive drop in the comics division's output left Stan Lee in the unenviable position of laying off his creative talents and reducing others to part-time status.[8] This was bad enough in the late '50s when the comics industry was already slowing down. It would become a nightmare when the number and popularity of the new Marvel heroes experienced a much greater demand. To solve this problem, while some heroes—the Fantastic Four, Spider-Man, Daredevil—had their own titles, others—Iron

Man, Doctor Strange, Nick Fury, and Captain America—would need to double up, at least for a while. Iron Man had been introduced and continued to be published under the title of a previous Atlas comic, *Tales of Suspense*. As with all the new Marvel comics of the 1960s, Stan Lee was the primary writer of all of Cap's new adventures, with Kirby providing the art throughout the decade.

Captain America officially entered the Marvel Comics Universe with *The Avengers* #4. Rather than having him merely show up, unchanged and unaged for decades, as Superman, Batman, and Wonder Woman were over at DC Comics, Lee and Kirby showed that Cap had been frozen in ice, having fallen into freezing waters after his last battle with the Red Skull near the end of World War II. He is found by Prince Namor, the Sub-Mariner (the sometimes villain/sometimes hero in the Marvel Comics Universe and, himself, a hero from the World War II era and a Golden Age ally of Captain America). Namor finds the block of ice being worshipped by Inuits and angrily takes it and throws it back into the sea (apparently unaware and unconcerned as to who the frozen individual was). As the block of ice floats southward, it melts, leaving the unconscious body of Cap for the Avengers to find. Once resuscitated—and calmed down—Cap agrees to join the new team of superheroes.[9] Though the Avengers are financed by Tony Stark (Iron Man), Captain America soon becomes the team's de facto leader. This becomes important by decade's end when the Avengers become a haven through which former criminals can redeem themselves. Many early Avengers—Black Widow, Hawkeye, Scarlet Witch, Quicksilver, and Vision—begin their careers as villains. Through Cap's example of the American Dream, where anyone can define who and what they become, these onetime villains will go on to become some of Earth's mightiest heroes.

Soon after Cap's return, Rick Jones—friend of Bruce Banner/the Hulk and, inexplicably, frequent hanger-on of several Marvel heroes—suggests becoming the new Bucky and partner to Captain America. Cap responds angrily to the suggestion, underscoring an ongoing storyline in the new adventures of Steve Rogers as Captain America. Steve suffers from survivor's guilt, a common malady of soldiers who have survived combat while losing close comrades-in-arms. Bucky is believed dead, dying in the same battle that Steve has miraculously survived. Bucky will join the list of Peter Parker's Uncle Ben and, later, Parker's girlfriend Gwen Stacy as characters that Marvel writers must never bring back from the dead. That list remained sacrosanct for decades (until Marvel realized that there is no money in dead characters).

The other primary aspect of the revived Captain is that Steve Rogers is a "man out of time." He is a modern-day Rumpelstiltskin, waking up after decades to a world he no longer recognizes. Steve has never seen a television set. He has never heard of an intercontinental ballistic missile. He has never witnessed the violent response to civil protest that is going on in the American South. He is not familiar with rebellious teenagers. When he went in the ice, the Soviet Union was America's ally. There had not been a presidential assassination in nearly half a century. Lastly, growing up during the Great Depression, he had never seen a financially thriving middle class. When one considers how much American society has changed from 2000 to 2020 with the advent of widespread internet, smartphones and social media, it is easy to imagine what an alien world 1964 America would be to someone essentially asleep since 1944.

In *Tales of Suspense* #58, the returned Captain America made his first non–Avengers appearance. Still titled *Tales of Suspense featuring The Power of Iron Man*, the Golden Avenger faces the conundrum of *two* Captain Americas: the real one, and the villain Chameleon impersonating him.[10] Beginning with the next issue, the title would be shared, *Tales of Suspense featuring Iron Man and Captain America*, with each hero's adventures covering half of each issue. In this Cap story, it is established that Iron Man has allowed Cap to move into Avengers Mansion in New York City, complete with the services of Tony Stark's butler, Jarvis (an actual human being rather than the A.I. made popular in the MCU films). In Cap's only visit to war-torn Vietnam, the hero goes behind enemy lines to rescue a captured American combat pilot, Jim Baker.[11] While the issue had a cover date of January 1965, it hit newsstands in October of the previous year, just two months after American pilot Lieutenant, Junior Grade (LTJG) Everett Alvarez, Jr., became the first American POW in the growing Vietnam War. Unlike Alvarez, however, the fictional Baker was a Black man. This is evidence of Lee's standing policy—long before he was allowed to create Black heroes—of wanting the background/guest characters in his superhero adventures to reflect the diversity of the real world.

In issue #63, Lee and Kirby retell the origin story of Captain America (issues 63–71 would be World War II adventures). Lee makes some subtle changes to the original 1940 story. Dr. Reinstein (the original scientist clearly a take on "Einstein") is renamed Dr. Erskine. Also, the project to create the Super Soldier is now shown to be "Operation Rebirth." Another change is that Private Steve Rogers is shown to be a bumbling soldier (akin to Clark Kent's persona versus that of Superman). Perhaps the most noteworthy change is the fate of the Nazi spy/assassin who kills Dr. Erskine. In the original 1941 comic, the newly transformed Steve Rogers punches the spy into a bank of electronic equipment (utilized in his transformation), accidentally killing the spy through electrocution; in the retelling, the spy purposely commits suicide (sparing the new Captain America of any suspicion of manslaughter).[12] While *Avengers* #4 explained that Captain America had been a hero during World War II, the war would mean nothing to the target audience of these new stories, none of whom had been born when the war ended. This nine-issue return to Cap's wartime adventures cements in the minds of the audience that Cap is indeed a "man out of time," a part of their parents' and grandparents' generation.

After the World War II adventures, Cap returns to the present, dreaming of his last wartime interaction with the Red Skull when the Nazi villain warned the Star-Spangled Avenger that 20 years after the war ended (so, in 1965), Nazi sleepers would awaken to once more return the Nazis to power.[13] This story of Nazi sleepers returning to reignite conflict—the sleepers being powerful giant robots—continues through issue #74. A few issues later, the Red Skull returns to the present, having his men attack Captain America while wearing devices that make them invisible to the public (hence making Cap look like a lunatic fighting people who are not there). The Skull recounts that he and his lieutenants were rescued after their last battle with Cap in World War II by the ultra-secret organization known only as "THEM," a committee of the Marvel terrorist organization known as Hydra, with its leader Baron von Strucker utilizing THEM to oversee two of Hydra's subdivisions: Advanced Idea Mechanics (AIM), a group of evil scientists, and the Secret Empire, which Cap will face in one of his most iconic stories in the following decade.[14] This is a key issue as it reintroduces Red Skull into the new Marvel Universe as well as the organization AIM and their creation, the Cosmic Cube (which will have many, many, *many* reappearances in Cap comics over the decades to come).

Most of the 1960s adventures of Captain America are essentially setting up plot devices and characters that will come to define the comic for the decades to come. Red Skull's return provides Cap with his most dangerous and deadly nemesis. In a rather ridiculous statement by the Skull, he states, "Haven't you [Cap] realized yet that ... the final triumph shall always be mine!"[15] There is quite a bit to unpack in that statement: (A) Cap has defeated the Skull every single time (though the Skull does have reason to believe Cap will lose *this* time); (B) the *final* triumph could only be decided when one of the two enemies is definitively dead (which both men at this point seem surprisingly adept at avoiding); and (C) how can the *final* triumph *always* be his? Are they going to have multiple final battles? The general gist of the Skull's statement seems to be fairly clear, but this quote does so through some unusually poor word choices for the legendary Lee. At one point, Cap will have to come to the aid of Nick Fury to face off against the Hate-Monger. Originally introduced in *Fantastic Four* #21 (December 1963) and created by Stan Lee and Jack Kirby, Hate-Monger was, in fact, Adolf Hitler, surviving World War II by having his consciousness uploaded into a cloned body (decades before Emperor Palpatine did it). The main modern-day Nazi, however, would continue to be the Red Skull. The Skull will of course continue to burden Captain America well into the 21st century, often utilizing the many assets of the terrorist organization Hydra.

Hydra becomes a standard foe for SHIELD (which, though it has held many acronyms over the decades, originally stood for "Supreme Headquarters, International Espionage and Law-enforcement Division"), acting as a precursor to the G.I. Joe vs. Cobra conflict originating in the 1980s (and covered in comic book form by Marvel). As stated earlier, the Hydra science division, AIM, creates the Cosmic Cube, a favorite weapon of the Red Skull from this point forward. The official Marvel database defines the Cube as "an item that can control matter and energy, answering to the will of the sentient beings that use them."[16] Essentially, the individual who possesses the Cube can make anything they imagine a reality. America loses World War II? Done! Captain America is a villain? Done! My burger should have been well-done? Done! The downside is, if one were to use the Cube for nefarious purposes (which Red Skull will do many, many, *many* times), all one has to do to *undo* what was done is to take possession of the Cube and reverse the effect. As a result, it becomes a rather lazy plot device to bring what could have been very interesting stories to a close. Eventually, if anything completely outlandish or unbeatable appears to be happening, it is usually just the Cosmic Cube, and Cap need only wish things back to normal. (Ideally, one would use the Cube to make the world as they want it and destroy the Cube, but human nature would negate any possibility of anyone doing that. Who knows when you might want a burger and fries after everything is closed?)

Other nemeses that debut in the 1960s are the Super Adaptoid, another AIM creation that is essentially an android that can take on the appearance of anyone it needs to, and Batroc the Leaper, a French mercenary that can ... jump ... a lot. Another outlandish villain that debuts in Cap's '60s adventures is MODOK. This villain—originally AIM scientist George Tarleton—is a "Mechanized Organism Designed Only for Killing" (though, from time to time, the "M" has stood for "Mobile" or "Mental"). It consists of Tarleton's massively engorged head encased in a yellow flying barrel with his normal-sized arms and legs protruding (with his giant head giving him enhanced intelligence and psionic powers).[17] While Red Skull and Batroc primarily face off only against Captain America, MODOK will appear in numerous comics over the decades, facing off against an array of Marvel heroes.

Shortly after Captain America begins appearing in *Tales of Suspense*, readers were introduced to Sharon Carter, Agent 13 of SHIELD. In her first appearance, it is revealed that Captain America's love interest in World War II had been Peggy Carter (as shown in the MCU films). Sharon Carter is introduced as Peggy's sister (with apparently a 20-year age gap between the siblings). Of course, Peggy Carter would now be a woman in her mid-40s/early 50s (and though she is still alive, and working with SHIELD, she is now too old for the long frozen hero). As such, *Sharon* Carter will now be Steve Rogers's continuing on-again/off-again love interest, on into the 2020s (brief pause for the collective "Gasp!" and/or "Ew!"). Agent 13 is one of Nick Fury's most dependable and qualified field agents, placing her alongside Captain America on numerous SHIELD-sponsored missions. This is something the old-school World War II soldier cannot wrap his mind around, once proclaiming, "I can't bring a *girl* on such a mission!" (This is a rather odd take for Cap considering that, in the late 1940s, his girlfriend Betsy Ross becomes his sidekick Golden Girl with no apprehension on Cap's part.)[18] Cap's chauvinism, disguised as chivalry, will become more and more an issue in the 1970s as the couple becomes more romantically involved.

Nick Fury, the eye-patched director of SHIELD, debuted in *Sgt. Fury and His Howling Commandos* #1 in 1963, a comic telling daring tales of World War II. When he is introduced later as the director of SHIELD, it is eventually explained that some formula has allowed him to dramatically slow his aging (or maybe he is a robot, or a series of robots—the mystery continues). Though Captain America joins the Avengers on his arrival in the 1960s, the international spy boss cannot resist making full use of America's single greatest soldier, sending Cap on numerous SHIELD missions throughout the 1960s and '70s (just as the MCU version will do in the 2014 film *Captain America: The Winter Soldier*). Fury's need to keep some information secret from the Star-Spangled Avenger will be the cause of many disagreements between these two very different concepts of the patriotic hero.

By far, the most historically important issue of Captain America adventures in the 1960s is *Captain America* #117 (September 1969). Having been body-swapped with the Red Skull, Cap is trapped on an island *within* the Cosmic Cube (with Skull in Cap's body watching from outside). While trapped, Steve meets Sam Wilson, who has also been trapped by the Skull for some reason. Sam has developed a psychic link with a falcon named Redwing. Once both men escape—and Steve returns to his own body—Sam agrees to become Cap's partner, the Falcon.[19] Not yet possessing his trademark wings, Falcon originally gets around via swinging on a cable that contains a bird-like claw, with trusty Redwing at his side. When not at work as the Falcon, Sam will work as a social worker in New York's Harlem, doing what he can for the Black community there throughout the 1970s. While Black Panther had been the first Black comic book superhero in 1966, Falcon holds the distinction of being the first Black *American* superhero.

Captain America's comic book adventures in the 1960s differ little from their 1940s and 1950s counterparts, essentially simple, basic "beat up the bad guy of the month" superhero stories. That was by design. When asked during a radio interview why Cap was not out there supporting the war effort in Vietnam as he had in Europe and the Pacific during World War II, Stan Lee said, "I don't know if it's in good taste to take something as serious as the situation in Vietnam and put a character like Captain America … we would have to start treating him differently and taking the whole thing more seriously."[20]

The stories do, however, set the stage for the character's perspective as a literal "man out of time," viewing the turbulent decades to come through the heroic eyes of America's Greatest Generation. They also set up vital characters—both enemies and allies—that will come to define the hero and his comic adventures on into the 21st century (and in his feature films). One key difference in the Cap comics of the 1960s is the addition of letters pages, publishing the thoughts and opinions of Captain America's dedicated readers. While on the surface this provides an excellent window into the minds of comic book readers of the period, it turns out these "letters" are not always what they appear to be.

The Letters to Cap

One aspect of comic books that emerged in the 1960s was the printing of fan letters at the close of each issue. This feedback allowed fans to interact with the creative teams behind their favorite superhero adventures. While letters to editors had originally been primarily comments on the quality of the *condition* of a book—"My issue was missing a staple," "My issue was missing a page," etc.—fan letters in the Silver Age increasingly included commentary on the quality of the content. Stan Lee strongly promoted this interaction, presenting his bullpen of creative talents as individual characters in and of themselves (with himself being the biggest character of all). This made the relationship between company and customer feel more personal. The titles of each comic's letters page were usually witty puns on either the title of the comic or the superhero featured within. For *Tales of Suspense*, the letters page was titled "Mails of Suspense."

In the 1960s—and well into the following decade—the conclusion of comic book marketing was that the primary audience was children (most notably 8–12-year-old boys). Why would anyone over that age read superhero stories? The fan letters in the '60s strongly suggest that not only were many older readers reading these comics (even readers who began reading during the Golden Age of World War II), but many of these older readers were professionals: university professors, lawyers, and even astronauts! Many of the letters to *Tales* were calling for Captain America—and Iron Man—to have their own titles. Fans were, of course, unaware that the reason for the doubling up was the severe publishing limit placed on Marvel by its printer/distributor (the aforementioned eight issues per month). Once that limit was lifted, Marvel was free to take off, and the separate titles were established, with Cap's adventures continuing with the numbering from *Tales of Suspense* #99 to *Captain America* #100. This numbering is somewhat misleading. The final issue of Cap's official 1940s run was #75, followed by 76–78 in the 1950s, but returning in issue #58 of *Tales of Suspense*. (Once the character enters the 2010s, all sense of "numbering" will become essentially nonsensical.)

One interesting aspect of these letters pages is that fans could actually interact with each other. Decades before internet chat rooms, a letter from one fan expressing a certain opinion of the character, a certain story, or the creative team could be answered months later by another fan's letter either supporting or disagreeing with the earlier opinion. When one considers that it could take months for a letter to make it to print, and months more for the response to be published, the fact that such interaction was attempted at all is quite fascinating. With entire digital copies of these comics now available at the touch of a finger, the interactions can be read similarly to an online chat, but the original back-and-forth took much longer, with no real expectation that any response would be published at all.

While these letters are fascinating windows into the thoughts and political leanings of comics readers for historians to sift through, it is important to note that they cannot always be trusted to be authentic. Several editors over the past decades have come forward admitting that if letters tended to lean a certain negative direction (either the quality of the content or an interpretation of character or plot), editors would invent letters expressing the opposite viewpoint. Unfortunately, without the actual physical letters to examine (they were not kept on file), it is impossible, from a research standpoint, to determine which published letters are genuine and which are the creation of the company itself. What can be deduced is that readers of Captain America stories in the 1960s did represent a socioeconomically and age diverse group of Americans.

Modern Takes

Overall, Captain America in the 1960s was not too different from what he had been in the 1940s and '50s: a standard superhero, having

Chapter 3. Man Out of Time

never-ending battles against an array of bad guys who threaten the status quo of American society. The primary difference in the '60s—and going forward—was the growing difference in what status quo would mean in American society itself. In the '40s and '50s, consensus was the standard in American towns and cities, schools and churches, workplaces and playgrounds: consensus against the Nazi threat in the 1940s, and against the communist threat in the 1950s. But beginning in the 1960s, consensus was a word that would very rarely apply to American society ever again. As America began to acknowledge, accept, and (eventually) respect the considerable diversity that had always been present in the country, consensus would often necessarily give way to diversity of thought, belief, and opinion as well, and as *that* diversity collided with the ever-growing distrust of government and authority, consensus would become as ancient a concept as silent movies, full-service gas stations, and comic book newsstands.

In 2009, Matthew J. Costello, professor of political science, published his book *Secret Identity Crisis*, an examination of how the Cold War affected American national identity through the lens of Marvel Comics. His research confirms this breakdown of general American consensus during the 1960s. On Captain America, he points out, "Captain America is the most ideological [of the Marvel superheroes]: he is, in fact, an avatar of American ideology and, thus, offers the most direct commentary on the character of the Cold War."[21] In regards to how the character transitions from his Golden Age persona into a character more recognizable to fans today, Costello points to Cap's relationship with Sharon Carter and the question of which identity defines him, Steve Rogers or Captain America, pointing out that this question of identity will become a core concept explored in Cap's adventures going forward.[22] As discussed earlier, the many societal changes occurring throughout the 1960s culminated in this growing question of what America is, and what that means going forward. This breakdown of national consensus will be both cause and result of the events of the decade to come.

As to the "man out of time" concept, in media studies professor J. Richard Stevens's study of concepts of masculinity in Captain America adventures, he points out, "This Captain America [of the 1960s] is morose, seeming to sit in his room nearly paralyzed with confusion and regrets. Between battle sequences…, the character broods about his place in the modern world and whether his mission is anachronistic … to the changing values of modern society."[23]

While this aspect of the character is used to point out the stark contrasts between the America of World War II and that of the 1960s, Stevens goes further, suggesting that this new aspect of the character could be attributed to Jack Kirby, a World War II veteran who likely felt much the same way (Stevens does not mention Lee—who wrote the stories—as playing a factor in this choice, possibly because while both men served in the war, only Kirby saw actual combat, giving him a very different perspective on the war than Lee would have had).[24]

Continuing this examination of the "man out of time" concept and its role in the development of the character over the succeeding decades, Jason Dittmer wrote, "Beyond his connection to World War II, Captain America's continued, embodied existence produces a tangible link to the past that marks him as a distinct kind of symbol to which the more recent or intermittently published nationalist superheroes can only aspire."[25]

It is true that while other Golden Age superheroes such as Superman, Batman, and Wonder Woman simply continue decade to decade as if their heroic adventures had only begun in recent years, Captain America is continuously connected to World War II America. In the 1960s comics, Cap had been on ice (literally) for 20 years, but in the MCU films, he was not removed from the ice until 2011 (giving him a sleep of nearly *seventy* years). No matter when you have Captain America return, he always begins in that fixed point in time, forever making him a product of the Greatest Generation and therefore a literal "man out of time." When one considers how idealized the World War II era is in the hearts and minds of Americans throughout the decades since (despite how that era may have actually been), it is easy to understand why all of the other Marvel heroes hold Cap in such high regard. He is never truly one of us; he is a living memory of who we think we were and wish we could still be.

The Aftermath of Chaos: Cap and America Face a New Decade

Throughout the 1960s, the Black civil rights movement in the American South influenced a plethora of similarly themed movements from the Hispanic, American Indian, women's and LGBTQ+ communities. The tragic and mysterious deaths of popular political and social leaders created a constant air of uncertainty throughout the country; and the decade was bookended by the terror and anxiety of mounting Cold War tensions in 1962 and the hope and pride of the moon landing in 1969. A decade that had seen social unrest, a controversial war, political assassinations, and overall doubt concerning America's future ended with "One small step for a man … one giant leap for mankind."[26] As Americans hoped that the massive accomplishment of putting a man on the moon suggested that the chaos of the last decade was over, and that this new event would usher in a new decade that would be defined by further great accomplishments and a new Golden Age for America, little could they imagine the seemingly endless drama that was about to unfold.

While Captain America may have sat events out as more of a medium of escape for presumably young readers, this would be the last decade in which he would do so. As a new decade dawned, a new generation of comic book creators was taking over from the generation that invented it. These new artists and writers were raised on these superhero adventures, and as the country continued to face new challenges, these young men were going to use the medium that helped define their childhood to become their mouthpiece for discussing political, economic, and social issues. From here on out, the writers of Captain America stories would utilize the character to represent the American Dream, avoiding taking a side other than the side of what was morally and ethically right. America was growing up, and with that growth would come growing pains. The 1970s would take an already weary population and push them to their limits politically, economically, and socially. As bad as many may have thought the '60s to be, the next decade was about to get much worse (in very different ways). Captain America would transform from simple kiddy fare and begin to take a stand.

CHAPTER 4

Man Without a Country

Captain America and a Nation in Crisis, the 1970s

The 1960s had been the most divisive decade of American history since the Civil War of a century before but had ended with hope for a better tomorrow. Socially, the decade that began with a focus on civil rights for Black Americans had, by decade's end, expanded that focus to include similar pushes for other racial/ethnic minority groups, women, and the LGBTQ+ communities. Politically, it had begun with a continued general consensus in America's struggle against the expansion of international communism, but ended deeply divided over American efforts to stop that expansion in Southeast Asia. On television, Americans had gone from the accepted norm of American families as presented in sitcoms such as *Ozzie and Harriet* and *Leave It to Beaver* to beginning to accept that, even within our own country, familial beliefs, values, and traditions were actually far more different throughout the nation than most had considered, with shows such as *The Beverly Hillbillies* and *Petticoat Junction* being wildly popular even in big cities. At the movies, studios went from historical epics such as *Cleopatra* and *Lawrence of Arabia* to more fantastical futuristic fare such as *2001: A Space Odyssey* and *Planet of the Apes*. In comic books, superheroes went from simple two-dimensional heroic figures to more complex, flawed, and haunted figures to whom the changing youth culture could more closely relate.

As the '60s drew to a close, the first generation of comic book creators was beginning to retire, replaced by a generation that had grown up on the mythical adventures that Greatest Generation had originated. This second generation of writers and artists had grown up witnessing the dramatic changes in American culture in the decades since World War II. They were aware of—and deeply invested in—the major issues facing the country and its populace in the wake of the turbulent decade that was coming to a close. The future seemed bright. America had won the space race and landed the first man on the moon. Groups of Americans long oppressed and subjugated by the predominantly white straight male system were gaining freedoms and liberties long denied. With all the fear, heartache, and conflict of the 1960s seemingly in the past, things could only get better! Right?

In fact, America was facing a decade that would see society pummeled again and again. By the end of the 1970s, the country would never be the same again, politically, socially, or economically. All that Americans had come to accept as set in stone—trust in government, the strength of the traditional family unit, and the power of the American economy—would be shown to be built on feet of clay. A criminal president, a redefining of family and marriage, and a stagnant economy that would only get worse year by year, tearing away at the middle class that had thrived since the war, would all combine to wear down American morale to depths not seen since the Great Depression of four decades earlier. The American Experiment appeared to be failing. Tradition meant nothing. Beliefs were questioned. Confidence was in crisis.

For the first time in his long history, Captain America would give voice to these changes, attempting to continue to be a beacon of hope in a time of seemingly endless hopelessness.

From Watergate to the "Crisis of Confidence"

Had it not been for the Watergate scandal, Richard Nixon would have likely been remembered fondly in American history. For the first time since World War II, the Cold War appeared to be nearing an end during the Nixon years. In 1972, Nixon signed the Strategic Arms Limitation Treaty (SALT I) agreement with the Soviet Union, placing limitations on construction of additional nuclear weapons by both countries. Nixon also initiated the policy of détente with the Soviets, bringing decades of tensions to a more moderate level of essentially "live and let live." That same year, Nixon became the first U.S. president to visit the People's Republic of China, opening the door for normalized relations with the communist country by decade's end. This "triangular diplomacy"—along with ending the war in Vietnam—would have been Nixon's legacy. Instead, his legacy is one of corruption and criminal activity due largely to exposure of what would come to be known as the Watergate scandal.

Prior to Watergate, the cracks in the system were already beginning to appear. The assassinations of Dr. King and the Kennedy brothers in the previous decade were already beginning to convince a growing number of Americans that their government was not being entirely honest with them. In 1968—just prior to the deaths of Dr. King and Bobby Kennedy—the disastrous Tet Offensive, though an American military "victory," made very clear that all in Vietnam was not going as well as the American people had been led to believe by their government. The next domino of trust to fall would be in 1971, with the release of the Pentagon Papers. In 1971, former Defense Department analyst Daniel Ellsberg—originally a strong supporter of the war in Vietnam who changed his mind after seeing the war firsthand—stole and copied a multi-volume report compiled by the Defense Department since 1967. The purpose of this report was to preserve the facts of American involvement in Southeast Asia for use by future historians. The vast majority of these facts, however, remained hidden from the American public, as they did not shine a good light on the American government. Ellsberg felt the people should know, and he gave his copies of the report to the mainstream news media, primarily *The Washington Post* and *The New York Times*. The report clearly showed that Presidents Eisenhower, Kennedy, and Johnson had all been less than honest with the American people concerning U.S. involvement in Vietnam. Though sitting president Richard Nixon was not shown in too harsh a light (his policies in Vietnam were essentially public knowledge), the fact that such a massive leak of classified information occurred under his watch did not make him look good. Nixon attempted to prevent the press from publishing the report's contents, but the Supreme Court decided otherwise. Though Ellsberg was arrested and convicted for espionage, his sentence was commuted once it was discovered that the Nixon administration had undertaken illegal activities in assisting in gaining evidence against Ellsberg.

The involvement of Nixon's White House in illegal activities in the Ellsberg case should have been a red flag, but the matter was not seriously followed up on. The following year, 1972, Nixon ran for reelection (a campaign that would win him the largest electoral majority of any American president in history to date other than George Washington's two unanimous victories). Unfortunately, his ultimate victory would prove to be his ultimate downfall. During the election, five members of the Committee to Re-Elect the President (which often went by the ironic acronym of CREEP)—Nixon's official reelection campaign—were arrested in the early morning hours of June 17, having been caught burglarizing the offices of the headquarters of the Democratic National Committee, located in the new and luxurious Watergate Hotel and Office Complex in Washington, D.C. (the scandal became known as Watergate, leading every presidential scandal since to have the suffix "-gate" added to it). Originally discounted by the White House as a third-rate burglary, two young reporters at *The Washington Post* smelled blood. Their dogged reporting would ultimately lead to the downfall of Nixon, causing him to become the only U.S. president to date to resign from office.

Chapter 4. Man Without a Country

Just prior to the Watergate scandal dominating the national news, Nixon was set to enjoy what should have been his crowning achievement: the end of the war in Vietnam. With his national security advisor, Henry Kissinger, holding secret negotiations with the North Vietnamese throughout 1972, the administration could announce just prior to the election that peace was at hand, only for the communists to change their mind just after the election. Nixon's reaction was a nonstop bombing campaign of the North for eleven straight days in December of '72. In January, the North capitulated and a cease-fire between the North Vietnamese and the U.S. was declared, officially ending America's long nightmare by the end of January 1973. Nixon's victory lap would be short-lived, however, as Congress wanted answers concerning Watergate.

The U.S. Senate would investigate the matter for over a year beginning in February 1973, slowly exposing more and more criminal activity by the Nixon administration, eventually implicating the president himself. Due to the seriousness of the situation, and Americans' growing obsession with the story, the investigative hearings were televised. The four TV networks—ABC, CBS, NBC, and PBS—juggled coverage, giving each a chance at the ratings grab while also giving each the opportunity to continue to partially air paid-for advertised programming. The terms "Watergate," "redacted," "smoking gun," and "expletive deleted" became part of popular vernacular. As did the overall question, "What did the president know ... and when did he know it?" Nixon did all he could to resist cooperation without appearing to do so, even appealing to the U.S. Supreme Court to protect his personal conversations with staff under the umbrella of executive privilege (which they did not do). Once a recording was discovered clearly showing that Nixon knew the full details of Watergate within days of the crime and actively sought to cover it up, the president had little recourse left, resigning on August 9, 1974.

Once resigned, Nixon could have been charged, convicted, and imprisoned had it not been for the new president, Nixon's recently appointed vice president Gerald Ford, granting Nixon a full pardon for any crimes committed as president. This looked particularly suspicious, as Nixon had not yet even been charged. Though Ford would explain the pardon by suggesting that it was in the best interest of the country to put all the ugliness of Watergate behind them, to many in the press, the American populace, and even Congress, it looked like a deal had been struck. Unlike most vice presidents, Ford had not been elected. The elected vice president, Spiro Agnew, had been forced to resign nearly a year before Nixon on unrelated criminal charges. Nixon then appointed Ford, fully aware that— should the investigations into him continue to go badly—he was handing the American presidency to him. This pardon—on top of a stagnating economy, to be discussed later—would play a key role in Ford's defeat in the election of 1976. Ford would run against the former Georgia governor, Democrat Jimmy Carter. During the campaign, Carter would promise to never lie to the American people. While this was refreshing after the events of the last five years, it would actually prove detrimental to Carter's own bid for a second term in 1980.

As Americans' despair grew over the next few years with high energy costs, insufficient fuel supplies, and inflation and unemployment both on the rise, the country turned its weary eyes to their president for words of comfort. But what they received in the summer of 1979 has come to be known as the "malaise speech." Expressing concern for the "crisis of confidence" that had clearly taken over throughout the population, Carter suggested that it was partly the fault of Americans themselves. The breakdown of community and family and an increased focus on the accumulation of wealth (or as much wealth as one could hope to attain) was driving America down a dangerous path that only the American people could reverse. This take on "God helps them who help themselves" did not go over well. Though initial reactions praised the president's wisdom, the popular tide soon turned against him, suggesting that such widespread societal problems were the president's to fix, not the American people's. Going into the fall of '79, Carter's popularity was diving fast ... and was about to experience an all-out crash.

On November 4, young radical revolutionaries in Iran overtook the American embassy in the capital of Tehran. Fifty-two American embassy personnel were taken hostage. The revolutionaries were angry that their recently overthrown monarch, the Shah, had been allowed to go to the United States for cancer treatment. The new Islamic Republic of Iran, under the leadership of the Ayatollah Ruhollah Khomeini, denounced the United States and President Carter, fully supporting the hostage takers. The Americans would be held for 444 days (coinciding with the number of days left until Carter left office to be replaced by the newly elected Republican Ronald Reagan). Though Iran claimed that they were holding the hostages to have an impact on the 1980 election and would only release them once Carter left office, they could have made their point once Carter lost the election in November 1980. Releasing them the following January—literally as Reagan was being sworn in—suggested more that they feared retaliation from the new wild-card president, giving the new leader a considerable political boost in the process.

As Americans experienced this seemingly never-ending cycle of political chaos, so too would Captain America. Throughout the decade, Cap would question his own definition of patriotism in regard to the Vietnam War as well as his own confidence in the U.S. government and its elected officials.

As American politics appeared to be in one crisis after another throughout the decade, each one further eroding Americans' faith in their political leaders, American society was in chaos as well. Aside from the crisis of confidence in government, the core unit of society—the family—seemed to be in a similar downward spiral. Long-standing givens were now in question. "Till death do us part" became more of a hope than an expectation. The man as king of the castle quickly became a thing of the past. Sexual mores long viewed as inflexible proved to be far more fluid far more quickly than many were comfortable accepting. Television—by now the nation's preferred medium of entertainment—would do its part to ease these transitions, educating as it entertained, but so much change at such a rapid pace would prove far more than most could handle, and by decade's end, the family—like the government—appeared to be on the brink of collapse.

Expanding Equality and Redefining the Family Unit

The various civil rights movements of the 1960s had experienced considerable successes (often in the wake of considerable bloodshed). As the decade ended, two more groups sought social equality: women and the LGBTQ+ movements. While the women's movement would be quite successful—though, like the racial/ethnic movements of the '60s, not as successful as one would hope—the LGBTQ+ movement, while making just as much impact at the time as the women's, would be less successful in the short term. Their efforts would be hit with the double whammy of the evangelical Christian movement and the new and mysterious AIDS crisis, both beginning as the national election of 1980 rolled around. Both would stem the tide of the movement for a generation.

The women's liberation movement, organized largely by the National Organization for Women (NOW), had been increasingly active since the mid-1960s. In 1972, Congress passed the Equal Rights Amendment. This would have had an historic effect on American society, giving equal pay, equal opportunities in the workplace, equal rights of property ownership, economic opportunities and more with a clear and definitive constitutional protection. Though it did not ultimately pass the required three-fourths state approval, its support—and the basic arguments of what is right and fair—provided women much-needed popular support for many of the gains they achieved on their own through the movement and in American courts. Also in 1972, as part of the "education amendments" enacted by Congress, Title IX protected young women from discrimination in any school/education program (something that, though it seems limited in scope, would have far-reaching ramifications for rights across the board). In 1973, the U.S. Supreme Court's decision in *Roe v. Wade* guaranteed a woman's right to safe and legal access to abortions nationally. While many since this decision have focused on the issue of right or wrong regarding terminating a pregnancy, the decision had wider implications. Women were no longer at the whims of their husbands or fathers when it came to their personal health, reproductive rights, and overall issues of bodily autonomy. In 1974, women were given the right to have a credit card in their own name rather than as part of their husband's or father's accounts. By 1980, American women enjoyed more opportunities than at any point in history. In the comics, throughout the 1970s, Captain America—the relic of the Greatest Generation—would be forced to question his own values concerning equality for women and their place in society.

The gay rights movement launched in 1969 after the legendary Stonewall Riots in Greenwich Village, New York. Though not receiving as much popular or legal support as the women's movement, the bravery of the gay men of Stonewall inspired a generation of LGBTQ+ Americans to come out, publicly admitting who they are and how they identify on the gender spectrum. Annual parades on the anniversary of Stonewall (still celebrated today) broke out in more and more American cities throughout the decade. In 1973, the American Psychiatric Association removed homosexuality from its list of mental illnesses. This diagnosis had been used for decades not only to institutionalize or incarcerate LGBTQ+ Americans, but also to "treat" them with cruel and painful tactics designed to "cure" them. It was also used to criminalize non-heterosexual sex (something that remained in many state law codes until it was finally decriminalized by the U.S. Supreme Court in 2003). While the LGBTQ+ community was quite successful in changing many hearts and minds by decade's end, the noticeable connection between gay men and the new, mysterious AIDS epidemic, opening the door for the religious right wing to gain political leverage over them, meant that the entire community would be ostracized for another generation.

The women's liberation movement and the push for LGBTQ+ rights led by such groups as the Gay Liberation Front were both part of a much wider sexual revolution that dominated American society in the 1970s. This revolution covered an array of issues: redefining manhood and womanhood, redefining gender roles within both marriage and society, expanding individual rights for women, and testing—and in many ways permanently changing—sexual mores of what was acceptable both within and apart from the institution of marriage. Marriage itself underwent considerable change, with divorce rates skyrocketing as the decade progressed. This can be largely attributed to both the sexual revolution and to the declining economy (money often being an issue of division, particularly in newer marriages).

There is a chicken-and-the-egg aspect to the feminist movement of the 1970s. Did feminism push more women into the American workforce, or did the necessity of women having to join the workforce to help families make ends meet drive the feminist movement? One thing that is clear is that American manufacturing—the backbone of the strongest economy on Earth since World War II—was decreasing dramatically, with more and more developing countries building a manufacturing base that offered the same products produced here at home but at much cheaper cost to consumers. The middle class that had been thriving since Japan's surrender was beginning to see a decline in its overall standard of living for the first time since the Great Depression. This shift would require the American housewife—for decades strongly encouraged to resign herself to her standard *Leave It to Beaver* role—to enter the workforce to provide additional income in order to maintain the standard of living that the new Baby Boomer parents had enjoyed in their youth.

This financial need for more housewives to enter the workforce coincided with a considerable rise in divorce rates, creating more single-parent homes than at any point in the nation's history (aside from the aftermath of the Civil War). This lack of parental presence at home created a new phenomenon among America's Generation X youth: the latchkey kid. With no room in the family budget for childcare (and little in the way of available childcare outside of babysitters), children as young as 8–10 years old were left to their own devices, having to rely on their own self-discipline to do their homework, feed themselves, or ready themselves for bed. Children would be left a house key and instructed to lock the door once they arrived home from school. This would have a fascinating effect on the young Gen Xers: with very little parental presence during their formative years, much of their ethics, values, and morals would not be taught to them by their parents—as had been the case since the Garden of Eden—but rather by their only present parental figure: the television. Ultimately, even if the women's and LGBTQ+ equal rights movements in the 1970s had not been as successful, the family unit would still have experienced dramatic change as a result of the ever-declining American economy.

The New Economy: Stagflation, Oil, and Despair

Since World War II, the booming American economy had been driven largely by the continuing militarization due to the Cold War, Korea, and Vietnam (even the massive spending of the Interstate Highway Act was due largely to the Cold War threat), and the space race with Russia. These big-money projects had a ripple effect that could be felt throughout the economy. Manufacturing was the heart of this postwar economy, and the emerging and thriving middle class enjoyed a higher standard of living than most Americans had ever experienced. That would change in the 1970s. President Nixon's policy of détente with the Soviets kept the Cold War cool throughout the decade, with Presidents Ford and Carter following his example. That, and the end of the conflict in Vietnam, slowed military spending considerably, having a similar ripple effect. Other events would make this economy in transition far, far worse.

In 1973, Egypt, Jordan, and Syria launched a coordinated attack against Israel in what came to be known as the Yom Kippur War. Israel not only successfully repelled the attacks, but also gained ground from their aggressors. When the U.S. came out publicly against the attack, the oil producing countries of the Middle East—making up most of the oil cartel OPEC (Organization of Petroleum Exporting Countries)—placed a six-month embargo on oil sales to the United States. From the late 1800s through World War II, the U.S. was the world's primary oil producer, drilling enough for our own needs and more to sell to the world. After the war, international agreements led America to scale back oil production to make the global market more equitable for those poorer countries that had nothing but oil to sell. This led to America becoming dependent on this foreign oil, making the embargo particularly painful.

While the U.S. could increase oil production, it could not do so at such a speed to provide immediate relief. Added to that, the country did not—and still does not—have the refining capacity to turn that oil into enough gasoline to meet demand. Though the embargo itself was short-lived, it had a ripple effect throughout the decade, made even worse by another brief embargo before the end of the decade. This would lead to long lines at gas pumps, rationing how much consumers could purchase per stop, and even limiting who could purchase gas on certain days (based on license plate numbers). The oil/gas crisis, then, also created an overall energy crisis, as it also affected home heating and cooling units.

Watergate cannot be overstated in its impact on the economy as well. As much of the American economy is based on projections and faith in the system, the scandalous resignation of the highest officeholder in the land delivered a massive blow to American—and global—confidence in the country's immediate future. Two areas of the economy that took a negative turn in the years immediately following Watergate were unemployment and inflation. Normally, these two things have an inverse effect on the other: one goes up as the other goes down. By mid-decade, however, both were rising at an alarming rate. The result came to be known as stagflation (a stagnant economy plus inflated consumer prices).

Nixon's successor, conservative Republican Gerald Ford, was philosophically opposed to the New Deal–esque type of government incursion into the economy more associated with liberal policies. Instead, Ford suggested a two-pronged approach to fight stagflation: (1) his WIN policy ("Whip Inflation Now"), essentially making the first 10 percent of an individual's income tax free; and (2) voluntary conservation, which was essentially "if you can't afford a TV, don't buy a TV" and "if you can't afford to drive to work, walk to work." Unfortunately, neither of these policies had the desired effect, and the economy would continue to worsen beyond Ford's administration, through that of his successor, President Jimmy Carter, and into the first two years of *his* successor, President Ronald Reagan. At a time when more and more Americans were finding themselves unemployed, oil, gas, home heating, and basic foodstuffs such as milk, eggs, and cereal were becoming increasingly out of most Americans' ability to purchase. As difficult as the American economy was overall, it was particularly hard in America's inner cities, which were predominantly minority Black and Hispanic Americans by this time. This is something that Captain America's partner, the Falcon, would experience firsthand in the comics.

As the 1970s drew to a close, America was in pretty rough shape. Faith in the political system had dwindled to historic lows. The family unit was in disarray due to increasing divorce rates, changing ideas concerning gender roles, the entire concept of sexual normality, and an increasing number of young Americans left to their own devices. The powerful economy that had essentially ruled the world for the last quarter century seemed on the very verge of all-out collapse. In the two previous decades, television would have acted as a much-needed diversion from the unpleasant events transpiring outside of American living rooms. In the 1970s, however, television—and comic books—would take a very different approach to their media: as much educators as entertainers.

Pop Culture in the 1970s: The Age of Social Relevance

Television took a dramatic turn as the nation transitioned from the '60s into the '70s. Traditional westerns like *Gunsmoke* and *Bonanza* would give way to historical family dramas *The Waltons* and *Little House on the Prairie*. Silly sitcoms such as *I Dream of Jeannie* and *The Beverly Hillbillies* would be replaced with more socially relevant sitcoms such as *All in* the Family and Good Times. Entertainment-driven variety programs such as The Ed Sullivan Show and The Lawrence Welk Show would give way to political commentary-driven variety shows such as Rowan and Martin's Laugh-In and The Smothers Brothers Comedy Hour. Americans were about to be force-fed a relentless diet of the traditional importance of the family unit and the necessity of progressive ideas and open-mindedness in adapting that unit to an ever-changing world.

The dramas The Waltons (set during the Great Depression) and Little House on the Prairie (set during late-1800s westward expansion), and the sitcom Happy Days (set in the 1950s) underscored to viewers what families used to be in American society. Ironically, these series were being written and produced as the American family unit was undergoing historic change. Their overall message—though timely—was likely largely unintended. The socially relevant sitcoms—notably the aforementioned All in the Family and Good Times, as well as The Mary Tyler-Moore Show, Maude, The Jeffersons, and M*A*S*H—provided American audiences with a seemingly nonstop diet of conservative versus liberal values (with conservative values consistently presented as being on the side of wrong), race/ethnicity issues, gender issues, LGBTQ+ issues, economic issues, and a healthy dessert of sociopolitical commentary. Even the new concept of the miniseries was not immune, with two of the biggest examples of the period being Holocaust (a story of European Jews in World War II) and Roots (the saga of a Black family through the last century of American slavery). While viewing ratings for all of the above programs were massive compared to 21st-century programming, the fact that viewing options were limited to ABC, CBS, NBC and PBS meant that the choice was essentially "watch this or spend time with your family ... we thought so!"

For the new phenomenon of latchkey kids, the launching of children's programming on the new Public Broadcasting Station (PBS) could not have been more timely. Just in time for kids returning from school Monday through Friday, PBS offered the triple-decker programs of Sesame Street, Mister Rogers' Neighborhood, and The Electric Company. While Sesame Street taught kids their ABCs and 123s, Fred Rogers provided kids with an emotional education, teaching them how to understand and cope with their feelings. The Electric Company taught phonics, adding to the lessons taught by Big Bird and company. On Saturday mornings—when Gen X kids watched cartoons as their parent or parents slept in—ABC aired segments of Schoolhouse Rock during commercial breaks (three-minute vignettes designed to teach kids math, grammar, history, and government through catchy songs with animated video).

As TV sought to expand kids' minds, a new form of entertainment would focus their eye-to-hand coordination. A new medium of popular culture in the 1970s was that of video games (arcade, home video systems, and electronic handheld games). Though the phenomenon would really take off in the early 1980s with the massively popular *Pac-Man*, the game that became the first obsession for the first generation of gamers was *Pong*. Initially released by Atari in 1972, the game was an electronic version of tennis (or ping-pong): two rectangular "paddles," guided by revolving knobs, volleying a square "dot" back and forth, following the rules of tennis/ping-pong. By 21st-century standards, the game is archaic, but the novelty of it inspired the massive gaming industry that exists today. Going from arcade to the Atari 2600 video gaming system, *Pong* started a phenomenon. Handheld electronic games such as *Football* (literally simple blinking dots guided to avoid the other team in order to score) and *Simon*, a game that required players to repeat growing chains of lights/colors/sounds in order, created an industry worth billions over the decades to come.

On the big screen, a new generation of filmmakers made their mark, giving birth to some of the most successful careers in film history. Francis Ford Coppola's 1972 *The Godfather*—based on the popular novel by Mario Puzo—is still considered one of the greatest films ever produced. Steven Spielberg essentially invented the summer movie craze with 1975's *Jaws* (based on a popular novel of the same name by Peter Benchley). The modern horror genre emerged with the groundbreaking films *The Exorcist* (1973), *The Texas Chainsaw Massacre* (1974), and *Halloween* (1978). After considerable success with his comedic film *American Graffiti* (1973), writer/director George Lucas went on to break all box office records (which had recently already broken by Spielberg's *Jaws*) with 1977's *Star Wars*. The following year, Warner Brothers Studios sought to get in on this new blockbuster craze with their own offering: *Superman: The Movie*, with relative newcomer Christopher Reeve embodying the Man of Steel for a generation of new comic book fans.

Though television was the primary medium of entertainment available in the 1970s, it did not hold a monopoly on social commentary. Comic books began to be voices of sociopolitical commentary—something the medium continues to do well into the 21st century—with a new generation of superhero comics creators replacing the old-school progenitors of the genre. At DC Comics, writer Denny O'Neil and artist Neal Adams turned *Green Lantern/Green Arrow* into a year-long journey through America's social issues. In response to Marvel's Stan Lee publishing an anti-drug issue of *The Amazing Spider-Man* (at the request of the federal government and against the recommendation of the Comics Code Authority), O'Neil and Adams likewise did an anti-drug issue of *Green Lantern/Green Arrow*. Marvel continued to produce Black heroes with Blade the Vampire Hunter,

Luke Cage, Brother Voodoo, and Storm of the X-Men. By decade's end, Marvel introduced more women heroes with She-Hulk (the Hulk's cousin), Spider-Woman (in no way connected to Spider-Man, ironically), and Ms. Marvel (originally Carol Danvers, today's Captain Marvel, not Kamala Khan, today's Ms. Marvel). While comic book sales throughout the decade began to sag significantly—perhaps due to the more real-world-relevant stories—the superhero creative teams did use their medium and genre to do what they could to educate their (still presumably) young readers as to what was going on in this ever-evolving American sociopolitical climate. Key among these new socially relevant superheroes was Captain America.

Cap in the 1970s

The 1970s would see Stan Lee leave his writing duties at Marvel for the first time since the company's early pre–World War II years. Lee did write Cap adventures through the first three-quarters of 1971, with art from Gene Colan and John Romita, Sr. Romita would continue as artist as Gary Friedrich took over as writer before turning art duties over to Sal Buscema. Buscema would continue as artist as writing duties switched once more, this time to Gerry Conway (all of this throughout 1972 alone). For the last third of 1972, Steve Englehart would begin his iconic run on the hero, with Buscema continuing on pencils. Englehart would stay on the title through the first half of 1975, with Frank Robbins stepping in on art for his last few issues. In 1976, the country's bicentennial, Cap cocreator Jack Kirby took over writing and drawing *Captain America*, staying on the title through 1977. In 1978, Don Glut took over writing duties, then passing them on to Steve Gerber and Roger McKenzie, with Buscema returning on art. A handful of bullpen talent would then finish out the last four months of the decade. This frequent turnaround of creative talent on *Captain America* was unprecedented, and would not be repeated again within the spate of one decade.

With social relevance being the watchword of the era, and an emphasis on diversity spreading across all forms of popular media, the title of *Captain America* would be changed to *Captain America and the Falcon* for most of the decade (specifically from issue #134, February 1971, to issue #222, June 1978). Coming into the 1970s, with American society already so different from the era of World War II, Captain America was beginning to truly feel his "man out of time" status. At the beginning of the decade, Cap opined, "I'm like a dinosaur ... in the cro-magnon [sic] age! An anachronism ... who's outlived his time! This is the day of the anti-hero ... the age of the rebel ... and the dissenter. It isn't hip ... to defend the establishment! ... Only to tear it down!"[1]

Chapter 4. Man Without a Country

In the Great Depression, the establishment, as Cap puts it, was FDR and the New Deal, the system that had kept America afloat. That was immediately followed by World War II, with FDR once again the symbol of the establishment, and a hero to most Americans at the time. The nation was united against the back-to-back threats of economic collapse and global fascism. Cap then "slept" through the late '40s and 1950s, as cracks in national consensus began to show. He reemerged in an era of widespread, large-scale social protest, and a war where young men, rather than running to enlist, were running to leave the country to avoid the draft. Little could Cap have known at the time that the foundations of what he believed and what he believed he stood for were about to be tested even more.

Since the title was renamed *Captain America and the Falcon* for most of the decade, many stories centered on the Falcon, aka Sam Wilson, Harlem social worker. This allowed for some examination of post–civil rights movement America. Though there had been much progress for Black Americans, particularly in the South in the 1960s, economic opportunity was not an area that had seen significant change. This was particularly true of the inner cities throughout the country, where populations were predominantly racial and ethnic minorities. After successfully dispersing an angry Black mob in Harlem (swayed into violence by the Red Skull), Captain America makes a comment that some "little something" will eventually cause the Black residents of Harlem to "explode again."[2] Cap's comment clearly disturbs Falcon, who needs to split off from his partner for a while. It also expresses just how much white America still did not understand the plight of non-white Americans, the obstacles they faced, and their limited opportunities due to systemic racism, which is worsened in periods of overall economic decline.

As the comic book audience continued to age, with readers continuing to follow their favorite heroes well into teenage years and adulthood, the problem of continuity emerged in the decades-old industry. Comic book characters like Captain America are, by necessity, static (meaning that they are commercial products that must remain the same decade to decade in order to continually attract new readers in each generation). If Superman, Batman, Wonder Woman, Spider-Man, or Cap were to show growth as characters, new readers could be put off because they are not familiar with the hero's journey to that point. On the flip side, longtime readers may get bored if month to month, year to year, the character simply repeats the same tropes over and over, ad infinitum, ad absurdum. This is a fine line for writers to attempt to traverse. In their defense, they have continued to do so, decade after decade, in particularly imaginative ways. This is particularly the case with Captain America.

In 1972, writing duties for *Captain America* were passed to now-legendary comics author Steve Englehart. The first story he chose to tell was an explanation of how Captain America could have been frozen in ice for two decades beginning in 1944 when he was frequently seen fighting bad guys throughout the rest of the 1940s and the Commies in 1953. After Cap's and Falcon's latest adventure, Cap departs for a long-overdue vacation. Shortly thereafter, Falcon comes across a young Black man of his acquaintance being beaten up in an alley ... by Captain America! Unmasking the presumed imposter, Falcon stares into the face of Steve Rogers. When a young—and very much alive—Bucky emerges from the shadows, "Cap" introduces them as "the REAL Captain America and Bucky!"[3]

Referring to Black people as "coloreds," this "Captain America" is clearly *not* the hero readers had come to know. As the Harlemites observe Falcon, their local hero, being beaten by the very symbol of America, word spreads (particularly fast, considering these pre-internet days).[4] In this story, Englehart observes how much America has changed in the last two decades through an examination of how the character of Captain America has likewise changed, from the stalwart defender of the system to the more open-minded and respectful hero 1970s readers had come to know (even though, as seen in the earlier story, Cap still viewed himself as part of the old school). Englehart fixes Cap's continuity issue by explaining that, with the actual Captain America inexplicably vanished near the end of the war, the U.S. government saw a need to convince any potential enemies that Cap was alive and well, eventually concocting a new (and apparently faulty) Super Soldier Serum and giving it to someone else. In 1953, the man they chose also had surgery and vocal training to appear to be Steve Rogers as well (though, as Cap's identity was always secret in those days, and he wore a mask, it is unclear why this might be a necessity, other than to create confusion for Falcon—and the audience—now). As such, *this* Cap (and Bucky, who was apparently also copied) represent America as it was in the 1950s: loyalty first and foremost to the government and the flag; women and minorities "knowing their place"; and any deviation from that labeled as communist.[5] This tale kills two birds with one epic stone: it fixes the continuity issue for longtime readers, and it takes a moment to look back at the considerable social progress America has undergone since the 1950s (albeit in a very hyperbolized and oversimplified manner).

As the anti-communist craze of the early 1950s subsided somewhat, this new Cap went the other direction, growing increasingly violent and seeing communists in every social movement (as the radical right wing had done at the time). This led to the new Cap and Bucky being frozen (intentionally), only to be thawed out in the '70s by an angry radical anti-communist government worker ... unleashing the sins of America's

Chapter 4. Man Without a Country

recent past onto an unsuspecting present.[6] As real-world politics began to grow further and further divided between left and right, the introduction of this 1950s Captain America provided a "dark mirror" villain for the real Cap to face off against in future adventures (similar to Bizarro and Superman, Ra's Al Ghul and Batman, and Venom and Spider-Man). Like many of this new generation of comics creators, Englehart was of a more liberal bent than some of his predecessors, particularly in the politically divided 1970s. His Cap would be a more left-of-center hero than he perhaps was in the 1940s, '50s, or even the '60s under Stan Lee.

The conflict of '70s ideologies would emerge a few issues later when Cap fights the Serpent Squad. While talking with his former paramour Peggy Carter, Cap meets a Vietnam War veteran named Dave Cox. This is the first real mention of Vietnam in the pages of Cap adventures since his one-off rescue mission the previous decade. Cox was a POW (prisoner of war) and lost his left arm in service to his country. His ordeal has caused him to rethink his ideology regarding war, conflict, and violence. Cox is now a conscientious objector, swearing off violence as a means of conflict resolution. Being a man of war, created for war, Captain America finds this ideology unpatriotic (and, though not specifically mentioned, unmanly). However, when Cox later is willing to die to protect Cap and Peggy while still refusing to give in to violence against the attacking Serpent Squad, Cap realizes that this man "is no coward."[7] This shaking of Captain America's traditional values establishes an open-mindedness that will come to define the character more and more in the decades to come.

The event that will shake Captain America to his foundations is that of the *Secret Empire* storyline. A conservative organization calling itself the Committee to Regain America's Principles (or CRAP for short, a clear poke at the Watergate-connected CREEP) launches a media campaign to turn public sentiment against Captain America. A portion of their television ad proclaims: "Who is Captain America? He wraps himself in our nation's proud flag, yet no one in our government is responsible—or will take responsibility for—his actions."[8]

The ad goes on to point out that Cap no longer works with the respected government agency SHIELD and that his powers are chemically induced.[9] From the perspective of the time this issue was published (roughly October/November 1973), the crimes of CREEP were well known to the American people (likely even to younger Cap readers), and President Nixon's involvement and removal from office appeared more and more likely. From the perspective of the 21st century, the ad rings chillingly similar to those commonly seen during every current election cycle. In their book *Fault Lines*, historians Kevin M. Kruse and Julian E. Zelizer identify the Watergate scandal as the turning point when American politics began its slippery slope into radical division (though widespread distrust of government had already been somewhat established, giving the political parties sufficient ground in which to plant such seeds of division).

Over the course of the "Secret Empire" story, Captain America—joined at one point by the X-Men, characters whose own book had been in reprints since 1970 but would soon return in a massive way just a year after this appearance—discovers that there is a top-secret cabal of politicians and business leaders who are pulling the strings of government and society, unbeknownst to the American people. At the story's climax, Captain America corners the cabal's mysterious leader, Number One, chasing the cloaked and hooded villain into the White House. Once captured, Cap removes his adversary's hood and the following discourse occurs:

> **CAPTAIN AMERICA:** Now let's just have a look underneath your cowl before.... Good Lord! YOU!!! ... But you ... you're...
> **NUMBER ONE:** Exactly! But high political office didn't satisfy me! My power was still too constrained by legalities! ... I gambled on a coup to gain me the power I craved ... and it appears that my gamble has finally failed! I'll cash my chips then! ... [pointing a gun to his head]
> **CAPTAIN AMERICA:** No Wait...![10]

The character's suicide is not shown on panel, but Cap's reaction at the sound—"KRAK"—clearly shows his shock and horror at what has happened. The identity of Number One is never definitively stated, but to older readers it was clear: "high political office" and "the power I craved" (and the fact that the villain sought refuge from Cap in the White House) were obvious hints that the identity of Number One was none other than President Richard Nixon himself (Nixon had been established in previous Marvel comics as the president at this time).

Hitting newsstands in the spring of 1974, months before the "smoking gun" tape would expose Nixon's criminal activity and lead him to resign, the climax of the "Secret Empire" story is clear commentary from one American—Englehart—that Nixon was a threat to America and needed to be removed from office. In the issue's epilogue, the narration box reads:

> A man can change in a flicker of time ... this man trusted the country of his birth ... he saw its flaws ... but trusted in its basic framework ... its stated goals ... its long-term virtue. Trusted. This man now is crushed inside. Like millions of other Americans, each in his own way, he has seen his trust mocked! And this man is Captain America![11]

Englehart expresses the hurt and outrage of a nation in this closing chapter of a superhero adventure. After a decade of events that led many to question their institutions, the Watergate scandal would shatter

Americans' trust in government and government officials (a shattering that has not only never healed, but has been continuously exacerbated by events ever since). Captain America's experience with the Secret Empire, and the discovery of who was behind it, led Steve Rogers to begin to question his own identity. If America was not what he thought it was, then who was "Captain America"?

The cover of the following issue shows civilian Steve Rogers walking away from fellow Avengers Thor, Falcon, and Iron Man as he drops his Captain America uniform to the ground. Thor states, "Hold Steve Rogers! Thou knowest not what thou dost!" To which Rogers replies, "Wrong, Thunder God! I know exactly what I'm doing! I'm renouncing my Captain America identity.... FOREVER! [emphasis in the original]"[12] The story inside begins with a brief retelling of Captain America's World War II origins, remembered by Cap himself. He concludes his retelling: "But so much has happened since then. I've seen America rocked with scandal ... seen it manipulated by demagogues with sweet, empty words ... seen all the things I hated when I saw those newsreels [of Nazis prior to World War II]."[13] After the Avengers attempt to console Cap with all the good he has done, Peggy Carter (Cap's World War II love interest and the older sister of Sharon Carter, Cap's new love interest ... ew...) points out all the good *America* has done and all it stands for. In response, Cap states:

> Nothing's that simple. Americans have many goals ... some of them quite contrary to others! In the land of the free, each of us is able to do what he wants to do ... think what he wants to think. That's as it should be ... but it makes for a great many different *versions* [emphasis in the original] of what America is ... so when people the world over look at me ... which America am I supposed to symbolize?[14]

This is a question that the character will frequently ask over the decades that follow, as America becomes more and more fractured politically and socially. Rogers would—briefly, for four issues—give up the stars and stripes, put down the shield, and become a (tacky) caped blue/black and yellow-clad alter ego called Nomad, the Man Without a Country.[15]

At mid-decade, Marvel editor-in-chief Len Wein greenlit a new comic that could once again focus on Cap's World War II adventures. In *Giant-Sized Invaders* #1, writer Roy Thomas retconned the All-Winners Squad from Timely Comics' World War II library, renaming the team-up of Cap, Bucky, Sub-Mariner, the original Human Torch, and the Torch's young sidekick Toro as the Invaders. The adventures would continue in an ongoing series throughout the mid-1970s. The stories would closely resemble the type of adventures in the original Timely comics, but with a modern approach to art and narrative.

As America approached the bicentennial celebration of 1976, Americans were politically, morally, and economically exhausted. The country had already been through so much and, unbeknownst to them at the time, still had so much more to endure before the decade's end. In January of '76, comics legend Jack Kirby returned to Marvel Comics and the pages of *Captain America*, working as writer, artist, and editor of his co-creation for the first time. His yearlong storyline focused on a device called the madbomb, a device that emitted an inaudible transmission that created anger and violence in the population. The villain—calling himself Lord Taury (a play on Tory, those Americans loyal to England during the Revolution)—hoped to split America into civil war/revolution to return it to its pre–Revolutionary War roots.[16] He also sought revenge against the descendant of the man who had killed his ancestor during the American Revolution. That patriot's name was Captain Steve Rogers (an ironic twist that, even for comic books, strained credulity). The madbomb story would run for the entirety of the bicentennial year (along with a special issue, *Marvel Treasury Special: Captain America's Bicentennial Battles*, cover dated June 1976), but Kirby would remain on the title through most of 1977 before being replaced by a revolving door of talent for the remainder of the decade.

The considerable progressive changes of the previous 20 years laid the groundwork, by 1979, for a growing conservative movement in American politics. The failed policies and leadership of the Carter administration only added fuel to this growing fire. That conservative revolt was also made evident in the pages of *Captain America* (which by that time had already dropped the more inclusive "*and the Falcon*"). In the final storyline of the decade, Captain America faces off against the National Force, a neo–Nazi organization led by the previously established *1950s* Captain America, who boldly proclaims: "The only way to insure (sic) America's strength is to make her pure! Because a white America is a strong America!"[17]

This continued depiction of the 1950s Captain America as racist underscores the perception of many on the political left that the "simpler times" of the 1950s, which many conservatives longed for (idealized in films like *American Graffiti* and television series like *Happy Days*), was a more racist period, and therefore anyone longing for those times must likewise be racist. This is the type of broad generalization and stereotyping that has become the norm in American politics in the 21st century.

A look back at the "Commie Smasher!" Cap adventures of the 1950s show no overt textual signs of racism in the character of Captain America, but the absence of any Americans of color in those stories does provide

Chapter 4. Man Without a Country

the subtext of the deep systemic racism of the day. Americans of color were essentially invisible. In the end, the evil '50s Cap and his National Force were just pawns of the more serious threats: MODOK (the comical-looking cyborg established in the 1960s) and the newer Cap villain Dr. Faustus, an evil psychiatrist. Like the Secret Empire, the true threats to America were those manipulating the already deep-rooted political, economic, and social divisions within the country, preventing the American people from achieving consensus and true, lasting progress.

In the wake of the National Force crisis, Captain America gives a press conference, attempting to clear his name by pointing out that his own fascist remarks had been made under mind control. He's informed that the American Nazi Party and the Ku Klux Klan are suing him for violating the National Force's rights to free expression and peaceful assembly, to which Cap points out that the Constitution does not "condone arson, kidnapping, terrorism or murder."[18] When asked by a reporter whether, since America is not at war and has eliminated the draft, "Captain America" has outlived his usefulness, Cap responds, "To be perfectly honest ... I ... don't know."[19] This expresses not only the character's frustrations with the events of the last decade, but also the thoughts of many across the nation as the decade drew to a close: were America's days of greatness, power, and influence a thing of the past?

One of the sad outcomes of the National Force storyline was the death of Agent 13 of SHIELD, Sharon Carter, Cap's love interest throughout the decade (though it should be clearly understood that death in superhero comics is by no means permanent, and that Sharon Carter will return ... someday). Steve Rogers's relationship with Sharon Carter had been one of the less-liberal aspects of 1970s Cap. Early in the decade, Carter was established as having a PhD in metaphysical psychology and being a member of SHIELD's Super Psyche Squad, a group of female agents skilled in predetermining threats. SHIELD director Nick Fury referred to the group as "hyped-up women's intuition."[20] Carter soon joined a new group of SHIELD agents: Femme Force. Throughout the decade, Carter would frequently comment upon the fact that she and other SHIELD agents were not seen as equals to their male counterparts. Likewise, Steve Rogers consistently underscored his belief that Sharon—and presumably all women—should stay at home while the men faced danger. By mid-decade, Sharon would leave SHIELD to respect Steve's wishes. This seemingly anti-liberal approach to an important female character appears in hindsight to be an attempt on the part of Cap's writers throughout the decade to point out that, as much as women had accomplished and were accomplishing, they were still not being given the respect and opportunities due to them. Even Captain America appeared to have limits to his progressivism.

Modern Takes

One of the earliest academic analyses of Captain America as a character was actually published in the 1970s. Originally published in 1973, Robert Jewett's *The Captain America Complex* utilized this star-spangled character as the central symbol of all that was wrong with the American mythology. As William Sloan Coffin pointed out in a foreword to the book's second edition in 1984, "*The Captain America Complex* is about American self-righteousness, about all the things in our history and culture that keep prompting the thought in American minds that of all the nations on earth, God smiles the most on ours."[21]

Jewett would return to this thesis with two more books cowritten with John Shelton Lawrence: *The Myth of the American Superhero* (2002) and *Captain America and the Crusade Against Evil* (2004). While the overarching themes of rampant nationalism in many heroic narratives throughout American pop culture since World War II (of which Captain America is, of course, one) are clearly outlined, the connections of this thesis to Captain America as a character—aside from the obvious connection of his very appearance—are tenuous at best, citing very few examples of the textual (or even subtextual) content of the comics themselves. Their thesis ties much more closely to the cowboy symbol addressed more deeply in *Myth of the American Superhero* (with which Captain America shares very few similarities). It's still a fascinating read and perspective on American hero fiction overall.

The Englehart stories are of particular interest to scholars of both the genre and the period. The social commentary of retconning the 1950s Captain America adventures to be very much not in keeping with the ideal of Captain America is significant not only to a study of the hero, but to American memory concerning its own identity. In his study of retconning, Jason Dittmer noted—as previously discussed in Chapter 2—that this move to retcon the "Commie Smasher" 1950s Cap as a different individual was an attempt to connect the idealism of World War II with the more progressive idealism of the 1960s, establishing the anti-communist 1950s as an anomaly in American history, inconsistent with the nation's values.[22] It is not meant to imply, however, that the American people were any more racist in the 1950s than they were in the 1970s, but that America as a *nation* was, in popular memory, a more racist and intolerant country than it currently was in the more "enlightened," post–civil rights movement 1970s.

In his study of masculinity and the monomyth of the superhero in Captain America, J. Richard Stevens wrote of the 1950s Cap:

> Though the [1950s Captain America] is stronger, the narrative portrays him as inferior in several ways: his costume rips during the battle, his shield is easily

Chapter 4. Man Without a Country   111

dented [the original shield would have been buried in the ice at the time of the '50s Cap], he makes wild logical errors, his prowess is not on par with the original Captain America. In this way, the narrative asserts that the conservative fervor of the 1950s is a "cheap copy" of the earned patriotism of the generation that served in World War II.[23]

The overall message is underscored in the physical combat: the progressive/multicultural argument is stronger than the conservative/intolerant viewpoint. This conflict would be more subtly addressed in the *Secret Empire* storyline when conservative President Richard Nixon is implied as being the head of the criminal cabal.

Meanwhile, Cap's interaction with the pacifist Dave Cox is also an interesting area of study in regard to thinking at the time. The story appeared in the summer of 1973, hitting newsstands mere months after President Nixon had declared American involvement in Vietnam to be over, and Americans were beginning to see firsthand how horrible the war had been as the POWs like Cox returned home, many crippled and disillusioned as Cox was. Dittmer said of this storyline: "The introduction of pacifist Dave Cox critiqued the relationship between Captain America's violence and the U.S. war in Vietnam in a way that the readership found acceptable.... Cox's principled objection to the war in Vietnam causes Captain America to consider his position on the war, which he had so scrupulously avoided."[24]

Stan Lee had avoided connecting Cap to the war in Vietnam, believing that doing so was not consistent with the primary mission of entertainment that he felt comics served at the time. Stevens adds to the discussion thusly:

> Cap's initial encounter with Cox causes him to wonder about the man's fortitude, considering his views as a conscientious objector, but after Cox is tortured by [the Serpent Squad] but doesn't betray his friends, he gains Cap's respect. This adjustment in attitude provides Cap with yet another opportunity to embrace the progressive values of his age.[25]

These interactions with the 1950s Captain America and Dave Cox shake Steve Rogers's thinking to its core. It causes the character to reexamine his own beliefs, views, and allegiances. The final trial of Cap's core identity will come in Englehart's next historic storyline: the *Secret Empire* and the Nomad aftermath.

The reveal of the sitting president, Richard Nixon, as the evil leader of the Secret Empire at a time when, in the real world, he was being slowly revealed as a dark and sinister character was a rather stark and alarming occasion of art imitating life. This is something I personally addressed in an earlier analysis of the storyline:

From time to time, a real-world event so shocks society that the creators of popular fictions feel an overwhelming compulsion to express their concerns and anxieties in the pages or frames of their respective media. At those times, our fictional heroes are given the opportunity to bring justice to our actual demons. This type of crossover provides society with a deep sense of catharsis at a time when it is most desperately needed… [Steve Englehart] saw a problem, and he addressed it.[26]

Ultimately, the *Secret Empire* story arc does more than hold the proverbial mirror to American society. It pulls up a couch to provide some psychoanalysis and provide a cathartic release.

While the *Secret Empire* storyline is clearly a commentary on the corruption of the Nixon administration that was becoming more and more public even as the final installment of the story was going to press, the fallout of that story—Rogers's renouncing of the Captain America identity and becoming Nomad, the Man Without a Country—has a far deeper subtext, calling on readers to question their own ideas of America and their own commitment to the beliefs that were once connected to that identity. Peter Coogan, one of the earliest analysts of superheroes as significant subjects of study, noted, "[The Nomad] stories drew into question whether or not a superhero could legitimately support constituted authority and whether the status quo was worth defending when it seemed to benefit oppressors and inequality."[27]

Shortly after the Nomad stories were originally published, Andrew and Virginia MacDonald connected the Nomad identity and the questions that led to it to the now-grown Baby Boomers and their own distrust of the system as they had grown to recognize it: "[Nomad] reflects the disillusioned Seventies when young people have seen the values this land has historically represented crushed by the corruption and hypocrisy of 'high-placed officials.'"[28]

Additionally, comic book scholar Richard Reynolds noted that the post–*Secret Empire* adventures of Captain America—and other superhero comics more generally—would begin to more closely scrutinize what it is that they stand for, and to what degree the status quo should be respected and defended.[29] When Rogers retakes the mantle of Captain America seven issues after giving it up (and four after donning the mantle of Nomad), he does so in the wake of a would-be Captain America dying at the hands of the Red Skull. This leads Rogers to realize that the nation *needs* a Captain America, and that only he—due to his Super Soldier Serum—can fill that role.[30] Of this realization, Matthew J. Costello wrote: "Captain America's crisis of faith is not merely political but personal as well. He defines the problem not as one of good government, but of authentic identity. In resolving this crisis he regains his faith, loses the costume of Nomad, and redone the flag-colored garb of Captain America."[31]

Stevens analyzes these events: "Having declared his sense of evolution [when retaking the mantle of Captain America], Cap returns to his public mission and is greeted by thousands of citizens who turn out to express their support of him, representing the resolution [in the real world] of the Nixon administration's cultural betrayals."[32]

As was the case with many Americans in the wake of Watergate, Steve Rogers questions America as a whole, not simply the actions of a handful of corrupt officials. In the end, Captain America—and the idea of America itself—is not representative of a president, presidential administration, or even the institution of government. He represents the ideals of liberty, freedom, and justice that the nation has claimed to stand for from its beginning. Though individuals or groups may fall short of those ideals, the ideals themselves must live on.

Ultimately, the Secret Empire would not be Cap's last crisis of confidence in the American government (or America itself). With a conservative wave building as the 1970s drew to a close, the nation was once more about to redefine itself ... for better or worse.

From Malaise to the Reagan Revolution

As the 1970s drew to a close, Americans could not be confident that there would still *be* an America ten years hence. The nation's morale was at historic lows. The political climate was so bleak that congressional committees actually had discussions about amending the Constitution to eliminate the American presidency due to the failures of the recent occupants of the office—Carter, Ford, Nixon, and Johnson—suggesting that the office had become too much for any one person to handle (a fact only exacerbated by the continuing Iran hostage crisis). Women were emboldened with new optimism for their futures, while the LGBTQ+ community faced an impending return to ostracization as a strange and mysterious "gay cancer" would lead an uninformed populace (though, to be fair, they were being led by equally ill-informed politicians and medical "experts") to see them as more than the moral threat they had traditionally been viewed as being; they were now a *physical* threat. Even Captain America seemed less than optimistic concerning the future of the American Dream.

America's crisis of confidence would bleed into the early months of the 1980s. The American experiment suggested in the wake of the American Revolution appeared to be failing. The nation needed a rejuvenation of faith in itself. The country needed a cheerleader! They needed a traditional cowboy hero to ride into Washington, D.C., waving the American flag and rallying the American people to fear nothing but fear itself and ask what they can do for their country! If only they could cast some charming actor to *play* the role of the leader they knew they needed.... As a struggling economy, political division and malaise, and decades of progressive social change pushed more and more Americans in a more politically conservative direction, this longed-for hero would emerge ... and the Reagan Revolution would begin.

CHAPTER 5

Captain America No More (Again)
Captain America in the Age of Reagan, the 1980s

In popular memory, the 1970s and 1980s were as different as night and day, as if the election of Ronald Reagan to the American presidency in November 1980 ended American malaise and the nation emerged to a once more strong economy and flag-waving patriotism, all to the backdrop of MTV. While it is true that the two decades have very distinct personalities and are *very* different in politics, culture, and economics, the transition was slower than many remember. Reagan would indeed be a national cheerleader right when the country needed one most, but while the American economy did experience a considerable rebound, core issues of race, class, and gender remained largely unchanged. The sociopolitical fault lines from the decade before were not healed, and, in many ways, fractured far more. Through it all, American popular culture would remain a steadfast escape from the stresses of the day as well as a reflection of who we were ... and who we were yet to become.

The American economy would boom during the decade, primarily from a combination of a massive investing push on Wall Street and Americans going on a seemingly never-ending shopping spree. America's youth—the coming-of-age Generation X—became a major sales demographic, due in no small part to the advertising phenomenon that was MTV (Music Television). American popular culture became one of the country's leading exports, especially to those countries still under the yoke of communism. The music of Michael Jackson and Madonna, the movies of Sylvester Stallone and Arnold Schwarzenegger, and television series such as *Dallas* and *Knight Rider* appealed to the peoples of the communist world, giving them a taste of what freedom—and capitalism—looked like.

The comic book industry—on the ropes once again as the 1980s began—would see a massive resurgence by decade's end. Comics such as *Batman: The Dark Knight Returns* and *Watchmen* garnered respect from literary critics and showed the non-comic book world that comics were not just for kids anymore. A dip in the stock market led cautious investors to begin looking at comic books as wise investments. The resulting collectors' bubble would bring the industry to never-before-seen heights ... only to come crashing down before the century's end. Through it all, as through the prior decades since the Great Depression, Captain America would be there, showing us who we were, warning us of where we were headed, and inspiring us as to who we could become.

The Age of Reagan: The Cold War Re-Heats and AIDS Runs Rampant

After two decades of progressive political and social reform, the American electorate took a dramatically conservative turn going into the 1980s. The perceived failures of Democrat president Jimmy Carter—the continued bad economy, the energy crisis, and the Iran hostage crisis—left even independent voters soured on President Carter and, to a lesser degree, on the Democratic Party in general. In the 1980 election, Republican candidate Ronald W. Reagan won 489 electoral votes (270 were needed to win), making up 91 percent of the overall electoral vote. He gained 50.7 percent of the popular vote to Carter's 41 percent.[1] This was the second-highest electoral victory for a presidential candidate in U.S. history to date (the first being President Nixon's reelection in 1972).[2] Four years after the American hostages released as Reagan was sworn into office in 1981 and the U.S. economy was on a massive rebound from the previous decade, Reagan won reelection with 525 electoral votes (97.6 percent of the total) and 58.8 percent of the popular vote.[3] President Reagan would leave office in 1989, still one of the most popular presidents in American history, making the 1980s truly "The Age of Reagan."

Richard Nixon's policy of détente with the Soviet Union and opening relations with communist China had left the Cold War essentially cooled off throughout the 1970s. That ended in 1979 when the Soviets invaded the neighboring country of Afghanistan. This aggression, from President Carter's perspective, ended détente. Additionally, that same year, the communist Sandanista regime took over the government of Nicaragua, leading Carter to begin providing money and weapons to the anti-communist Contras in response. In 1981, President Reagan inherited a very much reignited Cold War. The conservative cowboy embraced this, viewing the Soviet Union (and communism in general) as an "evil empire." Throughout the 1980s, Reagan would dramatically increase the national debt by pouring billions of dollars into America's conventional and nuclear weapons programs.

Chapter 5. Captain American No More *(Again)*

The Reagan Era was nearly cut short before it could even begin when, on March 30, 1981, while leaving a luncheon with the AFL-CIO labor union, President Reagan, Press Secretary Jim Brady, a Secret Service agent, and a D.C. policeman were hit by would-be assassin John Hinckley, Jr., firing a revolver from close range. Reagan was rushed to George Washington University Hospital to undergo emergency surgery, the bullet having entered the left side of his chest from the left armpit.[4] Reagan's popularity soared due to both public sympathy for the wounded leader and the president's own reported wit and charm throughout his ordeal (he allegedly said to the doctors and nurses surrounding him when he regained consciousness in the emergency room, "I hope you're all Republicans," and to his wife, Nancy, on her arrival, "Honey, I forgot to duck").

In 1983, Reagan spoke on national television announcing a plan that he had concocted: the Strategic Defense Initiative (which the press dubbed "Star Wars"). The plan, essentially, was to arm satellites with lasers that could shoot down Soviet ICBMs (intercontinental ballistic missiles) before they reached American shores. Though defense officials and scientific advisors suggested to the president that this plan was unfeasible, Reagan pushed it forward anyway. He was aware that it was not necessary for the program to actually work. It was only necessary to spend hundreds of millions of dollars in an attempt to make it work, forcing the Soviets to up their own military spending in response (something that the Communist nation was in no economic position to do, further destabilizing their economy and the Soviet hold on power in their country). Less than a year after Reagan left office in 1989, the Berlin Wall separating communist East Berlin, Germany, from the city's capitalist western half fell, leading to a cascading effect throughout communist Eastern Europe and culminating in the fall of the Soviet Union over Christmas 1991, ending the 45-year Cold War.

Oil from the Middle East had been a major economic and political issue in the U.S. throughout the 1970s. This would be a leading factor in events that transpired during the Reagan years. In response to Iran's taking of American hostages in 1979, the U.S. began supporting Saddam Hussein's new regime in Iraq. The U.S. would provide military equipment for Hussein to launch an eight-year war against Iran throughout the 1980s. Additionally—though not quite the Middle East—the U.S. would provide weapons support for freedom fighters in Afghanistan, fighting against the Soviet invasion of their country. One of these U.S.-trained jihadists was a young college graduate named Osama bin Laden. Both of these policies would come back to haunt the U.S. in decades to come. It was also in the 1980s when terrorists claiming to be jihadists began hijacking commercial airlines, holding the crews and passengers hostage until their demands were met. It was for this reason that commercial airlines began the policy of simply allowing hijackers to take control, assuming all would be safe as long as the hijackers were unmolested. This, too, would come back to haunt America as the new century dawned.

Though Reagan continues to be hailed as a hero of American conservatism, some of his policies were diametrically opposed to the more conservative Republican Party of the 21st century. Reagan strongly supported a ban on assault weapons, something that the no-limitations-on-the-Second-Amendment Republicans of the 2010s would never support. Likewise, by signing the Immigration Reform and Control Act of 1986, Reagan granted total amnesty to roughly three million undocumented immigrants living in the U.S. at the time. Thirty years later, these policies would negate any conservative credentials on the American political right.

Support for the alleged freedom fighter Contras in Nicaragua was less successful. After Congress refused continued funding for the Contras in 1984, Reagan officials found methods to subvert the order and continue to provide funding for the Nicaraguan group. Appearing to be another Watergate—this time called the Iran-Contra Affair due to the scheme of selling weapons to Iran (which was also a violation of Congressional dictates) and funneling the funds from those sales to the Contras in an attempt to receive assistance from the government of Iran in locating other Americans held hostage throughout the Middle East—the scandal threatened to bring down President Reagan's administration. This failed when mid-level military/CIA operative Colonel Oliver North, USMC, essentially took full blame for lying to Congress and overseeing the operation. Reagan emerged from the scandal relatively unscathed and just as popular with the American people as before news of the scandal broke.

Due to his considerable political—and financial—support from the new evangelical Christian right wing of the Republican Party, President Reagan refused to sign off on government funding to find a cure—or even a treatment—for the exploding AIDS epidemic. This disease, Acquired Immune Deficiency Syndrome, was caused by HIV (human immunodeficiency virus), and in the early 1980s appeared to affect only homosexual men. The religious right utilized this apparent "fact" to stigmatize the entire LGBTQ+ community, setting back its quest for equal rights by more than a decade and stigmatizing all victims of HIV/AIDS, regardless of sexual orientation. As the disease spread throughout the straight community as well, over 100,000 people would die by decade's end. Once Reagan's successor, Republican George H.W. Bush, *did* approve funding for research, a treatment was found very soon thereafter, showing that thousands—possibly tens of thousands—could have been saved

Chapter 5. Captain American No More *(Again)*

had it not been for the politicizing of the disease and the stigmatizing of one group of Americans.

Ultimately, however, how a president is remembered relies largely on their response to national tragedy (like FDR in the wake of Pearl Harbor). In Reagan's administration, that tragedy was the explosion of the space shuttle *Challenger* on January 28, 1986. Due to a leak in the solid rocket boosters, the boosters and fuel tank disintegrated. The shuttle itself, despite popular misconception, did not explode, instead breaking up due to its lack of boosters. The crew survived the breakup, the crew cabin falling into the ocean, causing the seven crewmembers (including civilian teacher Christa McAuliffe) to likely die from lack of oxygen as the cabin fell. Reagan's heartwarming speech—as he acted in his official role as mourner in chief—ended with "We will never forget them, nor the last time we saw them, this morning, as they prepared for their journey and waved goodbye and 'slipped the surly bonds of earth' to 'touch the face of God.'"[5]

When his two terms were up, Reagan's loyal vice president George H.W. Bush sought to succeed him. However, while Reagan possessed the tough, rugged personality of the cowboy hero, Bush was a leaner, more soft-spoken man, giving him the overall appearance of being less manly than the powerful and charismatic Reagan. This is ironic, however, as Bush was a true hero of World War II, while Reagan was unfit for military service due to poor eyesight. After stiff competition for the Republican nomination in 1988, Bush faced off that November against the Democrats' pick, Massachusetts governor Michael Dukakis. Due largely to Reagan's continued popularity (and the economy continuing to do well overall), Bush won with 79 percent of the electoral vote (426) and 53 percent of the popular vote.[6] Bush promoted a "kinder, gentler nation" and would finally approve funding for AIDS research as well as signing the Americans with Disabilities Act in 1990. While certainly a continuation of the so-called Reagan Era, most of what distinguishes Bush's term in office would technically take place in the '90s (to be discussed in the next chapter).

Despite the Iran-Contra Affair and his response to the AIDS crisis, President Reagan continued to enjoy high regard among the American electorate long after leaving office, up to his death in 2004. This popularity was due to many factors: American victory in the Cold War; Reagan's own charming personality and considerable gift in speaking to the American people (he was often referred to as "Great Communicator"); and, perhaps most of all, the booming economy of the 1980s. Though not as roaring as the 1920s, or as widely impactful as the post–World War II economy, many Americans did prosper throughout the decade, due largely to greater involvement in Wall Street. The '80s was when Americans first became aware of a New York real estate developer named Donald Trump and launched him into his own distinct area of celebrity. Many have referred to the 1980s as the "Decade of Greed."

The Decade of Greed

In his first inaugural address on January 20, 1981, Reagan said, "Government is not the solution to our problem; government *is* the problem."[7] Following in the footsteps of previous conservative Republican presidents Calvin Coolidge (1923–1929) and Herbert Hoover (1929–1933), the Reagan administration would take a very laissez-faire approach to the American economy. Reagan's economic policies—dubbed "Reaganomics" by the press—centered primarily on tax cuts, particularly for the wealthiest Americans and corporations. For example, in 1980, the highest personal (single) income tax bracket was 70 percent, kicking in at $108,300 of personal income, while the lowest was 14 percent, kicking in at $2,300. By 1990, the code was significantly simplified, with the high end being 28 percent for all making more than $20,350, and 15 percent for all making less than that.[8] The primary thinking behind this policy was that if so-called job creators are able to keep more of their money, they will then invest that money, creating more jobs, which will lower unemployment and raise incomes for more Americans. It is often called trickle-down economics due both to the slowness of this process and the idea that eventually benefits will start "trickling down" to the lower classes. Though this may contain some soundness on paper, to actually make it work for the benefit of all requires many, many other factors (both at home and abroad) to go in a particular way that can never be adequately assured. However, a rudimentary examination of the changes in tax brackets shows clearly that wealthy Americans benefited greatly from these policies while many in the lower income levels actually saw tax increases. How much it affected the American economy in the 1980s has been debated ever since.

Wall Street investors took full advantage of Reagan's more hands-off approach to oversight of their financial activities. That did not, however, prevent several government investigations leading to arrests of financial wrongdoing by infamous people such as Ivan Boesky and Michael Milken, to name but a couple. In a post–80s analysis of the decade, reporter Bill Taylor stated:

> According to Harvard Business School professor Michael Jensen, one of the most influential finance academics of his generation, and the source of the value-creation estimates on RJR Nabisco, the decade represents a triumph of financial innovation. The restructuring of corporate America "generated

large gains for shareholders and for the economy as a whole." It came crashing down, Jensen argues, largely at the hands of a political backlash from Big Business, Big Labor, and Big Media, "groups whose power and influence have been challenged" by the forces of change.[9]

As the character Gordon Gekko (Michael Douglas) stated in the 1987 film *Wall Street*, "Greed ... for lack of a better word ... is *good*."[10] However, like Americans' nostalgic memory of the 1950s, the economic boom of the '80s also relies heavily on nostalgia for what most remember as a better time. As Kruse and Zelizer point out in their in-depth analysis of America since Watergate:

> [In the '80s] The income of the top 20 percent of families grew by about $10,000 a year; the income of the lower 20 percent steadily declined.... Working class Americans without a high school degree saw a 6 percent drop in an average week of earnings between 1980 and 1990.... The "capitalist blowout" policies of the Republicans, [Kevin] Phillips [Republican strategist] concluded, had ushered in "a second Gilded Age," one in which "many Americans made and spent money abundantly" but far too many more were left behind.[11]

In the 1970s, one could realistically expect to find a well-paying job with no more than a high school education. That would be the last decade in which this would be the norm. Families that had gotten by on one source of income in the '70s would be forced to rely on two (or more) in the 1980s just to maintain the same standard of living.

Television exacerbated the romance with big business that defined the decade, both through scripted programs such as the wildly popular nighttime soaps *Dallas* and *Dynasty* and reality-based programs such as *Lifestyles of the Rich and Famous*. The idea of striking it rich on Wall Street in the 1980s was akin to those who rushed to California in 1849 with dreams of gold or Texas in the 1930s with dreams of oil. Fictional businessman J.R. Ewing and real-world businessman Trump became role models for the up-and-coming Generation X, a generation of Americans who were not only raised on popular culture but would come to monetize it like no generation before. American pop culture became the nation's leading export in the 1980s, with ramifications that were social, economic, and political.

American Pop Culture Fights the Cold War

American popular culture, a staple of American leisure since before the Great Depression, became so globally popular in the 1980s that it has remained the country's leading export in the decades since. Television—limited since its inception in the late 1940s to the four broadcast networks

ABC, CBS, NBC and PBS—expanded exponentially throughout the 1980s due to the advent of cable television. Rather than transmitting television signals through the air, multiple channels could be transmitted through coaxial cable. Premium channels such as HBO and Showtime—broadcast via satellite in the '70s—could now be pumped into every American home (for an additional monthly fee). Of all the myriad viewing choices that cable channels offered, perhaps the two most historically important cable channels were CNN and MTV.

CNN (Cable News Network) launched on June 1, 1980, ushering in the first of many decades the channel would cover live. The brainchild of cable entertainment magnate Ted Turner, CNN promised to bring 24-hour news coverage. The world was a big and complicated place, with plenty of news to fill a full day's programming. As it turned out, however, Americans had little interest in news events that did not affect them personally. Political instability in South America, famine in Africa, and the ravages of monsoon season in Asia had no interest for American audiences. Neither did they particularly want "human interest" stories here at home. As a result, in the absence of breaking news (such as the space shuttle *Challenger* disaster or the drama of Baby Jessica being trapped in a well), 24-hour news—which would be joined by FOX News and MSNBC in the 1990s—would ultimately become more like an hour of news and 23 hours of discussing (i.e., arguing about) the news. By the 2010s, cable news would play a major role in the increasing political divide in the country.

MTV launched on August 1, 1981, with a voiceover announcement: "Ladies and gentlemen ... rock and roll," followed by transmission of its first music video, "Video Killed the Radio Star" by the Buggles. Music videos were not yet staples of the industry, and MTV's early years relied heavily on video of live performances of rock bands from the previous decade. That would change dramatically when the channel decided to go against its initial "rock only" policy and begin playing the videos of the popular Motown kid artist from the '70s, Michael Jackson, later dubbed "The King of Pop." By the time of the first MTV Video Music Awards in 1984, the channel was not only reflecting popular music, but was also influencing popular culture. American teenagers of the 1980s and '90s centered their lives around MTV, from the artists the channel promoted to the fashions, hairstyles, and gadgets that celebrities wore. What was cool was whatever MTV said was cool. It was both the soundtrack and the trendsetter of the period. The channel would continue to drive American pop culture throughout the 1990s, but would eventually see a massive decline in both viewership and influence in the early years of the 21st century.

Much of the decade's perception of a booming economy came from the consumer culture of the period. Americans were out to buy whatever advertisers told them to (even more so than during the 1950s, when the phenomenon was truly born). Among these consumer dollars, America's youth was the primary advertising demographic. From Rubik's Cubes to Swatches, Sony Walkmans to boom boxes, and Reeboks to skateboards, American preteens and teenagers could not buy enough to satiate their need to be cool. Corporations moved from spokespeople such as Ronald Reagan and Martha Rae to spokes-characters like canine Spuds McKenzie and the allegedly CGI Max Headroom (who was actually a real actor in impressive makeup).

On television, nighttime soap operas such as *Dallas* and *Dynasty* personified this decade of opulent consumption. The networks saw the last of their heyday with milestone events such as the "Who Shot J.R.?" mystery on *Dallas*, which garnered 83 million viewers for the episode revealing whodunit, and the final episode of the sitcom *M*A*S*H*, which had 85 million viewers. Outside of Super Bowls, the original networks would never again see viewing figures like that for their programming. Overseas, pirated broadcasts of American television were finding their way beyond the Iron Curtain. In the communist country of Romania, broadcasts of *Dallas* helped inspire millions of Romanians to shake off the yoke of communism and overthrow their dictator, Nicolae Ceausescu, on Christmas Day 1989, signaling the near end of the Cold War.

On the big screen, the Cold War played out in films such as *Red Dawn* (1984) and *Rocky IV* (1985). America came to terms with its collective trauma regarding Vietnam with films such as *Born on the Fourth of July* (1985), *Platoon* (1986), and *Full Metal Jacket* (1987). Chuck Norris, Sylvester Stallone, and Arnold Schwarzenegger became synonymous with action films; as the 1970s had given rise to the blockbuster, the '80s gave rise to the franchise, with *Star Wars, Star Trek, Indiana Jones,* and *Back to the Future* (just to name a few) leading movie audiences to not only expect, but to demand continuing adventures of their favorite characters. All the while, writer/director John Hughes documented the life of the teenage Gen X with massively popular films such as *Sixteen Candles* (1984), *The Breakfast Club* (1985), and *Pretty in Pink* (1986). The popularity of some films such as *Top Gun* (1986), *Wall Street* (1987), and the *Rocky* and *Rambo* franchises would endure to such an extent that sequels would be made well into the 21st century.

Another area of pop culture that would gain international success was the video game. The release of *Pac-Man* in 1980 led to the phenomenon called "Pac-Man Fever," a seemingly infectious obsession with the game (ultimately leading to sequel games *Ms. Pac-Man* and *Pac-Man Jr.*). Arcades became popular hangouts for American youth for the first half of the decade, and video game companies amassed large fortunes, one quarter at a time. As the concept of personal home computers became a sign of things to come, video games would increase in popularity and quality going into the 1990s. Other popular games of the period included *Centipede, Space Invaders,* and *Q-bert.* The worldwide popularity of the 1980 sequel *Star Wars: The Empire Strikes Back* and the 1982 film *E.T.: The Extra-Terrestrial* led Atari to create video games based on the two films, but the games ultimately went down in history as the two worst video games of all time (leading to rumors still present in the 21st century of a mysterious landfill somewhere, filled with unsold Atari *E.T.* games).

The decade would also give rise to another phenomenon that has very much come to define 21st-century American pop culture: the superhero movie franchise. The massive success of *Superman: The Movie* in 1978 led to three more Superman films (and one Super*girl* film) throughout the 1980s, followed by 1989's *Batman* by director Tim Burton, starring Michael Keaton (known to that point as a comedic actor) as the Caped Crusader and Hollywood legend Jack Nicholson as the legendary supervillain, the Joker. By the time *Batman* hit theaters in June 1989, the comic book industry was experiencing its own economic boom. After two decades of barely hanging on as an industry, superhero comics were seeing heights not seen since World War II. Batman played a major role in that renaissance.

The Decline and Rise of the American Comic Book Superhero

Though the comic book industry had seen a bump in the late 1950s with the rise of the Silver Age and had done well throughout the 1960s, sales saw a considerable decline as the 1970s progressed. Marvel, in fact, was kept afloat largely due to its deal with Lucasfilm to produce new, original adventures set in Lucas's *Star Wars* universe. The decline can also be attributed to the advent of home video game systems in the late '70s, as well as the action figure craze established by Kenner Toys' massively popular line of—again—*Star Wars* action figures (making *Star Wars* at once comic books' enemy and their only saving grace). This decline continued into the first half of the 1980s. Facing the apparent end of the medium, no one—comic book creators most of all—could have foreseen the chain of events that would turn things around and not only save the industry but take it to heights not seen since World War II.

In 1986, two publications from DC Comics would not only rejuvenate but also revolutionize the superhero comic book industry. The British creative team of writer Alan Moore and artist Dave Gibbons produced the twelve-part miniseries *Watchmen*, which deconstructed the entire concept of superheroes while at the same time helping them to become more popular than ever. Likewise, Frank Miller's four-part miniseries *Batman: The Dark Knight Returns* told the tale of a near-future Batman, coming out of a ten-year retirement to continue his war on crime as a middle-aged man facing the realities of age and a society that both needed and despised superheroes. The previous year, DC had published a year-long event by writer Marv Wolfman and artist George Perez titled *Crisis on Infinite Earths*, dealing with the growing problem of half a century of continuities by zeroing out all the superhero stories and starting over across the board. *Watchmen* and *Dark Knight Returns* garnered the attention and praise of literary critics, with many articles announcing what the industry had been saying for years: comics aren't just for kids anymore.

Marvel had done okay for the first half of the '80s with the continued *Star Wars* comics. By the time they ended in 1986, writer Chris Claremont and (to that point) artist John Byrne had turned *The Uncanny X-Men* from a book facing cancellation in 1975 to the company's best-selling book, turning Marvel's merry mutants into a superhero soap opera due to hit stories such as "The Dark Phoenix Saga" and "Days of Future Past" and the growing popularity of the X-Men's breakout star, Wolverine. Meanwhile, new artists Todd McFarlane and Jim Lee excited fans with their takes on old favorites Spider-Man (McFarlane) and the X-Men (Lee).

Oddly enough, a major factor in the burgeoning collectors' bubble that would commence in the latter years of the decade came from outside the industry altogether. On October 19, 1987, the American stock market saw its largest one-day drop since the Great Depression of nearly 60 years earlier. Around the same time, an original copy of *Detective Comics* #27 (the first appearance of Batman) sold for tens of thousands of dollars. This led some editorials to speculate that comic books might be a better investment than stocks (the comic book had originally sold for just ten cents). This suggestion—along with the attention given the industry by the non-comic-reading world—converged to create the bubble, which would run from roughly 1988 to 1995. Almost overnight, both fans and non-fans were buying potentially valuable comic books in massive numbers, reading some and sealing others in mylar bags further protected by cardboard backing.

With comic book companies noticing this explosion in interest, gimmicks were immediately implemented to connect the idea of value to as many books as possible. Such gimmicks included relaunching long-running titles with new "#1" issues (suggesting to consumers that this issue would be valuable in years to come) and "event" stories such as the famous "Death of Superman" storyline of the early 1990s and the equally *in*famous "Clone Saga" in the Spider-Man books. The release of Burton's

1989 *Batman* likewise led to a multimedia craze, with everything Batman selling like hotcakes, especially the comics. As a result, DC launched additional Batman books and added him to most of their existing books; meanwhile, Marvel began putting an "X" on everything they could to take advantage of the still-growing popularity of their X-Men. By the end of the decade, the comic book industry was riding higher than at any time in the last fifty years.

The social relevance that became prominent in comic books in the 1970s would prove a mainstay throughout the subsequent decades. The popularity of Marvel's X-Men was due largely to its ongoing message of diversity and inclusivity. Always promoted as a team that protects a world that hates and fears them, the mutants truly saw hatred from their non-mutant brethren in the 1980s. The relaunching of the comic in 1975 with a racially and nationally diverse team spoke to all readers who considered themselves as "other." This spoke most directly to racial/ethnic minorities, young women, the LGBTQ+ community, and overall nerd/geek culture. This was most profoundly felt in the 1982 graphic novel *X-Men: God Loves, Man Kills* by writer Chris Claremont and artist Brent Anderson, where a religious zealot declares war on all mutants, viewing them as an abomination before God. This would have resounded familiar to even young readers as television evangelists at the time were making similar remarks against the gay community.

While Captain America did not enjoy the success of some of his sexier counterparts, the overall success of the market did allow for the Star-Spangled Avenger's adventures to continue without threat of cancellation. Under the guidance of writers J.M. DeMatteis, Mike Carlin, and Mark Gruenwald (one of the longest-running Cap writers of all time), *Captain America* would come to document the decade perhaps better than any other single comic and would present a stalwart contrast to another popular Marvel hero of the era: the Punisher. The violent, murderous vigilante was wildly popular during Reagan's America, while the truly patriotic Captain was appearing more and more an anachronism with every passing year. Who was America in the 1980s? Captain America sought to answer that question.

Cap in the 1980s

The American military—and the symbol of the American soldier—experienced a considerable rise in popularity in the patriotic fervor of the Reagan Era. From movies such as the *Rambo* and *Missing in Action* franchises to television series such as *The A-Team* and children's cartoons/toys

Chapter 5. Captain American No More *(Again)*   127

such as *G.I Joe: A Real American Hero*, the U.S. military and the American soldier were more popular than at any point since World War II. With Captain America representing the ultimate comic book example of the American soldier, one would expect Cap comics to do very well in the '80s. Interestingly, *Captain America* would not see the degree of success enjoyed by *The Uncanny X-Men* or even *The Punisher* (the latter of which far more "Rambo-esque" than Captain America). The book would, however, touch considerably on the militaristic ideology of the Reagan Era, though not in as complimentary a way as many of the earlier examples listed.

Like the '70s, the 1980s saw quite the revolving door of talent in the pages of *Captain America*. The first creative team was J.M. DeMatteis and various artists from late 1981 through 1984 before Mark Gruenwald took over in 1985, beginning what would be one of the longest runs on the comic (continuing as Cap's primary writer through 1995). Cap's writers would continue to discuss social issues of the day, particularly DeMatteis, who would introduce the first openly gay character in comic books (though he could not so actually say so within the pages of the book at the time). Gruenwald would focus some criticism on Reagan's America just as British writer Alan Moore had been doing regarding Margaret Thatcher's United Kingdom. As the decade opened, Captain America would face off against another war veteran hero—or, rather, *anti*hero—the Punisher.

Introduced in *The Amazing Spider-Man* #129 (February 1974) as an antagonist to the web-slinger, in the 1980s, the character would become one of Marvel's best-selling heroes. This was consistent with Reagan's America: the embittered Vietnam War veteran out to enforce justice (or, actually, vengeance) on wrongdoers. The Punisher is Frank Castle, a former U.S. Marine and veteran—originally—of the Vietnam War. When a mob war in New York City results in his wife and children being killed in the crossfire, the distraught Castle, a trained killing machine, embarks on a never-ending battle against criminals big and small, forgoing the leftist, bleeding-heart due process and enacting justice by the barrel of a gun (or guns, knives, hand grenades ... whatever gets the job done). In *Captain America* #241 (January 1980), the Punisher comes up against the Star-Spangled Avenger for the first time, and two dueling ideas of justice and the American way are presented: one a relic of a bygone era, the other the voice of a new generation of heroes.

When Captain America stops the Punisher from threatening a mob courier, Punisher points out that he was merely scaring the young man in order to get information on a mob meeting where he plans to assassinate the mob bosses. When Cap suggests that even mob bosses have rights, the Punisher responds, "Rights?! They gave up their rights when they chose the path of crime! Now it is my job to punish them ... and the Punisher never misses!"[12]

Cap pleads with the vigilante that if heroes subvert and ignore the rights of wrongdoers, then no one truly has rights. While philosophically correct, the rampant and growing urban crime of the 1970s had left many questioning by 1980 if there was, indeed, any true justice in America, with those who obey the laws living in constant fear of those who ignore them. Four years later, life would imitate art.

On December 22, 1984, New Yorker Bernhard Goetz shot four attackers on a New York subway. Goetz had allegedly been attacked on the subway years earlier and had since decided to arm himself. Dubbed the "subway vigilante," Goetz ultimately served eight months for illegal possession of a firearm, but one of his victims—left paralyzed and brain damaged by Goetz's attack—successfully sued the vigilante for millions of dollars. For the most part, public opinion was on Goetz's side, which was indicative of Reagan's America. The cowboy president inspired a cowboy ethic among a large number of Americans, and vigilante justice was seen by many as preferable to a system that was seen by many as far too lenient. Cap's interaction with the Punisher shows once more that American society is moving farther and farther away from the ethics on which Captain America had been based so many decades before.

In *Captain America* #250, Cap considers a run for the American presidency. By the spring of 1980, it seemed clear that Reagan would be victorious. American values were shifting to the right after decades of progressive social change. Captain America—though ideologically more left of center—still appeared to many to be a symbol of the right, with his patriotic clothing and flag-waving rhetoric. When first confronted by the New Populist Party claiming that the nation owes Captain America, Cap responds, "I owe the nation, Mr. Underwood! It's been very good to me!"[13] This comment is reminiscent of President Kennedy's call to "Ask not what your country can do for you, ask what you can do for your country." To the established Cap reader, it is not clear in what way America has been "very good" to Cap outside of giving him the Super Soldier Serum and making use of him as a soldier, and yet the hero feels that what he can do for his country is more important than anything the country can do for him. Though heroes and civilians alike strongly urge Cap to run, underscoring that what America most desperately needs is a leader they can trust (an argument of the Reagan campaign despite the fact that President Carter had never done anything dishonest or dishonorable while leading the country), Cap chooses not to run, explaining to a waiting crowd, "In the early 1940s, I made a personal pledge to uphold the [American] dream ... and as long as the dream remains even partially unfulfilled, I cannot abandon it!"[14]

Chapter 5. Captain American No More *(Again)*

In the 1980 presidential campaign, Reagan's conservatism did appear to uphold that dream more than President Carter's liberalism. To many voters—conservative, independent, and even some of a more liberal bent—liberalism equaled soft on crime and declining family values. Reagan promised to oppose those things and "make America great again" (a quote used many times by candidates from both political parties long before it became an official Trump mantra). It would not take long before it became clear that Reagan's America fell short in many ways of Cap's ideal dream.

One could ask what would make Captain America even consider a move to politics. Just a few months prior, Cap had battled a new superpowered villain. However, rather than being a villain out for money or power, this one seemed bent on revenge: an attack on a New York City Board of Education head and on a social security office (harming no one, but ransacking the office itself). The villain turned out to be a former actor, Joe Smith, who had gained super strength and stamina by accident. Smith was now a distraught father whose mentally disabled child had recently died. Believing his son's untimely death to be the fault of an American system that had abandoned them, Joe struck back.[15] Cap laments, "We've got to keep fighting these fights [to better the system] until we win, because if we lose them ... there's no hope for any of us."[16]

In this story, there are no true villains, only victims. While it is a sad reality that the system cannot save everyone, it is just as much a sad reality that it could save more than it does. This was just one of many issues facing voters in the 1980 presidential election, and one of the many issues that the victor—Ronald Reagan—would be entrusted with addressing.

It would not take long for Cap's ideologies to come into conflict with that of Reagan's America. In 1983, President Reagan spoke to a group of evangelical Christians, promoting their ideas of family values as the primary pillar of American society. His speech was titled "The Need for Moral Reform," and hit particularly at the social liberalism embraced by the previous decade. Cap faced a similar group in the pages of his comic, there referred to as the "Coalition for an Upstanding America" (CUA). In opposition to their ideologies, Cap said, "What happens to the individual in a land where morality is wielded like a club? Where decency is dictated by those with the loudest voices ... and the greatest wealth?"[17] Like President Carter's warnings in his 1979 "malaise speech," this question by Captain America in 1983 is very relevant in 2020s America.

While Sam Wilson/the Falcon had played a prominent role in Cap comics of the 1970s—even sharing the title of the comic for much of the decade—the character would see his last meaningful presence in the book for some time in 1982. That midterm election year, J.M. DeMatteis presented a story where Wilson runs for Congress. What drives him to do so is—after discovering that a Harlem boy that he (as Falcon) had recently rescued was, in fact, the murderer of Wilson's own brother-in-law—a conversation with the boy's mother that underscores to Sam the plight of black Americans in the inner cities. In her lament to Falcon, she tells him that due to the economic decay of the inner cities—which are, by 1982, predominantly Black and Hispanic Americans—drugs and crime are unavoidable for a young man like her son, no matter how hard she may try to shield him from it.[18] While America as a whole had not yet risen from the economic malaise of the previous decade by 1982, that economic change was coming soon … unless one lived in the inner cities. As much as Americans today may look back on the 1980s as a decade of excess, consumerism, and economic boom, it was not the case for all Americans. A major downside of the period was that poor Americans—of which racial/ethnic minorities represented a larger than proportional number—would see a worsening of their plight (as partially pointed out in the earlier layout of the tax cuts of the Reagan Era).

By the time that issue hit comic book racks, Cap readers had already been introduced to Arnie Roth as a friend of Steve Rogers long before the latter had become Captain America. By the early 1980s, Roth was a balding middle-aged man. He was introduced as searching for Steve because he needed Captain America to find his missing "roommate," Michael, who was being held hostage by Baron Zemo (one of Cap's enemies, introduced in the 1960s) in order to pressure Roth into luring the Star-Spangled Avenger into a trap. The visual imagery of their eventual reunion suggested something more intimate than simply being roommates: when Cap visits Michael's hospital room, the patient is in a semi-sitting position, with Arnie sitting on the bed close to Michael's hip (a much closer stance than a casual friend would normally take by sitting nearer the foot of the bed). When Michael was taken once more—this time dying during his rescue attempt—Arnie screams, "My Michael's dead!" confirming in the eyes of attentive readers that Arnie and Michael were, indeed, a romantic couple, making Arnie Roth the first gay character in American comic books.[19]

Later, Arnie himself would be captured—along with Sam Wilson and Cap's Jewish American girlfriend, Bernie Rosenthol—by the Red Skull as examples of Cap's radical leftist ways. Arnie was forced to dress as a clown and sing a song denouncing his "abnormality," after which he was forced to lament,

> A funny song, isn't it, Steve? A funny song … about a funny little man. A pot-bellied, bald-headed wretch … who doesn't know a thing about real human love. No wonder the Nazis wanted my kind—the weak, the misfits—locked away in the concentration camps with the other pariahs! I'm a menace to society … a disease! And you Star-Spangled idiot … you call me friend! Most

Chapter 5. Captain American No More (Again)

people simply hate men like me ... yet you always treated me w-with respect, because ... you're one of us? Is it because, deep inside, under all that macho bravado you're really a sorry excuse for a man ... like me? Wh-what kind of man are you h-hiding underneath that chain mail? You st-stupid ... silly.... NO!! No more! I can't! I w-won't! Oh, Steve ... it hurts! Help me! M-make them s-stop! MAKE THEM STOP!![20]

The agony that artist Mike Zeck portrays on Roth's face is heartbreaking. Red Skull was voicing what many on the political right were saying in the early 1980s: that to support the LGBTQ+ community must mean that you are in some way a part of that community. At no point could DeMatteis clearly identify Arnie (or Michael) as gay due to the strictures of the Comics Code (although considerably lessened in the 1970s, it still remained in effect).

One area where Reagan and Cap were more in line in their thinking was in the area of nationalism (not to be confused with the radically racist "nationalism" discussed in Chapter 1, but rather the idea of a strong sense of nation and respecting national borders). When a villain called Flag-Smasher destroys flags at the United Nations (which is odd, considering that Flag-Smasher opposes national identities, instead preferring one human society, and the U.N. is the closest representation of that very approach to civilization). Flag-Smasher defends his ideology by stating, "When you say, 'I'm an American,' what you're saying is that you are separate from anyone who cannot make a similar statement. Every nation fosters the idea that it is better than all the others! This is what has brought us to warfare with our fellow beings. What has brought us to the brink of nuclear destruction!"[21]

While his statement is true—both world wars were fought primarily due to radical nationalist ideologies—Captain America sees the United States as the proverbial city on a hill, representing freedom and justice to a world largely devoid of it. Were borders to be brought down, would other nations rise to the American standard, or would America fall to theirs? This is the Reagan version of nationalism that even Captain America upholds, as he defends it:

> I believe my opponent was wrong. There is nothing harmful about having a sense of national identity or ethnic heritage. America is made up of a multitude of different ethnic groups. Each of which has had its own part to contribute to American culture. Be proud of your heritage, but never let that pride make you forget that beneath it all, we are all human beings who have the same wants and needs and deserve the same respect and dignity.[22]

Cap's defense of America as he sees it fails to take into account the suffering that "different ethnic groups" were still encountering and would continue to encounter well into the century to come.

Mark Gruenwald's run on *Captain America* is one of the comic's most iconic. Of his many stories over his ten-year run, perhaps the most significant is that of "Captain America No More." When confronted with an allegedly presidential appointed group calling itself the Commission, tasked with overseeing super people, Captain America points out that he reports to no government agency, at which point he is given the choice: report to the Commission, or cease being Captain America (including giving up the shield and no longer wearing the stars and stripes, as the Commission sees "Captain America" as the property of the U.S. government). Steve Rogers chooses the latter.[23] The first long-running story arc in *Captain America* then begins, with a new "Captain America" and Steve Rogers continuing his super-heroing as simply "The Captain." Steve's choice in this matter, choosing to give up being Captain America because following the mandates of a committee would deprive him of his right to choose his actions (an argument he would later make in the MCU's *Captain America: Civil War*), seemed at the time to be quite out of character. Steve's initial choice to become Captain America in 1940 was due to his desire to serve his country as a soldier, which he did as the Sentinel of Liberty. Throughout his tenure as Captain America, he has served the American people by protecting them from those threats that standard defenses could not stand up to. *This* choice seems to be less about a refusal to serve as a soldier and more about not serving the current commander-in-chief (Ronald Reagan).

The Commission's choice for the "new" Captain America is a former professional wrestler named John Walker (a fairly obvious nod to the very manly Johnnie Walker whiskey, made even more obvious when the character later changes his name to Jack Daniels). This story, too, would appear later in the MCU in the Disney+ series *The Falcon and the Winter Soldier* (although there Walker was a decorated American soldier, not a wrestler). Walker's previous profession was also very likely a nod to the real-world World Wrestling Federation (WWF)—later renamed World Wrestling Entertainment (WWE)—which had gained considerable national popularity in the late 1980s through the popularity of such pro wrestlers as Hulk Hogan and Andre the Giant. Likewise, the storyline of the new Cap villain, Power Broker, dosing his wrestlers with a version of Super Soldier Serum was a nod to the real-world scandal in the latter half of the decade when Hulk Hogan admitted that he—and other wrestlers in the WWF—had used steroids to gain their impressive physiques. WWF owner Vince McMahon very much appeared to be the real-world embodiment of Power Broker.

Walker would be a much more hard-lined and violent Captain America, much more in line with the popular Punisher. Walker had already gained much media attention fighting crime as Super-Patriot, clad in a

Chapter 5. Captain American No More (Again)

patriotic-themed costume alongside three other former pro wrestlers as up his sidekicks, the BUCkies (Bold Urban Commandos), an obvious nod to Cap's World War II sidekick. Super-Patriot was a media hog first and foremost. He would ignore small-time crime to focus on bigger events that the media was more likely to cover. Once chosen by the Commission to be the new Captain America, Walker chooses one of his BUCkies—Lemar Hoskins—to serve as his "Buck" (Hoskins's superhero name was changed to Battlestar when it was pointed out by a reader that the term "buck" had once been used as a term for male slaves, and Hoskins was a Black character).[24] The new Cap and Battlestar soon take on the radical conservative/ultra-nationalist/racist organization the Watchdogs.

After some contemplation of his own future, Steve Rogers chose to continue to fight evil—though swearing to never fight the U.S. government—as the Captain. Steve's new costume (debuting in *Captain America* #337, January 1988) was a dark reflection of his original: an exact copy of the style of the Captain America costume (winged cowl included), but all black, with an inverted triangle of red and white stripes with a black star in the upper right corner on his chest; the same red boots and gauntlets as his original Cap costume; no "A" on his forehead; and a shield similar in style, design, and imagery as the original (which was now, presumably, in possession of the new Captain America). The Captain would continue to hold his leadership position with the Avengers as the new Captain America fought solo (with his sidekick).

In an interview with *Comics Week* magazine in 1987, Gruenwald discussed his inspiration for the *Captain America No More* storyline:

> I decided what I've gotta do is show what it means to support the ideals of America and support its political system, without necessarily supporting its policies.... I wanted to put Captain America through the worst time of his life, which is my job as a writer. I wanted the readers to find out how difficult it is to be Captain America. I think certain people take him for granted; they didn't know how hard it is to be Captain America. It's not an easy job to do—trying to represent the ideals of an entire nation.[25]

In this storyline—lasting a full eighteen months, one of the longest Cap stories of all time—Gruenwald goes deeper than perhaps any Cap writer to date to examine the question, "Who *is* Captain America?" In the 1940s and '50s he had been a stalwart defender of the nation against foreign enemies and ideologies. In the 1960s, he was a man out of time, a modern-day Rumpelstiltskin, a relic of the past somewhat overwhelmed at how the world has passed him by. Beginning in the 1970s, in the wake of Watergate, as America slowly but definitively begins to divide from within, where does Captain America fit? How can he represent the American ideal if that very ideal is a subject of stark divisions along political party lines? If John Walker is that representation in Reagan America, can Steve Rogers ever truly be Captain America again?

The contrast between Walker and Rogers is perhaps nowhere more apparent than in issue #338 (February 1988). In one of the most graphic pages in the long history of Captain America comics, Captain America (Walker) literally beats a villain to death. Crouching over a fallen Professor Power, Walker begins pummeling the villain's face. With each punch, Captain America's red glove becomes more bloodied; Walker's face at one point is literally red with rage.[26] This is the "New Captain America." This is the representation of Reagan-era America ... and Reagan-era Americans. The massive popularity of Stallone's *Rambo* films, Schwarzenegger's *Terminator* and *Commando*, popular support for real-world subway vigilante Bernard Goetz, and Marvel's own *The Punisher* and *Punisher: War Journal* comics are all testament to that fact. As is the case with many U.S. presidents, the cowboy actor Reagan was a reflection of who we were in the 1980s.

Perhaps the sharpest criticism of the Reagan Era to appear in Cap comics was the storyline featuring the villain Viper and her scheme to turn the population of Washington, D.C., into serpents. The benefit of the "new Cap" storyline was that it allowed the creative team to tell two stories: Walker's Captain America and Rogers's the Captain. In the Viper storyline, it is Rogers as the Captain who saves the day, eventually fighting against a serpentine Ronald Reagan. While saving the day and (presumably) returning the denizens of D.C. to normal, the closing panels of the story show a returned to normal President Reagan praising the Captain. A closeup of the 40th president of the United States clearly shows fangs in his smile.[27] The message is clear: the president was already a vile, venomous creature. The president's closing statement: "As for those of you who may have been concerned about the welfare of the First Lady [Nancy Reagan] and myself ... well, you can rest assured that we were never in any danger whatsoever."[28]

This leaves the reader to wonder: is the statement merely political spin to downplay the danger they were in, or were they truly in no danger because they were already serpents?

Following along this general thesis of Reagan America, the "new Cap" storyline comes to a conclusion with a resurrected Red Skull being disclosed as the true power behind the Commission and all of Steve Rogers's woes over the last eighteen months. Now living in a new body cloned from Rogers himself, the Skull proudly proclaims, "I have become an American dreamer. I now embrace the American dream for what it is—the realization of one's personal ambitions by whatever means necessary."[29]

Chapter 5. Captain American No More *(Again)*

This statement is a clear representation of all that 1980s America had come to embody: from J.R. Ewing to "Greed is good," from Donald Trump to Wall Street. America—and Americans—in the 1980s had come to idealize winning ... at any cost. Once Rogers is reinstated as the official Captain America, Walker—himself a Super Soldier—will continue (in Rogers's Captain uniform) as the U.S. Agent.

This point was driven home in an issue that would be published early in the new decade (but still within the Reagan Era). An image of a tall Washington, D.C., office building with a glass façade, the image of the Capitol building reflected in the glassy surface. With this one image, artist Kieron Dwyer summed up the 1980s. What the American people believed to be the seat of national power—Congress, located in the Capitol—was actually nothing more than its own façade, nothing but a mere reflection of the true seat of power: American corporations.[30] The question facing Gruenwald (and future Cap writers in the 1990s): Once the '80s were over, what would come next? Who would America *be* next? And how would Captain America fit into that America? For the 1980s, at least, the creative teams on *Captain America* have provided considerable material for scholars to dissect regarding the period, pulling back the curtain on the Reagan Era and showing the truth of its wizard.

Modern Takes

The 1980s issues of *Captain America* provide ample fodder for historians examining the Decade of Greed. The first (cover dated) issue of the decade was Cap's face-off with the Punisher. In his analysis of Cap and Punisher over the decades, Cord Scott points out, "Both are working for an ultimate goal (a just society) but how they approach it is very different in methodology and outcome. [In this issue] the Punisher gets the drop on Cap, but the battle ends with an outcome acceptable for both: the bad guys are halted."[31]

This will be an ongoing theme for the two characters. Both are former soldiers. Both are patriotic and love their country. Both want a safe, crime-free society for all Americans. The key difference is a monumental one: Captain America still firmly believes in the system and the concept of due process; the Punisher feels that the system has failed too many times, and too many dangerous criminals go unpunished, leaving people like his family (killed in the crossfire of a gang war) unsafe. The Punisher's answer is simple: eliminate the threat. There are many, many Americans who still share the Punisher's beliefs, and the character's increasing popularity throughout the Reagan years strongly suggests that they did then as well.

In President Reagan's previously discussed assertion that "government is not the solution" to America's problems, there is some similarity to President Carter's more infamous malaise speech: The problems facing America must be addressed first and foremost by the American *people*, putting the betterment of society over personal gain and advancement. In his study of Marvel Comics in the Cold War, Matthew Costello points out that

> [T]he contrast between the American dream and American reality posed by Captain America [in response to the push for him to run for president] … suggests that there is something fundamentally wrong with the reality of the American system.… Government is not seen as the venue through which American values can be made real; it will instead by the private realm to which people turn to secure their dreams of America for themselves and for their families.[32]

This analysis—and the original source material—does not go as far as to imply that, as Reagan said, government *was* the problem, but it underscores that, fundamentally, if the American people simply sit back and rely on politicians to fix America's problems, they are going to be disappointed—and continue to be burdened with those very problems—over and over again (and never more so than in the present political climate). It is important to keep in mind that by this time (and well into present times), American politicians have become as much consumer products as comic book superheroes. They sell themselves as products to the American voter with the ultimate end of ensuring future profits for American corporations.

A key part of the conservative revolution of 1980 was popular exhaustion with 20 years of progressive social change. As Costello points out, "Reagan attempted to rebuild an American consensus using the rhetoric of progress, freedom, and individualism in much the same way that rhetoric was used in the 1950s."[33]

This nostalgia for a simpler time was a major part of Reagan's (and Republicans') message in the 1980s, one to which straight white male America in particular (who likely saw themselves in Captain America) was quick to respond. While ensuring equal rights to all Americans does not take away from the rights of those who already enjoy them, ensuring equal *opportunity* to all Americans could, theoretically, reduce future opportunities for those who have enjoyed the monopoly of them to date. That possibility breeds fear, which—as Master Yoda pointed out—leads to anger, hate, and suffering.[34]

In J. Richard Stevens's analysis of masculinity in the character of Captain America, he provides the following analysis of Cap's politics in the Era of Reagan:

Chapter 5. Captain American No More *(Again)* 137

Although Captain America represented the image and spirit of 1980s America, his politics were hardly Republican, although they were influenced by the Republican manner. Despite his continuing to hold the liberal views he gained from his 1960s and 1970s adventures, his expression of his political views in the 1980s was much more measured and cautious.[35]

Though this analysis is debatable, it does have considerable backing in the source material. As Captain America is both a fictional character and a commercial product, the sociopolitical climate of the day must also be considered. President Reagan—even at the height of later scandal—remained wildly popular throughout his terms in office (and beyond). As such, statistically, a considerable portion of Cap readers were likely fans of the president (and, one presumes, his message).

In the overall context of Captain America adventures from 1941 to 2021, while Cap is markedly less vocal about social inequalities and societal problems in the 1980s than the two decades prior, when one considers him (as he clearly considers *himself*) a symbol of the American ideal, it is important to also consider what that ideal was in the overall zeitgeist of the period. Stevens concludes his analysis of Cap in the 1980s thusly:

> Like much of the American population, Captain America [in the 1980s] appears to have internalized his opinions about social injustice or the need to reform.... In contrast to his outspokenness in each of his earlier eras, Captain America remained relatively mute in the 1980s, just at a time when his symbolism appeared to convey powerful messages beyond his control.[36]

This observation of Cap's symbolism being more in line with conservative politics is a sad reality that appears to have begun (or at least become cemented) in the 1980s. Although the "liberal agenda" of the 1960s and '70s consisted of a push for a more liberated, more equal, and more just society (exactly what the red-white-and-blue should stand for), Reagan's brand of more "traditional" values (despite how unequal those traditions were) all but made the American flag their symbol, a symbol of the status quo, and a symbol against the ideologies of the left.

One of the more recent scholarly analyses of Captain America is Jason Olsen's *Mark Gruenwald and the Star Spangled Symbolism of Captain America, 1985–1995*. In this examination of the Gruenwald's long run on the series, Olsen spends considerable time on Cap's most prominent 1980s storyline, *Captain America No More!* Of Steve Rogers, Olsen concludes:

> When Steve Rogers declines to be Captain America in [issue] #332, he is not turning his back on the responsibilities of the title and he is not rejecting his country. Ultimately, his decision to stop being Captain America is a remarkably patriotic act, perhaps the most patriotic act he undertakes during

Gruenwald's run. He sees an unfairness in the system, detects that a good thing (his role as Captain America) could be exploited, and he says, "No More." Captain America's [i.e., Steve Rogers's] patriotism is not the flag-waving stuff of manipulative political rallies. Cap's patriotism is about knowing when America needs Steve Rogers more than it needs Captain America, and then finding a way to reconnect the two and ... doing it in a way that maintains the integrity and value of the personal patriotism that he cherishes.[37]

While of John Walker, Cap's replacement, Olsen states:

When the character first appears [as the Super-Patriot], Walker is convinced that the present is not ideal and a positive future needs to take a cue [from America's albeit darker and more flawed] past... [Walker] genuinely loves his country (albeit with a love that is naïve and lacking in complexity) and is manipulated by others as a result of that simplistic patriotism. Once his patriotism is exploited and he realizes where it has led him, Walker does not give up his love of country. Instead, he invests further, taking on a new identity and becoming a different hero, one still willing to serve and trust his country, but doing so with the experience of one who was misled as a result of his trust.[38]

While Walker does recognize how both he and Rogers have been manipulated by the Commission (and, by proxy, the Red Skull), as he continues to act as the U.S. Agent, his overall conservative political view does not change. He maintains his political identity and core beliefs—and future stories will exhibit the contrast between Walker's more hard line and Rogers's more egalitarian beliefs—and well into the 21st century continues to be a symbol of this Reagan Era of American history.

Exiting the '80s: A New World Order

As the 1980s drew to a close, Americans could have never imagined in their wildest dreams just how much politics, the economy, and society would change in the decade to come. The massive military spending and stock speculation on the Wall Street of the Reagan years would soon take its toll with the worst recession since the 1970s, before experiencing the biggest economic boom in the nation's history, primarily through a new infrastructure that would have seemed science fiction in 1989: the internet. As the Cold War comes to an abrupt end, Americans—for the first time in half a century—will have no more enemies ... no one left to hate or fear. As a result, they will turn their collective fear and loathing inward, finding enemies at home to build up as being as much a threat to American values as the Nazis or the Communists.

The two U.S. presidents of the coming decade—Republican George

Chapter 5. Captain American No More *(Again)*

H.W. Bush and Democrat Bill Clinton—personify this growing political division, though in hindsight they were far more alike than 21st-century presidents from the two parties. The epidemic consumerism and quest for wealth that came to define the 1990s created a "me first" mode of thinking that was very much what President Carter had warned against in 1979. The America that emerged from the 1980s was a very different society than that which had entered them. Americans were becoming increasingly disinterested in their neighbors and fellow Americans. The world's primary superpower was becoming a nation of entitlement: to wealth ... to power ... to being *right*, whether facts supported them or not. The lessons taught by superheroes were increasingly falling on deaf ears.

The comic book boom of the 1980s would meet a harsh crash by the mid–1990s. With no more enemies abroad, Americans would no longer have need for superheroes (and, as those heroes have become increasingly liberal over the last few decades, the political divide in America will lead to half the nation being turned off to the message of acceptance and tolerance those superheroes promoted). In a world with no threats, who needs heroes? This is a question that comic book creators would be forced to deal with. World War II and the Cold War had maintained a certain level of anxiety for America's youth that superheroes were largely successful in easing. The presumably peaceful "new world order" promised by the post–Cold War '90s lifted that anxiety ... until the new century brought about new threats, at home and abroad, that would revive the need for our spandex-clad heroes.

CHAPTER 6

Heroes Reborn

Captain America, the 1990s, and a New World Order

Over Christmas 1991, the Soviet Union experienced a complete governmental collapse, at least partially due to the country's attempt to stay competitive with Reagan's U.S. military spending increases of the 1980s (as well as the monumental costs of the 1986 explosion at their nuclear facility at Chernobyl). In February 1992, American president George H.W. Bush held a joint press conference with the new Russian president, Boris Yeltsin, to announce the official end to the Cold War. Forty-five years of political wrangling and nuclear brinksmanship ended, not with a bang, but with a whimper. For the first time in half a century, the United States possessed no external threats. The result would be a "new world order," a global society no longer threatened by the whims of the world's two superpowers (with one, Russia, no longer technically a superpower at all). With China not yet an economic challenger, Cuba without its primary benefactor, a relatively quiet North Korea, and al-Qaeda still an unknown entity to the American people, it seemed that the world was, for the foreseeable future at least, truly at peace. Capitalism had won out over authoritarian communism.

As America—and Americans—sought to find themselves in this new world order, a society-altering technology emerged: the internet. A new online economy would lead to the largest economic expansion in American history, and a redefining of every aspect of daily American life would begin. However, as the overall American economy boomed, the comic book industry would once more face almost certain collapse, the collectors' bubble of the last few years bursting (as all economic bubbles inevitably do). With no more external threats, the American people—inclined by this point toward the idea of never-ending conflict—would turn inward, the two political parties pointing at each other as the greatest threat to the nation. The result would be a culture war that would, over the next thirty years, tear the very political fabric of American democracy apart. Meanwhile, as the "American Century" drew to a close, a new threat emerged from the sands of the dawn of civilization ... determined to bring the world's only remaining superpower to its knees.

Within this decade of peace—between Cold War and war on terror—the very concept of superheroes comes into question. In a world with no threats, what are superheroes to do? The genre had emerged as the flames of World War II began to be lit and sustained a frightened society through the dangerous decades of the Cold War. With no more threats to truth, justice, and the American way, what role was left for America's spandex-clad defenders? Marvel Comics would face bankruptcy as movie superheroes became parodies of themselves, only to be saved by a half-vampire vampire hunter (while television introduced its own superhero vampire slayer). Generation X would dominate television with a show about nothing and one about a group of unbelievably attractive friends. The decade would see the death of Superman, as Captain America also died ... and died again ... and then, as the new century neared, yet again.

Politics in the 1990s: The Culture War Begins

President George H.W. Bush was proving a moderately successful and popular president as the 1990s began, made even more so with the successful Operation Desert Shield/Desert Storm expelling Iraqi dictator Saddam Hussein from the neighboring country of Kuwait in late 1990/early 1991. Here at home, a controversial Supreme Court appointment, Justice Clarence Thomas, brought the issue of sexual harassment in the workplace into the sphere of public discourse for the first time. Those events were followed by a major economic recession in 1992, awakening fears that the doldrums of the 1970s might be returning. The economic slump alone may not have hurt President Bush's reelection chances, but the rise of Texas billionaire H. Ross Perot as an independent conservative third option in that year's presidential race would succeed in splitting conservative votes, all but ensuring a Democratic victory that November.

At the 1992 Republican National Convention—mere months after the Cold War officially ended—Republican pundit and former Nixon administration official Pat Buchanan gave a speech, warning voters of the threat that liberal Democrats posed to American society:

> The agenda that [Bill] Clinton and [Hillary] Clinton would impose on America—abortion on demand, a litmus test for the Supreme Court, homosexual rights, discrimination against religious schools, women in combat units—

that's change ... but it is not the kind of change America needs.... This election is about much more than who gets what. It is about who we are. It is about what we believe. It is about what we stand for as Americans. There is a religious war going on in our country. It is a cultural war, as critical to the kind of nation we will one day be as was the Cold War itself.[1]

In that speech lay the foundations of the culture war that has increasingly divided the nation throughout the decades since. Issues that initially inspired political debate—abortion rights, LGBTQ+ rights, the military, immigration, minority rights, etc.—were now fodder for political war. This radical divergence would worsen even more as more cable news networks emerged, each choosing a political side to spin. From this point forward, presidents and presidential candidates (and eventually candidates for all elected office) would face not merely dislike or disagreement from the opposition party, but hatred. By the 2020s, friendships and familial ties would be torn asunder based on who someone had voted for in the last election, culminating in an all-out civilian invasion of the Capitol building on January 6, 2021, over misinformed disagreement over election results. American politics would now resemble a professional wrestling match more than a professional and informed debate.

The rise of H. Ross Perot as a conservative independent alternative to the more moderate President Bush, bringing about the division of conservative votes throughout all fifty states, all but guaranteed the victory of Democrat and former Arkansas governor Bill Clinton with only 43 percent of the popular vote. Had Perot not run in '92 (and again four years later), President Clinton would likely have lost and President Bush reelected.[2] In his final month in office, President Bush signed the North American Free Trade Agreement (NAFTA). The agreement formed a free-trade zone between Canada, the United States, and Mexico. Unfortunately, the agreement cost the U.S. more than a million manufacturing jobs (while creating double that in transportation jobs, which was of little concern to manufacturing workers who were now unemployed and forced to retrain for the changing economy). While Bush had negotiated and signed the agreement, since it went into effect in January 1994, Republicans would use the job losses as political fodder against President Clinton (who had nothing to do with the details of the agreement at all). This false politicizing would work, gaining Republicans control of Congress in that year's midterm elections.

With a Democratic majority in Congress initially, President Clinton did call for a national health care system (essentially proving Buchanan's warning of a liberal agenda). The result would be a new conservative wave in the 1994 midterm elections, with incoming Speaker of the House Newt Gingrich supporting a "Contract with America," blocking anything resembling liberal or progressive change. Republicans kept their word immediately, forcing a shutdown of the federal government in January 1995, which would have far more long-term political ramifications than it would on the short-term government funding.

During the shutdown, all nonessential government personnel were forced to leave work. This left an unusually high amount of daily work in the hands of unpaid interns. At the White House, one such intern, Monica Lewinsky, would be granted closer than usual access to the president of the United States. The notoriously womanizing President Clinton began an illicit affair with the intern. As the Republican Congress investigated the president and First Lady for their involvement with the questionable Whitewater real estate deal, the president's affair was brought to the attention of Whitewater special prosecutor Ken Starr. Starr's team—aware that Clinton had denied rumors of this affair while testifying under oath in a sexual harassment case brought against him by former Arkansas hotel employee Paula Jones—stepped away from Whitewater (which had led essentially nowhere) and began investigating the president for perjury and obstruction of justice (which they could far more easily prove). On December 19, 1998, President Bill Clinton became only the second U.S. president to be impeached by the House of Representatives. While he avoided removal from office by the U.S. Senate, the scandal forever tainted Clinton's presidency (and all but ruined the life of Lewinsky, whose only offense was being young and naïve in the face of a master manipulator). Despite the scandal, Clinton's popularity remained relatively unchanged, due primarily to the emerging new online economy.

Americans Become More (and Less) Connected: The Internet and Cellular Phones

With a long history of development behind it, the internet went fully commercial in 1995. By 1996, television commercials were including a company's website along with traditional marketing information. As early as 1994, developer Jeff Bezos had launched his online book-selling service, Amazon. Six months earlier, the search engine Yahoo had been launched, followed in 1996 by Ask Jeeves and in 1998 by Google. Incrementally, the sum total of human knowledge would be available at the stroke of a keyboard (along with an equally sum total of worthless misinformation). Chat rooms also emerged, allowing people of similar interests from around the nation (and the world) to meet in one place to discuss the topic of their choice. Everything from politics to comic books to conspiracy theories could gain large followings of like-minded (and opposition-minded) individuals. The advent of the internet naturally led to an explosion in the selling of personal computers, from roughly one million in 1993 to approximately 83 million by 1998.[3]

By mid-decade, cellular phones were also increasingly available—and affordable—for a growing number of Americans. A far cry from 21st century smartphones, the first commercially successful flip phones were merely that: telephones. Eventually texting capabilities would be introduced, but early cellular companies would charge customers for every call made, every call received, and every text sent (initially charging per character). With the cost being so high, many professionals in the 1990s continued to rely heavily on pagers (commonly called beepers), devices that would inform the owner that they had received a call or request for a call so that the owner could then seek out a phone to follow through. Though these new technologies dramatically changed America, the internet/cell phone age of the 1990s was still a far cry from where it would be by 2010. As the 20th century came to a close, Americans had still never heard the terms "social media" or "iPhone." The limits of these communications outlets would become evident when America faces its darkest day in 2001 ... a day that was already in the planning throughout the 1990s.

A New Threat Emerges

In 1988, a new radical Islamist jihadist international terrorist organization was born: al-Qaeda. Founded by wealthy, Saudi-born Osama bin Laden, the group opposed continued western influence in the Middle East and western support for the nation-state of Israel. Throughout the '80s, bin Laden had been a member of the CIA-backed mujahideen, freedom fighters opposing the Soviet invasion of Afghanistan. With al-Qaeda, however, bin Laden turned his focus—and that of his followers—against the very western powers that had supported his efforts in Afghanistan. The group became particularly outraged during 1990's Operation Desert Shield, when U.S. military forces—including female soldiers—occupied Muslim holy sites in Saudi Arabia (under the proclaimed auspices of protecting the region from potential invasion by Iraq). In 1993, the organization assisted with the attempted truck-bombing of the World Trade Center in New York City. In 1998, al-Qaeda conducted simultaneous bombings of the U.S. embassies in the African nations of Kenya and Tanzania. In October 2000, suicide bombers from the group drove a small boat (loaded with bombs) into the side of the U.S. Navy vessel USS *Cole*, killing seventeen American sailors. When the new century dawned, they would conduct their largest and deadliest attack to date.

Chapter 6. Heroes Reborn 145

By 1990, jihadist terrorism was not new news to Americans. However, with very few exceptions, the attacks and/or hijackings were almost always conducted within the Middle East. This gave the idea of terrorism very much an "over there" feel for most Americans. It was something that could never happen here (other than extremely rare homegrown terrorists such as the 1995 Oklahoma City bombing of the Alfred P. Murrah Federal Building by American terrorists Timothy McVeigh and Terry Nichols, which killed 168 people). Furthermore, when jihadist terrorists hijacked commercial airlines, it was always to demand transport to some other Middle Eastern location, leading airlines to implement a policy of allowing terrorists to simply take the plane if threatened. This policy—and Americans' relative apathy toward the possibility of such terrorism within the U.S.—would come back to haunt Americans at the dawn of the next century.

Gen X Neuroses: Pop Culture in the 1990s

As America entered the 1990s, Generation X (those born from roughly 1965 to 1980) was coming of age. With no memory of Pearl Harbor, or the assassination of President Kennedy, these were the latchkey kids, that generation of American children who essentially raised themselves, with both parents (or just the one in single-parent homes) forced to work to make ends meet while simultaneously unable to afford a babysitter. This generation did not learn about issues of race or gender from their parents; they learned them largely from *Sesame Street*, *Mister Rogers' Neighborhood*, and *Fat Albert*. They remembered the socioeconomic malaise of the 1970s and the boom times of the 1980s, and they were well aware that the future was theirs ... and they were not comfortable with that responsibility.

The two biggest television programs of the decade underscore the self-absorption and questioning of overall identity: *Seinfeld* and *Friends* (both airing on NBC). Both series focused on a tight-knit circle of friends who are closer to each other than they are their own families (a defining aspect of Gen X). Created by comedians Jerry Seinfeld and Larry David, *Seinfeld* was the iconic "show about nothing." Running from 1989 to 1998, the series centered on four friends in New York City—Jerry (Jerry Seinfeld), George (Jason Alexander), Elaine (Julia Louis-Dreyfus), and Kramer (Michael Richards)—who, though devoutly loyal to each other, are otherwise completely self-absorbed, concerned more about how they were perceived by others than how they actually felt about others. Similarly, *Friends* ran from 1994 to 2004, centering on a slightly larger group of friends—Monica (Courtney Cox), Rachel (Jennifer Anniston), Phoebe (Lisa Kudrow), Chandler (Matthew Perry), Joey (Matt LeBlanc), and Ross (David Schwimmer)—living, again, in New York City and dealing with their own personal neuroses with the support of the rest of the group. Both series were massive hits for NBC, calling for the highest paydays for cast in television history to that date (and beyond). Both shows emphasized the difficulties of navigating the complexities of modern life. This is the generation that would first be introduced to—and begin centering their lives around—the internet, which would only add to their collective uncertainty concerning the future and their ability to maneuver in it.

Another group that would see considerable representation on TV screens was the LGBTQ+ community. By 1990, the stigma of HIV/AIDS was less of an albatross for the movement, with more and more Americans learning about the realities of the disease (due largely to President Bush finally granting government funding for research); by mid-decade, there was a cocktail of drugs to provide hope to those infected, with the disease no longer an automatic death sentence. Series such as *Will & Grace* (originally running on NBC from 1998 to 2006) made great strides in humanizing what had, to date, been nothing more than a stereotype in popular culture. Likewise, when popular comedian Ellen Degeneres utilized her own sitcom, *Ellen* (ABC, 1994–1998) to come out as a lesbian, it opened a dialogue long overdue. Though it initially hurt her career (and resulted in her sitcom being canceled), her important role in helping the nation to heal post–9/11 would, itself, do much to open the doors of acceptance and social advancement to a group too long denied.

On the big screen, franchises continued to dominate (and many began to fail). The *Star Trek* and *Batman* franchises both began the decade strong, only to severely fizzle out by decade's end (leading to the need for reboots in the 2000s). Gen X writer/director Kevin Smith became the de facto voice of his generation with films such as *Clerks* (1994), *Mallrats* (1995), and *Chasing Amy* (1997). For many, the defining Generation X film was 1994's *Reality Bites*, starring Winona Ryder, Ethan Hawke, Ben Stiller, and Janeane Garofalo, about navigating the difficult years from teen to young adulthood while simultaneously not desiring to do so. Gen X writer/director Quentin Tarantino exploded onto the scene with his iconic *Pulp Fiction* (1994), with a star-studded cast telling a nonlinear story revolving around a handful of dark and colorful characters spouting equally dark and colorful dialogue that inspired the phrase "Tarantino-esque." In 1997, director James Cameron's historical fiction film *Titanic* became the highest grossing film of all time, bringing in over $2 billion (as of 2023, the film remained the third highest grossing film).

Superhero fare did not fare as well. Tim Burton's 1992 sequel to his

Chapter 6. Heroes Reborn 147

1989 hit *Batman*, *Batman Returns*, with Michael Keaton returning as the big screen Dark Knight, did well with critics and audiences. However, 1995's *Batman Forever*, directed by Joel Schumacher and starring Val Kilmer, began to see a decline; Schumacher's 1997 follow-up, *Batman & Robin* (this time with television superstar George Clooney donning the cape and cowl), was a total disaster, killing the franchise until owner Warner Brothers risked a reboot in 2005. Another superhero offering in 1997 was *Spawn*, based on Todd McFarland's wildly successful Image Comics antihero, similarly bombed. Coming just after the collapse of the comics industry's collectors' bubble as these films did, these simultaneous events underscored a growing theme in the 1990s: the days of the superhero appeared to be over. As the decade drew to a close, however, a surprising offering from the pages of Marvel Comics signaled that there might be some breath in the old genre still. *Blade* (1998) starred Wesley Snipes as the titular vampire hunter. The film's considerable success led to two sequels and more offerings from Marvel characters as the country entered the 21st century. Just the year prior, upstart television network the WB launched the similarly themed series *Buffy the Vampire Slayer*, starring Sarah Michelle Gellar as the cheerleader-turned-hunter of the undead. Based on the 1992 film of the same name by creator/writer Joss Whedon, the series was a cult success, running from 1997 to 2003, and reopening the door, originally cracked in the 1970s, of female-led superhero properties.

As Gen X reached adulthood, video gaming remained more popular than ever. Nintendo's release of the Super Nintendo gaming system in 1990 launched a new era for the industry, soon driving longtime industry leader Atari deep into the background. A home video version of the wildly popular *Mortal Kombat* was released in 1992. With the advent of the internet, the gaming community could communicate as never before, eventually leading to 21st-century gaming systems PlayStation and Xbox, which allowed players from across the world to play the same game simultaneously. By the beginning of the 21st century, video gaming would be as cemented a part of American popular culture as television and film.

As the '80s came to a close, the popularity of superhero films both boosted and was boosted by superhero comic book sales. That continued into the 1990s, but by mid-decade, the decreasing popularity of superhero films was likewise in tandem with the end of the boom in comics sales. Though there were many factors involved, Gen X played a role. By 1995, Gen Xers were starting families, making their way in the rapidly changing economy, and finding themselves no longer in possession of the finances necessary to continue to support their old comic book hobby. As a result, the industry faced possible collapse (again).

Comics in the '90s, Part I: The Bubble Bursts

The late 1980s had seen a rapid boom in the comic book industry. There were several factors converging at this point in time to create what has come to be known as the collectors' bubble:

- major "event" miniseries such as Marvel's *Secret Wars* and DC's *Crisis on Infinite Earths* and "special events" such as the wedding of Spider-Man/Peter Parker and Mary Jane Watson in *The Amazing Spider-Man Annual* #21 (1987), as well as the enduring popularity of the soap-operatic X-Men titles at Marvel raised the interests of traditional comics readers;
- the two 1986 miniseries by DC—*Watchmen* and *Batman: The Dark Knight Returns*—had won attention and acclaim from more mainstream literary critics, alerting those who were not reading comics that something had changed;
- the 1987 stock market crash coinciding with high-dollar auctions of Golden Age comic books;
- the massive success of the Tim Burton *Batman* film in 1989; and
- the rise of new superstar comics artists Todd McFarlane and Jim Lee.

Hopeful "investors" were buying comic books that appeared to have future value (particularly any issue showing as #1, or issues tied to special "event" storylines) and immediately boarding and bagging them.[4] Longtime comics collectors found themselves buying two copies of potentially valuable comics: one for bagging and one for reading.

The two major comics companies—Marvel and DC—picked up quickly on this growing trend and began marketing products accordingly. Suddenly there was a plethora of new #1 issues hitting newsstands. As that trend began to wane, other gimmicks were implemented such as the foil-embossed cover issues: essentially embedding a foil card onto the cover of certain comics, with images in the foil; perhaps the most famous example of this is the *Robin II* miniseries in 1991. With so many buyers choosing titles based on images rather than text (because they weren't actually reading them), story became less important than art, and artists such as McFarlane, Lee, and Rob Liefeld drew large paydays for output. As those initial gimmicks began to fail—due largely to constant repetition—the gimmick "event" began to be implemented, signaling the beginning of the end of the boom.

By 1993, when potential investors were wising up to the #1 and foil-

Chapter 6. Heroes Reborn

embossed cover gimmicks—and the superstar artists pushing sales left the "Big Two" and started their own company, Image Comics (to be discussed later)—Marvel and DC turned once more to story to drive sales, putting their most popular characters through the greatest challenges of their decades-long careers. The biggest example of this would be *The Death of Superman*. Running from December 1992 through October 1993, and overseen by DC's Superman editor Mike Carlin, the *Death of Superman* storyline ran through the pages of all of the Superman books at the time: *Action Comics*, *Superman*, *The Adventures of Superman*, and *Superman: The Man of Steel*. The story culminated in *Superman* #75 (the title had relaunched with a new #1 in the wake of 1985's *Crisis on Infinite Earths*), written by Dan Jurgens with art by Jurgens and Brett Breeding, delivering the event title's promise of the demise of the Man of Steel. The event made headlines in major news outlets, creating even more buzz and driving up sales even farther. Ultimately, that one issue sold approximately six million copies. Those familiar with comics knew that heroes dying was not uncommon (and never permanent), but those less familiar with the industry viewed this issue as holding potential value that would one day make them rich (not considering that the reason why *Action Comics* #1 from 1938 was so valuable was that by 1988, so few intact copies remained, while six million bagged, boarded, and boxed copies would never rise in value).

Other major event gimmicks at the time included *Knightfall* in the Batman titles. Running from April to October 1993 (in tandem with *The Death of Superman*), primarily in the pages of the two Batman books—*Detective Comics* and *Batman*—and overseen by Batman editor Denny O'Neil, the story centered on Batman facing a new foe, Bane, who puts the Dark Knight through a constant 24/7 quest to recapture escaped maniacs before fighting him one-on-one and breaking Batman's spine (presumably permanently ending the career of Bruce Wayne as Batman). At Marvel, what began as a similarly short-run gimmick storyline ended up getting out of control, running for over two years (from October 1994 to December 1996). "Spider-Man: The Clone Saga" ran primarily through the Spider-Man titles—*The Amazing Spider-Man*, *Web of Spider-Man*, *The Sensational Spider-Man*, *Spider-Man*, and *The Spectacular Spider-Man*—as well as additional "special" titles. Primarily the brainchild of Gerry Conway, Terry Kavanagh, and Howard Mackie, the story suggested that the Spider-Man/Peter Parker whose adventures fans had been reading for decades had actually not been the *real* Spider-Man/Peter Parker since the early 1970s; that he had been replaced at that time with a clone who believed himself to be the real Peter Parker. *The Clone Saga* sought to discover the truth, constantly taking unexpected turns and bringing in false leads and numerous clones, making it unclear who was real and who was a clone. While an intriguing storyline, the longevity of the story led many readers to simply give up, convinced no true answer was forthcoming. Meanwhile, longtime readers were angered that they might have not been reading adventures of the "real" Spider-Man for the last two decades (never stopping, one supposes, to consider that none of them were real).

By 1995, these events—all of which promised "permanent" changes to popular characters—ultimately ended with everything returned to normal (showing that even longtime readers failed to fully understand that Clark Kent, Bruce Wayne, and Peter Parker were all commercial products first and foremost, and therefore can never truly, permanently be gone).

Perhaps the most obvious gimmick of the period was the Amalgam experiment. Giving longtime comics fans what they had actually been demanding for decades, Marvel and DC—both facing rapidly diminishing sales—put aside their decades-long rivalry to pit their heroes against one another in the ultimate event. Readers could finally see Superman fight the Hulk, Batman fight the Punisher, and Flash test his speed against Quicksilver. The fights, naturally, largely ended in some manner of draw, but after the issues dealing with the battles ended, the two companies launched the joint endeavor of Amalgam Comics, a one-year experiment merging popular characters from each company into all-new heroes with powers and origin stories being an amalgamation of two characters. Batman merged with Wolverine to create the Dark Claw; Superman and Captain America merged to form Super-Soldier. Super-Soldier would have an origin and powers similar to Superman, but would be blond-haired, wearing the traditional Captain America costume, and carrying a shield bearing the shape and symbol of Superman.

While DC Comics had for some time been a subsidiary of Warner Brothers Studios, Marvel Comics had been an independent entity for years. The sales boom brought on by the collectors' bubble inspired Marvel to go public in 1991, selling stock on the New York Stock Exchange. When the sales bubble burst by 1995, Marvel stock plummeted, leading the company to declare bankruptcy in December 1996. Two years later, the company merged with ToyBiz to save it from bankruptcy, with the new owners understanding that though Marvel held nothing in actual physical assets, it possessed a wealth of intellectual property (i.e., the thousands of fictional characters owned by the company, many of which were ripe for monetizing through movies, television series, and merchandise). The release of *Blade* in 1998 showed that there was considerable profit potential with Marvel characters. Over the next four years, the massive back-to-back successes of 20th Century–Fox's *X-Men* and Sony Pictures' *Spider-Man* franchises would further underscore the point.

In the end, the collectors' bubble of the late '80s and early '90s would burst due to nearly as many factors as had caused it: fans and investors tiring of continual gimmicks to further boost sales; investors finding a newer and more promising investment in the burgeoning e-market of the internet; the end of the Cold War—and a half century of potentially world-ending hostilities—and the promise of a future defined more by peace and tranquility leaving a society no longer in need of heroes; and the movie industry seemingly being less and less interested in the antics of spandex-clad protagonists. The cracks were evident early on, as the large publishers—more interested in profit than in product quality—showed insufficient appreciation for the creators largely responsible for product interest and sales. That lack of appreciation would lead to a massive walk-out and the emergence of a new competitor.

Comics in the '90s, Part II: A Rival Emerges

The late '80s and early '90s had seen the rise of several superstar artists and, to a lesser extent, writers in the comics industry. Artist Todd McFarlane's wildly popular run on *The Amazing Spider-Man* inspired Marvel to give the artist his own separate Spider-Man title, fully drawn and written by him. The resulting *Spider-Man* #1 (August 1990) sold roughly 2.5 million copies. The following year, having enjoyed success as an artist on *The Uncanny X-Men*, Jim Lee was given art duties on a new "X" title with longtime X-Men scribe Chris Claremont (which was odd, considering both had already been working on *Uncanny*). *X-Men* #1 (October 1991) sold over 8 million copies.[5] Meanwhile, artist Rob Liefeld had been a contributing factor to a boost in sales for another Marvel "X" title, *The New Mutants* (issue #98 of which—cover dated February 1991—introduced Liefeld creation Deadpool, who would go on to be one of the most popular characters in Marvel Comics). This led to the book being relaunched as *X-Force* #1 (August 1991), featuring art by Liefeld and cowritten by Liefeld and *The New Mutants* scribe Fabian Nicieza.

Although Marvel was making massive profits due to these new artists, and overall sales were higher than ever, the company did not fully appreciate the degree to which sales were driven solely by the strengths of the artists (feeling that it was the characters driving sales rather than the artists themselves). Feeling unappreciated (and not sufficiently compensated) by the Big Two publishers, McFarlane, Lee, Liefeld and others—Erik Larsen, Whilce Portacio, Marc Silvestri, and Jim Valentino—collectively went rogue and formed Image Comics in 1992. Their business model provided creators with not only full creative control of their creations but also full ownership. As such, the company was actually an amalgam of smaller entities, all under the overall Image banner: McFarlane ran Todd McFarlane Productions (which produced the company's biggest success, *Spawn*) and Lee controlled WildStorm Productions (producing the comic *WildC.A.T.s*), while Liefeld operated Awesome Comics (with its biggest seller being *Youngblood*). Each of the other cofounders likewise ran their own distinct creative studios.

Marvel and DC (particularly Marvel, for whom all the Image founders had worked) soon saw the error of their ways as the strengths of these artists' names did, indeed, sell massive numbers of books. Image immediately cut its own significant portion of the overall comics sales pie (a pie that would very quickly get smaller as the sales bubble burst). However, with no clear executive structure and each owner having an equal voice (while having no input on each other's productions), problems soon arose, with Lee (among others) eventually selling out their subdivisions of Image to the larger publishers. Image continues to be a major player in the comics industry well into the 2020s, but nowhere near its initial success during the collectors' bubble of the early '90s.

Comics in the '90s, Part III: In a World with No Threats, Are Heroes Needed?

A contributing—though impossible to quantify—factor in the popularity of superheroes over the decades since the Great Depression was the fear and uncertainty of the real world. When superheroes first hit the market, America was still coming out of the decade-long Great Depression and was hit immediately afterward by the global threat of World War II. Once the war was over—and the economy continued to boom—superheroes fell out of fashion, not returning to prominence again until the late 1950s/early 1960s, when news headlines were dominated by the civil rights movement at home and the Cold War abroad. Sales would once more take a considerable dip during the doldrums of the 1970s, only peaking again during the collectors' bubble. Once the Cold War ended in 1992, the only thing keeping a need for superheroes afloat was the investors' bubble. Once that burst by 1995, the industry tanked once more, seemingly for good ... until the events of September 11, 2001. After that, the industry would once more take off, sustained by continued fear and uncertainty both at home and abroad, as well as the massive success of superheroes on the big screen due to the advent of CGI technology.

This rapid dip in superhero sales during the decade between the Cold War and 9/11 poses the question: Do we (as a society) *need* heroes? The rise

Chapter 6. Heroes Reborn 153

in sales during times of national crisis would suggest some corollary exists. Though the overall fear and uncertainty created by the events of 9/11 had subsided considerably by the time *Iron Man* and *The Dark Knight* hit theaters in 2008 (quickly becoming the two most successful superhero films to date), that year did see the rise of a new period of uncertainty in the U.S. political arena. The political divisions of the culture war were exacerbated that year by the rise of Democratic presidential candidate (and eventual president) Barack Obama, the first Black president in American history. If the Culture war should subside at some point in the 2020s, will superheroes once more see a similar dip?

In the 1990s, this overall sense that heroes were no longer needed, as no apparent threats seemed to exist for Americans as a whole, left comics creators with the conundrum of what to do with these characters in such a world. They could kill Superman, cripple Batman, and give Spider-Man the ultimate identity crisis, but eventually these commercial products would need to return. To do what?

Perhaps no single superhero attempted to address this issue more than Captain America. In that one decade, Captain America would not only die, he would do so *three times* between 1992 and 2002. Throughout that time, the Red Skull would return again and again to taunt the Star-Spangled Avenger with this very question. Finally, just weeks before 9/11, the Red Skull would confront Captain America with a terrifying prophecy, one that the real world would soon be forced to confront.

Cap in the 1990s

When the Cold War ended, decades of patriotic/nationalistic messaging were no longer relevant. Ironically, this transition to a "new world order" had been predicted in American popular culture only weeks before the Soviet Union fell. On December 6, 1991—less than three weeks before the fall of Soviet communism—*Star Trek VI: The Undiscovered Country* was released in the U.S., presenting an end to the "cold war" between the United Federation of Planets (an analogy for the U.S. in the *Star Trek* franchise) and the Klingon Empire (the franchise's analogy for the Soviet Union). They discuss tearing down the Neutral Zone (their Berlin Wall) and ending all hostilities.[6] At the core of this story was the idea of how cold warriors—those who have spent decades being taught to hate and distrust the other—adjust and adapt to an atmosphere of peace and an end to unremitting hostility.[7] This was the political atmosphere that America would find herself in throughout the early '90s, and was an issue the very patriotic Captain America would have to navigate.

During this period of apparent uncertainty as to what to do with Captain America in the waning days of the Cold War, one of the longer storylines was a werewolf story. This resulted, as one would expect, in Captain America becoming a werewolf (though not transforming back and forth as one would normally think of such a character, but rather being in permanent wolf mode for the duration of his affliction). It is one of the sillier Cap stories from his long and storied career—not to mention one of the odder Gruenwald stories—but it is relatively entertaining (though most would agree that it went on *far* too long). Aside from this outlandish tale, most of Cap's transitional stories (from Cold War to post–Cold War) would center on his interpersonal relationships with characters developed over the Gruenwald run.

Prior to the official end of the Cold War, as the 1990s open it is unclear where Captain America will be going in the new decade, as communist nations in Eastern Europe fall one by one and turn against the Soviet Union. Throughout 1990, Captain America begins a romantic relationship with the reformed Serpent Society villain, Diamondback. Meanwhile, the Red Skull faces a different kind of threat than ever before: an attack by a fellow Marvel villain. Magneto—the mutant master of magnetism—hunts down Red Skull. By this time it had been established that Magneto, as a child, had been one of the millions of European Jews taken, tortured, and nearly killed by the Nazis. Now, Magneto wants to see Red Skull pay for his crimes against humanity (ironic, considering Magneto's own crimes against humanity as he pushes for mutants to emerge as a "master race").

Captain America #383 (cover dated March 1991) is the 50th anniversary issue for the hero. Captain America encounters Father Time, who leads him on a magical mystery tour where the Star-Spangled Avenger meets Johnny Appleseed, Pecos Bill, John Henry, Paul Bunyan, and finally Uncle Sam. Of the group, Uncle Sam explains to Cap, "Doesn't matter where we seem to originate, my boy. On a poster, in a campfire tale, as a flesh-and-blood historical figure ... what matters is that we take hold of the American public's imagination, embody a specific heroic archetype, and assume mythic stature. That I've done, and so have you."[8]

He goes on to lament that in modern America, "the mass media replacing the deep truth of tall tales with the shallow truths of everyday events"[9] has led to the sad watering down of the concept of American legends. As Uncle Sam and Father Time suggest it is time for Cap to retire and join them in the world of legends, Cap refuses: "I can't accept that. I'm not ready to stop striving to make America a place where men can realize their dreams."[10]

Even before Americans were confronted with their post–Cold War identity crisis, the clear signs that the end of the conflict is near had some

Chapter 6. Heroes Reborn

already pondering what was next for America. The rest of the anniversary issue features three other stories: a World War II tale of Cap and Bucky, a self-reflection story for U.S. Agent, and a tale of the Red Skull—still living in a perfect body cloned from Steve Rogers—donning a Red Skull mask in order to fully express the Skull's psychological power.

As the rest of the industry focused on big gimmick storylines, the pages of *Captain America* rolled along relatively traditionally. The character's biggest '90s moments begin mid-decade, when Cap will die ... and die again ... and, presumably, die *again* as America enters the new century. Cap confronts a second Super-Patriot and a new foe, Americop, both of which essentially repeat the John Walker/Punisher dynamic of an anti-Steve Rogers.

The most startling event—perhaps of the entire run of the character—came in 1994 with the discovery that Cap's Super Soldier Serum had finally been pushed beyond its original design limits, quickly losing its ability to repair cells that become damaged or worn through use. Steve Rogers must refrain from superheroics or face total physical paralysis—or even death—within a year.[11] Gruenwald does not rush this story, allowing it to progress slowly as the doctor suggested, with only occasional reminders that the deterioration is continuing. In issue #438 (April 1995), Cap's body has nearly given out, and Tony Stark provides him with a suit of armor that will allow him to continue (similar to the mechanized leg braces Tony gives to Rhodey/War Machine after his paralysis in the MCU film *Captain America: Civil War*). Only issues later, Cap's empty armor is found at Avengers Mansion, leading the other Avengers to presume that the Star-Spangled Avenger is no more (which is an odd conclusion, as there is no body, so either Steve Rogers has gone off to die alone, or his body has been stolen; neither possibility is investigated by the Avengers).

Cap's first death in the '90s is short-lived. Awakened yet again from a block of ice, this time by the presumed-dead Sharon Carter/Agent 13, Steve Rogers notices that his strength is returning—he is no longer dying (or dead). Meanwhile, a funeral is held for Steve Rogers/Captain America, with President Bill Clinton acting as one of his pallbearers. Readers soon discover that Steve has been saved through a total blood transfusion from the only other person with an exact copy of his blood ... the Red Skull.[12] Gruenwald's last issue on *Captain America* had ended with the mysterious disappearance of Steve Rogers's body. It was up to new writer Mark Waid to write out the hero's return (both to life and to full health). The story of Captain America possessing blood given him by the Red Skull was controversial among readers, to be sure (though, if one considers that Red Skull's body was actually an exact clone of Rogers, then it actually was Rogers's blood and not the Skull's ... it's comic books, people!). However, Steve

Rogers's return to life would be short-lived, as he would die once more just a year later to save the world from the villain Onslaught.

Onslaught had been a storyline featured in the X-Men books of the mid-1990s, a new villain born from the psionic connection of Professor Charles Xavier (leader of the X-Men) and Magneto (former head of the Brotherhood of Evil Mutants). This odd creature (for lack of a better word) kidnapped and absorbed the two most powerful minds on Earth: Professor X and Franklin Richards, young son of Reed and Sue Richards of the Fantastic Four. As the X-Men attempted to take down the threat, they discovered that close interaction with mutants only made Onslaught more powerful. As a result, the non-mutant heroes (the Avengers and the Fantastic Four) and villains would have to sacrifice their lives to destroy Onslaught by allowing him to absorb their… "normalness" (it wasn't a popular ending).[13] For the first time since its inception in 1961, the primary timeline of the Marvel Comics Universe was without most of its founding heroes. This death, too, would not last long.

Facing bankruptcy—as well as the collapse of the sales bubble—Marvel Comics needed to do something desperate to boost sales. While the Spider-Man and X-Men titles were still doing comparatively well, the Avengers and Fantastic Four titles were not. As this was coinciding with the internal strife over at Image Comics, Marvel pulled off a coup: they would kill off some of their long-standing but poor-selling heroes and relaunch them in an entirely separate universe under the creative control of artists Jim Lee and Rob Liefeld. Lee would helm the "Heroes Reborn" issues of *Fantastic Four* and *Iron Man*, and Liefeld would take over creative duties on *The Avengers* and *Captain America*, each title restarting with all-new #1 issues (continuing to beat a dead horse). Each hero's origin story would be retold as the presumed-dead heroes awoke in a new reality, a new timeline, with no memory of their past lives. (It would not be the hit Marvel was hoping for.)

The relaunched and rebooted *Captain America* begins a different story for Steve Rogers. Waking up from a dream of a red-white-and-blue costumed hero fighting Nazis (oddly with the trademark "A" on his forehead replaced with an eagle), Steve Rogers finds himself in bed with his wife, alive and well in 1990s Philadelphia, Pennsylvania (Bill Clinton will appear later, setting a time stamp on this new universe). He is living a middle-class life with his wife and child, unaware that he was the Sentinel of Liberty of World War II. The opening offering also introduces young teenage girl Rikki Barnes (Cap's new Bucky) and a new Nazi villain, Master Man. With the new Nazi menace, Captain America must be reawakened, his entire life as he knew it no more than a ruse to keep the Super Soldier hidden and pacified until needed once more.[14]

Chapter 6. Heroes Reborn

The remainder of the short thirteen-issue run reintroduces the primary characters of the Cap comics: Nick Fury/SHIELD, Agent 13/Sharon Carter, Sam Wilson (this time a soldier, as he would later be in the MCU), Baron Zemo, MODOK, Crossbones, and of course the Red Skull. Though it's likely the heroes were always meant to return to the primary timeline, the shortness of the run of all four books was probably largely due to diminishing sales after the first issues. Ultimately, Cap and the others would learn that before their "deaths," young Franklin Richards utilized his powerful mind to create a "pocket universe" inside of his toy ball and sent his family and their friends there just as their lives appeared to end. As that universe collapsed due to the boy's continuing grief (apparently unaware of what he had done), the heroes found a way home, back to their original lives. Hence launching a *third* "volume" of *Captain America*.

Upon the heroes' return, many around the world begin worshiping Thor in a religious way. This opens a discussion between Cap and Thor:

> **CAP:** What keeps you from becoming arrogant about it?
> **THOR:** Should we someday lose the attentions of those who believe in us ... would we cease to exist?[15]

This seemingly unimportant interaction at the beginning of a new Cap adventure actually speaks to the very questions facing superhero comics by 1998: Are superheroes still relevant? Are they still needed? If so, for what?

Though this chapter is subtitled as an examination of the 1990s, it more accurately focuses on the period of peace between the Cold War and 9/11 (so, from 1992 to 2001). As America left the 1990s and entered the 2000s, the final year of the 20th century would see oddly prophetic storylines emerge in the pages of *Captain America*. The Hate-Monger would return, once more bent on beginning a race war in America. A new villain would seek to harness all of the information on the internet, and Captain America would see firsthand how the new technology began to feed conspiracy theorists around the nation. America had changed considerably, but in many ways remained very much the same. The 21st century would, indeed, see a massive rise in racial violence and conspiracy theorists. While the internet would be helpful in connecting people like never before, it would also connect people whose intents and motives were inherently dangerous.

Captain America would prove eerily prophetic in other ways as well. During the height of the 1998 "Skrull War" storyline, a destroyed downtown Manhattan is labeled "Ground Zero."[16] In the last issue of *Captain America* produced prior to the events of September 11, 2001 (though hitting newsstands a month later), the Red Skull explains to Captain America how the United States will ultimately fall: "All by itself, from within. Your nation is a cauldron of hate waiting to erupt. A cesspool of violent thoughts looking for release. It's a fuse extending from one coast to the other, waiting for someone to ignite the flame."[17]

The final issue of this third volume of *Captain America* (a multi-story issue) would hit newsstands in February 2002, while the nation had still not recovered from the events of the previous September. In that issue, Captain America appears to die once more, blowing up in a building after being attacked by an army of people in Red Skull masks.[18]

In the next story, a grade school classroom watches on television as the death of Captain America is announced. The children suddenly gang up on a Middle Eastern child, beating him because people "not from here" must have killed Captain America. Another child—later presumed to be the boy's friend—simply stands by and watches. When this boy goes home, readers see that he too was a fan of Captain America (a picture on his wall shows that Cap had once saved him), but that now, with Cap dead, his anger toward his classmates may have a longer lasting impact. Incidentally, this is the first published Captain American story written by a woman.[19] The closing image of this final issue is of the Marvel heroes standing around the grave of Steve Rogers, Captain America.

Of course, Cap will return, especially when America needs him most.

Modern Takes

Matthew J. Costello's examination of Marvel's Avengers and Avengers-related titles throughout the Cold War discusses this transitional period where comics—and the world—were attempting to understand exactly what the post–Cold War world would look like. As he points out:

> Between 1986 and 1996 [which would include Gruenwald's entire run on *Captain America*], twenty-eight issues of the Captain America, Iron Man, and relaunched Nick Fury series would focus on communist threats; twenty-one of those came after 1991 [when the Soviet empire collapsed] and focused on the potential threats of held-over Soviet technology (often superheroes) falling into the hands of international terrorists, or unreconstructed Soviet leaders attempting to recapture past Soviet glory. Secret organizations, now defined as terrorists or anarchist organizations rather than totalitarians bent on global domination, were more common; thirty-eight stories in the three books had the heroes battling Advanced Idea Mechanics, Hydra, or other secret global organizations.[20]

This was an ongoing issue throughout politics and popular culture in America at the time. For 45 years, the Soviet Union (and the threat of

Chapter 6. Heroes Reborn 159

global communism) had been a constant source of fear and uncertainty for people all over the world, particularly in the United States, which was a target of possible nuclear war from both the Soviet Union and China.

The 1990s see the end of the "official" run of *Captain America* that had been published—on and off—since before American involvement in World War II. The *Heroes Reborn* 13-issue run constituted a Volume II of the *Captain America* title, while the run that followed—the fifty issues published between *Heroes Reborn* and 9/11—constituted Volume III. By that time (1998), the Cold War was long past, and no one could have possibly imagined the events of 2001. Of this period, Costello points out: "Throughout its fifty-issue run, *Captain America* volume [III] returned to the visual and verbal narratives of the 1960s and 1970s.... In each of the stories the character of Captain America is treated more as a nationalist icon than has been true of the character since the mid-1960s."[21]

One of the concerns expressed by the conservative right in America at the time was this idea that without a foreign threat around which to rally the nation, the United States could instead become just one part of a more globalized community (and economy). As such, more nationalistic—meant here as "national identity" rather than the more modern negative connotation of xenophobia and "us versus them" mentality—icons such as Captain America became more embraced by the political right as liberal/leftist ideology bent more toward America pulling back regarding its international standing as a superpower and becoming more of a partner with nations around the world (believing more that in the rising tide of international peace, all boats should float).

Just as the 1990s represented this period of America seeking to redefine itself in a world with no more external global threats, it was also a period where Captain America was forced to redefine himself as well. This made addressing social issues, as he had during the 1970s and '80s, more difficult as it was not clear who Cap (or America itself) would be in the years and decades to come. As J. Richard Stevens points out:

> Though Captain America would confront salient political issues of his day, his actions (if any) are usually constricted to the physicality of the immediate moment. He rarely acknowledges the policy implications of the problems he faces, nor does he do much to approach problems from a systemic level. Captain America's politics can be largely summed up as progressive but tied directly to his overarching narrative of rugged individualism and willpower.[22]

This speaks to another issue facing America in the late 1990s: the concept of manhood. Captain America represented the old-school macho/cowboy idea of manhood in America that was being redefined as the 20th century drew to a close, particularly with the resurfacing of the LGBTQ+ movement and popular television programs such as *Will & Grace*, where heterosexuality was no longer being considered a defining aspect of what it was to be a man.

Stevens also commented upon the more conservative nature of Captain America (and comic book superheroes overall) due to the economic importance of the character as a commercial property:

> This decision [in the late 1980s and going into the 1990s to drop Marvel's contracts with outside licensed products such as *G.I. Joe* to focus more on properties owned directly by Marvel] would encourage conservative editorial directions for many Marvel comic books as the company began to increase its focus on holding the image of its characters in a recognizable stasis to reduce confusion among the readers, viewers, and toy collectors approaching them from different experiences. Comic books became a vehicle to promote characters and products, preventing the creators from writing stories that would result in significant changes.[23]

This has actually been a driving facet of comic book superheroes from the very beginning (and continuing well into current productions). Comic book superheroes are first and foremost commercial products. While they may promote progressive ideologies intended to inspire readers to be more open to a diverse and representative world, the characters themselves essentially promote the status quo, fighting to protect society as it currently exists. This is viewed as a sales necessity by the industry. If, as publishers assume, every month's new issue represents someone's first comic, the characters must remain essentially unchanged by the events they encounter. Captain America and Iron Man, for example, may debate various issues—as will be seen in far more detail in the decade to come—but, in the end, the two must come together and go forward as friends and allies, because that is the relationship that has been established as the status quo.

In his examination of Captain America as a nationalistic hero, Jason Dittmer provides insight that adds to this argument (as well as Cap's and America's corresponding identity crises in the 1990s):

> Beyond his connection to World War II, Captain America's continued, embodied existence produces a tangible link to the past that marks him as a distinct kind of symbol to which the more recent or intermittently published nationalistic superheroes can only aspire. This is true both within the narratives and among the readers. Within the narrative, Captain America's continuity is associated with American continuity.[24]

All societies throughout history are conservative in one particular area: they are resistant to change. America—despite its liberal founding and constant push for a more progressive society—is very resistant to

Chapter 6. Heroes Reborn   161

rapid change. This is most evident in the nation's slow progress in regard to areas such as racial/ethnic rights, women's rights, and LGBTQ+ rights. This resistance was most recently seen in the political conservative backlash to decades of social change in the 1980s. In the 1990s, America faced several immediate and long-term changes: the end of the Cold War, the rise of the importance of computers and the internet, and the return of the national push for LGBTQ+ rights.

The most detailed examination of this era to date has been Jason Olsen's analysis of Mark Gruenwald's 1985–1995 run on *Captain America*. The last of Gruenwald's stories—and perhaps the most relevant to the overall discussion of the abrupt change brought on by the end of the Cold War—was the story arc titled *Fighting Chance*, where Captain America came face to face with his own mortality just as America faced its possible irrelevance in the new world order. In his summary and analysis of this storyline, Olsen points out:

> Through "Fighting Chance" and its aftermath, Cap's mentality only leads him to fight, despite the inevitability of his demise as a result. His thoughts of retirement are, if not insincere, unlikely. The title "Fighting Chance" is ultimately appropriate because "fighting" is the only way Cap can see himself surviving a problem (even one made tangibly worse through the physical exertion of fighting).[25]

This same analysis can be applied to America at the same time (1994). For fifty years (1942–1992), America knew only fighting (first the Nazis and then the Soviets). The post–Cold War brought that to an end, literally overnight. The fighting hero America had been for that half century appeared to be dying just as Steve Rogers was dying on the printed page. The more effort he exerted, the quicker his impending demise; the more America fought to resist its new reality, the more it was eating away at itself, as the political climate of the upcoming decades would testify.

Gruenwald was the first Cap writer forced to deal with the impact of the new world order on the superhero genre. In his analysis of the many deaths of Captain America (up through the Gruenwald era), David Walton said:

> Receiving word that he had only twenty-four hours to live, Captain America's assessment of his legacy was darkened by a continuing string of frustrations that culminated with the revelation that a former associate, who had idolized [Cap] since [the associate] was a boy, no longer believed in heroes because his mother had recently been shot on her way to church.... Rogers' reading of his "failure" was symptomatic of the fall from Captain America's timeless ideals into the market pressures of history, or from democracy in principle to democracy in practice.... Because conflict is symptomatic of the desire that moves history forward, [Stan] Lee implied, Captain America and Steve Rogers could

never be fully reconciled. In death, the conflict between national symbol and the individual continued.²⁶

The end of the Cold War—and, presumably, the end of external conflict for America—created an identity crisis for superheroes, and Captain America in particular. If, at its heart, the character of Captain America was not an inspirational hero or source of escapism from the anxieties of daily life, then what was he to be other than just another standard commercial product?

The 1990s becomes a difficult decade of Captain America to study from a scholarly angle because there appears, on the surface, to be no there there. The decade provides a series of essentially disjointed stories that end, again and again, with the hero's "death" for lack of any other available option. However, each "death"—at the end of *Fighting Chance*, *Onslaught*, and the close of Volume III—represents the same conundrum: what to do with Captain America (and all superheroes) in a world that apparently no longer needs them. Had it not been for the return of Americans' need for heroes in the wake of 9/11, who is to say what would have happened to comic books as a medium or superheroes as a genre?

The End of the "American Century"

While every decade sees its share of societal change, perhaps no decade was as widely transitional as the 1990s. The advent of widespread access to cell phones and the internet would forever change every aspect of American society (and all industrial societies throughout the world). The end of the Cold War opened an era of hope, a new world order that could finally focus more on peace and prosperity ... or so it was thought. The ominous threat of the growing political divide throughout the country was also met with the return—and comparatively rapid success—of the LGBTQ+ rights movement. Despite his unseemly scandal, President Clinton's economic policies put America on course to completely pay off its national debt by 2010. China and India were still developing economies, and the United States had emerged early on as the world's only remaining superpower.

Peace at home and abroad—and American investors' interests shifting from comic books to the internet—seemed a death knell for superheroes. On the big screen, the genre crashed until, near the end of the decade, it showed a modicum of hope for the future. As the American Century came to a close, the future appeared to be brighter than ever before, but as the nation would soon see, the next problem is always waiting in the wings. A massively divisive presidential election would be followed less than a year later by the darkest day in American history. The 21st century would not be as bright as initially hoped. The nation would see increasing threats both at home and abroad, more dangerous than ever before, and a nation would once more turn its weary eyes to their costumed crusaders ... especially Captain America. The up-in-the-air argument of who America (and Captain America) would be in a post–Cold War new world order came to an abrupt end on September 11, 2001. America's role as a superpower was not, in fact, a relic of the past. It was needed once more to face a global threat, and Captain America would likewise rise to the challenge ... all the while attempting to temper our anxieties and measure our response to fear.

CHAPTER 7

Civil War and *The Death of Captain America*
America in the 2000s

In the waning weeks of the 20th century, the United States encountered one of the most divisive and controversial presidential elections in the nation's history. Less than a year later, the country would endure the darkest day in its history. Things were not looking good for the 21st century. Before that first decade ended, America would fall into its worst economic crisis since the Great Depression; with the election of the first Black man to the office of president of the United States, the nation that was briefly unified in the face of its darkest hour would once more divide politically, widening the chasm of the culture war and beginning an era that would destroy families and friendships, all in the name of political ideology. The nation that just fifteen years before was faced with a hopeful future free of conflict or threat would now once more seek out conflict and threat from within.

The culture war that had increasingly divided the nation came to a head with the 2000 presidential election, with liberals feeling that the election had been stolen by a conservative Supreme Court. Less than a year later, the nation would unite around that very same controversial president as he led a righteous crusade against those who sought to hurt America. As the decade waned, however, war-weary Americans once more became politically divided. When all were hit by the Great Recession of 2008, that shared experience did not heal the divisions as 9/11 had, and a president controversial for entirely different reasons would ascend to the country's highest office, making history as he made enemies. Chants of "hope and change" fell on largely deaf ears, as all were aware that the city divided against itself could not stand.

Popular culture would likewise be affected by real-world events. A new age of heroes was born as Americans once more woke up every morning to the anxieties of an uncertain—and increasingly unhopeful—future. The wake of the 9/11 attacks would prove a boon for the superhero industry as Americans once more sought the comfort of believing in heroes. The idea of the cowboy hero and his brand of singular justice would return in characters like Jack Bauer of the spy thriller television series *24*, and hero cop Jim Gordon would wage a one-man war on crime in a pre–Batman *Gotham*. Throughout this first decade of the 21st century, Marvel Comics would prove the box-office viability of their intellectual properties with big screen successes for *X-Men* (2000) and *Spider-Man* (2002). Then they would launch their own film studio, which would go on to dominate the global box office in the decade to come with the release of their first self-produced film, *Iron Man* (2008). As he had for decades prior, Captain America would once more answer the call of a nation facing fear, again holding a mirror up to American society, confronting its fears, exposing its flaws, and providing an example of how the American Dream can continue in an age of despair and uncertainty.

The Election of 2000: A Nation Divides

As the 1990s closed, the United States appeared to be facing a hopeful and prosperous future in the new 21st century. The world was—relatively—at peace, and the American economy appeared to be booming, due largely to the new internet-driven economy. Democratic president Bill Clinton had successfully negotiated with the Republican-held Congress to implement a plan that would eliminate the U.S. national debt by 2010. In 2000, President Clinton's two terms were coming to an end, with a new presidential election due to be held. The Democrats chose Clinton's loyal vice president, Al Gore of Tennessee. The Republicans chose Texas governor—and son of former president George H.W. Bush—George W. Bush. As the nation was deeply divided over the growing culture war, a roughly 50/50 split in the Electoral College left Florida the deciding state to determine the winner. On Election Night that November, the major cable news outlets had confirmed that Bush had won Florida and therefore the presidency. But just as Gore was about to publicly concede defeat, new information came in suggesting that the Florida vote totals were in doubt, requiring a recount.

The next four weeks became a political nightmare, with each side accusing the other of wrongdoing. A major factor in the confusion came from punch ballot voting machines—largely in poorer, Democrat-leaning districts—that had not been sufficiently cleaned over the years, making punching the ballots difficult and, in many cases, ineffective. Democrats successfully sued in state courts for recounts in heavily Democrat districts. With each successive recount, Bush's margin of victory diminished. Finally, with the most recent recount giving Bush a thin victory of only a few hundred votes, the Bush campaign sued directly to the U.S. Supreme Court, which by a vote of 5–4 (along political party lines) ordered the recounts stopped and the victory given to the Republican Bush.

Ultimately, Bush officially received 271 electoral votes (one more than was needed to win), but with only 47.9 percent of the popular vote (to Gore's 48.4 percent).[1] What added to the controversy was the fact that the Florida attorney general, Katherine Harris, had been personally involved with the Bush campaign (which was not unusual, but considering all the controversy that followed, it provided fodder for conspiracy theorists). With Republicans likewise in control of both houses of Congress, many assumed that the controversial new president would attempt to maintain a low profile in order to avoid any further controversy. Circumstances would demand otherwise.

9/11: A Nation Unites

On the morning of Tuesday, September 11, 2001, 19 al-Qaeda terrorists hijacked four passenger airliners (a 20th was actually stopped and prevented from boarding his assigned aircraft by airport security). While this had been a common phenomenon in the 1980s, Middle Eastern jihadist terrorists had never done so within the United States. It would soon be discovered that these were not traditional hijackings. Two of the planes were flown directly into the Twin Towers of the World Trade Center in New York City. A third was flown into the side of the Defense Department headquarters at the Pentagon in Washington, D.C. The fourth plane—planning to hit either the White House or the Capitol in D.C.—experienced an uprising by the passengers (made aware of events by loved ones on the ground due to the more widespread use of cell phones). Rather than giving up control of the plane, the terrorists crashed United Airlines flight 93 into a field in Pennsylvania, killing all aboard. By the end of the attacks, 2,977 passengers from the four flights were killed (not counting the 19 terrorists who died as well).

Within hours, al-Qaeda leader Osama bin Laden claimed responsibility for the attacks. The event brought a nation to its knees. Suddenly, all controversy regarding Bush's election was cast aside as the country moved away from the culture war to unite around their leader in the face of a new international threat (this quick reversal—and return to form as the threat subsided—is further evidence that the entire culture war is nothing more than a fabrication concocted by the major political parties to play into Americans' inherent need for an enemy). Bin Laden had received safe haven from the nation of Afghanistan, whose government had been usurped by the radical Islamist Taliban organization. President Bush declared a "war on terror," committing the United States to pursuing international terrorists wherever they were found, including those governments or individuals who aligned themselves with terrorists, as well as any nation or individual who threatened terrorist activity. In October 2001, President Bush—with the backing of NATO (North Atlantic Treaty Organization), for the first time in the organization's history—ordered the invasion of Afghanistan, which would last for 20 years before ultimately resulting in an American pullout and the return of the Taliban to power.

Also in October, Congress passed—and President Bush signed—the USA PATRIOT Act ("Uniting and Strengthening America by Providing Appropriate Tools Required to Intercept and Obstruct Terrorism"). More commonly referred to as the Patriot Act, the law gave government intelligence and criminal justice organizations widespread powers to monitor electronic communications such as cell phones, text, and email (social media was not yet a factor in electronic communications). While the act was widely accepted by the American people, who were still reeling from the fear and anxiety from the month before, as the nation once more regained its calm and began thinking more clearly, the question of security versus freedom quickly became part of the national discourse, harkening back to the quote often attributed to Founding Father Benjamin Franklin that those who are willing to give up liberty for the sake of security deserve neither (while this quote did originate with Franklin, it was in relation to a completely different matter[2]).

The events of September 11 could have raised domestic violence against Arab and Muslim Americans to horrifying levels, and while there were incidents of violence—and many more of simple verbal assaults—President Bush, despite the popular conception that the Republican Party is inherently pro–Christian and anti–Muslim, was adamant in pointing out that the war on terror was *not* a war on Islam or those who followed the Muslim faith. As Kevin M. Kruse and Julian E. Zelizer point out in their in-depth analysis of American society since the mid–1970s, *Fault Lines*,

> [Bush] was especially concerned about Muslim immigrants, most of whom had arrived from South Asia (Bangladesh, India, and Pakistan), Iran, and Arab-speaking countries, reaching significant numbers in the 1990s. In contrast to Europe, where Muslim immigrants had been geographically concentrated, new arrivals in America had scattered themselves all over the country in forming communities.[3]

Bush would promote Muslim involvement in the many faith-based initiatives backed by his administration, as well as having public recognitions of Islamic holidays at the White House. This was a stark contrast to the more popular and more beloved FDR during World War II, who rounded up and locked away Americans of Japanese, German, and Italian descent during that conflict.

In his State of the Union address in early 2002, Bush identified what he called the "Axis of Evil": the nations of Iran, Iraq, and North Korea, declaring all three supporters of terrorism around the world. That fall, Iraqi dictator Saddam Hussein once more threatened his neighboring countries, claiming that he possessed weapons of mass destruction (a claim the dictator had repeatedly made, retracted, made, and retracted repeatedly over the previous decade). President Bush declared that even the threat itself—whether backed up by facts or not—was a violation of the United States' new policy on terrorism (popularly referred to as the Bush Doctrine, a doctrine of preemptive military strikes against all who threaten terrorism). Bush gave Hussein six months to either back up his claims of weapons with proof or face reprisals. That spring, the U.S. led a multinational military strike against Iraq, removing Hussein from power (and resulting in the U.S. and allies remaining in the country for more than a decade to provide security in the face of the overnight power vacuum in the country). As Bush's second term in office came to an end in 2008, Americans' support for the wars had significantly waned, their fears and anxieties long subsided. As the nation returned to its pre–9/11 political divide, another crisis emerged that would have a significant impact on that year's elections. The winner would be the one forced to find a way out of it.

The Great Recession

The economic crisis of 2008 had been brewing for some time. It revolved to a large degree around the practice of subprime mortgages. The practice preyed heavily on the American dream of owning a home and was heavily pushed by President Bush in the years following 9/11. Essentially, the policy involved banks convincing potential homeowners that they could afford to buy a home even though their finances strongly suggested they could not (with customers trusting their bankers to know more than they did on whether they could afford the investment). The banks would then approve a mortgage at an affordable rate for the borrower that would balloon at a later date, often to such a high level that the buyer could no longer afford payments, allowing the bank to foreclose and then cash in insurance policies that the banks had taken out on their initial investment

Chapter 7. Civil War and The Death of Captain America   169

(therefore keeping the money already paid by the borrower, gaining the money from the insurance policy, and keeping the house to then resell to another potential buyer ... and over and over again). As this policy was profitable for banks, they continued to repeat it unabated while untold numbers of borrowers suffered by losing their homes and damaging their own credit history. Many of these investment banks would then bundle these questionable mortgages together and sell interest in them to investors. Banks would then attempt to hide the bad investments in what were called credit default swaps. A perfect storm of economic chaos, building over years of greed over ethics, came to a catastrophic head in the fall of 2008.[4]

In September of that year, two financial institutions—Fannie Mae and Freddie Mac—were placed in conservatorship due to mismanagement after already having received a bailout from the Treasury Department in exchange for preferred stock in the institutions. The following week, Lehman Brothers—a major Wall Street bank—was forced to declare bankruptcy when the Treasury Department refused to offer it a similar bailout to the ones given Fannie and Freddie. Announcement of the bankruptcy caused a 504-point drop in the American stock market. The following day, the Federal Reserve invested $85 billion in AIG (American International Group), the nation's largest insurer, which had posted severe losses due largely to the collective claims from subprime mortgage defaults. Treasury Secretary Hank Paulson and Federal Reserve Chair Ben Bernanke met with congressional leaders to brief them on the impending financial crisis and the probable need for congressional intervention. Paulson then provided Congress with a three-page bill requesting a $700 billion bailout for "mortgage-backed securities that were in danger of defaulting." In the final week of that month, three major events happened: two more Wall Street banks—Goldman Sachs and Morgan Stanley—filed to be recognized as commercial rather than investment banks in order to guarantee Federal Reserve protections; another bank, Washington Mutual, filed for bankruptcy protection; and the U.S. stock market collapsed, leading the Federal Reserve to help shore up foreign markets to prevent a global economic meltdown.[5]

The last-ditch attempt did not succeed, and global markets began collapsing as October 2008 began. Congress passed TARP (the Troubled Asset Relief Program), which allowed the U.S. Treasury Department to buy portions of failing financial institutions (including AIG *and* the Big Three U.S. automakers: Ford, Chrysler, and General Motors). The ripple effect of these transactions led to more than a million bank workers losing their jobs (while high-ranking bank leaders—largely responsible for the crisis—received golden-parachute severance packages worth millions).[6]

By the time newly elected President Barack Obama took office in January 2009, the American unemployment rate was at 7.6 percent (2.7 points higher than the year before), and the number of unemployed was approximately 11.6 million (in January of 2008 that number had been around 7.5 million).[7] In 2010, the unemployment rate would hit 10 percent, the highest since the early 1980s. It would take the Obama administration—and the nation—years to recover from this financial collapse, leading to its being called the Great Recession. These events proved that for all the math, science, and numbers, the American economy relies heavily on faith, and once that faith is shaken, the ramifications are far-reaching and can be long-term.

Because the meltdown happened in the final months of the 2008 presidential election, the sitting president, Republican George W. Bush, took much of the political hit, hurting Republican prospects in the November elections. With the wars in Afghanistan and Iraq, the disastrous government response to Hurricane Katrina in 2005, and now the potential collapse of the American economy as his legacy, Bush would leave office one of the most unpopular presidents in modern U.S. history.

The Election of 2008: A Nation Divides … Again

After heated battles in both parties, the nominees facing off in the 2008 U.S. presidential election were Republican John McCain (U.S. senator from Arizona) and Democrat Barack Obama (U.S. senator from Illinois). McCain was a Vietnam War veteran who had been taken prisoner in 1967. He was offered early release in 1968 when his father was named commander of U.S. forces in the conflict. McCain refused release unless his fellow prisoners were likewise released and remained a POW until the war's conclusion in 1973. He was later elected to the U.S. House of Representatives in 1982 and the U.S. Senate in 1987, where he served until his death in 2018. Obama was the son of an American mother and a Kenyan father, raised by his mother and American grandparents. He gained widespread political attention as a community organizer in Chicago, Illinois. In 2004, he was elected to the U.S. Senate, where he served until receiving the Democratic nomination for president in 2008, narrowly defeating fellow senator—and former First Lady—Hillary Clinton for the nomination.

Obama's choice for vice presidential running mate was his former challenger for the presidential nomination and longtime U.S. senator, Joe Biden. McCain—originally wanting fellow senator and conservative Democrat Joe Lieberman for his vice president—gave in to party pressure and

Chapter 7. Civil War *and* The Death of Captain America

chose Alaska governor—and radical conservative—Sarah Palin as his running mate. This made the 2008 election historic for two reasons: the first Black man to lead a major party presidential ticket, and the second woman to appear on a major presidential party ticket (after Geraldine Ferraro). By that time, America's unified front against our foreign attackers had subsided, and the culture war was once more ignited. The nomination of a Black man for the Democratic ticket inflamed more radically racist conservatives across the country; while McCain resisted the support of such elements within his party, Palin played up to that base, welcoming any support from any wing of the party.

Aside from the financial crisis brewing in the campaign's final weeks, the key issue that the two candidates focused a great deal on was the American health care system. Health care costs had been rising for decades, reaching nightmare proportions for many Americans. One policy that was hitting millions of Americans was the concept of preexisting conditions. Health insurance companies refused to cover these preexisting conditions. An example of this would be if a person has cancer, becomes too ill to continue working, loses their employer-based health insurance, manages to beat the cancer anyway, regains their job, receives a new insurance policy, and the same cancer returns, their health insurance does not cover it. Another example would be if a person receives a new job, gains health insurance through their employer, discovers that their spouse became pregnant a week before their health insurance went into effect, the insurance company declares the pregnancy a preexisting condition. Both candidates acknowledged that this policy needed to change. President Obama's eventual solution would include many McCain/Republican ideas, presuming that bipartisan support should be imminent.

Along with the race element, there was also a wing of the Republican Party pushing for deeper tax cuts (beyond what Bush and the Republican Congress had passed in 2001). Once Obama took office, this wing would launch the Tea Party movement ("Taxed Enough Already"), and a group of like-minded Republicans in Congress would create the Tea Party Caucus. Obama's campaign would ride his message of "hope and change" to victory that November, proving the campaign's own mantra, "Yes We Can!" Obama would win a significant victory with 365 electoral votes and 53 percent of the popular vote, becoming the best popular showing for a presidential candidate since 1984.[8]

On January 20, 2009, Barack Obama became the first Black man to become president of the United States. His two terms as president would see even deeper political divisions in the country as both political and social movements spurred the culture war to potentially dangerous levels. By opening the door for any supporters that were anti-liberal, the

Republican Party had allowed a dangerous faction into their party that would prove difficult to remove. Throughout the 2000s, as Americans endured a massive terrorist attack, a two-front war on terror, and deepening political divisions, popular culture would once more be relied upon to provide some escapism from the uncertainties of the day. Once more, it would not disappoint.

Pop Culture in the 2000s: Heroes Return

With the back-to-back national crises of the 2000 presidential election and the terror attacks of 2001, cable news dominated Americans' viewing habits as the 20th century bled into the 21st. While to date the longtime king of cable news—and progenitor of the medium—CNN had been "the most trusted name in news," the increasing political divisions of the 1990s had dented the onetime powerhouse's armor. The network was often derided by conservatives throughout the '90s as "the Clinton News Network" or the "Commie News Network" for their very obvious preference for Democratic president Bill Clinton. This left-leaning perspective on the day's news events was further backed up in the summer of 1996 with the launch of MSNBC. In response to this, 20th Century–Fox owner Rupert Murdoch launched a third—and decidedly more conservative—news network in October of '96: Fox News. Claiming to be "fair and balanced," Fox provided a distinctly conservative spin on daily national and international events. While most news consumers translated fair and balanced to mean that Fox would be presenting a non-biased version of the facts, the mantra actually referred to the fact that a conservative news outlet provided fairness and balance to what had heretofore been a liberal-leaning medium.

As Americans continued to divide along political party lines, audiences chose not only the perspectives they preferred but, over time, the facts they preferred. In the wake of 9/11, Fox News took a very "my country, right or wrong" approach, fully backing every policy undertaken by the Republican Bush administration (an approach they would all but abandon when the White House changed party hands). Meanwhile, MSNBC became far more critical of Bush policies and practices, leaving CNN to attempt to find an audience somewhere in the middle (unfortunately, while the political middle constitutes the largest number of Americans, it also constitutes the smallest number of cable news viewers). While all three networks presented a relatively united and consistent front in the immediate wake of 9/11, once fears and anxieties subsided, each turned

Chapter 7. Civil War *and* The Death of Captain America

sharply to their respective political spins, playing a significant role in the ever-widening political divide in America.

The devastation and terror brought on by the events of 9/11 led to an immediate need in American society for the return of heroes. The term "hero" had received a great deal of use in the days and weeks after the attacks with stories of first responders and their devoted actions in their desperate attempts to save lives as events unfolded. The NYC firefighters who sacrificed their lives to evacuate as many people as possible from the Twin Towers of the World Trade Center as the buildings literally came down around them were, until then, often seen as the stuff of Hollywood fiction. In the realm of entertainment—and its role as an escapist balm in the heat of social fear and anxiety—heroes (and their cousins, superheroes) were once more desperately needed. Ironically, television networks already had two such series in the works, already produced and scheduled to air in the weeks following 9/11.

On October 16, 2001, upstart network the WB launched the series *Smallville* (2001–2011), starring Tom Welling as a teenage Clark Kent, following his journey to becoming America's most famous fictional hero: Superman. Essentially copying the framework of the WB's other hit series, *Buffy the Vampire Slayer*, the series pitted its central superpowered hero and his non-superpowered friends against ever-escalating levels of threats against Smallville, Kansas, America, and the world. Running for ten seasons, the series naturally culminates with its hero donning his red cape and blue tights to become an American icon. The teaser for the series' pilot, however, drew controversy, exhibiting a shirtless Clark Kent, red "S" spray-painted on his chest, crucified on a scarecrow post in a cornfield. The combination of Christian and comic book iconography could not have summed up the country's collective feelings more perfectly.

A few weeks later, on November 6, 2001, Fox TV aired the pilot episode of *24* (2001–2010, returning for one more season in 2014). This series—set to unfold in real time, each episode presenting one hour of narrative—centered on counterterrorism agent Jack Bauer (Kiefer Sutherland), who over nine seasons total worked diligently to investigate and stop potential terror attacks against Americans with only a 24-hour window to succeed. In its later years (after most of the post–9/11 fear and anxiety had subsided), the series would be criticized for its glorification of violence and stereotypical portrayals of Arab Muslims (though, to be fair, most terror schemes stopped by Bauer were actually led by homegrown white Americans). For millions of Americans, however, the fictional adventures of macho heroes were not enough of an escape from the anxieties of the day. They preferred more realistic entertainments.

Scripted series are, by nature, more expensive to produce than the cheaper fare of reality programming. The networks had already dipped their toe in reality shows prior to 9/11 with *Survivor*, debuting in the spring of 2000 on CBS. Featuring a revolving cast of contestants each season, *Survivor* pitted individuals against one another in a "survival of the fittest" scenario in various wilderness island settings, with contestants voting to remove one of their number at the end of each episode (often based entirely on who was the most disliked by the other contestants). *The Amazing Race* debuted on CBS just a week prior to 9/11, featuring contestants on a global race against each other, solving various problems to be the first to reach the final destination. Both series gained popularity in the years immediately following 9/11 (and continue airing new seasons well into the 2020s). The 1999 ABC game show *Who Wants to be a Millionaire?* likewise became even more popular after the terror attacks, airing multiple nights a week under the charismatic hosting of longtime television icon Regis Philbin. The "real" lives of celebrity families became fodder for widespread audience obsession, with the exploits of rocker Ozzy Osbourne, hotel heiress Paris Hilton, *Playboy* publisher Hugh Hefner, and model Kim Kardashian being just a few to gain further icon status from their respective reality shows. The originally documentary-centered cable network the History Channel made a hard turn toward reality programming in 2009 with the wildly popular *Pawn Stars*, where average people would negotiate with employees of the Gold and Silver Pawn Shop in Las Vegas, Nevada, over objects of historical importance (or, at the very least, historical novelty or curiosity).

In 2004, television producer Mark Burnett approached celebrity businessman Donald Trump—who was experiencing considerable financial difficulties as the 21st century began—to host a new reality-based game show called *The Apprentice*. Trump would sit as chairman, tasking contestants with various money-making schemes as they competed for an opportunity with the Trump Organization (with losers facing down Trump's soon-to-be trademarked phrase, "You're fired!"). In 2008, the franchise would be expanded to include *Celebrity Apprentice*, where various celebrities (though more pessimistic viewers could use the term "has-beens") competed in similar competitions to raise money for various charities. In addition to saving Donald Trump's financial situation, the two series also provided him with considerable visibility that would be particularly useful in the decade to come.

On the big screen, legendary director James Cameron topped himself once more as the decade drew to a close with the release in 2009 of his 3D CGI phenomenon, *Avatar*, surpassing the previous decade's *Titanic* (also from Cameron) as the highest-grossing film of all time, earning $2.9 billion at the global box office (passing *Titanic*'s $2.2 billion). Holding the top two positions on the all-time box office chart for the next decade, the two films would meet repeated challenges from the continuously increasing popularity of the superhero genre.

The hero theme experienced a massive comeback at the U.S. feature film box office throughout the 2000s. Here is a list of some of the bigger superhero films of the post–9/11 to pre–MCU period: *Spider-Man* (2002); *X2: X-Men United*, *Hulk*, and *Daredevil* (all in 2003); *Spider-Man 2* (2004); *Fantastic Four*, *Elektra*, and *Batman Begins* (all in 2005); *X-Men: The Last Stand* and *Superman Returns* (both in 2006); *Fantastic Four: Rise of the Silver Surfer*, *Spider-Man 3*, and *Ghost Rider* (all in 2007); and *The Dark Knight* (2008, coming out a few months after *Iron Man*).

Marvel Enterprises experienced a massive economic recovery in the 2000s. Aside from the bump in comics sales and merchandise inspired by the film debuts of their catalog of heroes, the comics were also boosted by such powerhouse storylines as *Civil War*, *The Death of Captain America*, and *Secret Invasion*, all of which likewise addressed the fears and anxieties of post–9/11 America while providing careful commentary on the dangers of reactive versus proactive policies. That success would culminate in 2008 with the release of Marvel Studios' first theatrical release, *Iron Man*, and the launching of what would come to be known as the Marvel Cinematic Universe, or MCU. As they had during World War II and the Cold War in decades prior, comic book superheroes proved a welcome and safe harbor in uncertain times. A key player in this improved lot for Marvel was the very hero whose future was so uncertain prior to 9/11 ... a hero that the nation now needed more than ever.... Captain America.

Cap in the 2000s

Never one of Marvel's bigger sellers over the decades since his 1964 return, *Captain America* would nonetheless play a major role across the Marvel Comics' Universe in the 21st century, becoming to both readers and fellow characters the iconic leader he was always meant and written to be. His example as the American ideal had never been more important than in post–9/11 America, as a symbol of hope, bravery, and perseverance both in the years immediately following the terrorist attacks, and on through the following decades of increasing sociopolitical division. His eventual physical embodiment in the form of actor Chris Evans within the MCU (odd to use that acronym for Marvel Cinematic Universe when it also technically could stand for Marvel Comics Universe) made the character more real within the American zeitgeist. Before that would happen, however, Cap must first return from the dead once more ... and reassure a terrified nation that he remains a stalwart of protection.

The fourth "volume" of *Captain America* opens with a reminder of what has transpired in the real world: the shadow of a plane against the clouds ... an interior shot of unsuspecting passengers ... two men with boxcutters rise from their seats ... an undisclosed cave ... shadows of men ... waiting for word ... men sitting around a man clearly identifiable by now as Osama bin Laden ... raising their fists and weapons in triumph ... a fog-shrouded area ... a lone shadow becoming visible ... tossing debris from wreckage ... the caption reading, "Oh God.... How could this happen here? ... We've got to be strong.... Stronger than we've ever been.... If we lose hope here.... Bury our faith in this darkness.... Then nothing else matters.... They've won."[9]

The lone figure becomes discernible as a powerfully built blond white man, "Steve Rogers" written on his arm as he clings to hope that the next body he discovers will still be alive. Captain America is at Ground Zero, in the rubble of the Twin Towers.[10]

The shadowy black-and-white art depicting the area looks as if it were ripped directly from news broadcasts from the day following the attacks. It is powerful, particularly placed in the context of this being less than a year since the tragedy, when the horror and anxiety remained fresh in the minds of anyone reading it. As Steve continues his work, contemplating how the attackers believed they were doing this for their god, his reverie is broken by the appearance of SHIELD director Nick Fury. The country needs Captain America. At first refusing the call, choosing to stay and continue the search for survivors, a walk home, witnessing an attack on an innocent Arab American, in a moment Steve suits up and Captain America is ready to once more heed his nation's call.[11]

This was Captain America's return to a post–9/11 world: not as the macho hero storming a terrorist cell and beating the crap out of Muslim extremists, but as a soldier solemnly contemplating the events that have transpired and concluding that his role in the events to follow must be to lead once more by providing an example of who we can be—who we *should* be—and not who we necessarily want to be at the moment. Cap concludes the issue with more inner dialogue, now assured that America will survive this, because, once the fear and anger subside, "We share ... we are ... the American Dream."[12] This begins John Ney Rieber's run on *Captain America*, a run that will address what Americans are feeling while simultaneously attempting to provide clear and sober thinking at a time where popular culture would be under pressure to give in to popular sentiment and promote violence and anger.

The cover of the second issue contains the message, "Fight Terror!" On the third cover: "Are You Doing Your Part?" The fourth reads "Never Give Up," and the fifth—and last to contain such a message—"Honor Them."

Chapter 7. Civil War *and* The Death of Captain America 177

These first five covers of the post–9/11 *Captain America* read like old World War II propaganda posters, rallying a nation against the common foe. However, the messages are misleading. While a reader might have picked up one of these issues expecting to see foreign terrorists receiving their just deserts from the Star-Spangled Avenger, the stories instead have a much deeper meaning. They show that the United States is not an innocent victim, not always the good guy, and that many "innocent" civilians here at home are in fact contributing to horrors overseas, some of which have at least partially inspired the recent horrors here at home. As a terrorist leader states in issue #3, "When innocent Americans die ... it's an atrocity. But when we die ... we are 'collateral damage.'"[13] Before Cap's first post–9/11 adventure concludes, the hero of World War II will see similarities between the allied bombing of Dresden, Germany, and the 9/11 attacks on America in relation to the civilian casualties of both.

With issue #10, creative duties began to be shared with the writer/artist team of Chuck Austin and Jae Lee. In their first issue, Cap's past is retconned, with the U.S. government purposely putting Captain America "on ice" in order to prevent him stopping America's use of atomic weaponry to end World War II. As the U.S. embarks on a similarly deadly approach to the war on terror, Nick Fury questions Cap's loyalties regarding government policy: "You were *made* by the government at *your* request [emphasis in the original] ... I consider you my friend, Captain America. But Steve Rogers is a confused man, and his confusion has led to some terrible things that aren't his fault ... you're the perfect soldier who won't kill, who doesn't always follow orders."[14]

The more Captain America has learned about the war on terror, the more he has remembered his own actions during World War II, and the more he has come to question "heroic" America's actions in a situation where "heroism" is defined almost entirely by victory or loss: that of warfare.

The same year that "Volume IV" of *Captain America* launched, 2002, Marvel launched another title, *The Ultimates*. This was part of their new Ultimate line of comics. Similar in concept to the previous decade's *Heroes Reborn*, the line was designed to reboot all new titles around their most popular heroes—Spider-Man, the X-Men, the Fantastic Four, and the Avengers—in an alternate universe, beginning each story with younger versions of the decades-old characters at the beginnings of their respective careers. *The Ultimates* was this universe's version of the Avengers, and its first issue introduced Captain America. Beginning in 1945, at the start of a mission during World War II, Cap—with his original badge-shaped shield—mentions his upcoming wedding to his girlfriend, Gail, as he stands alongside a young (but adult) battlefield reporter, Bucky Barnes.[15]

This issue, for really the first time, shows in detail the mission that led to Steve Rogers disappearing into the ice near the end of World War II. At one point referring to the cowering soldiers on his team as "ladies," this is a very different Steve Rogers/Captain America than readers have seen before: more realistic than idealistic. It is in the pages of this Ultimate universe of stories that Nick Fury is presented for the first time as a bald Black man rather than his traditional form of a white man with a full head of hair graying at the temples (this new image both inspired by actor Samuel L. Jackson and the inspiration for hiring that same actor for the MCU role just five years later).

The following year, writer Robert Morales and artist Kyle Baker produced the miniseries *Truth: Red, White & Black* (later sold in graphic novel form as *Captain America: Truth*). Though not officially continuous with the main *Captain America* title (or the Ultimate universe), the story has since made its way into proper continuity and even been added in an altered state to the on-screen MCU. Making rather stark comparisons to some of America's more abhorrent history—such as the infamous Tuskegee experiments—it would prove quite timely in the 21st century's continuing conversation regarding race history in the U.S. Though an important part of Captain America's story in the 2000s, however, *Truth* and its impact on Marvel Comics will be discussed in a later chapter.

In 2005, a fifth "volume" of the main *Captain America* title would launch under the creative team of writer Ed Brubaker and artist Steve Epting. With American anxieties post–9/11 beginning to subside, the wars in Afghanistan and Iraq raging on, and President Bush easily reelected to a second term, the time had come for Captain America to return to more traditional stories, continuing to keep one eye on sociopolitical events in the real world, but building more toward the larger Marvel Universe stories unfolding elsewhere. In issue #8, Cap begins investigating a mysterious assassin known only as the Winter Soldier. By that time, readers had already been alerted to the possibility that this assassin was Cap's World War II partner, Bucky Barnes. While characters returning from the dead is by no means uncommon in superhero comics, for decades there was a small list of characters—namely Peter Parker's Uncle Ben, his former girlfriend Gwen Stacey, and Bucky—whose deaths were considered sacrosanct and essential to defining who Spider-Man and Captain America, respectively, had become.

Brubaker's story, however, was nothing short of fantastic. Since Cap's return in 1964, the story had been repeatedly told that, on a mission to stop an enemy drone, the drone launched but exploded shortly after takeoff, blowing Cap into the water where he eventually froze, but leaving Bucky to explode with the device. Brubaker's retcon, however, showed that Bucky, too, was blown clear, losing his left arm in the explosion. Discovered by a Soviet submarine, he was taken back to the Soviet Union where he was given a cybernetic arm, brainwashed, and turned into a master assassin, the Winter Soldier. Throughout the Cold War, he was kept on ice, thawed out for important missions, and returned to stasis once the mission was completed.[16]

While the term "Winter Soldier" does sound very Russian, the moniker can also be connected to Thomas Paine's *The American Crisis*, published in 1776, where he wrote: "These are the times that try men's souls. The summer soldier and the sunshine patriot will, in this crisis, shrink from the service of their country; but he that stands by it now, deserves the love and thanks of man and woman."[17]

If one interprets—and I believe rightly so—that the "summer soldier and the sunshine patriot" refers to Americans who supported the Revolution only during good times (warm weather, sufficient food and supplies, frequent American victories), but turn their backs once things go badly (bad weather, no food or supplies, and frequent American losses), then a winter soldier, by contrast, would continue to fight no matter what, never wavering, and never giving up. That definition would definitely apply to the character that Bucky Barnes became.

The Winter Soldier's discovery of his true identity, and the ramifications of his guilt from his actions as an assassin against his will for decades would become a major storyline in *Captain America* in the years that followed. Bucky Barnes/Winter Soldier would then become a major character in both Marvel Comics and the MCU, where he would eventually be played by Sebastian Stan. By the time the Winter Soldier storyline arrived at its dramatic conclusion, real-world events were once more breaking the fourth wall into the superhero world. Four years after its inception, the ramifications of the Patriot Act were raising the age-old question of liberty versus security. The political parties were taking sides, and so would the Marvel superheroes.

By far the most important Marvel storyline of the decade was *Civil War* (2006–2007). In the wake of a catastrophic 9/11-esque disaster, largely caused by young and untrained superheroes, the American populace demanded that the government begin regulating superhero activity, requiring training, certification, and registration of their secret identities. While some of the more prominent heroes—Iron Man, Yellowjacket, and Reed Richards of the Fantastic Four—supported registration, others—led by Captain America—strongly opposed it. Their arguments were largely, first, that registration of secret identities created the danger of leaks, which would endanger the loved ones of the heroes, and second, that giving the government control over superhero activities could lead to the politicizing of exactly who constituted a threat or was seen as a villain. When new SHIELD director Maria Hill, orders Captain America to assist in subduing heroes unwilling to comply, the following interaction takes place:

> **CAP:** You're asking me to arrest people who risk their lives for this country every day of the week.
> **HILL:** No, I'm asking you to obey the will of the American people, Captain.
> **CAP:** Don't play politics with me, Hill. Super heroes need to stay above that stuff or Washington starts telling us who the super-villains are.
> **HILL:** I thought super-villains were guys in masks who refused to obey the law.[18]

As predicted, the debate drives a wedge through the superhero community, leading to all-out war, spilling blood, costing lives, and affecting relationships for years to come.

What makes *Civil War* analogous to American society at the time was its core issue of security versus liberty. By 2006, Americans—once so terrified of another 9/11 they were happy to turn over all liberties to the government in exchange for tighter security—were becoming increasingly uncomfortable with the extent of the security measures outlined in the Patriot Act. Allowing the government essentially unfettered access to the cell phone conversations, texts, and emails of private citizens was no longer as appealing, with 9/11 nearly five years past and overall anxieties and fears of repeated attacks now mostly settled. The Marvel superheroes faced much the same question: Would government oversight of superhero activities cut down on the collateral damage of potential civilian casualties? If so, would the benefits of such oversight outweigh the risk of a superhero's identity leaking to the public, endangering the lives of the loved ones of said hero? Would the government's power to oversee superhero activities then give the government the authority to dictate who the bad guys are? While the U.S. government has proven mostly successful at keeping secrets, their history both of leaks and of abusing their power is also considerable (said abuse likewise analogous to the handling of the personal correspondence of American citizens).

As the story reaches a climax and the forces of Captain America go head-to-head with the forces of Iron Man, it is Cap who realizes that the fight has moved beyond the initial debate. Now the very citizens that superheroes swear to protect are themselves in danger of becoming collateral damage. Cap calls for a cessation of hostilities, surrendering to government forces:

> **CAP:** We're not fighting for the people anymore ... we're just fighting.
> **HUMAN TORCH:** Cap, what are you doing? They'll throw us in jail if you surrender.

Chapter 7. Civil War *and* The Death of Captain America

SPIDER-MAN: We were beating them, man. We were winning back there.
CAP: Everything except the argument ... stand down, troops.... That's an order.[19]

With that, Marvel's *Civil War* concludes, with a whimper rather than a bang, and the argument of liberty versus security comes down hard on the side of security (as the Patriot Act had done in 2001).

Another way that *Civil War* is analogous to American society—aside from the obvious contexts of America's post–9/11 discussion of security versus liberty as well as the series' namesake from nearly 150 years prior—is in the lack of compromise. This makes the story as important in the 2020s as it was at the time of its original publishing. In the Marvel story, in the context of post–9/11 Washington, the conflict over American slavery, and the current political climate of radical conservatism versus radical liberalism, the crises emerged from a lack of compromise from both sides. Americans' inability to come to terms with what the problem is, differing opinions on how to address the problem, and an utter intransigence when reaching a solution remains at the heart of most of the country's problems to this day.

The wake of *Civil War* would shock the world, making national headlines and causing Marvel editor-in-chief Joe Quesada to hit the talk show circuit to verify the truth and explain its meaning. In issue #25 of what was called "Volume V,"—the first issue of *Captain America* published after the events of *Civil War*—Cap is shot and killed while in federal custody, his dying words to longtime girlfriend Agent Sharon Carter of SHIELD: "Sharon ... the crowd ... get them to safety ... no more ... innocents ... hurt."[20]

Just like that, Captain America, the Star-Spangled Avenger, World War II's Sentinel of Liberty, was dead. As Quesada would explain in many interviews over the months that followed, this was no 1990s gimmick. Steve Rogers, the standing symbol of America's "Greatest Generation," was no more, his version of the American ideal now archaic in the 21st-century, post–9/11 America. The continuing war on terror and adherence to the Bush Doctrine would require a new "Captain America," one more consistent with the more violent society we had become. Above all, the death of Steve Rogers/Captain America (and Marvel's reasoning behind it) all but proves that the country as a whole did not learn the lessons taught in the "Fight Terror" storylines following 9/11 (nor, as it turns out, those in "The Death of Superman" nearly fifteen years earlier).

Ultimately, the mantle of Captain America would fall to Steve Rogers's World War II sidekick, Bucky Barnes, the now-reformed Winter Soldier. With an updated uniform (which many were quick to point out actually looked like the flag of U.S. territory Puerto Rico)—and now carrying a pistol and knife—the new Captain America, a longtime assassin, was now the symbol of the nation, with all that this would suggest. Agreeing to take up the shield as part of Steve's wishes, this new Winter Solder/Captain America proves a more violent hero, more in line with popular characters such as Wolverine and Deadpool. Unlike his MCU counterpart, the comics' version of Winter Soldier is not a Super Soldier, his only superhuman quality being his cybernetic arm (which will allow him to handle Cap's shield to the same degree as the original Super Soldier). Ultimately, the death of Steve Rogers proves more complicated than the simple act of a hired assassin, leading to discovery of the involvement of longtime Cap enemies Red Skull and the evil psychiatrist Dr. Faustus. After two years of carrying the shield, the new Cap would discover what comic book audiences had learned long ago: nobody dies forever.

On January 20, 2009, Barack Obama was inaugurated as the 44th president of the United States. With President Bush no longer in office, and the events of 9/11 now part of an increasingly distant past, a new era of hope and change emerged, and with it a hopeful return to the ideals and principles of that Greatest Generation of long ago ... and time for Steve Rogers to return. As Obama was being sworn in, a new limited series debuted from Marvel Comics: *Captain America: Reborn*. A rather complicated story—seriously ... he's dead ... but not really ... but, actually, yeah ... but ... oh well... (it seems like the creative team was trying to fix the problems of "The Death of Superman," but failed to)—brings the Sentinel of Liberty into the Age of Obama.

Going into the 2010s, Bucky Barnes would remain the "official" Captain America for some time, with Steve Rogers temporarily leading a team of "Secret Avengers." As chaotic as the 2000s had been for the Star-Spangled Avenger, the 2010s would prove even more so, seeing Rogers return to his traditional role, then give it up again, before finally sharing the title of Captain America with longtime ally Sam Wilson/the Falcon (America's first Black president serving alongside America's first official Black Captain America). As the country descended more deeply into political division by mid-decade, Cap would make national headlines once more, as the hero of World War II, the leader of the Avengers, and the pinnacle of all that the superheroes of the Marvel Universe stood for utters the horrific phrase: "Hail Hydra!"

Modern Takes

With 9/11, *Civil War*, and "The Death of Captain America" (not to mention the road to his return beginning in 2009), it is not difficult to see

Chapter 7. Civil War *and* The Death of Captain America

why the 2000s is perhaps the most closely analyzed and commented-upon period in Captain America's long history. For all of the previous decades where the character has reflected—and occasionally directly commented upon—events in the real world, the 2000s cements Captain America as a clear representation of what is going on in America at any given point in time; that will continue well into the 2020s. Of all the superheroes (from any publisher), Captain America stands as the most stark symbol of who we—as American readers—want our country to be: noble, self-sacrificing, possessing an unbending moral core, and, perhaps above all else, never compromising his values. Some of the following scholars take a firm stand on the side of Captain America in these iconic storylines; others do not. This is yet another testament to the power of the character, the divisions in American society (even the world of academia), and the never-ending question: "Who *are* we?"

Robert Jewett updated his *Captain America Complex* with the assistance of philosophy professor John Shelton Lawrence. Their earlier collaboration, *The Myth of the American Superhero*, examined the phenomenon of the cowboy mentality in the American monomyth. Their 2003 book, *Captain America and the Crusade Against Evil: The Dilemma of Zealous Nationalism*, takes the earlier "complex" and applies it to post–9/11 America. Along with "zealous nationalism," which they define as "seek[ing] to redeem the world by destroying enemies,"[21] they also examine the concept of prophetic realism: "It avoids taking the stances of complete innocence and selfishness. It seeks to redeem the world for coexistence by impartial justice that claims no favored status for individual nations.... It can be traced through the American experience in movements and writings that sometimes criticize aspects of the dominant consensus."[22]

In comparing the U.S. response to 9/11 to previous military incursions in Southeast Asia in the 1960s/70s and the Persian Gulf War of 1991, the two put forth, "It seemed that the United States, when it wished, could be like Captain America himself: strong, capable of acting without consulting or seeking direction, and exercising destructive power with few immediate repercussions."[23]

After over 300 pages of analysis—utilizing little in the way of direct sources from Captain America comics and outright ignoring texts and subtexts that disprove their analogy, Jewett and Lawrence conclude:

> The American sense of mission, scorned by cynics, secular realists, and disappointed idealists alike, needs to be transformed rather than abandoned. Its sense of how the world should be led to peace has been misguided by zealous myths. The absolutizing of our moral impulses, the delusions of the "grand conspiracy," the distortions of popular stereotypes, the mystique of violence, the idolatrous grasp of the Deuteronomic principle, and our crusades against

symbolic desecration have distorted our sense of mission and are driving us toward scenarios of mutual destruction.... It calls for a creative rechanneling of Captain America's impulse to "fight for right" toward a religious commitment that is shaped both by self-critical questioning and a sense of hope about the possibilities of peace.[24]

A simple glance back to the earlier discussion and quotes from the Rieber/Cassaday post–9/11 run on *Captain America* alone shows how the character did not (and quite frankly had not since the 1950s) express the ideas against which Jewett and Lawrence argue (though their general arguments outside of their analogy of Captain America are certainly sound). However, when one considers the general mental image of Captain America in the overall pre–MCU American zeitgeist, it does explain the attempted analogy.

Of Captain America's immediate response to 9/11 and the war on terror, Matthew J. Costello pointed out:

The equation of the U.S. firebombing of Dresden [during World War II] with the 9/11 attacks against the United States undermines the moral certainty of U.S. policy by implying both U.S. complicity in the rise of terrorism and a lack of moral purity to the nation's government.... Four decades of Cold War global activity have removed from the United States any vestige of its moral superiority in other nations.... Lacking moral core, the United States is generally portrayed as complicit in terrorism or incapable of confronting it.[25]

Many on the left—more so in the years since 9/11 than in its immediate aftermath—have pointed to past American actions overseas as planting the seeds for international jihadist terrorism today, and indeed, the U.S. does possess its share of past sins at which one can point. As Costello points out, however, such accusations take away from the argument of the moral right to avenge the deaths of presumably innocent Americans here at home. Wars, more often than not, take as many if not more civilian casualties than happen among soldiers on the battlefield (particularly in the modern era of larger and more powerful long-range weapons). Is America responsible for the rise of al-Qaeda? Has America set the precedent for terrorist attacks? It is a difficult issue to attempt to settle, and the answer, ultimately, is of no help in resolving the problem at hand.

In his in-depth and well-researched analysis of masculinity and violence in Captain American narratives, J. Richard Stevens points out the Rieber/Cassaday idea of making Steve Rogers's identity public knowledge:

Unlike previous Captain America narratives, the post–9/11 Captain America will not be a faceless symbol of his country. By revealing his identity, he removes from his arsenal the primary weapon that both sides in a "war on terror" really have: anonymity. Cap's unmasking serves as a statement that faceless action is an escape from personal responsibility.[26]

Chapter 7. Civil War *and* The Death of Captain America

To be fair to Captain America, he would have been on ice at the time of dropping the atomic bombs on Japan (which had been established previously in that storyline as an overall conspiracy to keep Cap from stopping the order). Overall, the post-9/11 fourth volume of *Captain America* did far more to criticize America's reactions (or overreactions) to foreign threats than it did to justify them. Additionally, it did a great deal to underscore Captain America's role as representing the American ideal more than any specific policy (or administration) of the American government.

The return of Bucky Barnes as the enigmatic Winter Soldier brought into question Steve Rogers's initial PTSD in the 1960s storylines, expressing survivor's guilt over the World War II loss of his young sidekick. Would the discovery that Bucky survived (although many would argue he faced a fate worse than death through his brainwashing and being used as an assassin for decades) alleviate Steve's guilt or worsen it (by not verifying his partner's death and possibly saving him from his enslavement earlier)? Robert G. Weiner refers to this story change in his essay regarding Cap's overall PTSD and survivor's guilt regarding the loss—and rediscovery—of his old sidekick:

> In the *Winter Soldier* storyline, as in previous examples [of Cap's dealing with the loss of Bucky], Captain America refused to let the memory of Bucky become tarnished. Perhaps all the grief, denial, depression, and trauma Captain America suffered turned out to be true, with Bucky now alive.... This, however, does not negate all the PTSD, depression, trauma, and survivor's guilt that Captain America went through.[27]

Since, by the time of his "return," Bucky has spent more time as the Winter Soldier than he did as Cap's sidekick (even subtracting time "frozen" between missions). His brainwashing and retraining as an assassin was so completely embedded in who the former Bucky Barnes was by 2005 that Steve Rogers could have easily dismissed his former partner as lost and beyond hope or redemption, but he does not. Redeeming the Winter Soldier is vitally important to Cap not only as a sense of duty to his former partner, but also as a salve for his survivor's guilt and a last-ditch effort to save what he for so long thought was permanently lost.

> In an essay written in response to the *Civil War* storyline, John McGuire points out the dilemma facing Bucky Barnes in the wake of Steve Rogers's death (corresponding with the real-world crisis of the economic crash of 2008): "The solution in the comic book to the [economic] crisis in America is the renewal of the Captain America identity, which works metaphorically as renewal of the American dream.... Bucky faces two representations of "Captain America" that stand in opposition to him [that of Steve Rogers and the 1950s "Commie Smasher"].[28]

The economic crisis began, relatively unnoticed by the majority of Americans, as the events of *Civil War* and the death of Steve Rogers came to a dramatic conclusion. The rise of the Winter Soldier as the new Captain America represented an era of change in the Marvel Comics Universe (much as the following year's election of President Obama would for the country). While Bucky represented a new and more violent Cap than Steve Rogers, he maintained the symbolism of Captain America, putting his own spin on his mentor's legacy.

Of course, the topic of Captain America—and Marvel Comics overall—that most appeals to modern scholars is that of *Civil War*. Although the event storyline encompassed the near entirety of the Marvel superhero universe, the two most central characters were the two leaders of the opposing sides of the argument: Iron Man/Tony Stark and Captain America/Steve Rogers. Despite the fact that the story was very well constructed in such a way as to make both arguments equally viable and defensible, the overall sentiments and opinions of readers appear to have fallen on the side of Captain America (evident, it can be argued, in the fact that when the storyline was adapted for the MCU, it was done in a Captain America movie rather than an Avengers or Iron Man film).

Beginning with J. Richard Stevens's analysis, basing his discussion primarily on modern perspectives of masculinity and violence, he points out the following of the two leading voices in the piece:

> [Iron Man] sees heroes as morally ambiguous yet allows his version of "right" to be trumpeted as "good," whereas Captain America's relative silence in the media discourse must appear to some as "evil" (or at the very least misguided). The ability to voice one's position in times of crisis would appear to be regarded according to social morality. Ultimately, dissenting voices are largely ineffective in times of social crisis because they are perceived to be part of the external threat and therefore not trusted. And critics cite concerns that even if a dissenting critique were to penetrate the manipulation of social control, it might cause great damage to society.... The *Civil War* narrative concludes with the voice of civil liberties constrained and then silenced through assassination.[29]

Indeed, on the real-world issue of the Patriot Act, conservative media outlets such as Fox News and radio hosts such as Rush Limbaugh and Glenn Beck touted the importance and patriotism of the act (and essentially all policies of the Bush administration in regard to the war on terror), discounting any opposition or outcry as liberal, defeatist, and even treasonous. Likewise, more liberal outlets such as CNN and MSNBC and the editorial pages of *The New York Times* and *The Washington Post* argued the exact opposite. One would be hard-pressed to find any information outlet that provided equal presentation of both sides. While the readers of

Chapter 7. Civil War *and* The Death of Captain America 187

Civil War were exposed to both sides of its argument, the heavy-handed tactics of Iron Man's side likely shifted overall audience sympathies toward Cap and his Secret Avengers.

In 2016, longtime comic book scholar Travis Langley edited a collection of essays examining the different psychological perspectives of Iron Man and Captain America. In her essay on "moral decisions," Mara Wood concluded:

> At times, [Captain America's and Iron Man's] adamant focus on the conflict [of *Civil War*] keeps them from remembering their values and principles, but the reasons and rationales behind their actions reveal what Captain America and Iron Man value most. In the end, both heroes want to protect their community, and their approaches demonstrate how difficult it can be to make moral decisions.[30]

Indeed, the issue of morality in decision-making is a debate as old as critical thinking itself. Particularly in a society as diverse as the United States, who decides what the standard morality is? On the issue of superhero registration, what is the moral route: the security society feels with superheroes registered and overseen by democratically elected officials, or the personal privacy of individuals who have chosen of their own accord to utilize their special powers to make society safer for everyone else? The same goes for the morality issue concerning the Patriot Act: the security society feels with government keeping close watch on everyone in order to find potential threats before they strike, or the personal privacy allegedly guaranteed in a society with government by the people?

Examining the issue more from a perspective of symbols, Tommy Cash and Travis Langley look at the outward appearance (or uniforms) of Cap and Iron Man and what those symbols say about what each stands for:

> The leader who dresses in the American flag [Captain America] fights for liberty, while the leader who wears a machine the color of money (usually gold but occasionally silver) [Iron Man] fights for a structured system. Neither side in the conflict needs to wave a banner because their leaders are their living emblems.... Both the audience and the other characters in the Marvel Universe see Captain America as a symbol of America, but maybe a historic America, while Iron Man might represent modern America or corporate America.[31]

Symbols have been vitally important to all human civilizations as far back as recorded history documents, and they have certainly proven vitally important throughout American history, particularly in the wake of the 9/11 attacks. This examination of the symbols that each costume represents is particularly astute. Symbols are paramount in the superhero genre, and as Cash and Langley point out, billionaire Tony Stark wears a (partially) golden suit of armor (except when it was briefly silver in the 1980s). With Iron Man firmly on the side of the U.S. government, this conflict symbolizes how the government sides more with corporate America than it does the people (who would normally associate more with the symbology of Captain America).

In a final selection from *Captain America vs. Iron Man*, Alan Kistler and Billy San Juan discuss the issue of masculinity in this clash of ideologies:

> Only when Captain America displays more insight into the mechanisms driving their actions and the repercussions on their conflict does he end the superhero civil war. Perhaps if they question the forces that define the Man in Iron Man and the Captain in Captain America, they can be more complete as individuals and more capable of saving the world.[32]

One aspect of the violent outbreak of civil war among the Marvel superheroes that often goes unnoticed is that of ego. In fact, the one thing that keeps Iron Man and Captain America so intransigent in their respective perspectives is their own personal pride in being "right." Throughout the storyline, two female characters—She-Hulk (reluctantly siding with Iron Man) and Sue Richards of the Fantastic Four (less reluctantly siding with Cap)—hint toward this idea, suggesting a more genial approach to the argument. It is only when Cap puts his pride aside when a crowd of bystanders begin attacking him (defending Iron Man) that he sees the unintended consequences of this superhero civil war and ends it by putting aside his pride (though never admitting he was argumentatively wrong). In the very long history of male-dominated societies, this aspect of ego/pride cannot be understated as a source of unnecessary conflict, pain, and suffering.

In another take on *Civil War*, Kevin Michael Scott edited a collection of essays titled *Marvel Comics' Civil War and the Age of Terror* (2015). One essay examines where the law sides in the issue of superhuman registration. Daniel Davis Wood points out that since superheroes (as vigilantes) had acted without oversight for so long, such registration had long since become a moot point:

> The flaw in the actions of the lawmakers was the expediency with which they drafted and approved the registration legislation, an expediency driven by the sense of a need for urgent action in the wake of [the event that caused societal outrage against superheroes]. What lawmakers should in fact have acted on was not the aftermath of that debacle, not the urgency they felt, but rather the sustained and incremental accession to the actions of independent administrators of justice who ... establish themselves as adjudicators of social disturbances [on basis of their super abilities] instead of respecting the slow, complex, and cumbersome dictates of due process.[33]

Chapter 7. Civil War *and* The Death of Captain America 189

The same could equally be said of real-world lawmakers and the Patriot Act of 2001. History has repeatedly shown the dangers of overreaction in response to crises, and America's reaction to the events of 9/11 (both legally and socially) were very clearly overreactive responses to the fear and anxiety caused by the sudden and tragic events.

In a reflection on how current conflicts can often be mistakenly viewed through the lens of conflicts from the past (or at least how societies remember the past), Kathleen McClancy examines *Civil War* through Iron Man as a creation of the Cold War and Captain America as a creation of World War II. The two heroes were created at very different times, during very different wars, and with very different ideas of what constitutes a hero. She concludes:

> In *Civil War*, both Captain America and Iron Man misread the signs left in the wake of [the catastrophic event that leads to the dispute], reading them through their 20th century preconceptions. They thus replicate the misreadings of American culture, which in an attempt to make sense of global terrorism has turned to nostalgic imaginaries of idyllic times that never existed. Neither World War II nor the Cold War are appropriate frameworks for the War on Terror.... Using these nostalgic frameworks blinds us to the realities of the actual conflict: that terrorists have no nation; that military action is inadequate; that not all terrorists are evil; that American foreign policies bear part of the responsibility for nurturing terrorism in the first place; and that the United States is not inevitably destined to emerge victorious.[34]

American response to 9/11 was, indeed, treated very much as foreign conflicts had been in the past. But al-Qaeda was not the Soviet Union or Nazi Germany. It was not a nation embracing a political philosophy. It was a scattered band of religious zealots striking at the most powerful target it could find. Likewise, Marvel's *Civil War* was not like any battle the heroes had fought in the past. It was not to stop a supervillain from doing harm. It was a disagreement over policy that was allowed to devolve into violence. As such, Iron Man and Cap responded in the same way as the nation responded to the conflicts which created them: Iron Man by standing by government decisions, right or wrong, and Cap by rallying the people in a call for liberty.

In the wake of *Civil War*, the former assassin, the Winter Soldier, is given the mantle of Captain America after the death of Steve Rogers. Many news outlets at the time commented upon what this said about Bush-era America. Costello concludes his analysis of Cold War America by pointing out that the death of Captain America implied that "without intention, and without reasoned control, Americans have destroyed the myth of the American self."[35] Of the new Winter Soldier Cap, he adds,

Bucky offers a different definition of the American icon. Carrying not only the shield but also a gun, he is more willing to take fatal action than was Steve Rogers.... Bucky as Captain America offers a more flawed, less virtuous ideal.... Rogers brought World War II values to the late twentieth century; Bucky upholds these ideals, tempered by the reality of four decades of Cold War transformations.[36]

In World War II, America stood as a shield against the global spread of Nazi fascism. During the Cold War, America stood against the spread of Soviet communism by always having an arsenal of world-ending nuclear weaponry at the ready. Like the new Winter Soldier Cap, America had a weapon of death ready if needed, but praying it never would be. Bucky will not turn to his gun as a first response, but he understands all too well that against unknown future enemies, it is better to be armed and not need it, than to need arms and not have them.

The examples cited above represent just a small portion of what has been written to date on Captain America—and *Civil War* more generally—in the first decade of the 21st century. As transformative as that decade was—and as rich as the comics material produced has proven to be—the decade will ultimately be a source of academic analysis for generations to come. As the decade opened, Steve Rogers was dead (and "Captain America" with him). The events of 9/11 demanded the return of comics' most patriotic hero. As social divisions returned, however, the hero was "killed" again, only to be brought back once the concept of hope appeared on the horizon. The 2010s would continue to see massive social and political divisions throughout the country, worse than at any point since the American Civil War. The divisions would prove more than even Captain America could hope to contain, which is possibly why the decade would ultimately give us three of him.

The Culture Wars Heat Up: Setting Up the 2010s

As the 2000s closed, the American economy was still steeped in the ramifications of the Wall Street collapse. America's first Black president caused the deepest, darkest realms of racist America to once more rear their collective heads, showing those who had chosen to believe that part of America long since buried in the past that they had been living in a fool's paradise. A push for President Obama to publicly release his birth certificate in order to prove his American citizenship gained momentum, largely through the support of longtime celebrity businessman and reality game show host Donald Trump, who would later use the effort to launch

Chapter 7. Civil War *and* The Death of Captain America

his own political ambitions ... and lead a dangerous new right-wing movement that, as the 2020s began, would be viewed by many to threaten the very foundations of American democracy.

Social media would springboard into a massive online community throughout the decade to come, with Facebook, YouTube, and Twitter leading the way to a more interconnected—and argumentative—America. Concepts of love and hate would have louder microphones than ever before in human history, and the concept of facts more debated than any just a decade prior could ever have possibly imagined. Would the internet become the savior of all mankind, or the architect of its ultimate destruction? Political speeches would have broader audiences than at any point in history, with radicalism (at both ends of the political spectrum) once more becoming an ideology embraced by millions.

With the massive success of Marvel Studios' *Iron Man*, a new phenomenon was about to dominate the global film box office: the Marvel Cinematic Universe. Over the course of the next decade, Marvel would release an astounding 20 films in their MCU franchise, four of which would make the list of top ten all-time box office movie successes by decade's end. Captain America would play a major role in that success. In the comics, America's first Black president would be joined by the first (official) Black Captain America, Sam Wilson. Diversity would become the name of the game across popular culture, nowhere more prominently than in Marvel Comics. From #BlackLivesMatter to #MeToo, a "more perfect union" once more became a goal for a growing number of Americans ... and would be fought by just as loud an opposition with their own definition of that same union. While the American president in 2010 would represent America's diversity, its president ten years later would represent its ever-widening division and opposition to that diversity.

CHAPTER 8

From *Two Americas* to "Hail Hydra!"

Captain America and a Divided Nation in the 2010s and Beyond

The culture wars that had been dividing America since the early 1990s came to blows in the 2010s. From radical conservative response to America's first Black president to liberal protest against police violence toward Black men, the issue of race became an explosive center of the growing national divide. On the left, social movements from #BlackLivesMatter to #MeToo (women coming forward with their personal stories of sexual assault and harassment) and from wokeness to cancel culture, plus the election of President Barack Obama in 2008, inspired a national push—or, more accurately, half a push—for diversity, social justice, and representation on all levels of society. On the right, responses to progressive change—and a push to preserve Confederate heritage in the South through preserving long-standing statues of Southern Civil War heroes—reawakened a nationwide movement of white nationalism that would eventually rally around the long-used political phrase, "Make America Great Again." The decade would begin under the leadership of President Obama and end under the leadership of President Donald J. Trump, the two ultimately becoming the most divisive presidents in American history (in very different ways, and for very different reasons). President Abraham Lincoln famously stated that a "nation divided against itself cannot stand," either eventually reunifying or falling completely apart—it cannot stand divided. The 2020s would then be left with the question: which will it be?

In popular culture, the geeks inherited the earth. San Diego Comic-Con would become a mecca for hundreds of thousands of pop culture aficionados. Superheroes would dominate the big screen as long-standing franchises *Star Wars* and *Star Trek* made triumphant returns. On television, the biggest programs of the decade—*The Walking Dead* and *The Big Bang Theory*—would cement the power of so-called nerd or geek culture in America. Facebook, Twitter, and YouTube would simultaneously bring people closer than ever before and exacerbate already existing divisions. The smartphone would forever change human society. Television—for decades the primary source of entertainment in America—would slowly but surely fall to streaming platforms such as Netflix, Hulu, and Amazon Prime. American society in 2020 would look very different than it did in 2010, more so than perhaps any decade prior.

Captain America would experience the most successful decade in his seventy years of existence. On the big screen, global audiences would be exposed to the exploits of the Star-Spangled Avenger like never before, making him more a part of the American zeitgeist than past creative teams on the comic could have ever imagined. In the comics, though Steve Rogers returned once more from the dead in 2009, Bucky Barnes—the Winter Soldier—would continue to bear the mantle of Captain America well into the new decade. Even when Rogers returned to carry the shield once more, it would be short-lived; another hero, Sam Wilson—the Falcon, the first Black American superhero—would step up to become the first (official) man of color to hold the title of Captain America. When Rogers returned once again to hold the title of Captain America simultaneously with his old partner (yes, two Captain Americas…. Captains America?), generations of Cap fans would gasp in horror when World War II's Sentinel of Liberty uttered the horrific words: "Hail Hydra!"

Obama America

Throughout the 2008 presidential campaign, America's long history of racism once more reared its ugly head—as everyone expected it would— and the Republican Party would see this unified radical front as a potential voting base (many on that fringe had supported the Republican Party for decades, since the radicalization of the left wing of the Democratic Party in the 1960s, but the Republicans had, to date, officially denounced them). Going forward, Republicans running for public office would have little choice but to embrace this small but loud demographic. In 2009/2010, a new conservative movement arose with the Tea Party, and a new racial conservative caucus of Republican members of Congress would begin to identify as the Tea Party Caucus (changing their name to Freedom Caucus when the Tea Party was exposed as being more corporate-backed than had been originally believed). Republicans would control both houses of Congress for the last six of Obama's eight years in office. As such, Obama's greatest legacy of his presidency would be passed early on in his term: the health care reform popularly known as Obamacare.

In the spring of 2010, the Affordable Care Act was signed into law. Prior to the economic collapse in late 2008, the primary issue in the presidential race had been the cost of health care and the tangential issue of preexisting conditions. For decades, Democrats had been pushing for universal or single-payer health care (a socialized system controlled by the government and paid for through taxes). Many believed that the Democratic Obama would push such a proposal, similar to that pushed by President Clinton in the mid-1990s. Instead, on entering office, President Obama gave Congress one year to develop serious health care reform. When they failed to do so, he stepped in and proposed what became the ACA. Republicans in opposition to anything supported by Obama dubbed the suggested bill "Obamacare," and the name stuck (as much in a positive way as in the intended negative).

Despite being suggested by Obama and supported by congressional Democrats, the Affordable Care Act was actually one of the most bipartisan bills ever to pass Congress. From the Democrat side, the ACA expanded Medicaid (the already existent government policy providing health care coverage for those who could not afford it). From the Republican side, the law required all adult Americans to purchase health insurance (if not already provided by their employer), providing tax rebates for those who needed assistance in paying the monthly premiums. Both sides favored the elimination of the preexisting condition policy, and the new law made such a distinction illegal in policies going forward. Republicans had been pushing for the forced purchase of insurance since the late '90s, with Republican Massachusetts governor Mitt Romney implementing a policy similar to the ACA in the 2000s. However, despite the bipartisan nature of the law—and the fact that tens of millions of Americans would now have access to health care coverage who had not before—since Republicans had attached Obama's name to it, they could not publicly support it at all, swearing to overturn Obamacare at their earliest convenience (in fact, for Obama's last six years in office, the Republican Congress would pass numerous bills to overturn the ACA... all vetoed by Obama).

With the economy still struggling by 2012, and the divisive nature of Obamacare, President Obama's chances of winning reelection were by no means certain. Republicans chose Mitt Romney as their candidate in that year's election, but despite his desperate attempts to prove otherwise, he failed to meet the increasingly radicalized standard of being conservative enough. A terrorist attack on an American outpost in Benghazi, Libya, on September 11, 2012, brought the war on terror once more into the political fray (a topic Republicans had dominated since the 9/11 attacks).

Chapter 8. From Two Americas to "Hail Hydra!"

The secrecy around the facts of the Benghazi attack would be a political sticking point for the next four years. However, despite all that was going against Obama, he prevailed, winning a significant victory for a second term.

The racist reaction to America's first Black president would continue with a radical right-wing push for Obama to produce his birth certificate to prove his natural-born citizenship status (something no president or presidential candidate in American political history had ever been pushed to produce). Even after giving in to pressure and producing the document, the right was not satiated, insisting that the document was not proof enough. Fox News—a conservative shouting post since its inception in 1996—became as radicalized as their viewer base, all but declaring all-out war on America's first Black president.

The loudest voice on the birth certificate issue was former real estate mogul, current reality show host, and unlikely future presidential contender Donald Trump. Trump would ride the political tide of anti-Obama-ism to the Republican nomination for president in 2016.

Trump America

When Trump announced his bid for the 2016 Republican nomination in June 2015, it was largely considered a joke, even by Fox News and major conservative voices (especially considering the wide array of better-qualified candidates vying for the nomination). His campaign was plagued by scandal—allegations of collusion with the Russian government, his refusal to release his income taxes for public scrutiny, the many undignified insults he launched at his fellow Republican candidates, discovery of his having had affairs with an adult film star and a former *Playboy* model (and his paying off both for their silence), and an audio tape of Trump bragging in the 2000s of his celebrity ability to sexually assault women without consequences—but his firebrand rhetoric and blatant hatred of Obama won him massive support with Republican voters.

On the Democratic side, the nomination appeared to be less a contest and more a coronation of Obama's former secretary of state (and 2008 rival), former senator and First Lady Hillary Clinton. Clinton's only real rival for the nomination was New Hampshire's socialist senator, Bernie Sanders. Sanders was hugely popular with younger voters (ironic considering the Senator's advanced age in 2016), but Clinton ultimately won the nomination (though she angered a significant portion of Democratic voters in the process). Despite the division in the Democratic ranks, Clinton's victory over the inexperienced and ill-qualified Trump seemed all but certain by analysts from across the political spectrum. Despite winning the popular vote by more than three million (the largest popular margin ever for a candidate that lost the electoral vote), Trump pulled out 306 electoral votes to Clinton's 232.[1] Footage from Election Night showed that both Clinton and Trump were visibly shocked by the results.

Throughout his troubled presidency, Trump's policies would repeatedly cater to his radicalized base of supporters. Though touted by said supporters (and by Trump himself) as a resounding success, the Trump administration had repeated failures: his promised wall along the nation's southern border was never completed (or paid for by Mexico); though Republicans controlled both houses of Congress for his first two years in office, Obamacare was not overturned and no Republican health care alternative ever even proposed; the infamous Mueller Report (commissioned by the Republican Congress), while failing to prove Trump's collusion with Russia in 2016, likewise could not disprove it (though it did prove ten instances of obstruction of justice on the part of the president, which were never followed up on by Democrats once they took control of Congress); and he was impeached twice by the House of Representatives (though never for activities that could be legitimately and definitively proven due to the failure to verify intent), becoming only the third U.S. president to face impeachment, the first Republican to do so, and the first to be impeached more than once. Add to all of that the president's slow and disorganized response to the COVID-19 pandemic of 2020, and his chances of reelection in 2020 seemed unlikely at best. In fact, Trump's only actual successes as president consisted of partial completion of his wall; establishment of the U.S. Space Force as a fifth branch of the U.S. military (eerily immediately following leaked footage of U.S. Navy aircraft clearly encountering unidentified flying objects); appointing three radically conservative U.S. Supreme Court justices; signing a tax cut passed by the Republican Congress; and fast-tracking multiple vaccines for the COVID virus (the last being a considerable feat and by far his crowning achievement as president).

While Obama and Trump were both highly divisive presidents, President Obama did at least attempt to heal the political divide with numerous gestures to meet Republican legislators halfway on policy. President Trump, by contrast, eagerly further alienated those who opposed him, frequently calling any such opposition disloyal and even treasonous. His frequent flouting of presidential tradition exposed just how easily the power of the American presidency could be abused (something that Democrats, retaking both houses of Congress *and* the White House in 2020, though losing the House of Representatives in 2022, have thus far failed to address). Continuing to garner considerable support among Republican

Chapter 8. From Two Americas to "Hail Hydra!"

voters long after the end of Trump's term, the "MAGA" movement continues to be a driving force in Republican politics well into the 2020s (far more so than Obama's or Clinton's influence has continued among the Democratic rank and file). Trump's refusal to accept his 2020 reelection loss—despite his own vice president, his own attorney general, his own head of cybersecurity, all 50 state governors, all 50 state attorneys general, all nine Supreme Court justices, more than 60 federal and state judges, and even Fox News confirming his defeat—rallied a violent response that culminated in an all-out attack on the U.S. Capitol by die-hard Trump supporters on January 6, 2021.

Of the Trump effect on American politics, Kruse and Zelizer, in their analysis of the dissolution of American politics since Watergate, concluded:

> The first year of the Trump presidency revealed the enormous wear and tear that forty years of bitter division has inflicted on the republic. Yet a divided nation did not mean a broken nation.... The question that the United States of America now faces as a divided country is whether we can harness the intense energy that now drives us apart and channel it once again toward creating new and stronger bridges that can bring us closer together.[2]

Despite what one hears through more liberal media outlets, President Trump was not the cause—or even, more particularly, a cause—of the divisions in American culture in the late 2010s. The causes had been building over time, widening the divide between political fringes to the point that anyone identifying as the political "center" comes across as simply not caring.

Ultimately, the 2010s will be remembered largely for the massive political division throughout the country (whether that division continues or is healed in the 2020s or beyond). Despite Americans turning on each other over the issue of political leanings, the nation was largely unified in the area of entertainment and popular culture. Most pop culture successes throughout the decade were enjoyed by a considerable majority of Americans, showing that some things do have wide appeal to all audiences. Contributing factors to both the political divisions in the country and the successes of pop culture sensations were, in fact, the same things: smartphones (particularly the wildly popular iPhone from Apple) and the various—and ever-growing—platforms of social media.

Getting Connected and Going Viral

In the 1990s, Motorola and Nokia were the leading names in cell phones in the U.S., but in the wake of 9/11, BlackBerry became the standard bearer with its early smartphone technology. During the 2008 presidential campaign, Barack Obama became well known for his constant connection to his BlackBerry (something that, as president, he would have to severely curtail). In 2007, Apple introduced the iPhone, which would take the world by storm. As the iPhone improved with each successive model throughout the 2010s, Apple's key competitor for smartphone dollars would be the Samsung Galaxy. Ironically, though many computer users testify that the Apple Mac computer is more difficult to navigate and less user friendly than the more popular PC, the Apple iPhone appears to be the more user friendly when compared to the Galaxy (though much of this is more a matter of opinion than hard science). Regardless of which is "better," between the iPhone and the Galaxy, Americans—and people around the world—grew to become completely dependent on the devices as the 2010s progressed. Indeed, it is difficult for many to realize that the smartphone as it currently exists has only been around since 2007, as many cannot remember how society functioned without them (in the 1990s, one's local weather forecast being announced every eight minutes on the Weather Channel was considered state-of-the-art). With constant handheld access to the internet and all that it encompasses, Americans in the 2010s literally had the world at their fingertips, from weather to photographs to music to movies to television series to past messages as well as current.

In the 2000s, three websites launched that would come to completely define the 2010s: Facebook (2004), YouTube (2005), and Twitter (2006). While other sites like Google and Amazon would continue to grow in popularity (and profitability), still others—Spotify, Instagram, and Snapchat to name but a few—would be added to this number as the concept of social media came to dominate American society throughout the 2010s. A post, video, meme, or Tweet could go viral (spreading across social media and seen by growing numbers online in a short amount of time). As of this writing, Facebook remains king of social media, with roughly 2.9 billion users worldwide. YouTube follows closely with over 2.6 billion, and Twitter, now known as X after its purchase by Elon Musk—possibly the most active throughout the 2010s—450 million. Social media would perhaps have its most significant impact in the area of political campaigns. In the presidential election of 2012, Republican candidate Mitt Romney far outspent Obama in the area of political advertising, but Obama made more use of social media (which is free). In 2016, Clinton outspent Trump on campaign ads, but Trump dominated social media. Ultimately, social media reaches more potential voters at essentially zero cost. In the area of business, email and texting would be joined by video conference calls. By 2020, Americans were connected like never before in its history ... for good or ill.

Chapter 8. From Two Americas to "Hail Hydra!" 199

The obvious downside to such easy connectivity is that it provides an equal platform for those with malicious intentions as well as the mentally unstable; both appeared to emerge in growing numbers throughout the decade. The 2016 election made particular headlines with the scandal of Russian intervention. While Russia—and the Soviet Union before it—as well as China have repeatedly utilized all mechanisms at their respective disposals to interfere in American elections (activities that America itself cannot claim innocence of), the power of social media made such interference far more likely to succeed. Ultimately, investigations by multiple agencies—as well as the U.S. Congress—proved that such interference did in fact occur, primarily in the form of spreading misinformation online (something that was as much evident from American sources as Russian). In the end, though many still tend to trust what they view online as fact, the wise user—as with the wise newspaper reader or cable news viewer—must look outside any singular source and investigate for themselves the true facts on any subject. By 2020, American politicians across the spectrum had become masters of circulating falsehoods, "alternate facts," and "fake news."

Smartphones and social media thus became part of American popular culture in the 2010s. They also held the powerful position of *influencing* popular culture, from politicians to entertainment. Within hours of a film's release, thousands of reviews are posted, many filled with spoilers that filmmakers would prefer to keep secret. As a result, a film can now have a blockbuster opening on a Friday night and become a box office bomb by Monday. A celebrity can post a controversial tweet and find themselves "canceled" by the end of the day. In 2018, the wildly popular 1990s sitcom *Roseanne* was rebooted to massive critical acclaim and audience reaction. By the end of its commanding first season, however, star Roseanne Barr posted a racist tweet regarding a former Obama administration official. The ABC network's immediate response was to cancel the overwhelmingly popular sitcom (until Barr agreed to give up all interest in the series, allowing it to go forward with the rest of its cast as *The Conners*, which would achieve strong audience numbers on its own). By the end of the decade, celebrities were finding their Twitter and Facebook posts being diligently researched for controversial material with which to end their careers. The "popular" in popular culture had never been more relevant than it now became.

The Geek Shall Inherit the Earth: American Pop Culture in the 2010s

For decades, many aspects of so-called geek culture—*Star Wars*, video games, comic books, etc.—had dominated pop culture dollars, but many still did not define themselves by the traditionally insulting moniker. That would change definitively in the 2010s. As television (both cable and traditional network) slowly fell in popularity to the more convenient streaming platforms, one network offering would come to define the decade perhaps more than any other entertainment in any other medium: the sitcom *The Big Bang Theory* (CBS, 2007–2019). With a weekly audience of nearly 20 million by the series' end, the show centered on four young men who are science geniuses, friends obsessed with all things popular culture—from *Star Wars* to *Star Trek*, *Lord of the Rings* to *Game of Thrones*, and superheroes to video games—who meet their new neighbor, an attractive young woman with no interest in geek culture, who opens their world to new possibilities of romance that none had ever imagined likely. One of their areas of obsession was the annual San Diego Comic-Con event.

SDCC had been an annual event since 1970, when it had only a couple hundred attendees. By 2000, that number had risen to 48,000, growing to approximately 125,000 by 2010. Throughout the 2010s, the convention—now featuring offerings from all of the major Hollywood studios to promote their most recent (and near-future) offerings—attendance would average around 130,000, peaking at 167,000 in 2015. The COVID pandemic would, of course, shut down the convention for 2020 and 2021, but it returned to figures around 135,000 by 2022. Though similar conventions are held in essentially every major city in the U.S. throughout the calendar year, the San Diego convention is considered the mecca for pop culture aficionados and all things geek or nerd.

While *The Big Bang Theory*—and a handful of other programs—kept network television relevant in the 2010s, cable television was dominated by one program: *The Walking Dead* (AMC, 2010–2022). Based on the wildly popular Image Comics book by Robert Kirkman and Tony Moore—running from 2003 to 2019—the series focused on a group of survivors as they navigated their way through the years following an apocalyptic zombie outbreak. Postapocalyptic narratives were popular in the U.S. throughout the 2010s, likely due to the fact that the daily news appeared to suggest that society was nearing an all-out collapse, if not in that decade, in the one to come. In 2016, as the Clinton/Trump presidential race exposed how America was more deeply divided than ever before, two of the biggest box office successes at movie theaters were the superhero films *Batman v. Superman: Dawn of Justice* and *Captain America: Civil War* (based loosely on the popular 2000s comics run discussed in the previous chapter). Ironic that in that divisive year, two superhero films from the two major superhero studios would each release big-budget blockbusters revolving around similar divisions. Throughout the decade, superheroes would dominate the big screen, particularly from the upstart Marvel Studios.

Chapter 8. From Two Americas to "Hail Hydra!"

After the massive success of its initial 2008 offering, *Iron Man*, Marvel Studios was on its way. In the 2010s, Marvel would dominate not only the American but also the global movie box office, releasing some of the highest-grossing films of all time:

- 2010—*Iron Man 2*
- 2011—*Thor* and *Captain America: The First Avenger*
- 2012—*The Avengers*
- 2013—*Iron Man 3* and *Thor: The Dark World*
- 2014—*Captain America: The Winter Soldier* and *Guardians of the Galaxy*
- 2015—*Avengers: Age of Ultron* and *Ant-Man*
- 2016—*Captain America: Civil War* and *Doctor Strange*
- 2017—*Guardians of the Galaxy, Vol. 2*; *Spider-Man: Homecoming*; and *Thor: Ragnarok*
- 2018—*Black Panther*; *Avengers: Infinity War*; and *Ant-Man and the Wasp*
- 2019—*Captain Marvel*; *Avengers: Endgame*; and *Spider-Man: Far from Home*

With a total of 23 films—including 2008's *Iron Man* and *The Incredible Hulk*—in 11 years, the new Marvel Studios found themselves dominating longtime studios such as Warner Brothers and 20th Century–Fox (each of which had similar—though considerably lesser—success with their own superhero offerings). Warner Brothers—owners of DC Comics—would have some considerable successes—*The Dark Knight Rises* (2012), *Wonder Woman* (2017), and *Aquaman* (2018)—as well as those that fell far short of critic/audience expectations (most notably the aforementioned *Batman v. Superman*, and the Zach Snyder/Joss Whedon amalgam *Justice League* in 2017). Meanwhile, 20th Century–Fox enjoyed some success with the reboot of its *X-Men* films (most notably the R-rated *Deadpool* in 2016 and *Logan* in 2017).

Other than superheroes, geek culture also celebrated an unexpected return to a galaxy far, far away. In 2012, writer/director George Lucas announced the sale of his wildly successful Lucasfilm studio to the Walt Disney Corporation. Disney immediately announced that it would have Lucasfilm—kept as its own separate entity—begin work on a new series of *Star Wars* films. Box office dollars would pour in with the new slate of films: *Star Wars, Episode VII: The Force Awakens* (2015); *Rogue One: A Star Wars Story* (2016); *Star Wars, Episode VIII: The Last Jedi* (2017); *Solo: A Star Wars Story* (2018); and *Star Wars, Episode IX: The Rise of Skywalker* (2019). Fan backlash over the last three films led to Disney/Lucasfilm putting future

Star Wars films on hold, moving the franchise more toward streaming series on the new Disney+ platform, which launched in late-2019 with their first offering, *The Mandalorian* (possibly the most popular *Star Wars* offering since the original trilogy of films).

Disney's purchase of Lucasfilm was preceded by their 2009 purchase of Marvel Entertainment and followed by their 2019 purchase of 20th Century-Fox (giving the 95-year-old Disney Corporation ownership of a considerable slice of American popular culture overall). Though hit hard in 2020 by the COVID pandemic—as were all businesses, all over the world—Disney would launch into the new decade with a massive slate of offerings from Marvel, Lucasfilm, Pixar, and more. Like Lucasfilm, Marvel was maintained as its own separate entity, owned by Disney but largely independent creatively. With the impressive success of its film division, the comics division could continue with far less pressure as paper magazines all but disappeared in the new digital age. Creative teams could experiment like never before with the wide array of Marvel characters at the company's disposal. In the trying times that were the 2010s, Captain America would provide commentary on the world at large like never before.

Cap in the 2010s

As the 2010s opened, *Captain America* comics made news again with the biggest controversy to ever hit the series. With Steve Rogers returned from the "dead" (once again), he took a much-needed vacation, leaving Bucky Barnes to continue in his role as the current Captain America. In the first storyline of the 2010s, Cap faces off against two old nemeses: the Watchdogs (the racist nationalist group that John Walker's Captain America faced in the 1980s) and the psychotic 1950s Captain America (now going by his birth name of William Burnside). The two team up with one mission in mind: to make America "great" again (showing how the idea—not yet cemented in that exact phrase—had become dogma for the radical right in Obama's America).[3]

In the opener of this storyline, Cap and Falcon travel encounter a right-wing political rally, with the crowd carrying placards that read "AMERICA NOT AMERICANT" (which would make more sense if there were an "N" at the end of "AMERICA," suggesting that the creator of the sign failed to get the joke he was trying to convey), and "NO GOVT IN MY MEDICARE!" (obviously suggesting that the creator of this sign was unaware that Medicare has always been a government program), and "NO NEW TAXES"[4] (a callback to the broken promise of the first President Bush in the late

Chapter 8. From Two Americas to "Hail Hydra!"

'80s/early '90s). All of these were signs likely to be seen in Tea Party rallies at the time. The one that made national headlines, however, was the sign that read: "Tea Bag the Libs Before They Tea Bag YOU!"[5] That image outraged the real-world Tea Party for three main reasons: (1) it directly identified them as villains to Captain America; (2) it suggested that the movement was racist (to be fair, their frequent referrals to President Obama essentially did that already); and (3) the fact that—as comedians around the country had already pointed out—the term "tea bagging" had sexual connotations that the Christian right found disgusting and insulting. For all future printings of the issue—as well as the digital copy posted to the Marvel Unlimited app—that sign would be shown as reading "AmeriCAN not AmeriCAN'T"[6] (inexplicably correcting the placard still visible on the previous page).

The next issue begins with explaining the perspective of William Burnside (the 1950s "Commie Smasher" Cap). Traveling across country in 2009, witnessing the results of the recent economic crash, Burnside is reminded of the Great Depression he grew up in, lamenting that the so-called liberal agenda of modern America had caused this (rather than the unethical corporate practices that were actually responsible) and that the Eisenhower 1950s had been more prosperous, wishing America could return to that era.[7] This nostalgia for the 1950s had been central to the philosophies of the American right since the 1980s Reagan Era and was central to the new Tea Party movement (which in and of itself suggests a lack of knowledge of the period on their part, as taxes—the central complaint of the movement—were *much* higher in the 1950s than during the Obama administration). In an interesting bit of retconning, this issue suggests that Bucky did not accidentally walk in on Steve Rogers changing into his Captain America costume prior to World War II, but was actually trained from the beginning to be the Sentinel of Liberty's partner.[8]

A key topic in the "Two Americas" storyline was the concept of the patriot. In the decades since 9/11, the term has been almost completely appropriated by the radical right wing, strongly suggesting that to be patriotic is to back policies that outright hurt and oppress anyone who cannot be identified as white, straight, and Christian. While the use of the insane 1950s Cap and the Watchdogs amplifies this with a degree of hyperbole, the differences between this fiction and reality would narrow considerably as the decade proceeded. Rather than simply vilifying conservatives, "Two Americas" gives voice to much of what was making the right so angry: economic disparity, increasing government intervention in all aspects of everyday life, and political liberals calling for the government to help specific groups rather than all Americans (which is not exactly what the Democratic Party was doing, but it is easy to see how one—or many—could interpret it that way).

In a bit of rather terrifying premonition, the '50s Cap explains his organization to a captured Bucky: "I didn't join up with the Watchdogs. They joined *me*. And there are a lot of other militia groups just like them living off the grid out there in the *real* America. Just waiting for a leader to rally around … just waiting for a sign the tide is turning in their direction" [emphases in the original].[9]

As the decade progressed and the Tea Party evolved into the Freedom Caucus, a leader did indeed rise to rally the various right-wing organizations that for years had been lying quiet in the fringes of society. Fear, anger, and hate are easy fodder for politicians of any philosophy, and since the last two Democratic presidents—Clinton and Obama—were far more popular than the last two Republicans—the two Bushes—the Republican Party needed something to rally a dedicated base of supporters. In lieu of popular policies, they opted for emotion.

While the "Two Americas" story was an opportunity to present a peaceful common ground between America's two competing philosophies—like the "Fight Terror" storylines attempted to do after 9/11—no such common ground is found. Ultimately, the only way Bucky can stop the radical fringe from their violent designs is to kill their leader (though, to be fair, by 2010 even novice comic book readers should be well aware that in comics, nobody dies forever). As the political right became more radicalized as the decade progressed, this storyline took on a far more frightening tone than likely originally intended. With the real-world Tea Party so clearly seeing themselves in the Captain America villains, what could have been a come to Jesus moment instead became a direct insult that further exacerbated already heated emotions. As the real-world political climate continued to deteriorate, *Two Americas* would not be the last time audiences see a "bad" Captain America; and the next time, the "bad" Cap would be the *real* Cap.

While Bucky continued to serve as Captain America, the newly resurrected Steve Rogers continued his own adventures in a new comic, *Steve Rogers: Super Soldier.* In this book, Steve wears a costume similar to the one worn by the MCU Cap in *Captain America: Winter Soldier* and *Avengers: Infinity War*, patriotic in theme but only blue and white (and no shield). His adventures open by investigating the grandson of the professor that created Steve's Super Soldier Serum, and the fact that a new serum is now being sold on the black market. This serum, however, is flawed, causing violent tendencies and fatal physical side effects such as brain aneurysms. Steve will go on to work with SHIELD and the Avengers in his role as Super Soldier.[10] Primarily, however, Steve will organize the Secret Avengers—made up of himself, Sharon Carter, Black Widow, Valkyrie, War Machine, Nova, Moon Knight, and Beast (of the X-Men)—to fight

Chapter 8. From Two Americas to "Hail Hydra!"

"the threats we don't know about."[11] It seems clear, then, that despite Steve Rogers surrendering the argument behind *Civil War*, he was still ideologically committed to trusted secrecy over the transparency pushed by Iron Man's side of that conflict.

In 2011, Bucky/Cap appears to have died, opening the door for Steve Rogers to return once more as Captain America. However, this turn would be short-lived when Steve Rogers encounters a villain called the Iron Nail who manages to remove Rogers's Super Soldier Serum, reverting him physically to the body of a 90–100-year-old-man (though still an oddly healthy one).[12] Steve chooses his successor once more, this time Sam Wilson, the Falcon. At the end of the final issue of this run of *Captain America* (Volume VII? Unsure if it matters at this point), readers—and the collected Avengers—see Sam in his new Captain America suit, with wings added. Steve gives Sam his iconic shield and the series continues in *All-New Captain America* #1 (January 2015). From this point forward, a continuous *Captain America* title is difficult to follow as there will be numerous short-lived books bearing *Captain America* as part of their titles, but in the short term at least, *All-New Captain America* and its immediate successor *Captain America: Sam Wilson* will provide some fascinating political commentary on the ever-widening American sociopolitical divide.

The 2010s saw a huge push throughout popular culture to promote more diversity of representation in popular media. While this would be evident in many franchises such as *Star Trek* and *Star Wars*, Marvel Comics would probably represent the most significant example of this long-needed change ... kind of. Aside from the new Sam Wilson Captain America, in 2013, Marvel introduced a new Ms. Marvel—the original character who held that moniker for decades, Carol Danvers, had in recent years changed her title to "Captain Marvel." The new Ms. Marvel was Kamala Khan, a Pakistani American Muslim teenager. Marvel also introduced a female Thor (the original no longer "worthy" of his heroic mantle), a young Asian man as the new Hulk (the original killed off ... for a while), a Black female Iron Man, dubbed Ironheart (with the original Iron Man, Tony Stark, also dying briefly), a new female Hawkeye (the original accused of murder), a young Hispanic woman as the new Wolverine (the original ... yes... "dying"), and three prominent gay characters: Wiccan (the reincarnated son of the Scarlet Witch and member of the Young Avengers); Hulkling (a green alien, member of the Young Avengers, and love interest of Wiccan); and Iceman of the X-Men (in a magnificently thought-out story exposing that the character had, in fact, been in the closet since the character's beginning). However, due to the rapidity of these characters emerging, this soon began to look very much like a gimmick, feeding into popular trends (this perception would not be helped when the original white male Captain America, Thor, Iron Man, Hulk, Hawkeye, *and* Wolverine all eventually resumed their respective roles alongside their replacements). Fortunately, whether the characters were a sincere push for change or simply a sales gimmick, these new heroes proved popular with readers, securing their continued place in the Marvel Comics—and eventually Marvel Cinematic—Universe.

The new Captain America's first adventure would see Sam Wilson facing off against not one but many legacy villains in the *Captain America* franchise, led by one of Cap's most dangerous foes: Baron Helmut Zemo and Hydra. Interestingly, while each of these old-school Cap foes mock and ridicule Sam for being the new Cap, none do so by making an issue of his race (not even the fascist Zemo or Sin, the daughter of the Nazi Red Skull), instead making light of Sam's decades as Cap's "sidekick," his lack of Super Soldier Serum enhancements, and his lack of military training and experience (the first two also being issues that the comics version of Bucky shared when he held the shield). They do, however, call him "Captain America."[13]

While Sam's Cap follows the traditions and beliefs of Steve Rogers (which was why he was chosen), the new Captain America also receives a new partner, Ian Rogers (the adopted son of Steve Rogers and Sharon Carter while they were trapped in an alternate dimension ... it's complicated) as the new Nomad. Confronting Baron Zemo while Captain America wins the day elsewhere, Nomad admits, "[W]hile I love [Steve and Sharon] dearly, we disagree on one thing. Sometimes doing the right thing means killing the necessary people."[14]

This mode of thinking has been seen before, in the forms of the John Walker Captain America of the 1980s (and his succeeding career as U.S. Agent), the Punisher, and, to a lesser degree, in the Bucky Cap. Meanwhile, readers learn that Sam's morals come not only from Steve's example, but also from Sam's own minister father and the lessons he learned from him prior to his father's death while attempting to stop a fight in the streets of Harlem.[15] This will help to define Sam Wilson in a way that had not been properly done to date, separating him from Steve Rogers and exposing him as his own man, his own Captain America.

The announcement of Sam as the new Captain America was the end of the *Captain America* title (for some time anyway). After the brief series *All-New Captain America*, Sam's adventures continued in the ongoing series *Captain America: Sam Wilson*. This is a departure from previous Steve Rogers replacements. In the '80s, the title remained *Captain America* for the entirety of John Walker's time in the role, and for Bucky's in the late 2000s/early 2010s. While the reason for the change of title was likely due largely to Marvel publishing several miniseries bearing the title

Chapter 8. From Two Americas to "Hail Hydra!"

Captain America (by this time the MCU films had made the character more popular than ever before) and wanting to make sure readers knew *which* Cap they were buying, the fact that the first Black Captain America doesn't hold the title that the character has always had is noticeable to those intimately following the character. Intentional or not, specifying the book as *Captain America: Sam Wilson* brings with it a subtext that the first Black Captain is not *the* Captain. The new series would examine the idea—already evident in the real world on social media—that many (within the fictional world of the Marvel Universe) would refuse to acknowledge Sam as Cap, and what that said about American society in the 2010s.

When it comes to political commentary on the events of the day, *Captain America: Sam Wilson* is, without a doubt, *Captain America*. In the very first issue, Sam updates the readers on the world they live in:

> Let's just be honest here ... this country is as divided as it's ever been. Red and blue, black and white, Republican and Democrat, North and South ... feels like we're constantly at each other's throats, we don't *trust* each other. We no longer see ourselves in our neighbor. And this is not some intellectual debate ... people are *dying*. Our streets are burning. Inequality is soaring.... The good guys—S.H.I.E.L.D., the N.S.A.—are getting caught doing things we never dreamt the *bad guys* would do.... But the even bigger, scarier problem for me? In all these struggles, all these debates, all these things tearing us apart.... I have a side.... I have opinions. Strongly held beliefs, even. And here's the thing ... the more I saw the people I believed I was standing up for being *walked* on ... the more I heard a noise machine spouting *intolerance* and *fear*, drowning common sense out ... the more I wondered ... shouldn't Captain America be *more* than just a symbol? [emphasis in the original][16]

While Sam is the new Captain America, he has forsworn any adherence to SHIELD or the U.S. government. His previous adventure in *All-New Captain America* had led him to believe that something ominous was occurring at the highest levels of security (and his beliefs would be proven all too soon). By 2015, the government was no less divided than American society, and there was no way that the American ideal could symbolize the American government as it currently was.

Sam continues to work as Captain America, but directly for the people, setting up a hotline for Americans to call if they need help. This is a callback to when Steve Rogers set up a similar hotline in the early 1980s, something that the U.S. government at the time did not like any better than they do with Sam. This time, however, Sam is able to advertise his hotline on social media, and Sam (and the readers) see examples of just what a nightmare asking Americans on the internet to tell you their problems has become. Rather than having a sidekick, Sam's Cap works alongside Misty Knight, former SHIELD agent (and Sam's volatile love interest).

Cap decides to investigate a group calling itself the New Sons of the Serpent, a militia group patrolling the U.S.–Mexico border in search of undocumented immigrants. The story shifts to the Sons coming upon a group of undocumented immigrants being guided across the border by a Samaritan looking to help. The Serpent leader announces, "Attention all trespassers! I am the Supreme Serpent! By invading this sovereign land, you defy the law of God, nature, and the United States Constitution! Therefore, I hereby apprehend you by the power vested in me by the aforementioned God, nature, et cetera, et cetera."[17]

While somewhat hyperbolic, this is representative of the real-world militias that were likewise "patrolling" the U.S. border at the time (which would increase under the administration that followed).

The Supreme Serpent goes on to suggest that those crossing bring with them "disease and crime,"[18] something that rings frighteningly similar to Donald Trump's own phraseology regarding undocumented immigrants coming across the Mexican border in his announcement of his run for the presidency just a few months prior. The Serpent even refers to an upcoming "mighty wall" to be built.[19] In yet another nod to conservative complaints of the period, the Serpent tells those crossing, "Also, you know how you make me press a one for English at the beginning of every call to my satellite provider? *That is something I cannot abide!* [emphasis in the original]"[20]

While a banal and ridiculous complaint, it was something that right-wing media repeatedly harped upon during the 2010s. When Cap arrives before things get violent, the Supreme Serpent calls him "Captain Socialism"[21] (conservative media frequently referred to President Obama as "socialist"). An interesting aspect to this new Cap book is that the narration boxes—usually utilized to communicate a character's inner dialogue—are, in fact, breaking the fourth wall. Cap is speaking to the reader, and the messages he conveys are strikingly similar to what President Obama had been lamenting for his entire term of office. However, just as Cap is about to save the day and beat the bad guys, he is ordered to stand down by SHIELD agents ... led by Commander Steve Rogers.[22]

A year later, while dealing with an uprising at a supervillain prison, Steve Rogers has his Super Soldier Serum reconstituted by a sentient form of the Cosmic Cube (the long-standing reality-bending apparatus frequently used over the decades by the Red Skull ... and by writers desperately in need of a quick fix to the status quo). With the Skull's return, Sam Wilson concludes that this threat will take more than one Captain America, and suggests sharing the title with the newly re-strengthened Rogers (with Sam continuing to carry the traditional round Cap shield while Steve carries a more badge-shaped shield reminiscent of his original pre–World War II shield).[23]

Chapter 8. From Two Americas to "Hail Hydra!"

In the debut issue, Red Skull addresses an audience of American "patriots." Lamenting that his homeland—Germany—is experiencing the same border/immigrant issues as America (referring to Middle Eastern refugees fleeing to Europe during the conflicts in Syria at the time), the Skull states, "Your entire culture is under siege. The principles your country was founded upon lost in the name of 'tolerance.' Your religion, your beliefs, your sense of community … all tossed aside like trash. And you cannot even speak out against it, lest you be called a bigot!"[24]

To read the arguments frequently touted on conservative media and by Republican politicians coming from the mouth of the most evil Nazi villain in Marvel Comics is terrifying (and no doubt intended to be). Writer Nick Spencer provides internal dialogue for a young man in the audience, and how the power of Skull's words speaks to him, driving his inner feelings to support what the Red Skull is saying. Spencer here provides an air of sympathy for those being swayed by such arguments in the real world. They are not evil. They are scared, frustrated, and feeling limited in where they can turn for protection. The Red Skull is preying on Americans' anger and fears to further his own goals, something that many were warning was happening on the far right in the real world.

As the first story of Steve Rogers returning as (a) Captain America closed, a terrifying event takes place that led to "Captain America" becoming breaking news in the real world's national newscasts for the fourth time in less than ten years. After once more saving the day, rescuing a hostage, and then inexplicably killing his own partner, Captain America turns to the hostage and says, "Hail Hydra."[25] As the adventure unfolded, flashbacks showed the childhood of Steve Rogers during the Great Depression, ultimately exposing for the first time that he and his mother were taken in and helped by a Hydra cell in New York City, introducing the young Steve Rogers to the terrorist organization years *before* he became "Captain America."[26] The subtle message was clear: Steve Rogers, the original Captain America, has always secretly been a Hydra agent. This led to the biggest Captain America story of the 2010s: *Secret Empire* (a nod to the iconic 1970s storyline by Steve Englehart exposing then–president Richard Nixon as the head of a national criminal cabal, discussed in more detail in Chapter 4).[27]

Public backlash to this story was immediate. By this time, Chris Evans had appeared in five MCU films, and Captain America had become as beloved a hero as Superman, Batman, and Spider-Man. Added to the storyline's implications was its timing. The 2016 presidential election was in full swing, and Donald Trump and his supporters were becoming an increasingly vilified presence in American politics. With the Red Skull—and the New Sons of the Serpent before him—proclaiming the ideology of the current conservative movement in America, placing Captain America firmly in that camp infuriated liberals and moderates alike (not to mention also insulting conservatives by presenting their arguments as an ideology of villainy). Oddly, what fans, critics, and those who only knew Captain America through the movies failed to stop and consider was that this—like the "death" of Captain America in the previous decade—was a *story*. Captain America—and more specifically, Steve Rogers *as* Captain America—is a commercial product first and foremost. The character is never going to truly and definitively die or become a villain so long as he continues to have a profitability factor (sorry if that spoils future controversial storylines).

The *Secret Empire* storyline feels very similar to the legendary 1962 film *The Manchurian Candidate*, where a decorated military hero is actually a programmed agent of America's enemies. In *Secret Empire*, however, Steve Rogers is not brainwashed. He firmly believes in the ideologies of Hydra because he has been raised with that ideology since childhood. In a calculated move, Steve—as the only Captain America now, with Sam being fired from the position and in hiding—manages to trap half of Marvel's heroes in space (with an impenetrable force field prohibiting their return to Earth) and the other half in New York City (encapsulated in a similar force field). Cap then utilizes laws passed by Congress—who believe Steve Rogers to be incorruptible—to declare martial law in America and assume absolute rule over the world's leading superpower.[28]

As the Marvel heroes are confused, convinced that Cap must be in some way being controlled by Hydra, Steve Rogers lifts Thor's mystic hammer Mjolnir, sending the message to the world that his mission, Hydra's mission, is a worthy one.[29] This leads to worldwide online discussion. What is the correct course of action when what appears to be the right thing to do is not a good thing to do? If one assumes that Hydra is evil, and that martial law and the denial of personal liberties in America is wrong, how can an object imbued with the mystical properties of acknowledging worthiness support that course of action? Readers were as flabbergasted as the plurality of Marvel heroes; as in *Civil War* a decade earlier, the question is once more posed: at what point does the importance of security outweigh the basic rights of liberty?

The story was initially well executed, its premise a fascinating examination of competing ideologies in American sociopolitical culture (as the pages of *Captain America* have consistently proven to be over the decades). The solution, while more or less satisfying, was convoluted. As with any reality-altering story concerning the Cosmic Cube (or some version of it), the climax will revolve one way or other around the fact that the Cube alters reality however the holder wishes to alter it. As such, what is real (or "real") in Marvel Comics is literally up for grabs. As *Secret Empire* concludes, there are two Steve Rogers (Rogerses?) and Sam is once more Captain America, but the damage done may well be irreparable.

In the Marvel Comics Universe—as in the real world—who are the laws designed to protect? Which ideology is "right" when "truth" is relative? *Secret Empire* answers the core story's specific questions: What happened to Steve Rogers? How was he able to lift Mjolnir? Who is Captain America and why? The larger questions—those that philosophers have debated for millennia—remain the objects of careful thought and discussion for the readers (and scholars needing to publish) to continue to consider. Love it or hate it, *Secret Empire* was a milestone event.

In the wake of *Secret Empire*, a one-shot comic, *Generations: Sam Wilson Captain America & Steve Rogers Captain America*, tells a special story explaining why Sam gives up the shield, returning it to Steve for him to reclaim the mantle of Captain America.[30] The following year, the main title *Captain America* relaunches with a new #1, with Steve Rogers once more the one and only Captain America, facing a world that no longer trusts him. While the Marvel superheroes—and the readers—are aware of what transpired, to John Q. Citizen in the Marvel Universe, all that anyone on either side understands is that Steve Rogers took over America in the name of Hydra. Those who supported him do not understand why his stance has changed. Those who opposed him do not trust that he will not do the same thing again. Sam returns to his role as the Falcon in his own ongoing series beginning in October 2017.

Marvel Comics in the 2010s saw three men bear the mantle of Captain America, with the original becoming a villain before the decade ended by attempting to return to the status quo. The aftermath of *Secret Empire*, however, would see Steve Rogers spend the remainder of the decade attempting to regain the trust of the American people. Meanwhile, Sam Wilson's run as Cap proved popular enough that he would return early in the 2020s to hold that role simultaneously with Steve Rogers once more. While Rogers spent most of the decade on the sidelines, on the big screen the world recognized him as *the* Captain America. In 2021, the MCU would finally pass the shield to their own version of Sam Wilson/the Falcon, making him the franchise's official Captain America. The 2010s, however, gave sufficient fodder for scholars to dissect for years to come: three Captains America, three controversial national news stories, a Black Captain America during the administration of America's first Black president, and continuous discussion of the growing divide in American society.

With a global pandemic, a national lockdown, a heated presidential election, and an attempted coup, the 2020s are already proving to be one of the most dangerous in modern American history; as the remainder of the decade promises to be just as dangerous, Captain America will continue to play his role in trying to make sense of the senseless, give hope to the increasingly hopeless, and be a symbol that aspires to inspire.

Current Takes

It remains too early at time of writing to have much of a selection regarding the 2010s Captain America storylines, especially on Sam Wilson/Captain America and *Secret Empire*. With roughly a decade since Bucky gave up the shield, there is some discussion of his era as Cap. Concerning the immediate aftermath of *Civil War* and the decision to have the former Winter Soldier become the new Captain America, John McGuire points out:

> The solution in the comic book to the crisis in America [the issue of liberty versus security at the core of both *Civil War* and the Patriot Act] is the renewal of the Captain America identity, which works metaphorically as renewal of the American Dream, detailing the process. In his early experiences as Captain America, Bucky faces two representations of "Captain America" that stand in opposition to him. The first is the shadow of the dead Captain America, Steve Rogers. Bucky fears that he cannot meet the legacy of Rogers and fears to even try. However, he is also prepared to defend his idea of this Captain America.... The other Captain America that Bucky contends with is the Captain America of the 1950s.... The 1950s Captain America is representative of a particular American ideology of the past—valorizing Hard Work but closed and rigid— and the idea that this conservative ideology should become dominant today.... In one way [Bucky] is indeed a new Captain America, but yet he retains elements of the original. Within the context of Obama's mantra of "being the change" (borrowed from Gandhi) and his promise of renewal of the American Dream, *Captain America* is complementary to the Obama campaign.[31]

This is a fascinating take on the Winter Soldier/Captain America. Most critics—and fans for that matter—thought the choice to replace Steve Rogers with Bucky was more a commentary on the more violent Winter Soldier being more representative of Bush America. This comparison to Obama, focusing more on Bucky being a continuation of Steve Rogers's original philosophy and idealism, is a refreshing counterpoint.

In his larger study of issues of masculinity and violence in *Captain America*, J. Richard Stevens discusses the more widely accepted interpretation:

> The Barnes Captain America debuted in *Captain America* volume 5, number 34, a controversial debut even before the comic was released because of the prominent presence of a handgun in the promotional images. Without the

supersoldier serum that gave Steve Rogers his fighting edge, Barnes relies on his more brutal tactics and weaponry to combat the more powerful enemies he faces.[32]

He then moves directly to a discussion of the *Two Americas* storyline from 2010. Regarding the controversy over the Tea Party association with the protester sign, Stevens points out that a simple internet search would discover that the exact sign that the Tea Party found so offensive was, in fact, present at Tea Party rallies.[33]

The adventures of Captain America—in all his identities—throughout the 2010s provided a nonstop roller coaster of commentary on the American sociopolitical climate. More and more books and articles will discuss these stories in the future, using the various narratives to hold the proverbial mirror to American society, reflecting both what that society would and would not like to see. By 2020, the comic book adventures of Bucky Barnes, Steve Rogers, and Sam Wilson—and, of course, Chris Evans's portrayal of Rogers in the MCU—provided a rich tapestry of differing ideals on America, its flaws, and its potential. Going forward, America will—for the foreseeable future—*need* two Caps to handle the load.

The State of Captain America in the 2020s: Two Captains, Two Shields, Two Americas

From a philosophical perspective, the fact that Marvel Comics in the 2020s would recognize two characters as "Captain America" is a perfect reflection of the fact that, societally, there appear to be two Americas. From a commercial standpoint, it makes even more sense: on the big screen Sam Wilson is Captain America, so he also needs to appear as such in the comics; the original Cap, Steve Rogers, continues to sell comics; and two Caps mean twice as much Cap merchandise. In 2021, the creative team of Christopher Cantwell and Dale Eaglesham produced the comics miniseries *The United States of Captain America*, where Steve and Sam go on a nationwide hunt for Cap's missing shield, meeting many Americans along the way ("The Captains") who have locally taken up the mantle of Captain America to do good in their own communities, proving Cap's value as a symbol of the American ideal. The book continues, through a succession of amazing talents, to provide commentary on the current state of America, regardless of what that state is. As long as Marvel Comics continues, Captain America—regardless of who bears the title—will continue to be what we most need him (or her) to be: a reflection of who we've been, who we are, and who we can be.

In the immediate aftermath of the *Secret Empire* storyline, Steve Rogers was put in a position of needing to regain the trust of the American people (none of whom knew anything about Cosmic Cubes or alternate realities). This quest was not helped by the sudden murder of General Thaddaeus "Thunderbolt" Ross, apparently at the hands of Captain America. When Sam retakes the mantle of Captain America alongside Rogers (a clear metaphor for two Americas), he returns to his red-white-and-blue costume and corresponding shield, but the actual "Captain America" shield remains in the hands of Steve Rogers. In 2021, the two Caps embark on separate adventures. Sam's Cap investigates an international plot involving several overlapping crimes: human trafficking of undocumented immigrants, weaponizing the rare element of vibranium, and creating discord between the United States and the new government of the African kingdom of Wakanda. Steve Rogers, meanwhile, investigates a century-long "game" between powerful clandestine elites in which both Rogers and Bucky Barnes have been pawns from the beginning of their superhero exploits, a game in which Cap's own iconic shield is a subtle symbol of the group's power and influence. Both Caps continue to portray their respective ideas of the American ideal, with Steve continuing to represent the idealistic symbol of "Captain America" as he has always done, and Sam representing a more realistic symbol, fully aware of America's flaws and sins as well as its hope and promise. Unlike the two Americas of the country's current sociopolitical reality, the two Captains America manage to fully represent who we are, who we have been, and who we can be. As America proceeds deeper into the 2020s, there has never been a time when Captain America has been more important. Thankfully, there is no sign that America will be without their Sentinel of Liberty or Symbol of Freedom any time soon.

The Divide Deepens: America Enters the 2020s

The presidential election in 2020 would be overshadowed by multiple debilitating factors: the COVID pandemic, which required a months-long shutdown of most public activities and ultimately leading to over a million American deaths; massive fearmongering and misinformation on the part of the sitting president and his supporters in both the news and on social media; and actions by the postmaster general that would drastically slow down the U.S. mail during an election that would rely more heavily than usual on mail-in ballots. The year began with President Trump becoming only the third president in U.S. history to be impeached by the U.S. House of Representatives. As dangerously divided as the nation had seemed in

Chapter 8. From Two Americas to "Hail Hydra!"

2016, the situation had only worsened over the four years that followed. When election results were announced that November, Trump refused to accept the results and concede defeat, further inflaming the ire of his supporters to do the same. The two months following the election would show that American democracy and the peaceful transfer of power between political parties was in more danger than ever before in its history.

By the spring of 2023, the political divide has grown even deeper (as difficult as that is to believe). Both sides have committed to the "politics of hate," with hatred of one another being the core value of both political extremes. As a result, politically moderate independent voters and citizens grow increasingly disillusioned with politics, which places the future of the country in a dangerous place: in the hands of eternally battling political extremes intent on the destruction of the other at all costs. In the early 1960s, Soviet leader Nikita Khrushchev allegedly suggested that the Soviet Union need not take any measures to "destroy" the United States because the very nature of American politics would eventually become the nation's downfall. This premonition has become dangerously close to reality.

In 2019, actor Chris Evans said goodbye to the role of Captain America, passing the shield to Anthony Mackie's Sam Wilson/the Falcon (as he had already done in the comics). Meanwhile, within the comics, both Steve Rogers and Sam Wilson would bear the name "Captain America" in the 2020s, perhaps more than ever symbolizing the fact that, as the 2010s ended, there were actually two Americas (as the 2010 Bucky/Cap storyline had already suggested). Just as the importance of Steve Rogers as Captain America in comics over the decades cannot be overstated, likewise the importance of Evans, in his MCU portrayal of Cap, playing a major role in the success of the MCU in the 2010s is also incapable of being overstated. Evans embodied the character to absolute perfection, and fans were devastated to say goodbye to him. He had shown the world the example of Captain America that comic book readers had known for seventy years and made him a firmly embedded part of the overall American zeitgeist.

Chapter 9

The Star-Spangled Man with a Plan
Steve Rogers and the Marvel Cinematic Universe

Captain America has been around almost as long as Superman and Batman, and a tad longer than Wonder Woman. However, until well into the 21st century, he was not as well known, nor as much a part of the American zeitgeist. Those three other contemporaries all enjoyed considerable success on television in the decades following World War II. Superman and Batman, in particular, have been national icons almost from their inception. Captain America, by contrast, has existed primarily in the shadows of the world of comic books, despite making occasional forays into other media. That would change with the massive success of the Marvel Cinematic Universe in the 2010s. Though the fourth man to play Captain America on screen, Chris Evans embodied the role like no one before (or likely to follow). While fictional characters are born from the words written for them, some characters—as comics icon Dennis O'Neil has stated—take on lives of their own, becoming larger than those who write them.[1] Steve Rogers has become such a character. While others have carried the shield (in comics), there is something about Steve Rogers that defines what it means to be "Captain America" more than any other character to fill that role.

Like Superman and Batman (and Fawcett Publications' Captain Marvel), Captain America was portrayed in a 1940s movie serial. While popular at the time, it was quite different from what fans were reading in the pages of *Captain America Comics*. He made a return in animated—or semi-animated—form in the 1960s, when he was key to the massive success of the newly dubbed Marvel Comics. In the 1970s, two television movies attempted to repeat the success of Marvel's *The Incredible Hulk* (CBS, 1977–1982), though, as in the '40s serial, the characterization fell short of its comics incarnation. A 1990 feature film was shot, then aborted, then sent straight to home video. That film, too, took some liberties with the source material. As such, 2011's *Captain America: The First Avenger* was the first true representation of Steve Rogers/Captain America seen by national—and, in this case, global—audiences. Since then, in six more films over the following eight years (plus a Disney+ series and more films to come), Captain America now has his proper place in American popular culture. A truly heroic and patriotic figure now inspires millions across America and around the world.

Getting Cap Wrong: 1944–1990

Captain America has been seen far less outside the realm of comics than his more famous Golden Age contemporaries: one 15-part black-and-white movie serial in the 1940s, 13 episodes of a syndicated animated series collectively known as *The Marvel Superheroes* in the 1960s, two made-for-TV movies in the 1970s, and an aborted feature film in the 1990s. Other than those projects, he did appear in single episodes of various Saturday morning cartoons featuring other Marvel heroes. By comparison, DC Comics' Superman appeared in the following: animated shorts, a live-action movie serial, and a daily radio program in the 1940s; a feature film *and* live-action television series in the 1950s; Saturday morning cartoons in the 1960s, '70s, '80s, '90s, and 2000s; a live-action *Superboy* series in the 1980s; three live-action television series from 1993 to 2023; and eight feature films from 1978 to 2017. Even Cap's fellow Marvel hero Spider-Man has had a larger presence outside of comics, with five Saturday morning cartoons from the late 1960s through the 2000s, a live-action television movie in the late 1970s, and three feature films between 2001 and 2011 (with two more after that before the character's introduction into the MCU). The road from the *Captain America* movie serial to 2019's *Avengers: Endgame* is a much shorter journey.

Movie serials were very popular in the 1940s. These short (5- to 10-minute) multi-chapter epics unfolded over a series of weekly adventures rather than a single, complete film (similar in almost every way to series on streaming services in the 2020s). Some of the more popular centered on pop culture icons of the day such as sci-fi hero Flash Gordon, cowboy adventurer Red Ryder, and the mysterious detective Green Hornet. From the pages of comic books, Captain Marvel (known better today as SHAZAM!) was the first to get the serial treatment in 1941, followed by Batman in 1943 and Captain America in 1944 (Superman would not make his live-action debut until receiving his own movie serial in 1948, though popular animated shorts were shown in theaters [17 from 1941 to 1943]).

Captain America, by Republic Pictures, was directed by Elmer Clifton and John English and starred Dick Purcell as the titular hero.

The main criticism of this first on-screen Cap adventure is that it does not actually portray Captain America, at least not the one that comic book fans knew all too well by 1944. This was not volunteer soldier Steve Rogers fighting America's enemies at home and abroad alongside kid sidekick Bucky Barnes. This is District Attorney Grant Gardner. He is investigating a series of mysterious suicides. This Captain America does not carry a shield but rather a gun (which he does use to kill villains ... he is apparently immune from prosecution from his own office?). He wears a costume very similar to that of his comics counterpart, but with no wings on the side of his cowl and a shiny belt buckle that bears an image of a badge similar to Cap's original comics shield.[2]

Those familiar only with the more modern take on Captain America might find the serial's main character's willingness to take a life unusual. However, the 1940s Captain America killed the bad guys at the end of the story more often than not (or, more accurately, engaged in hand-to-hand combat until the villain accidentally found himself in a situation where his life was ended, often pushed or punched toward their end by either Cap or, just as frequently, young Bucky). It is impossible to accurately determine how popular the serial was for one key reason: as each chapter was shown before that week's featured film presentation, it is impossible to know how many ticket buyers were there primarily to see the serial versus how many merely sat through it in order to see the featured film. Modern takes on the serial are relatively positive. It was extremely similar (to the point of being identical) to all other action/adventure movie serials of the day in tone, style, story, acting, direction, and production. It is mostly remembered for being the first attempt to bring comics' Sentinel of Liberty to the screen.

In 1966, Grantray-Lawrence Animation contracted to bring the new and massively popular Marvel superheroes to television screens across the U.S. Earlier that year, the campy live-action *Batman* series starring Adam West and Burt Ward as the Caped Crusaders had taken the country by storm. In all, *The Marvel Superheroes* consisted of 65 episodes airing between September and December of '66. Five heroes were featured, each given 13 episodes: Captain America and Namor, the Sub-Mariner (two of Timely Comics' 1940s heroes revived by Lee and company into the new Marvel line); the Incredible Hulk, the Mighty Thor, and the Invincible Iron Man. Composer Jaques Urbont created a distinct opening theme song for each of the five featured characters. Cap's opener featured the line, "When Captain America throws his mighty shield; all those who chose to oppose his shield must yield."[3]

Though considered animation, the term is used lightly in regard to

Chapter 9. The Star-Spangled Man with a Plan

The Marvel Superheroes. Each episode was a retelling of a recently published Marvel comic, with the panels merely reprints of the original Jack Kirby artwork with only the characters' mouths and, occasionally, limbs animated (in essence, an early form of the motion comic). Actor Sandy Becker provided the voice for Steve Rogers/Captain America, with Carl Banas voicing Bucky Barnes and Paul Kligman voicing the Red Skull. Compilations of each character's 13 episodes were released on VHS in the 1990s, but otherwise are largely available on YouTube. For fans of the Lee/Kirby era of Marvel Comics, these animated episodes will be highly enjoyable. Being derived directly from the comic book page, *The Marvel Superheroes* was the most accurate portrayal of Captain America outside of comics prior to the first MCU film in 2011.

Cap's next foray into television would be live action; while more loyal to the source material than its 1940s predecessor, 1979's *Captain America* and *Captain America II: Death Too Soon* would have their own issues regarding representation of the character.

In 1978, Marvel Comics appeared to be on the verge of a successful transition to television. CBS—one of the only four networks on television at the time—debuted *The Incredible Hulk*, starring Bill Bixby as "David" Banner (as opposed to the comics' name, "Bruce") and bodybuilder Lou Ferrigno as the titular, green-skinned goliath (and Mr. Hyde to Banner's Dr. Jekyll), which would run for five successful seasons. They also began the first season—or, more accurately, miniseries—of *The Amazing Spider-Man*, starring Nicholas Hammond as Peter Parker/Spider-Man. A pilot telefilm had aired in 1977, with the first of 13 episodes airing early in '78 (the remaining 12 episodes would air sporadically through mid–1979). Also in '78, CBS aired the movie *Doctor Strange* (which was ultimately a failed pilot for a third series), starring Peter Hooten as the Master of the Mystic Arts. By that time, production was well underway on bringing Captain America to the small screen as well.

Starring Reb Brown as Steve Rogers, the 1979 *Captain America* film took some liberties with the source material. Rather than a frozen relic from World War II, this Steve Rogers was a former U.S. marine from the Baby Boomer generation. His *father* had been a hero of World War II, developing a version of the comics' Super Soldier Serum and called "Captain America." Steve is given the serum, which enhances his strength and stamina, and he begins to fight America's enemies as the new Captain America. The costume was more screen accurate than that of the 1940s movie serial, but only slightly so. Rather than a winged cowl, this Cap wore a blue motorcycle helmet with a white "A" on the forehead and white wings painted on the sides. Unlike his '40s big screen incarnation, this Cap carried an indestructible shield (clear in the center ring rather than white) which, when thrown, looked more like an inflatable pool toy than a metal disk. The film was apparently more successful (or at least simply cheaper to produce) than *Doctor Strange* because it gained a follow-up film later that same year. *Captain America II: Death Too Soon* was less successful, and no further projects were produced.[4]

Though likely seen as cheesy by today's standards, both films were more consistent in acting, writing, directing, and production value than most other television fare from the period. Reb Brown was a believable Steve Rogers, and looked every bit the part (more so, in fact, than any other actor to take on the role prior to Chris Evans). They were very much a step up from the '40s movie serial or the '60s animated series in their portrayal of the character, and only a small step below the character's next multimedia incarnation, 1990s feature film, *Captain America*. That film, hot off the massive success of Tim Burton's *Batman* the year before, was completed but would never receive its planned theatrical release.

The 1990 *Captain America* film was, to date, the most accurate live-action portrayal of the titular character yet produced. Played by Matt Salinger, Steve Rogers was (finally) a patriotic volunteer for the Super Soldier Serum program during World War II (though, in this rendition, he had been disqualified from service due to polio rather than simply physical frailty) who found himself frozen in ice prior to the war's conclusion. One other difference is that this film's Red Skull (who, like Rogers—and his comics incarnation—likewise makes it to the modern world) was an Italian fascist rather than a German one. The Red Skull was played by Scott Paulin (his on-screen makeup falling far short of the brilliant work on Jack Nicholson's Joker just the year before). Ultimately, the film's theatrical release was canceled, but it did get a direct-to-video release and airing on American cable television in 1992. Like the two '70s films, the 1990 *Captain America* is very much a product of its time, better than some other superhero fare, but not as well done as others.[5] This would be the last Captain America project until the launch of the MCU in 2008.

It is difficult to fully identify how these early incarnations of Captain America got it "wrong." They each followed previously established criteria for their respective projects. The 1940s serial produced a Captain America fully consistent with the medium's portrayals of other superheroes: Captain Marvel, Batman, and Superman. The costume was there. The sense of duty and justice were there (though he was neither Steve Rogers nor a soldier). Likewise, the 1970s telefilms were very consistent in tone and production values as the other Marvel properties at the time (and even consistent with DC's one tele-project, *Wonder Woman*). This time Cap was Steve Rogers and did carry the shield. The unreleased 1990 feature film was the closest to the source material to date, and was once again consistent with other superhero projects of the period in tone, production values, and budget. But the one thing that all of those live-action projects got wrong was getting to the heart of the man behind the muscle—while Reb Brown's portrayal was perhaps the most accurate, his near-perfect physique from the very beginning prevented any definitive look beyond that to the heart beneath. Ultimately, it would take a very special kind of actor to walk the line between cheese and substance that a true representation of the Star-Spangled Avenger required. Ironically, it would be an actor known primarily for cheesy comedy who would emerge as the perfect fit.

An Unlikely Steve Rogers

Marvel Studios has existed since 1993, primarily overseeing production of animated series and advising on big-budget productions from other movie studios. Due to Marvel Entertainment filing for bankruptcy in 1996, the company was forced to sell the production rights to many of its licensed characters to larger studios: 20th Century–Fox received the rights to the X-Men and the Fantastic Four, Sony purchased the rights for Spider-Man and the Hulk, and New Line Cinema would produce Marvel's first big screen success, *Blade*, in 1998. After the back-to-back (-to-back) successes of the initial *Blade*, *X-Men*, and *Spider-Man* trilogies, Marvel Studios believed they could do a better job with their own content. However, with all of their highest-selling characters already partitioned out to various studios, Marvel had little to work with without including these other studios. The only major characters left in the company's complete control outside of comics were the Avengers: Iron Man, Thor, Black Widow, Hawkeye, Ant-Man, the Wasp, Black Panther, Captain/Ms. Marvel, Doctor Strange, and … Captain America. With the *Avengers* comics one of the company's lower sellers at the time (and the solo titles of these characters selling even less), big screen success seemed unlikely. However, when director John Favreau led their first feature—2008's *Iron Man*, starring Robert Downey, Jr.—to nearly $600 million in global ticket sales, Marvel Studios—and the MCU—was well on its way to making Hollywood history. Now they would need a new Captain America.

Prior to taking up the shield in *Captain America: The First Avenger*, Chris Evans was known for mostly comedic roles such as *Not Another Teen Movie* (2001) and *Scott Pilgrim vs. the World* (2010). He had even previously played a Marvel character, the comedy-centric Johnny Storm/Human Torch, in *Fantastic Four* (2005) and *Fantastic Four: Rise of the Silver Surfer* (2007), both produced by 20th Century–Fox. The announcement that he would be playing the very straitlaced Steve Rogers—like the

1986 announcement that popular comedy actor Michael Keaton would be the first big screen Batman—was met with considerable skepticism by Marvel fans (including this one). Audiences of those previous four films could only imagine that Marvel was planning to make their on-screen Steve Rogers/Captain America as campy as Adam West's 1960s portrayal of Bruce Wayne/Batman. However, as history had proven with Michael Keaton, those critics would be proven wrong. Not only would Evans prove to be more than up to the task, but he would also embody the character with more depth, humanity, and heart than anyone could have possibly imagined.

Getting Cap Right: 2011–2019[6]

Captain America: The First Avenger, directed by Joe Johnston (the director of *Jurassic Park III* and, more notable to hardcore pop culture fans, the man credited with George Lucas for creating the wildly popular *Star Wars* bounty hunter character Boba Fett) and starring Evans, Hayley Atwell, Hugo Weaving, Stanley Tucci, and Tommy Lee Jones, was given a production budget of $140 million. Roughly 99 percent of the film would be set during World War II, making it both a superhero film and a period piece. Rogers's/Cap's origin story was nearly identical to the comic book source material. Weaving's Red Skull—thanks to considerably better special effects than ever before on top of Weaving's phenomenal acting abilities—was terrifying and in no way as silly or campy as the character could easily have been presented. Above all was Evans's outstanding portrayal of a man with a heart much bigger than his muscles. Though focusing primarily on Cap's World War II origin (based largely on the original Simon/Kirby story), the film does conclude with bringing the frozen Steve Rogers into the 21st-century world of the MCU.[7] While not as financially successful as the MCU's three previous releases (not counting Sony's 2008 *The Incredible Hulk*), the film did make more than $370 million at the global box office, more than double its budget.[8] As Evans did not have the widespread appeal of *Iron Man*'s Downey, and Atwell and Jones lacked the big screen popularity of *Thor*'s Natalie Portman and Sir Anthony Hopkins—and the general cheesiness associated with the character in the overall zeitgeist—the success of *The First Avenger* is all the more considerable.

One deviation from the comic book origin that stands out and actually adds considerably to the future of the character is the immediate aftermath to Steve receiving the Super Soldier Serum. In the comics, as the only Super Soldier, Steve reports directly to the army, occasionally acting as "Captain America" against the nation's enemies. In the film, however,

Chapter 9. The Star-Spangled Man with a Plan

since he is the *only* Super Soldier, he is considered useless by the military (what can one man do?). As such, he is used as a propaganda tool, wearing his over-the-top costume in USO shows, recruiting programs, and newsreels and punching "Adolf Hitler" (an actor humorously portraying the dictator) in front of excited audiences (a reference, of course, to the cover of the first Cap comic in December 1940). The army's perspective is that one man (even a superpowered man) cannot make a difference; Steve's commitment—and a message of the film—is that one person can make all the difference.

Evans would reprise the role less than a year later in *Marvel's The Avengers*. Directed by Joss Whedon, *Avengers* did what no film in history had done before: it took the main characters of four different franchises and meshed them into a franchise all their own. Along with Downey and Evans, Chris Hemsworth returned as Thor, Scarlett Johansson reprised her *Iron Man 2* role as Black Widow, Jeremy Renner appeared as Hawkeye (previously introduced in 2011's *Thor*), and Mark Ruffalo debuted as the big screen's third Bruce Banner/Hulk. The film was a box office phenomenon, bringing in more than $1.5 billion in revenues (more than six times its initial budget).[9] Brought together by SHIELD's Nick Fury (with the iconic Samuel L. Jackson reprising his role from the first two Iron Man films as well as *The First Avenger*), the newly formed Avengers would unite to fight the Norse god Loki, adopted brother of Thor.[10] Once more, despite not being as "powerful" as Iron Man, Thor, or the Hulk, Evans's Captain America would prove the definitive leader, never saying die, never surrendering despite seemingly insurmountable odds. Audiences' one repeated criticism? At no time did Cap utter his iconic comics phrase, "Avengers Assemble!"

Avengers would bring to a close what is now called Phase 1 of the Marvel Cinematic Universe and was the first MCU film to be produced after Marvel Entertainment was bought by the Walt Disney Corporation. Once *Avengers* completed its theatrical run, the MCU was more than a mere franchise; it was a pop culture phenomenon. While DC Comics' Superman and Batman had dominated the movie box office for the last two decades of the 20th century, Marvel was dominating the 21st century on-screen as well as on the comic book sales racks. A growing key to the MCU's success was Evans as Captain America. He had taken what seemed at its core a rather ridiculous concept—a muscle-bound Boy Scout dressed in the American flag and carrying a giant frisbee as a weapon—and turned him into a character of honor and integrity, making the Golden Age comic book superhero an example for everyone—regardless of race, ethnicity, gender, religion, or nationality—to aspire to emulate.

Next for Cap—and Evans—would be 2014's *Captain America: The*

Winter Soldier. Once more taken to a large extent from the comic book page—this time Ed Brubaker's brilliant *Winter Soldier* story from the late 2000s—*Winter Soldier* would be directed by brothers Joe and Anthony Russo. While *First Avenger* had been a period piece/war film, *Winter Soldier* would be a spy film/political thriller, with Jackson returning as Fury, Johansson returning as Black Widow, and Sebastian Stan reprising his role as Bucky Barnes from the first Cap film. Added to the returning cast would be Anthony Mackie as Sam Wilson/the Falcon and Hollywood legend Robert Redford as Alexander Pierce, longtime friend of Fury's and member of the World Security Council, which oversees SHIELD.[11] This film would delve deeper into Steve Rogers as a "man out of time" and a veteran with survivor's guilt from World War II, as well as continuing to expand on Cap's comic book adventures from a new, 21st-century perspective. The film nearly doubled the box office of the first film, making over $714 million against a budget of roughly $170 million, securing not only the continuation of the Cap franchise, but the Russo brothers' direction of the third Cap film as well as the third and fourth Avengers films.[12] *Winter Soldier* would see Steve/Cap begin to question all he had ever believed in, with Evans providing a depth of emotional vulnerability to the stalwart and stoic Sentinel of Liberty that was difficult to achieve on the comic book page. Before the third Cap film, however, the character would unite once more with his Avengers teammates to face off against another global threat ... one of the Avengers' own creation.

With the massive success of *The Avengers*, the return of Joss Whedon to the director's chair for the inevitable sequel was a no-brainer. However, his second outing with "Earth's Mightiest Heroes," would not—despite being the MCU's second-highest grossing film prior to 2018's *Avengers: Infinity War*—be as beloved by fans as its predecessor. This could most likely be chalked up to the darker tone of the film, dividing the very team that the previous film had spent uniting. Ultimately, *Avengers: Age of Ultron* would be a cautionary tale of hubris and overreaction (both at the heart of the MCU's core character: Downey's Tony Stark/Iron Man). As with previous MCU offerings, *Age of Ultron* would unite previously established characters while introducing new ones. Once more Steve Rogers would prove his leadership abilities, even as his teammates faced different levels of confusion, despair, and uncertainty. Facing off against the mechanical menace of Ultron—created in the film by Stark and Bruce Banner rather than the character's comic book creator, Hank Pym/Ant-Man/Giant Man—the team is also introduced to new enemies (and future allies): Elizabeth Olsen's Wanda Maximoff (known to comics fans as the Scarlet Witch) and Aaron Taylor-Johnson's Pietro Maximoff (Quicksilver).[13] This was something of a surprise to in-the-know MCU fans as, in the comics, the Maximoff twins are mutants, and, as such, connected to the X-Men franchise (which at this time was still theatrically controlled by 20th Century–Fox). While Evans's heroic demeanor was still very present, and his leadership key to success, there was less of Steve Rogers as a distinct character than in his own films (or the *First Avenger* film). Fans of Cap were titillated, however, as the film closed with Cap saying, "Avengers ... A ..."[14] (The instantaneous shift from excitement to disappointment was palpable in the theater.) With the team clearly ideologically divided, MCU fans would not have long to wait to see where this new division was headed: for all-out civil war.

The third Cap film, *Captain America: Civil War*, was as similar to the Marvel comic event of the same name as it was dissimilar. As in the comic, a catastrophic event leads to a discussion of more governmental oversight regarding the activities of superheroes. A key difference is that in the film, this oversight would be conducted by an international body rather than simply the U.S. government (making the concept of bureaucracy all the more problematic). As in the comics, Iron Man and a handful of Avengers favor regulation while Captain America and an equal number of heroes reject it. Central to the film's story is the question of culpability of the Winter Soldier in yet another catastrophe. The divisions of ideology presented in *Age of Ultron* are underscored in *Civil War*. Like previous MCU films, *Civil War* introduces more characters into the film franchise: the MCU versions of Spider-Man (Tom Holland) and the Black Panther (Chadwick Boseman), as well as another Marvel Comics villain, Baron Zemo (Daniel Brühl). By the film's end, Captain America is on the run, a fugitive from international justice, without his team, without his shield, without a country ... a Nomad.[15] With a budget of a quarter billion dollars, *Captain America: Civil War* would continue the franchise's upward trend, earning more than $1 billion at the global box office (helped considerably by the fact that the film was really more of an Avengers film than a Captain America film ... which was also the reason for its larger budget).[16]

Steve Rogers is the primary voice opposing international regulation of superheroes. His experiences in *Captain America: The Winter Soldier* have taught him that political power changes hands, and in doing so, political agendas change as well. This was a prevailing issue in American politics at the time, with the Democratic and Republican parties more divided than ever on every single issue facing the country: from climate change to immigration, from abortion rights to marriage rights, and from social safety nets to corporate accountability. If governments begin to have authority over when superheroes can act, they will have authority over who superheroes act upon. As in the comics, the intention of the writers appears to have been to provide both sides of the argument, but also as in the comics, the side of right clearly appears to fall on the side of Captain America.

As stated in the previous chapter, the fact that *Civil War*—and the DC film *Batman v. Superman: Dawn of Justice*—arrived in theaters in 2016 was somewhat prescient, as that year's presidential election between Democrat Hillary Clinton and Republican Donald Trump was one of the closest, ugliest, most divisive, and most dangerous national elections in U.S. history. As Captain America and Iron Man—and Batman and Superman—came to blows, so too did the American people nearly do so as the culture war that had haunted and divided American society for the last 25 years came to its most divisive point to date. Though the heroes themselves reunite (to a degree) by the film's end, the regulations on superheroes become law, leaving half the MCU heroes labeled as criminals as the franchise goes forward. When a threat that has been building since the first *Avengers* film reaches its climax, the Marvel Cinematic superheroes are scattered, scarred, and utterly unprepared.

The third and fourth *Avengers* films tell one overarching story, including every single MCU character introduced since 2008. Since 2012's first *Avengers* film, the concept of the Infinity Stones had been slowly introduced, implying that bringing them together could bring about universally catastrophic consequences. Such is the plan of Thanos (known in the comics as the Mad Titan). While loosely based on the 1990s comics storyline *The Infinity Gauntlet*, *Avengers: Infinity War*—coming on the heels of *Civil War*—confronted the coming threat from a starting point of division (both physically—scattered across the globe and universe—and ideologically). When Bruce Banner returns to Earth—missing since the events of *Age of Ultron* and therefore absent from (and ignorant of) the events of *Civil War*—to warn the Avengers of the coming of Thanos, Cap and his cadre of fugitive heroes are nowhere to be found. Reactions to Thanos's arrival further divides the heroes. While Iron Man, Doctor Strange, Spider-Man, the Guardians of the Galaxy, and Thor work to prevent Thanos achieving his goals, Captain America, Falcon, Black Widow, War Machine, Black Panther (and the other heroic Wakandans introduced in the previous year's *Black Panther* film), Winter Soldier, Scarlet Witch, and Bruce Banner work to keep the final Infinity Stone—embedded in the android hero Vision—safe. At the film's conclusion, the heroes face their first real failure … and half of them are suddenly, unceremoniously, just gone.[17]

Though Steve Rogers never officially goes by the name "Nomad" in *Infinity War*, it is clear to those fans familiar with the hero's comics history that this is who the character now is. He is bearded, he has no shield, and his costume is now a dark blue and grayish white rather than the traditional red-white-and-blue. Once it is clear that Iron Man is gone and Earth has no organized heroes to defend it, Steve and his team rise to the occasion, putting aside their disagreements with the governments of the world to do their job and protect the world and its people. His never-say-die mentality evident in his proclamation, "We don't trade lives."[18] Even facing a superpowered foe with a superpowered army, Steve Rogers remains the clear, stalwart leader of the heroes. His inherent integrity, honor, and sense of duty are his greatest super powers, and a source of inspiration to heroes far more "powerful" than he.

Not since 1980's *Star Wars: The Empire Strikes Back* had an American blockbuster left audiences so emotionally distraught. Blogs, YouTube channels, and social media commentators would spend the next year speculating on what would happen next, and how—or if—the MCU heroes would survive the next film. Luckily, fans had only a year to wait. The pinnacle of the Infinity Saga would be 2019's *Avengers: Endgame*. With half the MCU characters absent from the bulk of the film, *Endgame* had much more time to focus on personal character moments, primarily with those heroes that had been in the franchise the longest. The final battle—with all of the heroes once more united—was nothing short of epic (which is insufficient to describe it, but no larger word exists). Near the end, after 20 films, hardcore comics fans received their much-anticipated goosebumps moment: Captain America uttering, "AVENGERS!!! ... Assemble!" (I literally just teared up writing that).[19] As expected—these characters are, after all, commercial products—the heroes win the day, but not without a horrible price. The film brings to a close not only the Infinity Saga, but also the storyline of Chris Evans's Steve Rogers/Captain America. The actor's contract complete with *Endgame*, Evans chose to step away from the character that made him a megastar. Since he had so completely embodied the character for so long, recasting Steve Rogers at this point was a nonstarter. The shield—and, with it, the mantle of Captain America—must be passed on to another ... but will that other accept it?

With a combined budget of $700 million, *Infinity War/Endgame* brought in a combined global box office of over $4.8 billion.[20]

The Cap the 2010s Needed

With 22 films in 11 years, Marvel Studios had become one of the biggest success stories in Hollywood history, and a major contributing factor of that success was Chris Evans and his performance as Captain America. A cheesy, flag-waving children's comic book hero from World War II had emerged as one of the greatest heroes in 21st-century cinema. Emerging in

2011 as American society began a dangerous trend toward social division not seen since the American Civil War, and appearing regularly throughout the decade that would need him so desperately, Captain America was finally able to do on a large scale what writers of the character in the comic books had been attempting to do for decades: provide an example of how we should act, what we should stand for, and who we can be. Going into the 2020s, comic book readers would still have Steve Rogers and his adventures as Captain America, but *non*-comics readers, those who relied solely on the MCU for their exposure to Cap, would have a new one.

In the 21st century, pop culture studies have exploded in the world of academia. Long derided as simply mass escapism, scholars have finally noticed that, by its nature, popular culture is a window into who we have been at any particular point in history. What is popular among a large swath of the population speaks to a large degree about what they are thinking, feeling, and believing. Essentially, popular culture defines who we are, what we fear, and what we hope for the future. While comic books—as the previous chapters have hopefully proven—provide such an example for a considerable and increasingly diverse portion of the population, television and movies provide an even larger sample of consumers. The massive popularity of the MCU films of the 2010s provide an immense canvas for academic study, and although they are relatively new (*Iron Man* debuted a mere fifteen years ago at time of writing), scholars have already begun to dissect this monumental pop culture phenomenon and what it says about Americans in the 2010s. In the area of Captain America, however, much has already been done to examine the character of Steve Rogers, a great deal of which applies as much to Evans's MCU version as to the character as presented in the comics.

In his in-depth analysis of Captain America as a fictional character and moral example, Mark D. White identified three key "American" ideals that Captain America stands for: justice, equality, and liberty.[21] In reference to *Captain America: The First Avenger*, J. Richard Stevens noted,

> Rather than jingoistic patriotism, the movie Cap's motivation is that he simply doesn't like bullies, and his humility and compassion are his enduring traits.... However the film version also maintains his position outside of society, so that he interacts only to leverage violent action to battle injustice (bullies) he sees.... It is difficult not to see the movie version of Captain America as representative of the American monomyth, if a gentler one than some of his predecessors (or, indeed, some earlier versions of himself).[22]

While it is certainly true that the first MCU portrayal of Cap is very similar to earlier monomythical portrayals of American heroes like John Wayne or Clint Eastwood, particularly in his bravery and dedication to American victory, it must also be taken into consideration that this first film was a story of World War II, a war that—both through propaganda at the time and enhanced in American memory since—has always been portrayed as a righteous and truly heroic "American" war. Also, while most of the movie indeed takes place "outside of [civilian] society," the early scenes do show that Steve Rogers's crusade against bullies begins long before he joins the army or becomes "Captain America." The character's MCU catchphrase of "I can do this all day!" is first uttered in a back-alley fistfight with a much larger bully.[23] The time spent on scrawny, pre–Cap Steve Rogers stands outside the traditional monomyth, focusing more on the heart of the character rather than his physical strength (the monomyth thesis would never emphasize a character that was physically scrawny or weak).

The first Avengers film brings Cap firmly from the past into the present and establishes him as the most qualified to lead this team of superheroes. As to Cap's presence in *The Avengers*, Stevens goes on to point out,

> The 2012 Marvel Studios film *The Avengers* served mostly to position Captain America as a natural team leader, though the character does spend some screen time exhibiting suspicion of the government and even questioning the appropriateness of his own patriotic uniform. Though possessing less raw power than some of his contemporaries, Cap's battlefield experience makes him the choice to organize the Avengers' efforts to repel an alien invasion.[24]

While Nick Fury brings these heroes together to form the team, and Iron Man is the most socially visible and well-known member of the group, and Hulk and Thor are far more physically powerful, Steve Rogers emerges as the voice to be listened to, the character to rally around in the heat of a battle against overwhelming odds. While many in the team exhibit doubt and a sense of "this is too much," Captain America never wavers, never shows fear, always exhibiting his "I can do this all day" attitude.

The last film to be discussed in Stevens's work was 2014's *Captain America: The Winter Soldier*, considered by many—including this author—to be the best MCU film to date. Stevens concludes:

> At the core of Cap's initial objection to S.H.I.E.L.D.'s plans to deploy the new superweapons is an indictment of the core neoconservative arguments of projected strength as defense. To drive that critique home, the film links this philosophy to the conspiracies of Hydra, the organization that originally grew (in the first film) from the excesses of Nazi totalitarianism.[25]

Post-9/11 American conservative political philosophy has increasingly been compared to totalitarianism: from the state denying marriage equality and women's reproductive rights to governors dictating the offerings in school classrooms and libraries. Is this analogy legitimate? That is a matter of debate. What is not debatable is that the more power is given to the state, the less power resides in the hands of the people, and that is a slippery slope. As Stevens also points out, Cap debates SHIELD's plan with Director Nick Fury, who represents the argument of security at the cost of personal liberty. Captain America—in *The Winter Soldier* and both the comics and film versions of *Civil War*—stands firmly opposed to the idea of too much power in the hands of too few people. This debate would become even more relevant in the remainder of the decade following the 2014 film.

Thanks to the timing of the MCU films—coming late in the game to the superhero film genre due primarily to the limitations of movie special effects prior to 1999—Steve Rogers (and Captain America) hit the overall American zeitgeist when the nation most needed him. Both on the page and the screen, Steve Rogers exemplifies the moral core and ethical values that Americans have come to associate with the World War II generation. As countries around the world—including the United States—possessed growing factions of nationalistic/fascistic authoritarianism in the 2010s, an unquestionable moral voice from World War II was more vitally important than ever before (even compared to that legendary wartime period itself).

Throughout the 2010s, the MCU Captain America presented the perfect example both of what a hero should be and what a person should be. While humanity will always fall short in their attempt to be Christlike (as the Christian religion purports to aspire to be), it is within everyone's ability to be more Cap-like. Though Steve Rogers may have left the MCU field (for now), his example lives on in those heroes inspired by his character. Sam Wilson may be a controversial choice to be Captain America (aside from the race issue, there is the fact that Sam is not, like Steve or the MCU's Bucky, a Super Soldier), but Anthony Mackie's portrayal of him has exhibited all the heart, dedication, and bravery as his serum-enhanced predecessor. As Steve Rogers was our on-screen Captain America in the 2010s, Sam Wilson will be our example for the 2020s, whatever that decade may bring about in the real world.

The Future for Cap in the MCU

Avengers: Endgame concluded with Steve Rogers passing the shield to Sam Wilson/the Falcon, as the character had already done in the comics, so fans had some confusion when one of the first MCU projects to be announced for the new Disney+ streaming platform was a series titled *The Falcon and the Winter Soldier*. If Sam now had the shield, why would he still be known as the Falcon? The series would answer that question. If Steve had passed the shield to Bucky (the Winter Soldier) as he had done in the 2000s, perhaps no follow-up commentary would have been needed, but this was 2019 America … and Sam Wilson is a Black man.

Chapter 9. The Star-Spangled Man with a Plan

The election of Barack Obama in 2008 had shown that America's deeply embedded history of racism was still not only present, but widespread. While all presidents face a constant barrage of criticism, ridicule, and insult, the diatribes launched at President Obama possessed a sense of menace, hostility, and seething hatred on a scale seldom seen in American political discourse prior to 2008 (even from news media and other politicians). There was no "post-racial" America as some had hoped the 2008 election would bring into being. This was covered to some degree in the comic books when Sam became the first Black Cap, but with the larger canvas of the MCU, it was an issue that would require a deeper commentary. Anthony Mackie's Sam Wilson *will be* the MCU's Captain America for the 2020s. The only question that remains is how Americans, the world, and—perhaps most importantly to Disney—the box office respond.

As the post-*Endgame* MCU would focus on the concept of a multiverse, with multiple universes and timelines with varied incarnations of the Marvel characters, in 2021 Marvel Studios launched the animated series *What If...?*, an anthology cartoon where each episode focused on a different version of a different Marvel character. In the debut episode, set in World War II, a strange twist of fate would lead to Peggy Carter receiving the Super Soldier Serum rather than Steve Rogers, emerging as "Captain Carter." Like her Steve Rogers counterpart, Peggy would find herself decades in the future, standing up against global and universal (and *multiversal*) threats. Hayley Atwell—Peggy in the MCU films—would return to not only voice Captain Carter, but also to play the character in the 2022 live-action film *Doctor Strange and the Multiverse of Madness*. Largely positive fan response to this version of Cap will likely see the character's return in many Marvel projects yet to come.

Like any long-standing pop culture franchise, Captain America has a considerable history on the issue of race in America. From traditionally racist portrayals of Black characters in the 1940s, to introducing the first African American superhero in the 1960s, to creating a racist organization as a villain in the 1980s, to a retconned history of race and the shield in the 2000s, to making a Black man the comic's primary protagonist during the administration of the nation's first Black president, the history of race in America unfolds in the pages of *Captain America*. This is as it should be, considering that the American ideal that Captain America has for so long stood for must by its very nature include a progression toward a post-racial America. Captain America—be that Cap white, Black, female, or LGBTQ+—has a duty to lead the way. The history of race in America plays a large part in the overall story of who we have been, who we are, and who we should strive to become.

CHAPTER 10

The Legacy of the Shield
Truth, The Falcon and the Winter Soldier,
and Race in Captain America Comics

While colleges and universities have offered classes in African American History for decades, the truth is that any course covering *American* history, if done correctly, must by definition include African American history to a large degree. Since the issue of race is so intertwined with the overall history of the nation, one topic cannot be fully explained without the other. As the previous chapters have (hopefully) shown, the nation's history since the Great Depression has unfolded hand-in-hand with that of Captain America. Though the comic can be criticized as to the extent that race has been discussed, it cannot be discounted that it has, over time, discussed it and established it as an issue in American society. However, since the character was a product of the industry's Golden Age of the 1940s, the subject of race was not handled well initially. Beginning in the 1960s, Captain America (regardless of who carries the name) makes several attempts to address race in American society, but ultimately does little more than skirt the issue, essentially doing no more than acknowledging that it *is* an issue. In the 21st century, however, the creative teams of Captain America have tackled race more than any period prior, opening the door for a wider discussion and a path to reconciliation and redemption for America's oldest sin.

Summing Up Cap and Race in the 20th Century

Racism was prevalent in most superhero comic books. In the pages of *Captain America Comics* and its sister title *Young Allies*, only two Black characters appear. In one brief panel in one Cap issue, a Black butler expresses fear at a possible ghost in his mistress's house. Aside from his

Chapter 10. The Legacy of the Shield

fear—a racist stereotype of Black people at the time—the butler also speaks in a broken, illiterate manner (another stereotype of the period). In *Young Allies*—as discussed in Chapter 1—one of the main child heroes was a Black boy named Whiplash Jones. The boy was shown with over-exaggerated racist features—thick lips creating a circular mouth and wide eyes—the broken English mentioned earlier, and (oddly) often wearing suits—completely out of sync with the other child characters—styled along the lines of famed Black musical artist Cab Calloway: loose pants and long coat of identical color and a wide, flat-brimmed hat. Like the butler character, Whiplash frequently expresses fear where his white friends do not (though occasionally his fear ultimately wins the day). Though the Cap comics of the '40s do not discuss the issues of race prevalent in American society at the time, these portrayals do act as a window to modern readers as to how easily racism was considered acceptable in pop culture.

As Stan Lee oversaw the creation of the Marvel Comics Universe in the 1960s, he was originally forbidden by his employer to include Black heroes, but Lee did insist that his artists include people of all races in the background scenes, so that the New York City presented in Marvel Comics reflected what the real New York City looked like. Once Lee successfully did introduce comics' first Black superhero, the Black Panther, in 1966—as popular support for the real world's civil rights movement continued to grow—he deduced that the time was ripe for the first *American* Black hero, and, in 1969, Captain America met Sam Wilson, the Falcon. Though many today—including fellow characters within the comics—refer to Falcon as Cap's sidekick, Steve Rogers consistently referred to them as partners, and for most of the 1970s, *Captain America* was retitled *Captain America and The Falcon*. For those years, standalone Falcon stories frequently examined the state of affairs in New York's inner-city borough of Harlem: rampant poverty, street crime, and seeds of militant violence. In the 1980s, under John Walker's tenure as Cap, Lamar Hoskins became the first Black man to hold the position of Bucky (or Battlestar, once it was made clear to Marvel writers that the term "buck" was a derogatory term aimed at Black men during slavery times), and the two took on the militia group the Watchdogs, a white nationalist organization that would return at the height of the Obama years.

Overall, what is Captain America's score on discussing the issue of race in America in the decades following World War II? That is a difficult judgment to make. On the one hand, considering how much time and attention the comic gave to issues in American society, the issue of race is barely touched upon. However, despite creators' decisions regarding the handling of real-world issues, it was not the job of a comic book superhero to provide any commentary on any sociopolitical issue. That would change in the 21st century. In the wake of 9/11, the creative teams for the various *Captain America* titles have taken their responsibility—and the character's responsibility—to provide insight and discussion on the issues of the day very seriously. Since 2001, any character to carry the mantle of Captain America would strive to be more than a Sentinel of Liberty or a Star-Spangled Avenger. No matter who is behind the mask or carrying the shield, they strive to not only represent the American ideal, but also to provide an example of what that ideal should be.

Cap in the 21st Century, Part I: *Truth*

In 2003, writer Robert Morales and artist Kyle Baker produced the seven-part miniseries *Truth: Red, White, and Black*. This tale, originally non-canonical, takes place as America begins to enter World War II. To date, the origin of Captain America had been presented thusly: weak, scrawny white man Steve Rogers, desiring to serve his country in World War II but unable to pass the physical, signed up for the army's Project: Rebirth, where he was to be injected with a Super Soldier Serum developed by a Dr. Erskine (originally Dr. Reinstein in the 1940s). Upon successful completion of the experiment, with Steve Rogers now the powerfully built Captain America, the scientist was killed by a Nazi spy, the secret of his serum dying with him, making Rogers the only Super Soldier produced. This is the tale told and retold for 60 years by this point. Morales and Baker present a pre–Steve Rogers story as a commentary on America's sinister history with race, basing it loosely on a real-world horror story.

In the 1930s, more than 300 Black men were subjected to what has become known as the Tuskegee Experiments. These men were told that they were being treated for syphilis. The *truth*, however, was that they were being used as guinea pigs to trace the long-term effects of syphilis in men. The experiment went on from 1932 to 1972. Despite the fact that the treatment for syphilis had been perfected in 1947, none of the patients in the Tuskegee cases were ever given that treatment. As a result, nearly half died either from the disease itself or complications derived from it, and several of the men had passed on the disease to their wives and, eventually, children. Of the many atrocities against Black Americans throughout the country's history, the Tuskegee Experiment remains one of the worst (and suggests that other such "experiments" could have happened that have simply not been discovered).

In Morales's and Baker's story, a group of Black men are subjected to an experimental version of Reinstein's Super Soldier Serum (making the story non-canonical, as by that time the name of the scientist overseeing the project had been changed to Erskine). Skeptical as to why Black soldiers should be given such an honor, the army is informed that before the serum is given to a white soldier, it needs to be tested, and Black soldiers would be these test subjects. The story focuses on three Black men: Maurice Canfield, an upper-class Black man who was also a social crusader for labor rights; Luke Evans, a veteran of World War I who has become disillusioned with the military's continuing racism; and Isaiah Bradley, an everyman with a wife and unborn child as America enters the war. Through the experiences of all three men, the plight of being a Black man in America in the 1940s comes alive on the page. Ultimately, only one survives the experiment, though—like those who survived the Tuskegee Experiments—not without long-term ramifications. The tale ends in the present, with Steve Rogers discovering the horrible "truth" of the serum that made him Captain America.[1]

The story is heartrending, graphically portraying some of the horrors experienced by people of color throughout U.S. history. It also gives a more realistic portrayal of how a project like the Super Soldier Serum would have come to fruition at that point in American history. The story presented in *Truth* was so well-received that it has since been woven into the regular canon of the Captain America comic books, with Isaiah Bradley's grandson, Eli Bradley, eventually emerging as the hero Patriot, a member of the Young Avengers. Likewise, an altered version of Isaiah would be introduced into the MCU as part of the limited series *The Falcon and the Winter Soldier*. Merging a portion of the *Truth* storyline into the MCU narrative provides additional context for the discussion of a Black man—Sam Wilson—taking up the mantle of Captain America.

Cap in the 21st Century, Part II: *The Falcon and the Winter Soldier*

In March 2021, the Disney+ streaming platform launched its second Marvel offering with the six-part limited series (at time of writing only the one season is expected) *The Falcon and the Winter Soldier*, with Anthony Mackie and Sebastian Stan reprising their roles from the MCU. Picking up some time after the events of 2019's *Avengers: Endgame*, the series opens with Mackie's Sam Wilson still operating as the Falcon, conducting classified missions for the U.S. military (with both the Avengers and SHIELD seemingly no longer standing organizations). Struggling with Steve Rogers's offer of the shield (and its implication that he should pick up the mantle of Captain America), Sam chooses to return the shield to the U.S. government for display at its Captain America museum. The whereabouts of Steve Rogers are unknown (he was alive when last audiences saw him, though considerably aged), leading to wild rumors as to where "Captain America" may be. Bucky Barnes is undergoing therapy for the trauma of his experience as the Winter Soldier, struggling to achieve a redemption he does not believe he deserves. When the government chooses to give the shield—and the job of Captain America—to decorated veteran John Walker (though with no corresponding Super Soldier Serum), both Sam and Bucky are unhappy with the decision, with Bucky blaming Sam for not adhering to Steve's wishes. This opens the series to dive deeper into the question of how the appointment of a Black Captain America would be received by the American populace, and the weight placed on a Black man to accept such a mantle considering the nation's history as regards the race issue.[2]

The limited series meshes multiple Cap storylines from the comics—John Walker Cap, the Power Broker, Sam Wilson Cap, *Truth*, and a particularly clever twist on the 1980s villain Flag-Smasher—weaving them into the new reality of the post–*Endgame* MCU. Aside from the new John Walker (a military veteran in the MCU rather than a former professional wrestler), the series also introduces *Truth*'s Isaiah Bradley (with veteran actor Carl Lumbly) to examine this issue of a Black Captain America more closely, what that means, and the weight of history behind the decision to take up the shield. In an interesting narrative choice, the MCU version of Bradley's story has the experiments being done on him *after* Steve Rogers became Captain America (as a military effort to recreate the original serum). This was likely done due to the fact that Stanley Tucci's portrayal of Dr. Erskine in *Captain America: The First Avenger* had established him as a noble person who would not have condoned the pre–Rogers experiments conducted in *Truth*. Though not as sad an ending for Isaiah as in the comics (but only very slightly better), Lumbly's Isaiah has had his own trauma due to the U.S.'s history of racism. With every line of his story, the haunting past of America's racism is brought to life. His anger and bitterness for America and his firm belief that no Black man with a shred of self-respect would ever *want* to be Captain America become slightly softened by Sam's firm devotion to the idea of what Captain America stands for, and the American ideal he both represents and strives to inspire.[3]

An important aspect of the discussion is Bucky's realization that as a white man, he is incapable of comprehending the issues that Sam faces in his decision to take up the shield. To Bucky, all that is important is that this is what Steve wanted, but Steve, too, is a white man incapable of fully grasping the Black man's reality in America. Many white liberals frequently fail to comprehend this in their own idealism. Despite their knowledge of America's race history, or their deep commitment to what is right, neither Steve nor Bucky (nor John Walker for that matter) have ever had to consider that a simple traffic stop could be the end of their life. They've never had to deal with the probability of being denied service due to their skin color. Likewise, while both Steve and Bucky experienced being used as guinea pigs for government research, neither man had experiences similar to Isaiah Bradley (even Bucky's imprisonment and enslavement by the Russians and Hydra were not as nightmarish as what Bradley experienced at the hands of the U.S. government). Sam takes up the mantle of Captain America fully aware that many of the people he swears to protect will hate him for it.

As the series concludes, the title card changes from *The Falcon and the Winter Soldier* to *Captain America and the Winter Soldier*. The torch has been passed. Sam Wilson continues into the 2020s as *the* Captain America of the MCU. At time of writing, Mackie is due to return as Captain America in *Captain America: Brave New World*, currently set to release in 2025, with Lumbly returning as Isaiah Bradley as well. Reviews of the series were mixed, with conservative viewers feeling the series was too preachy on the issue of race, and liberal viewers discontented that it didn't go far enough in its commentary. With such criticism coming from the two political fringes, it is safe to conclude that the series hit the mark exactly, driving the point home without overdoing it.

It is not the place for entertainments such as the MCU to provide solutions to society's problems, but rather to simply make a clear point of what those issues are and the importance for us as the consumer to take up the issue, have the necessary discussions, and seek out resolutions ourselves.

The Black Captains America on Page and Film

The comics and film media portray very different versions of the characters of Sam Wilson and Isaiah Bradley. In the comics, Sam is not a veteran. He is the son of a Harlem minister who becomes a social worker. He develops a psychic link with a falcon named Redwing, eventually becoming Captain America's longtime partner, the Falcon. In the MCU, Sam is a military veteran from Louisiana, given access to the "Falcon" program (mechanical bird wings) through his search and rescue job. Rather than a bird partner, Redwing is the name of a bird-shaped drone built into his Falcon flight suit mechanics. In the comics, Isaiah Bradley is given the experimental Super Soldier Serum before Steve Rogers, and the long-term effects of the serum deprive Isaiah of his mental faculties. In the MCU, Isaiah is part of a program to *repeat* the Super Soldier Serum, experimented upon by the government for years to determine why the serum worked on him. Meanwhile, Isaiah is used as a secret Super Soldier, at one point doing battle against the Winter Soldier (and is one of the few who live to tell the tale). In the MCU, though Isaiah is understandably angry and bitter toward the U.S. government for their treatment of him, he is in full physical and mental health. Both versions of both characters are excellent examples of the Black experience in American history; considering the enduring popularity of both—Sam Wilson has actually proven far more popular as Captain America than he ever was as the Falcon—there will likely be many more adventures for and explorations of these two powerful Black characters.

Of all the social issues tackled in the pages of *Captain America*, the issue of race is one that has only barely been touched upon. This is partly due to the reality of the character of Steve Rogers (and John Walker and Bucky Barnes) being a white man. While the white men who have carried the mantle of Captain America over the decades could observe racial oppression and inequality, it is impossible for any of them to adequately know what those experiences entail or feel like. While many have criticized the lack of tackling racial issues in *Captain America*, the writers over the decades have (thankfully) avoided the mistake of many white liberal commentators of claiming to "understand" the Black experience in America when they are utterly incapable of doing so. Through the characters of Sam Wilson, Isaiah and Eli Bradley, and many others in the pages of Marvel (and, to a lesser extent, DC) Comics, these experiences can be better explored, explained, and—hopefully—understood.

Conclusion
"We Can Do Better!"

The decades since the Great Depression have been the most consistently active, dangerous, and transformative in the nation's history. The world we know today would be seen as the wildest of science fiction by our great-grandparents. Our cars can tell us how to get where we are going, and often park themselves once arriving at our destination. We have access to the sum total of all human knowledge literally in the palm of our hands. Major news events are known to the entire world within seconds of them happening. Just in the last decade America has had its first president *and* vice president of color, the first woman to head a major political party ticket, and the first American Indian to oversee the U.S. Department of the Interior. Despite how the nightly news may present the world as being, America's goal to always try to do *better* continues to roll along unabated. Having said that....

While the road to progress is a long and slow one, the argument can fairly be made that in this country, progress takes too long and arrives far too slowly. All human societies are resistant to change. It is inescapable. It is part of our DNA. Change is frightening, even when we know that it is positive change. How many of us take the exact same route to work every day, becoming discombobulated when that route, for whatever reason, is forced to change? From a change in how you do your job, to how you eat, to how you are expected to interact with people, change brings with it uncertainty, anxiety, and often fear. Those who most suffer from this fear, however, are those who most desperately desire and need for things to change. This is where heroes (both real and fictional) come into play: to help alleviate our fears, to give us the courage to not only support but embrace change.

In hero narratives, the medium that brings the hero most closely to the day-to-day lives of everyday Americans is that of comic books. Whereas novels and films take years to complete, and months go by between the production and release of television and streaming programs, comic books come out every single month. From idea to page to newsstand, the time elapsed is normally only a matter of weeks. As such, a close chronological examination of superhero comic books opens a window into how these spandex-clad protagonists have experienced the decades since the Great Depression, their writers, artists, and editors literally living the history that we, in the present, can only experience through history books and documentaries. When comic books in early 1942 bore the message "Remember Pearl Harbor" on their covers, the men behind those books were still dealing with the shock and trauma of the attack, only weeks past for them. When President Richard Nixon was revealed as the head of the Secret Empire, taking his own life rather than being caught by Captain America, writer Steve Englehart likely had that day's newspaper lying next to him as he wrote, or had the Watergate hearings playing in the background, further feeding his own anger and frustration at the current events. When Steve Rogers cleared rubble from the site of Ground Zero in 2002, there were still undiscovered bodies lying beneath that rubble in the real world. Comic books are living testaments to their times, as much as contemporary newspapers or magazines.

While the Captain America of the 1940s and 1950s (and to only a slightly lesser extent in the 1960s) was a relatively cookie-cutter beat-up-the-bad-guy superhero adventurer, Captain America since the late '60s has very much been a social crusader, not so much calling for change, but very much pointing out the need for change and inspiring the bravery to *make* change. Through the pages of *Captain America*, readers have witnessed consistently progressive ideals regarding race, gender, and patriotism throughout the ever-growing sociopolitical divide in the U.S. He has repeatedly fought the enemies of change while simultaneously understanding and attempting to calm the hesitancy about such change. Throughout, Captain America has been used as a guidepost, defending pride in national identity while, at the same time, underscoring the importance of constantly questioning and, when wrong, opposing national policy and history. He claims to stand for the American *ideal*, but what to which "ideal" is he referring?

He is referring to the American ideals of justice, liberty, and equality on a universal scale, regardless of race, ethnicity, religion, national origin, gender identity, sexual preference, political ideology, or economic status. He firmly believes in the philosophy of the Declaration of Independence that "all men are created equal" (the word "men" in this context referring to mankind or humankind). Like America itself, Captain America is not—and never claims to be—without his own flaws. In the 1970s, Cap discovers that his chivalric ideology of protecting women and keeping them out of harm's way is sexist (and disrespectful of those women who are more than capable of handling any harm they may encounter). In the same decade, through his discussions with his partner, Sam Wilson, Cap discovers that the issues facing those who live in the inner cities are far more complicated than simply an issue of race. In the 1980s, Cap discovers that even though he signed up as a soldier, there are times when people of good conscience cannot simply follow orders, and that when the government is clearly in the wrong, it is the duty of good soldiers to stand up and say so—even if it means being dismissed from service.

In the 1990s—as America faced a future without enemies and the comic book industry struggled for its very survival—Captain America faced his own existential crisis ("dying" three times in a span of less than ten years). In the 21st century, having lived through all of the social changes (good and bad) of the latter half of the 20th century, Captain America has stood up more than at any point previous to be a symbol of that American ideal that we, as a nation, must also strive to live up to: the ideal that *we can do better*. Whether he is underscoring that "terrorism" and "Islam" are not synonymous, or warning against the sacrifice of personal liberty in favor of safety and security, or showing that the immigration issue on the southern border is not a race issue but an economic one, Captain America is there, month after month, as a mentor, guide, counselor, and symbol of what we, as Americans, should strive to be.

Now that Captain America has transitioned from four-color hero to big screen icon, appearing in some of the most profitable films in Hollywood history, the character is firmly part of the overall American zeitgeist, more so than ever before in his history. As bearers of the shield and the mantle of Captain America, Chris Evans and Anthony Mackie have perfectly embodied the character as presented on the written page (particularly the post–9/11, 21st-century incarnation) and become a positive symbol and hero to children of all races, ethnicities, and backgrounds (some still far too young to read their monthly magazine adventures). With both the comic book *Sam Wilson: Captain America* and the streaming limited series *The Falcon and the Winter Soldier*, the following question continues to be explored: Can a Black man stand as the symbol of a nation whose history—and a considerable portion of its population—continues to exhibit violence and hatred toward people of color? As Mackie's Cap beautifully states, "We built this country ... bled for it.... I ain't gonna let anybody tell me I can't fight for it."[1]

The history of America over the last 80-plus years is the history of Captain America as well. As the nation and its society move forward into the 2020s and beyond, the two will do so hand-in-hand with the Sentinel of Liberty of America's Greatest Generation. More troubles lie ahead.

Social conflict and political division will continue to grow. Racial tensions will continue to ebb and flow as we, as a society, strive to move forward toward that more perfect union that the Founding Fathers so hoped we would become. Though perfection will never be achieved, the effort will yield its own rewards. Like Captain America, we must all do our part to make that better world, for our children and theirs. He has provided the example, and—through his present and future creative teams—will continue to do so, forever reminding us and future generations that no matter how things may look, "We can do better!"

Chapter Notes

Introduction

1. Joe Simon and Jack Kirby, "Meet Captain America," *Captain America Comics* #1 (New York: Timely Comics, cover date March 1941).
2. "Captain America," *Official Handbook of the Marvel Universe—Master Edition, Vol. 1: Abomination to Gargoyle*, (New York: Marvel Comics, 2008). The original "Official Handbook" was published in several single issues published from 1991–1993 (no page numbers given).
3. Full Disclosure: *The Falcon and the Winter Soldier* (Disney+, 2021) is this author's favorite MCU project to date!
4. Two notes on sources: (1) As actual publication dates on early issues of comics is difficult to ascertain, in most cases the cover date will be used for dating purposes, and (2) as Cap has appeared in numerous titles over the decades—*All Winners Squad, The Avengers, Marvel Team-Up*, as well as one-shots, annuals, and special issues, in the interest of space—and with a few exceptions—only issues of the monthly *Captain America* comics will be used in discussions.

Chapter 1

1. H.W. Brands, *Traitor to His Class: The Privileged Life and Radical Presidency of Franklin Delano Roosevelt* (New York: Doubleday, 2008), p. 165.
2. Bradford W. Wright, *Comic Book Nation: The Transformation of Youth Culture in America* (Baltimore, MD: Johns Hopkins University Press, 2003), pp. 3–5; Sean Howe, *Marvel Comics: The Untold Story* (New York: Harper/Perennial, 2012), p. 11.
3. Larry Tye, *Superman: The High-Flying History of America's Most Enduring Hero* (New York: Random House, 2012), p. 29.
4. Howe, *Marvel Comics: The Untold Story*, p 16.
5. "1940 Electoral College Results," National Archives Online, https://www.archives.gov/electoral-college/1940.
6. Samuel I. Rosenman, Ed., *The Public Papers and Addresses of Franklin D. Roosevelt, 1940* (New York: MacMillan, 1941), p. 644.
7. Howe, *Marvel Comics: The Untold Story*, p. 20. While the first issue of *Captain America* posts a cover date of March 1941, cover dates originally had nothing to do with the date a comic book was published; it was the date on which newsstand vendors were instructed to remove a magazine from their racks, returning any unsold copies to the publishers.
8. Joe Simon, *My Life in Comics* (London, UK: Titan Books, 2011), p. 87.
9. Carolyn McNamara, "'Sentinel of Liberty': Captain America on the Home Front in WWII," UT Research Showcase, (Austin: University of Texas, October 2, 2015), https://research.utexas.edu/showcase/articles/view/sentinel-of-liberty-captain-america-on-the-home-front-in-wwii.
10. "Our Documents: Lend Lease," FDR Library Online, http://docs.fdrlibrary.marist.edu/odlendls.html.
11. Harvey Kurtzman, artist [no writer credited], *Four Favorites* #9 (New York: Periodical House, February 1943).
12. Charles de Gaulle Quote, https://www.goodreads.com/quotes/526167-patriotism-is-when-love-of-your-own-people-comes-first.

13. William A. Galston, "In Defense of a Reasonable Patriotism," Brookings Institute, July 23, 2018, https://www.brookings.edu/research/in-defense-of-a-reasonable-patriotism/.
14. Galston, "In Defense of a Reasonable Patriotism."
15. Jason Dittmer, *Captain America and the Nationalist Superhero: Metaphors, Narratives, and Geopolitics* (Philadelphia, PA: Temple University Press, 2013), p. 7.
16. Robert Jewett and John Shelton Lawrence, *Captain America and the Crusade Against Evil: The Dilemma of Zealous Nationalism* (Grand Rapids, MI: William B. Eerdmans Publishing, 2003), p. xiii.
17. Mark D. White, *The Virtues of Captain America: Modern-Day Lessons on Character from a World War II Superhero* (Oxford, UK: Wiley Blackwell, 2014), p. 171.
18. Paul Castiglia, "Introduction," *America's 1st Patriotic Hero: The Shield*, Paul Castiglia, ed. (New York: Archie Comics Publications Inc., 2002), p. 7.
19. Howe, *Marvel Comics: The Untold Story*, p. 18.
20. Daron Jensen et al, *Official Index to the Marvel Universe: Captain America* (New York: Marvel Entertainment, 2011), entries for all issues with cover dates in the 1940s.
21. Joe Simon and Jack Kirby, "Case No. 1: Meet Captain America," *Captain America Comics* #1 (New York: Timely Comics, March 1941).
22. Jack Kirby, *Captain America Comics* #2 (New York: Timely Comics, April 1941), cover; Al Avison, *Captain America Comics* #36 (New York: Timely Comics, March 1944), cover.
23. Mason Bissada, "First Comic Book Featuring Captain America Sells for Over $3 Million At Auction," *Forbes*, April 7, 2022, https://www.forbes.com/sites/masonbissada/2022/04/07/first-comic-book-featuring-captain-america-sells-for-over-3-million-at-auction/?sh=675035824b2e.
24. Dan Whitehead, "Kapow! A Talk with Joe Simon," www.simoncomics.com; Richard Hall, "The Captain America Conundrum: Issues of Patriotism, Race, and Gender in Captain America Comic Books, 1941–2001" (PhD diss, Auburn University, 2011), p. 32, https://etd.auburn.edu/xmlui/handle/10415/2760.
25. Simcha Weinstein, *Up, Up, and Oy Vey!: How Jewish History, Culture, and Values Shaped the Comic Book Superhero* (New York: Leviathan Press, 2006), 47.
26. Todd A. Burkhardt, "Captain America and the Ethics of Enhancement," *Philosophy Now* (November / December, 2007), 8, emphasis in the original; Hall, "The Captain America Conundrum," pp. 36–37.
27. Joe Simon and Jack Kirby, "Captain America and the Riddle of the Red Skull," *Captain America Comics* #1 (New York: Timely Comics, March 1941).
28. Brian Carnell, "Captain America's Sentinels of Liberty," April 10, 2021, https://brian.carnell.com/articles/2021/captain-americas-sentinels-of-liberty/.
29. Stan Lee and Al Avison, *Captain America Comics* #13 (cover) (New York: Timely Comics, April 1942), cover; Hall, "The Captain America Conundrum," p. 43.
30. Syd Shores and Al Avison, "The Tunnel of Terror," *Captain America Comics* #15 (New York: Timely Comics, June, 1942).
31. "Attention Americans!" *Captain America Comics* #15 (New York: Timely Comics, June 1942); Hall, "The Captain America Conundrum," pp. 44–45.
32. Stan Lee and Al Avison, "Your Life Depends On It" *Captain America Comics* #19 (New York: Timely Comics, October 1942).
33. Bill Woolfolk and Syd Shores, "Golden Girl," *Captain America Comics* #66 (New York: Timely Comics, April 1948).
34. "Captain America Comics Vol. 1 No. 66," Marvel database, https://marvel.fandom.com/wiki/Captain_America_Comics_Vol_1_66.
35. Howe, *Marvel Comics: The Untold Story*, p. 19–21.
36. Stan Lee, "Captain America Foils the Traitor's Revenge," *Captain America Comics* #3 (New York: Timely Comics, May 1941).
37. Paul S. Hirsch, *Pulp Empire: The Secret History of Comic Book Imperialism* (Chicago: University of Chicago Press, 2021), p. 46.
38. Paul Hirsch, "'This is Our Enemy': The Writers' War Board and Representations of Race in Comic Books, 1942–1945," *Pacific Historical Review* Vol. 83, No. 3 (Pacific Coast Branch, American Historical Association, 2014), p. 449.

39. Stan Lee and Charles Nicholas, "The Coming of Agent Zero," *Young Allies* #1 (New York: Timely Comics, June 1941).
40. Robert Jewett, *The Captain America Complex*, 2nd ed. (Santa Fe, NM: Bear & Company, 1984), p. 9.
41. Richard Reynolds, *Super Heroes: A Modern Mythology* (Jackson: University Press of Mississippi, 1992), p. 16.
42. Dittmer, *Captain America and the Nationalist Superhero*, p. 10.
43. Jason Dittmer, "Retconning America: Captain America in the Wake of World War II and the McCarthy Hearings," *The Amazing Transforming Superhero!: Essays on the Revision of Characters in Comic Books, Film, and Television*, Terrence R. Wandtke, ed. (Jefferson, NC: McFarland & Company, 2007), p. 40.
44. J. Richard Stevens, *Captain America, Masculinity, and Violence: The Evolution of a National Icon* (New York: Syracuse University Press, 2015), p. 55.
45. Stan Lee and Jack Kirby, "Captain America Joins... The Avengers!" *The Avengers* #4 (New York: Marvel Comics, March 1964).

Chapter 2

1. Richard M. Fried, *Nightmare in Red: The McCarthy Era in Perspective* (New York: Oxford University Press, 1990), p. 3.
2. Joseph McCarthy, "The Threat of Domestic Communism," speech delivered February 9, 1950, Congressional Record, 81st Congress, 2nd Session, 1950, Vol. 96, Pt. 2, 1954–57.
3. Matthew J. Costello, *Secret Identity Crisis: Comic Books & the Unmasking of Cold War America* (New York: Continuum Press, 2009), p. 32.
4. Robert Longley, "Communism vs. Socialism," ThoughtCo, December 1, 2022, https://www.thoughtco.com/difference-between-communism-and-socialism-195448.
5. Elaine Tyler May, *Homeward Bound: American Families in the Cold War Era* (New York: Basic Books, 1988), p. 113.
6. Hirsch, *Pulp Empire*, p. 169.
7. David Hajdu, *The Ten-Cent Plague: The Great Comic-Book Scare and How It Changed America* (New York: Farrar, Straus, and Giroux, 2008), pp. 233–234.
8. Frederic M. Thrasher, "The Comics and Delinquency: Cause or Scapegoat," *Journal of Educational Sociology*, Vol. 23, No. 4 (December 1949), pp. 195, 205.
9. Fredric Wertham, *Seduction of the Innocent* (Port Washington: Kennikat Press, 1972, c1954), pp. 12, 39, 72.
10. Hirsch, *Pulp Empire*, p. 193. Some information from excerpt originally footnoted as being taken from "Crime and Horror Comics Books in Foreign Countries," June 4, 1954, box 172, RG 46, NA.
11. "The Comics Code of 1954," Comic Book Legal Defense Fund, https://cbldf.org/the-comics-code-of-1954/.
12. Mark Evanier, "Wertham Was Right!" *Wertham Was Right!: Another Collection of POV Columns by Mark Evanier* (Raleigh, NC: TwoMorrows Publishing, 2003), pp. 176–195.
13. Daron Jensen, Al Sjoerdsma, and Stuart Vandal, *Official Index to the Marvel Universe: Captain America* (New York: Marvel Enterprises, 2011).
14. Simon, *My Life in Comics*, pp. 112–113.
15. Howe, *Marvel Comics: The Untold Story*, pp. 31–33.
16. Howe, *Marvel Comics: The Untold Story*, p. 29.
17. Stan Lee and Martin Nodell, "Captain America in the Red Skull Strikes Again!" *Captain America's Weird Tales* #74 (New York: Timely Comics, October 1949).
18. Don Rico, John Romita, Sr., and Mort Lawrence, "Back from the Dead!" *Young Men* #24 (New York: Atlas Comics, December 1953).
19. Stan Lee and John Romita, Sr., "The Betrayers," *Captain America* #76 (New York: Atlas Comics, May 1954).
20. Stan Lee and John Romita, Sr., "Captain America Strikes!" *Captain America* #76 (New York: Atlas Comics, May 1954).
21. Stan Lee and John Romita, Sr., "Come to the Commies!" *Captain America* #76 (New York: Atlas Comics, May 1954).
22. Lee and Romita, "Come to the Commies!"
23. Stan Lee and John Romita, Sr., "You Die at Midnight," *Captain America* #77 (New York: Atlas Comics, July 1954).
24. Stan Lee and John Romita, Sr., "The Man with No Face!" *Captain America* #77 (New York: Atlas Comics, July 1954).

25. Stan Lee and John Romita, Sr., "Captain America," *Captain America* #77 (New York: Atlas Comics, July 1954).
26. Stan Lee and John Romita, Sr., "His Touch is Death!" *Captain America* #78 (New York: Atlas Comics, September 1954).
27. Stan Lee and John Romita, Sr., "The Green Dragon!" *Captain America* #78 (New York: Atlas Comics, September 1954).
28. Stan Lee and John Romita, Sr., "The Hour of Doom!" *Captain America* #78 (New York: Atlas Comics, September 1954).
29. Simon, *My Life in Comics*, p. 188.
30. Joe Simon and Jack Kirby, "First Assignment: Break the Spy Ring," *Fighting American* #1 (New York: Prize Comics Group, April/May 1954).
31. Joe Simon and Jack Kirby, "Ask Fighting American and Speedboy about Space-Face," *Fighting American* #7 (New York: Prize Comics Group, April/May 1955).
32. Lee and Kirby, "Captain America Joins... The Avengers!"
33. Steve Englehart and Sal Buscema, "Captain America... Hero or Hoax?" *Captain America and the Falcon* #153 (New York: Marvel Comics, September 1972).
34. Dittmer, "Retconning America," pp. 48–49.
35. As of this writing, only a few of the 1940s issues of *Captain America Comics* are available on the app, but all three of the "Commie Smasher!" issues are available.
36. Stevens, *Captain America, Masculinity, and Violence*, pp. 67–68.
37. Wright, *Comic Book Nation*, p. 123.
38. Wright, *Comic Book Nation*, p. 183; Jeremy Dauber, *American Comics: A History* (New York: W.W. Norton & Company, 2022), p. 154.
39. Howe, *Marvel Comics: The Untold Story*, pp. 36–43; Wright, *Comic Book Nation*, pp. 201–215; Dauber, *American Comics: A History*, pp. 261–266 (and literally dozens of books, articles, and documentaries on the subject).
40. H.W. Brands, *American Dreams: The United States Since 1945* (New York: Penguin Books, 2010), pp. 82–84.
41. Brands, *American Dreams*, pp. 94–99.
42. Brands, *American Dreams*, pp. 84–91.

Chapter 3

1. Howe, *Marvel Comics: The Untold Story*, p. 38.
2. Stan Lee and Jack Kirby, *The Incredible Hulk* #1 (New York: Marvel Comics, May 1962), pp. 1–23.
3. Stan Lee and Jack Kirby, "Thor the Mighty and the Stone Men from Saturn!" *Journey Into Mystery* #83 (New York: Marvel Comics, August 1962), pp. 1–13.
4. Stan Lee and Jack Kirby, "The Coming of the Avengers," *The Avengers: Earth's Mightiest Heroes* #1 (New York: Marvel Comics, September 1963) pp. 1–23.
5. Stan Lee and Steve Ditko, "Spider-Man!" *Amazing Fantasy* #15 (New York: Marvel Comics, August 1962), pp. 1–11.
6. Howe, *Marvel Comics: The Untold Story*, p. 44.
7. Wright, *Comic Book Nation*, p. 217; Costello, *Secret Identity Crisis*, p. 1.
8. Howe, *Marvel Comics: The Untold Story*, p. 32.
9. Lee and Kirby, "Captain America Joins... The Avengers!"
10. Stan Lee and Don Heck, "In Mortal Combat with Captain America," *Tales of Suspense featuring the Power of Iron Man* #58 (New York: Marvel Comics, October 1964), pp. 1–18. In these issues, each story of an anthology title begins with page 1, but the above story was the first story of that issue.
11. Stan Lee and Jack Kirby, "The Strength of the Sumo!" *Tales of Suspense featuring Iron Man and Captain America* #61 (New York: Marvel Comics, January 1965), p. 5 of the second story.
12. Stan Lee and Jack Kirby, "The Origin of Captain America!" *Tales of Suspense featuring Iron Man and Captain America* #63 (New York: Marvel Comics, March 1965), pp. 1–10 of the second story.
13. Stan Lee and Jack Kirby, "The Sleeper Shall Awake!" *Tales of Suspense featuring Iron Man and Captain America* #72 (New York: Marvel Comics, December 1965), p. 4 of the second story.
14. Stan Lee and Gene Colan, "The Red Skull Lives!" *Tales of Suspense featuring Iron Man and Captain America* #79 (New York: Marvel Comics, July 1966), p. 5 of the second story.
15. Stan Lee and Gene Colan, "... And Men Shall Call Him Traitor!" *Tales of*

Suspense #90 (New York: Marvel Comics, March 1967).

16. "Cosmic Cube," Marvel online database, https://marvel.fandom.com/wiki/Cosmic_Cube (no original posting date given; accessed on November 30, 2022).

17. Stan Lee and Jack Kirby, "If This Be... MODOK!" *Tales of Suspense* #94 (New York: Marvel Comics, October 1967), pp. 4–5 of the second story.

18. Stan Lee and Jack Kirby, "The Sleeper Strikes," *Captain America* #102 (New York: Marvel Comics, June 1968), p. 7. After *Tales of Suspense* #99, Iron Man's adventures continued in *Iron Man* #1, but Captain America's self-titled book picked up with the numbering from *Tales*, his first issue being *Captain America* #100.

19. Stan Lee and Gene Colan, "The Coming of... The Falcon!" *Captain America* #117 (New York: Marvel Comics, September 1969); Lee and Colan, "Now Falls The Skull!" *Captain America* #119 (New York: Marvel Comics, November 1969).

20. Sean Howe, *Marvel Comics: The Untold Story* (New York: Harper/Perennial, 2012), p. 94.

21. Costello, *Secret Identity Crisis*, p. 13.

22. Costello, *Secret Identity Crisis*, p. 78.

23. Stevens, *Captain America, Masculinity, and Violence*, p. 95.

24. Stevens, *Captain America, Masculinity, and Violence*, p. 96.

25. Dittmer, *Captain America and the Nationalist Superhero*, p. 94.

26. Neil Armstrong's iconic quote from the moon (with the "a" added before "man," which is what he actually said).

Chapter 4

1. Stan Lee and Gene Colan, "The Sting of the Scorpion!" *Captain America* #122 (New York: Marvel Comics, February 1970), p. 3.

2. Gary Friedrich and John Romita, Sr., "Power to the People!" *Captain America and the Falcon* #143 (New York: Marvel Comics, November 1971).

3. Englehart and Buscema, "Captain America... Hero or Hoax?!"

4. Steve Englehart and Sal Buscema, "The Falcon Fights Alone!" *Captain America and the Falcon* #154 (New York: Marvel Comics, October 1972).

5. Steve Englehart and Sal Buscema, "The Incredible Origin of the OTHER Captain America!" *Captain America and the Falcon* #155 (New York: Marvel Comics, November 1972).

6. Englehart and Buscema, "The Incredible Origin of the OTHER Captain America!"

7. Steve Englehart and Sal Buscema, "Beware of Serpents!" *Captain America and the Falcon* #163 (New York: Marvel Comics, July 1973).

8. Steve Englehart and Sal Buscema, "When a Legend Dies!" *Captain America and the Falcon* #169 (New York: Marvel Comics, January 1974).

9. Englehart and Buscema, "When a Legend Dies!"

10. Steve Englehart and Sal Buscema, "... Before the Dawn!" *Captain America and the Falcon* #175 (New York: Marvel Comics, July 1974).

11. Englehart and Buscema, "... Before the Dawn!"

12. Steve Englehart and Sal Buscema, "Captain America Must Die!" *Captain America and the Falcon* #176 (New York: Marvel Comics, August 1974), Cover.

13. Englehart and Buscema, "Captain America Must Die!"

14. Englehart and Buscema, "Captain America Must Die!"

15. Steve Englehart and Sal Buscema, "The Coming of the Nomad!" *Captain America and the Falcon* #180 (New York: Marvel Comics, December 1974).

16. It's important to note here the difference between a revolution and a civil war, as both represent conflicts between governments and the population. A revolution occurs when the people are successful in overthrowing the standing government. If the government is successful in putting down the rebellion, it is labeled as a civil war.

17. Roger McKenzie and Sal Buscema, "Aftermath!" *Captain America* #231 (New York: Marvel Comics, March 1979).

18. Roger McKenzie and Sal Buscema, "From the Ashes...," *Captain America* #237 (New York: Marvel Comics September 1979).

19. McKenzie and Buscema, "From the Ashes...."

20. Stan Lee and John Romita, Sr., "The Unholy Alliance!" *Captain America and*

The Falcon #141 (New York: Marvel Comics, September 1971).
21. William Sloan Coffin, "Foreword," *The Captain America Complex: The Dilemma of Zealous Nationalism* 2nd ed., by Robert Jewett (Santa Fe, NM: Bear & Company, 1984), p. vii.
22. Dittmer, "Retconning America," pp. 48–49.
23. Stevens, *Captain America, Masculinity, and Violence*, pp. 106–107.
24. Dittmer, *Captain America and the Nationalist Superhero*, p. 137.
25. Stevens, *Captain America, Masculinity, and Violence*, p. 107.
26. Richard Hall, "Art Imitates Life: Nixon as Villain in the Pages of *Captain America*," *The Supervillain Reader*, Robert Moses Peaslee and Robert G. Weiner, eds (Jackson: University of Mississippi Press, 2020), p. 272.
27. Peter Coogan, *Superhero: The Secret Origin of a Genre* (Austin: MonkeyBrain Books, 2006), 212; Hall, "The Captain America Conundrum," p. 151.
28. Andrew and Virginia MacDonald, "Sold American: The Metamorphosis of Captain America," *Journal of Popular Culture*, Vol. 10, No. 2 (1976), pp. 249, 254; Hall, "The Captain America Conundrum," p. 151.
29. Reynolds, *Super Heroes*, 100–101; Hall, "The Captain America Conundrum," p. 151.
30. Steve Englehart and Frank Robbins, "Nomad: No More!" *Captain America and the Falcon* #183 (New York: Marvel Comics, March 1975).
31. Costello, *Secret Identity Crisis*, pp. 111–112.
32. Stevens, *Captain America, Masculinity, and Violence*, p. 112.

Chapter 5

1. "1980," The American Presidency Project, University of California, Santa Barbara, https://www.presidency.ucsb.edu/statistics/elections/1980.
2. As stated in the previous chapter, this claim discounts the two unanimous electoral victories of George Washington in 1788 and 1792, as the popular vote and campaigning had nothing to do with either of those elections.
3. "1984," The American Presidency Project, University of California, Santa Barbara, https://www.presidency.ucsb.edu/statistics/elections/1980.
4. "Assassination Attempt," (Online: Ronald Reagan Presidential Library and Museum), https://www.reaganlibrary.gov/permanent-exhibits/assassination-attempt (Accessed December 19, 2022).
5. Ronald Reagan, "Address to the Nation, January 28, 1986," (Online: NASA), https://history.nasa.gov/reagan12886.html (Accessed December 27, 2022).
6. "1988," The American Presidency Project, University of California, Santa Barbara, https://www.presidency.ucsb.edu/statistics/elections/1988.
7. "Inaugural Address 1981," Ronald Reagan Presidential Library and Museum, https://www.reaganlibrary.gov/archives/speech/inaugural-address-1981; "C-SPAN: President Reagan 1981 Inaugural Address," posted to YouTube January 14, 2009, C-SPAN, https://www.youtube.com/watch?v=hpPt7xGx4Xo.
8. "Historical U.S. Federal Individual Income Tax Rates & Brackets, 1862–2021," Tax Foundation, posted August 24, 2021, https://taxfoundation.org/historical-income-tax-rates-brackets/.
9. Bill Taylor, "Crime? Greed? Big Ideas? What Were the '80s About?," *Harvard Business Review* (Jan–Feb 1992), https://hbr.org/1992/01/crime-greed-big-ideas-what-were-the-80s-about.
10. *Wall Street*, Oliver Stone, writer/director (20th Century–Fox, 1987).
11. Kevin M. Kruse and Julian E. Zelizer, *Fault Lines: A History of the United States Since 1974* (New York: W.W. Norton & Company, 2019), p. 133.
12. Mike W. Barr and Frank Springer, "Fear Grows in Brooklyn!" *Captain America* #241 (New York: Marvel Comics, January 1980).
13. Roger Stern and John Byrne, "Cap for President!" *Captain America* #250 (New York: Marvel Comics, October 1980).
14. Stern and Byrne, "Cap for President!"
15. Peter Gillis and Jerry Bingham, "The Sins of the Fathers!" *Captain America* #246 (New York: Marvel Comics, June 1980).
16. Gillis and Bingham, "The Sins of the Fathers!"

17. J M. DeMatteis and Mike Zeck, "Sermon of Straw!" *Captain America* #280 (New York: Marvel Comics, April 1983).
18. J.M. DeMatteis and Mike Zeck, "Mean Streets!" *Captain America* #272 (New York: Marvel Comics, August 1982).
19. J.M. DeMatteis and Mike Zeck, "Yesterday's Shadows!" *Captain America* #275 (New York: Marvel Comics, November 1982); J.M. DeMatteis and Mike Zeck, "In Thy Image!" *Captain America* #277 (New York: Marvel Comics, January 1983).
20. J.M. DeMatteis and Paul Neary, "Things Fall Apart!" *Captain America* #296 (New York: Marvel Comics, August 1984).
21. Mark Gruenwald and Paul Neary, "Deface the Nation!" *Captain America* #312 (New York: Marvel Comics, December 1985).
22. Gruenwald and Neary, "Deface the Nation!"
23. Mark Gruenwald and Tom Morgan, "The Choice!" *Captain America* #332 (New York: Marvel Comics, August 1987).
24. Mark Gruenwald and Paul Neary, "Super-Patriot Is Here!" *Captain America* #323 (New York: Marvel Comics, November 1986); Mark Gruenwald and Tom Morgan, "The Replacement!" and "Basic Training!" *Captain America* # 333–334 (New York: Marvel Comics, September and October, 1987).
25. "Mark Gruenwald: 'New Captain America Here To Stay," *Comics Week* #2, July 20, 1987.
26. Mark Gruenwald and Kieron Dwyer, "Power Struggle!" *Captain America* #338 (New York: Marvel Comics, February 1988).
27. Mark Gruenwald and Kieron Dwyer, "Don't Tread on Me!" *Captain America* #344 (New York: Marvel Comics, August 1988).
28. Gruenwald and Dwyer, "Don't Tread on Me!"
29. Mark Gruenwald and Kieron Dwyer, "Seeing Red!" *Captain America* #350 (New York: Marvel Comics, February 1989).
30. Hall, "The Captain America Conundrum," p. 229.
31. Cord Scott, "The Alpha and the Omega: Captain America and the Punisher," *Captain America and the Struggle of the Superhero: Critical Essays*, Robert G. Weiner, Ed. (Jefferson, NC: McFarland & Company, 2009), p. 126.
32. Costello, *Secret Identity Crisis*, pp. 137–138.
33. Costello, *Secret Identity Crisis*, p. 157.
34. The original Yoda quote appeared in George Lucas's *Star Wars, Episode I: The Phantom Menace*. (Lucasfilm, 1999).
35. Stevens, *Captain America, Masculinity, and Violence*, p. 152.
36. Stevens, *Captain America, Masculinity, and Violence*, p. 182.
37. Jason Olsen, *Mark Gruenwald and the Star Spangled Symbolism of Captain America* (Jefferson, NC: McFarland & Company, 2021), p. 75.
38. Olsen, *Mark Gruenwald and the Star Spangled Symbolism*, p. 100.

Chapter 6

1. "Patrick Joseph Buchanan, 'Culture War Speech: Address to the Republican National Convention' (17 August 1992)," Voices of Democracy: The U.S. Oratory Project, https://voicesofdemocracy.umd.edu/buchanan-culture-war-speech-speech-text/.
2. "1992," The American Presidency Project, University of California, Santa Barbara, https://www.presidency.ucsb.edu/statistics/elections/1992.
3. Peter Bernstein, "Technological Change and First-Class Letter Mail," *Diffusion to the Wire: Studies in Diffusion and Regulation of Telecommunications Technology*, Allan Shampine, ed. (Hauppauge, NY: Nova, 2003), p. 94.
4. The term "boarding and bagging" refers to placing a comic book in a clear mylar bag, backing it with a white piece of cardboard (to prevent bending or otherwise damaging the book), and storing it—with other comics—in custom-built cardboard boxes. This phenomenon opened an entirely new area for the industry producing and selling the bags, boards, and boxes.
5. It is important to note that a major contributing factor to the large sales numbers on *X-Men* #1 was the added gimmick of selling *five* different covers for the single issue. Four of the covers could be placed side by side to form a larger mosaic, while the fifth was a fold-out cover featuring all four previous covers merged into

the larger picture. Both fans and investors sought to own all five versions.

6. *Star Trek VI: The Undiscovered Country*, Nicholas Meyer, dir. (Paramount Pictures, 1991).

7. *Star Trek VI: The Undiscovered Country*.

8. Mark Gruenwald and Ron Lim, "I Am Legend!" *Captain America* #383 (New York: Marvel Comics, March 1991).

9. Gruenwald and Lim, "I Am Legend!"

10. Gruenwald and Lim, "I Am Legend!"

11. Mark Gruenwald and Dave Hoover, "Fighting Chance, Part One: Super Patriot Games!" *Captain America* #425 (New York: Marvel Comics, March 1994).

12. Mark Waid and Ron Gamey, "Operation: Rebirth, Chapter One: Old Soldiers Never Die!" *Captain America* #445 (New York: Marvel Comics, November 1995).

13. Mark Waid and Adam Kubert, *Onslaught: Marvel Universe* (New York: Marvel Comics, 1996).

14. Jeph Loeb and Rob Liefeld, *Captain America* (Vol. II), #1 (New York: Marvel Comics, November 1996).

15. Mark Waid and Ron Gamey, "Power and Glory, Chapter One: Credibility Gap!" *Captain America* (Vol. III), #5 (New York: Marvel Comics, May 1998).

16. Mark Waid and Dale Eaglesham, "Power and Glory, Chapter Three: Hoax!" *Captain America* (Vol. III), #7 (New York: Marvel Comics, July 1998).

17. Dan Jurgens and Bob Layton, "America Lost! Part II of IV," *Captain America* (Vol. III), #46 (New York: Marvel Comics, October 2001).

18. Brian David-Marshall and Igor Kordey, "Relics," *Captain America* (Vol. III), #50 (New York: Marvel Comics, February 2002).

19. Jennifer Van Meter and Brian Hurtt, "A Moment of Silence," *Captain America* (Vol. III), #50 (New York: Marvel Comics, February 2002).

20. Costello, *Secret Identity Crisis*, pp. 164–165.

21. Costello, *Secret Identity Crisis*, p. 205.

22. Stevens, *Captain America, Masculinity, and Violence*, p. 207.

23. Stevens, *Captain America, Masculinity, and Violence*, p. 183.

24. Dittmer, *Captain America and the Nationalist Superhero*, pp. 94–95.

25. Olsen, *Mark Gruenwald and the Star Spangled Symbolism*, p. 244.

26. David Walton, "'Captain America Must Die': The Many Afterlives of Steve Rogers," *Captain America and the Struggle of the Superhero: Critical Essays* (Jefferson, NC: McFarland & Company, 2009), pp. 170–172.

Chapter 7

1. "2000," The American Presidency Project, University of California, Santa Barbara, https://www.presidency.ucsb.edu/statistics/elections/2000.

2. Benjamin Wittes, "What Ben Franklin Really Said," *Lawfare*, posted July 15, 2011, https://www.lawfareblog.com/what-ben-franklin-really-said.

3. Kruse and Zelizer, *Fault Lines*, p. 253.

4. This is a paraphrase (and likely oversimplification) of the description of the practice given in the 2011 HBO film *Too Big to Fail* (directed by Curtis Hanson), based on the 2009 Viking Press book *Too Big to Fail: The Inside Story of How Wall Street and Washington Fought to Save the Financial System—and Themselves* by *New York Times* financial journalist Andrew Ross Sorkin. There is also an excellent summation (for those who want more than the movie offers, but more concise than the book) in Kruse and Zelizer's *Fault Lines*, pp. 290–295.

5. Kimberly Amadeo, "2008 Financial Crisis Timeline: Critical Events in the Worst Crisis Since the Depression," The Balance, updated April 30, 2022, https://www.thebalancemoney.com/2008-financial-crisis-timeline-3305540.

6. Amadeo, "2008 Financial Crisis Timeline."

7. "The Economics Daily: Increase in Unemployment Rate in January 2009," U.S. Bureau of Labor Statistics, February 10, 2009, https://www.bls.gov/opub/ted/2009/feb/wk2/art02.htm.

8. "2008," The American Presidency Project, University of California, Santa Barbara, https://www.presidency.ucsb.edu/statistics/elections/2008.

9. John Ney Rieber and John Cassaday, "Enemy, Chapter One: Dust," *Captain America* Vol. IV, #1 (New York: Marvel Comics, June 2002).

10. Rieber and Cassaday, "Enemy, Chapter One: Dust."
11. Rieber and Cassaday, "Enemy, Chapter One: Dust."
12. Rieber and Cassaday, "Enemy, Chapter One: Dust."
13. John Ney Rieber and John Cassaday, "Enemy, Chapter Three: Soft Targets," *Captain America* Vol. IV, #3 (New York: Marvel Comics, August 2002).
14. Chuck Austen and Jae Lee, *Captain America* Vol. IV #10 (New York: Marvel Comics, May 2003).
15. Mark Millar and Bryan Hitch, "Super-Human," *The Ultimates* #1 (New York: Marvel Comics, March 2002).
16. Ed Brubaker and Steve Epting, "Out of Time, Part 6," *Captain America* Vol. V #6 (New York: Marvel Comics, June 2005); Brubaker and Epting, "The Winter Soldier, Part 1," *Captain America* Vol. V #8 (New York: Marvel Comics, September 2005).
17. Thomas Paine, "The Crisis," History. Org, https://www.ushistory.org/paine/crisis/c-01.htm.
18. Mark Millar and Steven McNiven, *Civil War* #1 (New York: Marvel Comics, July 2006).
19. Mark Millar and Steven McNiven, *Civil War* #7 (New York: Marvel Comics, January 2007).
20. Ed Brubaker and Steve Epting, "The Death of the Dream Part One," *Captain America* Vol. V, #25 (New York: Marvel Comics, April 2007).
21. Jewett and Lawrence, *Captain America and the Crusade Against Evil*, p. 8.
22. Jewett and Lawrence, *Captain America and the Crusade Against Evil*, p. 8.
23. Jewett and Lawrence, *Captain America and the Crusade Against Evil*, p. 14.
24. Jewett and Lawrence, *Captain America and the Crusade Against Evil*, p. 324.
25. Costello, *Secret Identity Crisis*, pp. 217, 219.
26. Stevens, *Captain America, Masculinity, and Violence*, p. 216.
27. Robert G. Weiner, "Sixty-Five Years of Guilt Over the Death of Bucky," *Captain America and the Struggle of the Superhero: Critical Essays*, Robert G. Weiner, ed. (Jefferson, NC: McFarland & Company, 2009), pp. 99–100.
28. John McGuire, "Captain America in the 21st Century: The Battle for the Ideology of the American Dream," *Marvel Comics' Civil War and the Age of Terror: Critical Essays on the Comic Saga*, Kevin Michael Scott, Ed. (Jefferson, NC: McFarland & Company, 2015), p. 159.
29. Stevens, *Captain America, Masculinity, and Violence*, p. 254.
30. Mara Wood, "Moral Decisions in Marvel's *Civil War*: Stages of Hero Development," *Captain America vs. Iron Man: Freedom, Security, Psychology (Unauthorized)*, Travis Langley, ed. (New York: Sterling Press, 2016), p. 21.
31. Tommy Cash and Travis Langley, "Punching Hitler: Symbols in Red, White, Blue, and Gold," *Captain America vs. Iron Man: Freedom, Security, Psychology (Unauthorized)*, Travis Langley, ed. (New York: Sterling Press, 2016), p. 61.
32. Alan Kistler and Billy San Juan, "Codes of Masculinity: The Road to Conflict," *Captain America vs. Iron Man: Freedom, Security, Psychology (Unauthorized)*, Travis Langley, Ed. (New York: Sterling Press, 2016), p. 87.
33. Daniel Davis Wood, "Whose Side is the Law On?: Living with Legalistic Absurdity in Marvel's *Civil War*," *Marvel Comics' Civil War and the Age of Terror: Critical Essays on the Comic Saga*, Kevin Michael Scott, Ed. (Jefferson, NC: McFarland & Company, 2015), p. 34.
34. Kathleen McClancy, "Iron Curtain Man versus Captain American Exceptionalism: World War II and Cold War Nostalgia in the Age of Terror," *Marvel Comics' Civil War and the Age of Terror: Critical Essays on the Comic Saga*, Kevin Michael Scott, Ed. (Jefferson, NC: McFarland & Company, 2015), p. 118.
35. Costello, *Secret Identity Crisis*, pp. 238–239.
36. Costello, *Secret Identity Crisis*, p. 240.

Chapter 8

1. "2016," The American Presidency Project, University of California, Santa Barbara, https://www.presidency.ucsb.edu/statistics/elections/2016.
2. Kruse and Zelizer, *Fault Lines*, p. 358.
3. Ed Brubaker and Luke Ross, "Two Americas," *Captain America* #602 (New York: Marvel Comics, March 2010). After

#50 of Volume V, all concepts of "volumes" were put aside, with the next issue listed as #600, placing all previous "volumes" in line with the original, for one continuous line of books.

4. Brubaker and Ross, "Two Americas."
5. Brubaker and Ross, "Two Americas."
6. Brubaker and Ross, "Two Americas."
7. Ed Brubaker and Luke Ross, "Two Americas, Part Two of Four," *Captain America* #603 (New York: Marvel Comics, April 2010).
8. Brubaker and Ross, "Two Americas, Part Two of Four."
9. Ed Brubaker and Luke Ross, "Two Americas, Part Three of Four," *Captain America* #604 (New York: Marvel Comics, May 2010).
10. Ed Brubaker and Dale Eaglesham, *Steve Rogers: Super Soldier* #1 (New York: Marvel Comics, September 2010).
11. Ed Brubaker and Mike Deodato, Jr., *Secret Avengers* #1 (New York: Marvel Comics, July 2010).
12. Rick Remender and Carlos Pacheco, "The Tomorrow Soldier: Conclusion," *Captain America* Vol. VII (?) #25 (New York: Marvel Comics, December 2014).
13. Rick Remender and Stuart Immonen, *All-New Captain America* #1–6 (New York: Marvel Comics, January–June 2015).
14. Rick Remender and Stuart Immonen, *All-New Captain America* #6 (New York: Marvel Comics, June 2015).
15. Remender and Immonen, *All-New Captain America* #1–6.
16. Nick Spencer and Daniel Acuna, *Captain America: Sam Wilson* #1 (New York: Marvel Comics, December 2015).
17. Spencer and Acuna, *Captain America: Sam Wilson* #1.
18. Spencer and Acuna, *Captain America: Sam Wilson* #1.
19. Spencer and Acuna, *Captain America: Sam Wilson* #1.
20. Spencer and Acuna, *Captain America: Sam Wilson* #1.
21. Spencer and Acuna, *Captain America: Sam Wilson* #1.
22. Spencer and Acuna, *Captain America: Sam Wilson* #1.
23. Nick Spencer and Jesus Saiz, *Captain America: Steve Rogers* #1 (New York: Marvel Comics, July 2016), title page.
24. Spencer and Saiz, *Captain America: Steve Rogers* #1.
25. Spencer and Saiz, *Captain America: Steve Rogers* #1, final page.
26. Spencer and Saiz, *Captain America: Steve Rogers* #1.
27. See Chapter 4 for full discussion of this storyline.
28. Nick Spencer, Rod Reis, and Daniel Acuna, *Secret Empire* #0 (New York: Marvel Comics, June 2017).
29. Nick Spencer and Andrea Sorrentino, *Free Comic Book Day 2017 (Secret Empire)* #1 (New York: Marvel Comics, July 2017), final page.
30. Nick Spencer and Paul Renaud, *Generations: Sam Wilson Captain America & Steve Rogers Captain America* #1 (New York: Marvel Comics, September 2017).
31. John McGuire, "Captain America in the 21st Century," pp. 159–161.
32. Stevens, *Captain America, Masculinity, and Violence*, p. 266.
33. Stevens, *Captain America, Masculinity, and Violence*, pp. 268–269.

Chapter 9

1. *Comic Book Superheroes Unmasked*, Steve Kroopnick, dir. (History Channel, 2003); "Comic Book Superheroes Unmasked (History Channel Documentary—2003)," posted to YouTube May 26, 2013 by DarkStar659, https://www.youtube.com/watch?v=Ygx_rUJ3XaI (accessed October 9, 2023).
2. *Captain America* (serial), Elmer Clifton and John English, dirs. (Republic Pictures, 1944); "1944 Captain America Movie," posted to YouTube May 15, 2017, Movies and Serials, https://www.youtube.com/watch?v=FjkZmESYVM4; Cord Scott and Robert G. Weiner, "A Selected Filmographic Essay," *Captain America and the Struggle of the Superhero: Critical Essays*, Robert G. Weiner, Ed. (Jefferson, NC: McFarland & Company, 2009), pp. 218–219.
3. "Captain America Intro (1966)," posted to YouTube February 18, 2012 by hewey1972, https://www.youtube.com/watch?v=8ZpQ9hZi34A.
4. *Captain America*, Rod Holcomb, dir. (Universal Television, 1979); *Captain America II: Death Too Soon*, Ivan Nagy, dir. (Universal Television, 1979); Scott and Weiner, "A Selected Filmographic Essay," pp. 221–222.

5. *Captain America*, Albert Pyun, dir. (20th Century–Fox, 1990); Scott and Weiner, "A Selected Filmographic Essay," pp. 222–223.

6. All MCU films discussed in this section are available for viewing on the Disney+ streaming platform.

7. *Captain America: The First Avenger*, Joe Johnston, dir. (Marvel Studios, 2011).

8. "Box Office History for Captain America Movies," *The Numbers*, https://www.the-numbers.com/movies/franchise/Captain-America#tab=summary.

9. "Box Office History for Marvel Cinematic Universe Movies," *The Numbers*, https://www.the-numbers.com/movies/franchise/Marvel-Cinematic-Universe#tab=summary.

10. *Marvel's The Avengers*, Joss Whedon, dir. (Disney/Marvel Studios, 2012).

11. *Captain America: The Winter Soldier*, Anthony and Joe Russo, dirs. (Disney/Marvel Studios, 2014).

12. "Box Office History for Captain America Movies," *The Numbers*, https://www.the-numbers.com/movies/franchise/Captain-America#tab=summary.

13. *Avengers: Age of Ultron*, Joss Whedon, Dir. (Disney/Marvel Studios, 2015).

14. *Avengers: Age of Ultron*.

15. *Captain America: Civil War*, Anthony and Joe Russo, dirs. (Disney/Marvel Studios, 2016).

16. "Box Office History for Captain America Movies."

17. *Avengers: Infinity War*, Anthony and Joe Russo, dirs. (Disney/Marvel Studios, 2018).

18. *Avengers: Infinity War*.

19. *Avengers: Endgame*, Anthony and Joe Russo, dirs. (Disney/Marvel Studios, 2019).

20. "Box Office History for Marvel Cinematic Universe Movies."

21. White, *The Virtues of Captain America*, pp. 182–186.

22. Stevens, *Captain America, Masculinity, and Violence*, p. 261.

23. *Captain America: The First Avenger*.

24. Stevens, *Captain America, Masculinity, and Violence*, p. 286.

25. Stevens, *Captain America, Masculinity, and Violence*, p. 287.

Chapter 10

1. Robert Morales and Kyle Baker, *Captain America: Truth* (Collected Volume) (New York: Marvel Comics, 2009). Originally published monthly as *Truth: Red, White, and Black* #1–7 (New York: Marvel Comics, January–July 2003).

2. *The Falcon and the Winter Soldier*, Kari Skogland, dir. (Disney/Marvel Studios: Disney+, 2021).

3. *The Falcon and the Winter Soldier*.

Conclusion

1. "One World, One People," *The Falcon and The Winter Soldier*, Season 1, Episode 6, Kari Skogland, dir. (Disney/Marvel Studios: Disney+, 2021).

Bibliography

Books / Articles

Bernstein, Peter. "Technological Change and First-Class Letter Mail." In *Diffusion to the Wire: Studies in Diffusion and Regulation of Telecommunications Technology*, Allan Shampine, ed., 94. Hauppauge, NY: Nova, 2003.

Brands, H.W. *American Dreams: The United States Since 1945*. New York: Penguin Books, 2010.

Brands, H.W. *Traitor to His Class: The Privileged Life and Radical Presidency of Franklin Delano Roosevelt*. New York: Doubleday. 2008.

"Captain America." *Official Handbook of the Marvel Universe—Master Edition, Vol. 1: Abomination to Gargoyle*. New York: Marvel Comics, 2008 (the original "Official Handbook" was published in several single issues published 1991–1993).

Cash, Tommy, and Travis Langley. "Punching Hitler: Symbols in Red, White, Blue, and Gold." In *Captain America vs. Iron Man: Freedom, Security, Psychology (Unauthorized)*, Travis Langley, ed., 55–64. New York: Sterling Press, 2016.

Coogan, Peter. *Superhero: The Secret Origin of a Genre*. Austin, TX: MonkeyBrain Books, 2006.

Costello, Matthew J. *Secret Identity Crisis: Comics Books & the Unmasking of Cold War America*. New York: Continuum Books, 2009.

Dauber, Jeremy. *American Comics: A History*. New York: W.W. Norton & Company, 2022.

Dittmer, Jason. *Captain America and the Nationalist Superhero: Metaphors, Narratives, and Geopolitics*. Philadelphia, PA: Temple University Press, 2013.

Dittmer, Jason. "Retconning America: Captain America in the Wake of World War II and the McCarthy Hearings." In *The Amazing Transforming Superhero!: Essays on the Revision of Characters in Comic Books, Film, and Television*, Terrence R. Wandtke, ed., 33–51. Jefferson, NC: McFarland, 2007.

Evanier, Mark. "Wertham Was Right!" In *Wertham Was Right!: Another Collection of POV Columns by Mark Evanier*. Raleigh, NC: TwoMorrows Publishing, 2003.

Fried, Richard M. *Nightmare in Red: The McCarthy Era in Perspective*. New York: Oxford University Press, 1990.

Hajdu, David. *The Ten-Cent Plague: The Great Comic-Book Scare and How It Changed America*. New York: Farrar, Straus, and Giroux, 2008.

Hall, Richard. "Art Imitates Life: Nixon as Villain in the Pages of *Captain America*." In *The Supervillain Reader*, Robert Moses Peaslee and Robert G. Weiner, eds., 266–273. Jackson, MS: University of Mississippi Press, 2020.

Hall, Richard A. "The Captain America Conundrum: Issues of Patriotism, Race, and Gender in Captain America Comic Books, 1941–2001." PhD diss., Auburn University, 2011. https://etd.auburn.edu/xmlui/handle/10415/2760.

Harmon, Jim, and Donald F. Glut. *The Great Movie Serials: Their Sound and Fury*. Oxford, UK: Routledge, 1973.

Hirsch, Paul. "'This is Our Enemy': The Writers' War Board and Representations of Race in Comic Books, 1942–1945." *Pacific Historical Review* Vol. 83, No. 3. University of California Press: Pacific Coast Branch, American Historical Association, 2014, 448–486.

Hirsch, Paul S. *Pulp Empire: The Secret History of Comic Book Imperialism*. Chicago: University of Chicago Press, 2021.

Howe, Sean. *Marvel Comics: The Untold Story*. New York: Harper/Perennial, 2012.

Jensen, Daron, Al Sjoerdsma, and Stuart Vandal. *Official Index to the Marvel Universe: Captain America*. New York: Marvel Entertainment, 2011.

Jewett, Robert. *The Captain America Complex*, 2nd ed. Santa Fe, NM: Bear & Company, 1984.

Jewett, Robert, and John Shelton Lawrence. *Captain America and the Crusade Against Evil: The Dilemma of Zealous Nationalism*. Grand Rapids, MI: William B. Eerdmans Publishing, 2003.

Kistler, Alan, and Billy San Juan. "Codes of Masculinity: The Road to Conflict." In *Captain America vs. Iron Man: Freedom, Security, Psychology (Unauthorized)*, Travis Langley, ed., 77–90. New York: Sterling Press, 2016.

Kruse, Kevin M., and Julian E. Zelizer. *Fault Lines: A History of the United States Since 1974*. New York: W.W. Norton & Company, 2019.

MacDonald, Andrew and Virginia. "Sold American: The Metamorphosis of Captain America." *Journal of Popular Culture*, Vol. 10, No. 2, 1976: 248–260.

May, Elaine Tyler. *Homeward Bound: American Families in the Cold War Era*. New York: Basic Books, 1988.

McCarthy, Joseph. "The Threat of Domestic Communism." Speech delivered February 9, 1950. Congressional Record, 81st Congress, 2nd Session, 1950, Vol. 96, Pt. 2, 1954–57.

McClancy, Kathleen. "Iron Curtain Man versus Captain American Exceptionalism: World War II and Cold War Nostalgia in the Age of Terror." In *Marvel Comics' Civil War and the Age of Terror: Critical Essays on the Comic Saga*, Kevin Michael Scott, ed., 108–119. Jefferson, NC: McFarland, 2015.

McGuire, John. "Captain America in the 21st Century: The Battle for the Ideology of the American Dream." In *Marvel Comics' Civil War and the Age of Terror: Critical Essays on the Comic Saga*, Kevin Michael Scott, ed., 150–163. Jefferson, NC: McFarland, 2015.

Nama, Adilifu. *Super Black: American Pop Culture and Black Superheroes*. Austin, TX: University of Texas Press, 2011.

Olsen, Jason. *Mark Gruenwald and the Star Spangled Symbolism of Captain America*. Jefferson, NC: McFarland, 2021.

Reynolds, Richard. *Super Heroes: A Modern Mythology*. Jackson: University of Mississippi Press, 1994.

Scott, Cord. "The Alpha and the Omega: Captain America and the Punisher." In *Captain America and the Struggle of the Superhero: Critical Essays*, Robert G. Weiner, ed., 125–134. Jefferson, NC: McFarland, 2009.

Scott, Cord, and Robert G. Weiner. "A Selected Filmographic Essay." In *Captain America and the Struggle of the Superhero: Critical Essays*, Robert G. Weiner, ed., 218–226. Jefferson, NC: McFarland, 2009.

Simon, Joe. *My Life in Comics*. London, UK: Titan Books, 2011.

Stevens, J. Richard. *Captain America, Masculinity, and Violence: The Evolution of a National Icon*. New York: Syracuse University Press, 2015.

Thrasher, Frederic M. "The Comics and Delinquency: Cause or Scapegoat." *Journal of Educational Sociology*, Vol. 23, No. 4. American Sociological Association, December 1949.

Tye, Larry. *Superman: The High-Flying History of America's Most Enduring Hero*. New York: Random House, 2012.

Walton, David. "'Captain America Must Die': The Many Afterlives of Steve Rogers." In *Captain America and the Struggle of the Superhero: Critical Essays*, Robert G. Weiner, ed., 160–175. Jefferson, NC: McFarland, 2009.

Weiner, Robert G. "Sixty-Five Years of Guilt Over the Death of Bucky." In *Captain America and the Struggle of the Superhero: Critical Essays*, Robert G. Weiner, ed., 90–103. Jefferson, NC: McFarland, 2009.

Weinstein, Simcha. *Up, Up, and Oy Vey!: How Jewish History, Culture, and Values Shaped the Comic Book Superhero*. New York: Leviathan Press, 2006.

Wertham, Fredric. *Seduction of the Innocent*. Port Washington: Kennikat Press, 1972, c1954.

White, Mark D. *The Virtues of Captain America: Modern-Day Lessons on Char-*

acter from a World War II Superhero. Oxford, UK: Wiley Blackwell, 2014.

Wood, Daniel Davis. "Whose Side is the Law On?: Living with Legalistic Absurdity in Marvel's Civil War." In *Marvel Comics' Civil War and the Age of Terror: Critical Essays on the Comic Saga*, Kevin Michael Scott, ed., 26–35. Jefferson, NC: McFarland, 2015.

Wood, Mara. "Moral Decisions in Marvel's Civil War: Stages of Hero Development." In *Captain America vs. Iron Man: Freedom, Security, Psychology (Unauthorized)*, Travis Langley, ed., 11–24. New York: Sterling Press, 2016.

Wright, Bradford W. *Comic Book Nation: The Transformation of Youth Culture in America*. Baltimore, MD: Johns Hopkins University Press, 2003.

Comic Books / Graphic Novels

[All Captain America comic books accessed via the Marvel Unlimited *digital comics app.]*

Austen, Chuck, and Jae Lee. *Captain America* Vol. IV #10. New York: Marvel Comics. May 2003.

Avison, Al. *Captain America Comics* #36. New York: Timely Comics. March 1944.

Barr, Mike W., and Frank Springer. *Captain America* #241. New York: Marvel Comics. January 1980.

Brubaker, Ed, and Mike Deodato, Jr. *Secret Avengers* #1. New York: Marvel Comics. July 2010.

Brubaker, Ed, and Dale Eaglesham. *Steve Rogers: Super Soldier* #1. New York: Marvel Comics. September 2010.

Brubaker, Ed, and Steve Epting. *Captain America* Vol. V #6. New York: Marvel Comics. June 2005.

Brubaker, Ed, and Steve Epting. *Captain America* Vol. V #8. New York: Marvel Comics. September 2005.

Brubaker, Ed, and Steve Epting. *Captain America* Vol. V #25. New York: Marvel Comics. April 2007.

Brubaker, Ed, and Luke Ross. *Captain America* #602. New York: Marvel Comics. March 2010.

Brubaker, Ed, and Luke Ross. *Captain America* #603. New York: Marvel Comics. April 2010.

Brubaker, Ed, and Luke Ross. *Captain America* #604. New York: Marvel Comics. May 2010.

Castiglia, Paul. "Introduction." *America's 1st Patriotic Hero: The Shield*. Paul Castiglia, ed. New York: Archie Comics Publications. 2002.

David-Marshall, Brian, and Igor Kordey. "Relics." *Captain America* Vol. III #50. New York: Marvel Comics. February 2002.

DeMatteis, J.M., and Paul Neary. *Captain America* #296. New York: Marvel Comics. August 1984.

DeMatteis, J.M., and Mike Zeck. *Captain America* #272. New York: Marvel Comics. August 1982.

DeMatteis, J.M., and Mike Zeck. *Captain America* #275. New York: Marvel Comics. November 1982.

DeMatteis, J.M., and Mike Zeck. *Captain America* #277. New York: Marvel Comics. January 1983.

DeMatteis, J.M., and Mike Zeck. *Captain America* #280. New York: Marvel Comics. April 1983.

Englehart, Steve, and Sal Buscema. *Captain America and the Falcon* #153. New York: Marvel Comics. September 1972.

Englehart, Steve, and Sal Buscema. *Captain America and the Falcon* #154. New York: Marvel Comics. October 1972.

Englehart, Steve, and Sal Buscema. *Captain America and the Falcon* #155. New York: Marvel Comics. November 1972.

Englehart, Steve, and Sal Buscema. *Captain America and the Falcon* #163. New York: Marvel Comics. July 1973.

Englehart, Steve, and Sal Buscema. *Captain America and the Falcon* #169. New York: Marvel Comics. January 1974.

Englehart, Steve, and Sal Buscema. *Captain America and the Falcon* #175. New York: Marvel Comics. July 1974.

Englehart, Steve, and Sal Buscema. *Captain America and the Falcon* #176. New York: Marvel Comics. August 1974.

Englehart, Steve, and Sal Buscema. *Captain America and the Falcon* #180. New York: Marvel Comics. December 1974.

Englehart, Steve, and Frank Robbins. *Captain America and the Falcon* #183. New York: Marvel Comics. March 1975.

Friedrich, Gary, and John Romita, Sr. *Captain America and the Falcon* #143. New York: Marvel Comics. November 1971.

Gillis, Peter, and Jerry Bingham. *Captain America* #246. New York: Marvel Comics. June 1980.

Gruenwald, Mark, and Kieron Dwyer. *Captain America* #338. New York: Marvel Comics. February 1988.

Gruenwald, Mark, and Kieron Dwyer. *Captain America* #344. New York: Marvel Comics. August 1988.

Gruenwald, Mark, and Kieron Dwyer. *Captain America* #350. New York: Marvel Comics. February 1989.

Gruenwald, Mark, and Dave Hoover. *Captain America* #425. New York: Marvel Comics. March 1994.

Gruenwald, Mark, and Ron Lim. *Captain America* #383. New York: Marvel Comics. March 1991.

Gruenwald, Mark, and Tom Morgan. *Captain America* #332. New York: Marvel Comics. August 1987.

Gruenwald, Mark, and Tom Morgan. *Captain America* #333. New York: Marvel Comics. September 1987.

Gruenwald, Mark, and Tom Morgan. *Captain America* #334. New York: Marvel Comics. October 1987.

Gruenwald, Mark, and Paul Neary. *Captain America* #312. New York: Marvel Comics. December 1985.

Gruenwald, Mark, and Paul Neary. *Captain America* #323. New York: Marvel Comics. November 1986.

Jurgens, Dan, and Bob Layton. *Captain America* Vol. III #46. New York: Marvel Comics. October 2001.

Lee, Stan. "Captain America Foils the Traitor's Revenge." *Captain America Comics* #3. New York: Timely Comics. May 1941.

Lee, Stan, and Al Avison. *Captain America Comics* #13. New York: Timely Comics. April 1942.

Lee, Stan, and Al Avison. *Captain America Comics* #19. New York: Timely Comics. October 1942.

Lee, Stan, and Gene Colan. *Captain America* #117. New York: Marvel Comics. September 1969.

Lee, Stan, and Gene Colan. *Captain America* #119. New York: Marvel Comics. November 1969.

Lee, Stan, and Gene Colan. *Captain America* #122. New York: Marvel Comics. February 1970.

Lee, Stan, and Gene Colan. *Tales of Suspense featuring Iron Man and Captain America* #79. New York: Marvel Comics. July 1966.

Lee, Stan, and Gene Colan. *Tales of Suspense* #90. New York: Marvel Comics. March 1967.

Lee, Stan, and Steve Ditko. *Amazing Fantasy* #15. New York: Marvel Comics. August 1962.

Lee, Stan, and Don Heck. *Tales of Suspense featuring the Power of Iron Man* #58. New York: Marvel Comics. October 1964.

Lee, Stan, and Jack Kirby. *The Avengers* #1. New York: Marvel Comics. September 1963.

Lee, Stan, and Jack Kirby. *The Avengers* #4. New York: Marvel Comics. March 1964.

Lee, Stan, and Jack Kirby. *Captain America* #102. New York: Marvel Comics. June 1968.

Lee, Stan, and Jack Kirby. *The Incredible Hulk* #1. New York: Marvel Comics. May 1962.

Lee, Stan, and Jack Kirby. *Journey Into Mystery* #83. New York: Marvel Comics. August 1962.

Lee, Stan, and Jack Kirby. *Tales of Suspense featuring Iron Man and Captain America* #61. New York: Marvel Comics. January 1965.

Lee, Stan, and Jack Kirby. *Tales of Suspense featuring Iron Man and Captain America* #63. New York: Marvel Comics. March 1965.

Lee, Stan, and Jack Kirby. *Tales of Suspense featuring Iron Man and Captain America* #72. New York: Marvel Comics. December 1965.

Lee, Stan, and Jack Kirby. *Tales of Suspense* #94. New York: Marvel Comics. October 1967.

Lee, Stan, and Charles Nicholas. *Young Allies* #1. New York: Timely Comics. June 1941.

Lee, Stan, and Martin Nodell. *Captain America's Weird Tales* #74. New York: Timely Comics. October 1949.

Lee, Stan, and John Romita, Sr. *Captain America* #76. New York: Atlas Comics. May 1954.

Lee, Stan, and John Romita, Sr. *Captain America* #77. New York: Atlas Comics. July 1954.

Lee, Stan, and John Romita, Sr. *Captain*

Bibliography

America #78. New York: Atlas Comics. September 1954.
Lee, Stan, and John Romita, Sr. *Captain America and The Falcon* #141. New York: Marvel Comics. September 1971.
Loeb, Jeph, and Rob Liefeld. *Captain America* Vol. II #1. New York: Marvel Comics. November 1996.
McKenzie, Roger, and Sal Buscema. *Captain America* #231. New York: Marvel Comics. March 1979.
McKenzie, Roger, and Sal Buscema. *Captain America* #237. New York: Marvel Comics. September 1979.
Millar, Mark, and Bryan Hitch. *The Ultimates* #1. New York: Marvel Comics. March 2002.
Millar, Mark, and Steven McNiven. *Civil War* #1. New York: Marvel Comics. July 2006.
Millar, Mark, and Steven McNiven. *Civil War* #7. New York: Marvel Comics. January 2007.
Morales, Robert, and Kyle Baker. *Captain America: Truth* (Collected Volume). New York: Marvel Comics. 2009. Originally published monthly as *Truth: Red, White, and Black* #1–7. New York: Marvel Comics. January–July 2003.
Remender, Rick, and Stuart Immonen. *All-New Captain America* #1–6. New York: Marvel Comics. January–June 2015.
Remender, Rick, and Carlos Pacheco. *Captain America* Vol. VII (?) #25. New York: Marvel Comics. December 2014.
Rico, Don, John Romita, Sr., and Mort Lawrence. *Young Men* #24. New York: Atlas Comics. December 1953.
Rieber, John Ney, and John Cassaday. *Captain America* Vol. IV #1. New York: Marvel Comics. June 2002.
Rieber, John Ney, and John Cassaday. *Captain America* Vol. IV #3. New York: Marvel Comics. August 2002.
Shores, Syd, and Al Avison. *Captain America Comics* #15. New York: Timely Comics. June 1942.
Simon, Joe, and Jack Kirby. *Captain America Comics* #1. New York: Timely Comics. March 1941.
Simon, Joe, and Jack Kirby. *Captain America Comics* #2. New York: Timely Comics. April 1941.
Simon, Joe, and Jack Kirby. *Fighting American* #1. New York: Prize Comics Group. April/May 1954.
Simon, Joe, and Jack Kirby. *Fighting American* #7. New York: Prize Comics Group. April/May 1955.
Spencer, Nick, and Daniel Acuna. *Captain America: Sam Wilson* #1. New York: Marvel Comics. December 2015.
Spencer, Nick, and Paul Renaud. *Generations: Sam Wilson Captain America & Steve Rogers Captain America* #1. New York: Marvel Comics. September 2017.
Spencer, Nick, and Jesus Saiz. *Captain America: Steve Rogers* #1. New York: Marvel Comics. July 2016.
Spencer, Nick, and Andrea Sorrentino. *Free Comic Book Day 2017 (Secret Empire)* #1. New York: Marvel Comics. July 2017.
Spencer, Nick, Rod Reis, and Daniel Acuna. *Secret Empire* #0. New York: Marvel Comics. June 2017.
Stern, Roger, and John Byrne. *Captain America* #250. New York: Marvel Comics. October 1980.
Van Meter, Jennifer, and Brian Hurtt. "A Moment of Silence." *Captain America* Vol. III #50. New York: Marvel Comics. February 2002.
Waid, Mark, and Dale Eaglesham. *Captain America* Vol. III #7. New York: Marvel Comics. July 1998.
Waid, Mark, and Ron Gamey. *Captain America* #445. New York: Marvel Comics. November 1995.
Waid, Mark, and Ron Gamey. *Captain America* Vol. III #5. New York: Marvel Comics. May 1998.
Waid, Mark, and Adam Kubert. *Onslaught: Marvel Universe*. New York: Marvel Comics. 1996.
Woolfolk, Bill, and Syd Shores. *Captain America Comics* #66. New York: Timely Comics. April 1948.

Online Sources

Amadeo, Kimberly. "2008 Financial Crisis Timeline: Critical Events in the Worst Crisis Since the Depression." The Balance, updated April 30, 2022. https://www.thebalancemoney.com/2008-financial-crisis-timeline-3305540.
"Assassination Attempt." Ronald Reagan Presidential Library and Museum. https://www.reaganlibrary.gov/permanent-exhibits/assassination-attempt.

Bissada, Mason. "First Comic Book Featuring Captain America Sells For Over $3 Million At Auction." *Forbes*, April 7, 2022. https://www.forbes.com/sites/masonbissada/2022/04/07/first-comic-book-featuring-captain-america-sells-for-over-3-million-at-auction/?sh=675035824b2e.

"Box Office History for Captain America Movies." The Numbers. https://www.the-numbers.com/movies/franchise/Captain-America#tab=summary.

"Box Office History for Marvel Cinematic Universe Movies." The Numbers. https://www.the-numbers.com/movies/franchise/Marvel-Cinematic-Universe#tab=summary.

"C-SPAN: President Reagan 1981 Inaugural Address." C-SPAN. Posted to YouTube January 14, 2009. https://www.youtube.com/watch?v=hpPt7xGx4Xo.

"Captain America Comics Vol 1 66." Marvel Database. https://marvel.fandom.com/wiki/Captain_America_Comics_Vol_1_66.

"Captain America Intro (1966)." Posted to YouTube February 18, 2012. https://www.youtube.com/watch?v=8ZpQ9hZi34A.

Carnell, Brian. "Captain America's Sentinels of Liberty." April 10, 2021. https://brian.carnell.com/articles/2021/captain-americas-sentinels-of-liberty/.

"Comic Book Superheroes Unmasked (History Channel Documentary—2003)." Posted to YouTube May 26, 2013. https://www.youtube.com/watch?v=Ygx_rUJ3XaI.

"The Comics Code of 1954." Comic Book Legal Defense Fund. https://cbldf.org/the-comics-code-of-1954/.

"Cosmic Cube." Marvel Database. https://marvel.fandom.com/wiki/Cosmic_Cube (no original posting date given).

"Economics Daily: Increase in Unemployment Rate in January 2009." U.S. Bureau of Labor Statistics, posted February 10, 2009. https://www.bls.gov/opub/ted/2009/feb/wk2/art02.htm.

Galston, William A. "In Defense of a Reasonable Patriotism." Brookings Institute, July 23, 2018. https://www.brookings.edu/research/in-defense-of-a-reasonable-patriotism/.

"Historical U.S. Federal Individual Income Tax Rates & Brackets, 1862–2021" Tax Foundation, August 24, 2021. https://taxfoundation.org/historical-income-tax-rates-brackets/.

"Inaugural Address 1981." Ronald Reagan Presidential Library and Museum. https://www.reaganlibrary.gov/archives/speech/inaugural-address-1981.

Longley, Robert. "Communism vs. Socialism." ThoughtCo, December 1, 2022. https://www.thoughtco.com/difference-between-communism-and-socialism-195448.

McNamara, Carolyn. "'Sentinel of Liberty': Captain America on the Home Front in WWII." UT Research Showcase, University of Texas–Austin, October 2, 2015. https://research.utexas.edu/showcase/articles/view/sentinel-of-liberty-captain-america-on-the-home-front-in-wwii.

"1980." The American Presidency Project. University of California, Santa Barbara. https://www.presidency.ucsb.edu/statistics/elections/1980.

"1988." The American Presidency Project. University of California, Santa Barbara. https://www.presidency.ucsb.edu/statistics/elections/1988.

"1984." The American Presidency Project. University of California, Santa Barbara. https://www.presidency.ucsb.edu/statistics/elections/1984.

"1940 Electoral College Results." National Archives Online. https://www.archives.gov/electoral-college/1940.

"1944 Captain America Movie." YouTube. https://www.youtube.com/watch?v=FjkZmESYVM4.

"1992." The American Presidency Project. University of California, Santa Barbara. https://www.presidency.ucsb.edu/statistics/elections/1992.

"Our Documents: Lend Lease." FDR Library Online. http://docs.fdrlibrary.marist.edu/odlendls.html.

Paine, Thomas. "The Crisis." History.Org. https://www.ushistory.org/paine/crisis/c-01.htm.

"Patrick Joseph Buchanan, 'Culture War Speech: Address to the Republican National Convention' (17 August 1992)." Voices of Democracy: The U.S. Oratory Project. https://voicesofdemocracy.

umd.edu/buchanan-culture-war-speech-speech-text/.

Reagan, Ronald. "Address to the Nation, January 28, 1986." NASA. https://history.nasa.gov/reagan12886.html.

Rosenman, Samuel I., Ed. *The Public Papers and Addresses of Franklin D. Roosevelt, 1940.* New York: Macmillan, 1941. Library of Congress website, https://web.mit.edu/21h.102/www/Primary%20source%20collections/World%20War%20II/FDR,%20Arsenal%20of%20Democracy.html.

Taylor, Bill. "Crime? Greed? Big Ideas? What Were the '80s About?" *Harvard Business Review.* January–February 1992. https://hbr.org/1992/01/crime-greed-big-ideas-what-were-the-80s-about.

"2000." The American Presidency Project. University of California, Santa Barbara. https://www.presidency.ucsb.edu/statistics/elections/2000.

"2008." The American Presidency Project. University of California, Santa Barbara. https://www.presidency.ucsb.edu/statistics/elections/2008.

"2016." The American Presidency Project. University of California, Santa Barbara. https://www.presidency.ucsb.edu/statistics/elections/2016.

Whitehead, Dan. "Kapow! A Talk with Joe Simon." Simon Comics. www.simoncomics.com [defunct].

Wittes, Benjamin. "What Ben Franklin Really Said." Lawfare, July 15, 2011. https://www.lawfareblog.com/what-ben-franklin-really-said.

Filmography

Avengers: Age of Ultron. Joss Whedon, dir. Disney/Marvel Studios. 2015.

Avengers: Endgame. Anthony and Joe Russo, dirs. Disney/Marvel Studios. 2019.

Avengers: Infinity War. Anthony and Joe Russo, dirs. Disney/Marvel Studios. 2018.

Captain America. Albert Pyun, dir. 20th Century–Fox. 1990.

Captain America (Movie Serial). Elmer Clifton and John English, dirs. Republic Pictures. 1944.

Captain America. Rod Holcomb, dir. Universal Television. 1979.

Captain America: Civil War. Anthony and Joe Russo, dirs. Disney/Marvel Studios. 2016.

Captain America II: Death Too Soon. Ivan Nagy, dir. Universal Television. 1979.

Captain America: The First Avenger. Joe Johnston, dir. Marvel Studios. 2011.

Captain America: The Winter Soldier. Anthony and Joe Russo, dirs. Disney/Marvel Studios. 2014.

Comic Book Superheroes Unmasked. Steve Kroopnick, dir. The History Channel. 2003.

Falcon and the Winter Soldier, The. Kari Skogland, dir. Disney/Marvel Studios: Disney+. 2021.

Marvel's The Avengers. Joss Whedon, dir. Disney/Marvel Studios. 2012.

Star Trek VI: The Undiscovered Country. Nicholas Meyer, dir. Paramount Pictures. 1991.

Star Wars, Episode I: The Phantom Menace. George Lucas, dir. Lucasfilm. 1999.

Wall Street. Oliver Stone, writer/director. 20th Century–Fox. 1987.

Index

Advanced Idea Mechanics 82–83, 159
Affordable Care Act 194, 196
Age of Ultron 201, 224–226
Agent 13 14, 83–84, 155, 157; death 109–110
AIDS 95–96, 116–120, 146; *see also* HIV
AIM *see* Advanced Idea Mechanics;
 American Indian Movement
Al-Qaeda 140, 144–145, 184, 189; *see also* 9/11
All-Negro Comics 15, 31
Amalgam Comics 150, 152, 201
Amazon *see* websites
American Indian Movement 72
American Nazi Party 109
assassinations 68, 75–76, 88, 186; *see also* Kennedy, John F.; Kennedy, Robert F.; King, Martin Luther, Jr.
Atlas Comics 15, 18, 57–58, 64–66, 77–80
Atwell, Hayley 222, 231
authoritarianism 51–52, 230
automakers 169; *see also* Ford, Henry
The Avengers 12, 15, 43, 78, 80–82, 84, 107, 133, 155, 156, 177, 204, 221–226; comic book 18, 62, 80, 82, 156, 221, 223; films 12, 201, 223–225, 229; modern take 158–162; secret 182, 186–187; young 206
Avengers: Age of Ultron see *Age of Ultron*
Avengers: Endgame see *Endgame*
Avengers: Infinity War see *Infinity War*
Avison, Al 35

Baby Boomers 54, 97, 112, 219; *see also* Greatest Generation
Baker, Kyle 16, 178, 234
bankruptcy: Marvel 13, 141, 150, 156, 221; 2008 Economic Crisis 168–169
Banks, Dennis 72
Barnes, Bucky *see* Bucky
Baron Zemo *see* Zemo
Batman 2, 5, 6–8, 14, 18, 25, 36–37, 40, 47, 65–66, 80, 88, 103, 105, 124–126, 146, 153, 165, 209, 216, 217, 226; comics 36, 55, 125, 148–150; film 13, 143, 124–125, 147, 175, 200, 201, 220, 222, 223; live action 218, 222
Batman: The Dark Knight Returns 115–116
Battlestar 133, 233
Bay of Pigs 73–74
Bellecourt, Clyde 72
Berlin 73–74, 117
Berlin Wall 77, 117, 153
Bezos, Jeff 143
Biden, Joe 170–172
Bin-Laden, Osama 117, 144–45, 166–168, 176
Black Panther 16, 84, 201, 221, 225–226, 233
Black Widow 15, 80, 204, 221, 223, 224, 226
BlackBerry 197–199
Bold Urban Commandoes *see* BUCkies
Boomers *see* Baby Boomers
Boseman, Chadwick *see* Black Panther
Bradley, Isaiah 7, 10, 16, 235, 236, 237–238
Brown, Reb 13, 219–221
Brown v. Board of Education of Topeka, Kansas 67–68
Brubaker, Ed 178
Bruce Banner 78, 80, 219, 223, 224, 226; *see also* The Hulk
BUCkies 133
Bucky 1, 7, 12, 14, 17, 36–40, 43–44, 58–61, 63–64, 80, 104, 107, 155, 156, 177–179, 181, 182, 185–186, 190, 193, 202–207, 212–2145, 218, 219, 224, 230, 233, 236–238; *see also* Captain America
Buscema, Sal 102
Bush, George H.W. 118–120, 139, 141–142, 165–168, 170, 171, 172, 178, 186, 188, 202–204, 212; doctrine 182
Bush, George, W. 1, 146, 165, 170

263

264 Index

The Captain 132
Captain America *see* Bucky; Rogers, Steve; Walker, John; Wilson, Sam
Captain America: comic 2, 7–8, 15–16, 17–18, 28, 34–37, 39, 57–59; death 158, 164–190, 210; film 5, 19, 12, 13, 14; letters 9–10; 1944 serial 57, 216; telefilm 219–222
Captain America and the Falcon 63, 102–103, 233
Captain America: Civil War 9, 132, 155, 200–201, 225
"Captain America No More" 132–133, 135
Captain America: Sam Wilson 205–207
Captain America: The First Avenger 2, 5, 8–9, 12, 14, 201, 217, 221–222, 228, 236
Captain America: The Winter Soldier 221, 225, 229
Captain America: Truth see Truth: Red, White, and Black
Captain America II: Death Too Soon 13, 219–221
Captain America's Weird Tales 58–59
Captain Carter *see* Carter, Peggy
Captain Marvel 6, 21, 25, 216–217, 220; *see also* Danvers, Carol
Carter, Jimmy 108, 116–117, 139; *see also* Malaise Speech
Carter, Peggy 7, 84, 105, 107, 231
Carter, Sharon *see* Agent 13
Castro, Fidel 74
cellular telephones 143–144, 162, 166–167, 197; *see also* iPhone
Challenger 119, 122
Chavez, Cesar 72
China 26, 50, 52, 60, 75, 91, 116, 140, 159, 162, 199
Civil Rights Act 71
Civil War 29, 68, 70, 75, 90, 97, 108, 175, 187, 192, 228
Civil War 17–18, 180–183, 185–186, 188–190, 205, 210, 212
Clinton, Bill 139, 141–144, 155–156, 165, 172
Clinton, Hillary 142, 171, 195, 226
"Clone Saga" 125, 149
CNN 1, 122, 172, 186
Coalition for an Upstanding America *see* CUA
Cold War 11, 15, 17, 41, 45, 46, 48–51, 52–53, 60, 62, 64–65, 67, 69, 72–75, 79, 87–88, 91, 97–98, 116–120, 122–124, 136, 139, 140–142, 151–155, 157–159, 161–163, 175, 179, 184, 189–190
Collectors' Bubble 116, 125, 140, 147, 152; burst 140–152, 156
Comics Code Authority 56, 101

"Commie Smasher" 8, 16, 17, 44, 46–68, 75, 108, 110, 185, 203
Committee to Re-elect the President 92, 105
Committee to Regain America's Principles *see* CRAP
Communism 47–55, 59, 61, 65, 67, 69, 73, 74, 75, 90, 115–116, 123, 140, 153, 159, 190
Congress for Racial Equality *see* CORE
consensus 3, 23, 50–55, 67–69, 87, 90, 103, 109, 136, 183
conservatism 6, 118, 129, 181
Containment Theory 53–54
Contras *see* Iran-Contra Affair
Coppola, Fracis Ford 101
CORE 71
Cosmic Cube 82–84, 208, 210, 214
COVID 196, 200, 202, 214
Cox, Dave 105, 111
CRAP 105
CREEP *see* Committee to Re-elect the President
"Crisis of Confidence" 91–95, 113
Crisis on Infinite Earths 125, 148–149
CUA 129
Cuba 51, 69, 73–75, 140; *see also* Bay of Pigs
Cuban Missile Crisis 74
Culture Wars 190–191, 192

Dallas 115, 121, 123
Danvers, Carol 102, 201, 205; *see also* Captain Marvel
Daredevil 2, 9, 13, 67, 78–79, 175
"Dark Phoenix Saga" 125
"Days of Future Past" 125
DC Comics 2, 24, 37, 43, 55, 57, 66, 79, 80, 101, 124, 150, 201, 217, 223, 238
"Death of Superman" 125, 141, 149, 181–182
Degeneres, Ellen 146
DeMatteis, J.M. 16, 126–27, 129, 131
democrat 22, 50, 51, 74, 94, 116, 119, 139, 141, 142, 153, 165–166, 170–171, 172, 193–194, 195–197, 203, 204, 207, 226; party 75–76, 116, 225
Desert Storm *see* Operation Desert Shield
détente 91, 98, 116
Disney 14, 23, 132, 201–202, 217, 223, 231, 235
Dittmer, Jason 32, 41–42, 63, 88, 110, 111, 160
Doctor Erskine *see* Erskine, Abraham
Doctor King *see* King, Martin Luther, Jr.
Doctor Reinstein 36, 81, 234; *see also* Super Soldier Serum

Index

Doctor Strange 67, 78, 80, 201, 219, 220, 221, 226, 231
Domino Theory 50
Downey, Robert, Jr. 221–223
Dynasty 121, 123

Eisenhower, Dwight D. 67, 92, 203
Ellsberg, Daniel 92
Endgame 5, 201 217, 227, 230–231, 235
Englehart, Steve 16, 63, 102, 104–105, 106, 110, 111, 112, 209, 240
Equal Rights Amendment 33, 95, 97, 118, 136; *see also* 1972
Erskine, Abraham 81, 234–236
Evans, Chris 1, 5, 12, 14, 175, 209, 213, 215, 216, 220, 221, 227, 241; *see also Captain America the First Avenger*
Evans, Orrin Cromwell *see All-Negro Comics*
Executive Order 8802 30
Executive Order 9066 30

Facebook 191, 193, 198, 199
Falcon *see* Wilson, Sam
The Falcon and the Winter Soldier 14, 18, 132, 230, 232, 235, 237, 241
fan letters *see* letters
Fantastic Four 13, 14, 16, 66–67, 75, 77–79, 82, 85, 156, 175, 177, 179, 188, 221
fascism 6, 17, 21, 30, 42, 44, 47, 51–53, 103, 190
FDR *see* Roosevelt, Franklin D.
The Feminine Mystique see Friedan, Betty
feminism 97
fighting American 62; comic book 61–62
Flag-Smasher 131; in MCU 236
Flash 43, 66, 150, 217
Ford, Gerald 93–94, 98–99, 113
Ford, Henry 22, 26; *see also* automakers 169
Fox News 122, 172, 186, 195, 197
Friedan, Betty 72–73
Friends 145

Gay Liberation Front 96
Generation-X 97, 100, 115, 121, 123, 141, 145–147
Generations: Sam Wilson Captain America & Steve Rogers Captain America
G.I. Joe 83, 160
Goetz, Bernhard 128, 134
Golden Girl 39, 59, 84
Goodman, Martin 25, 27, 39, 57–58, 66, 77, 79

Google *see* websites
Great Depression 6, 17–18, 22, 44–45, 47, 54, 65, 76, 81, 91, 97, 100, 103, 116, 121, 125, 152, 164, 203, 209, 232, 239, 240
Great Recession 164, 168–170
Greatest Generation 45, 54, 85, 88, 90, 96, 181, 182, 241; *see also* Baby Boomers
Ground Zero 74, 157, 176, 240
Gruenwald, Mark 126–127, 32, 132, 133, 137–138, 154–155, 158, 161

Harlem 63, 84, 104, 130, 233, 237
Harlem, Ace 31
Harlem Rennaisance 23
Hate-Monger 82, 157
Hawkeye 15, 80, 205, 206, 221, 223
"Heroes Reborn" 140–163, 177
"Heroes Return" 157, 172–175
Hill, Maria 180
Hitler, Adolf 6–7, 21, 26–27, 28, 32, 36, 44, 50, 51, 61, 82, 223
HIV *see* AIDS
Hoskins, Lemar *see* Battlestar
House Un-American Activities Committee 48
Huerta, Dolores 72
The Hulk 2, 13, 67, 79, 80, 132, 150, 175, 188, 205, 206, 218, 221, 223, 229; film 222; TV show 216, 219
Human Torch 14, 15, 25, 58, 60, 65, 78, 107, 180, 221
Hussein, Saddam 117, 141, 168
Hydra 1, 17, 82–83, 158, 182, 192–215, 229, 237

Image Comics 147, 149, 151, 156, 200
Immigration Reform and Control Act of 1986 118
impeach 143, 196, 214
Infinity Gauntlet 226
Infinity Saga 227
Infinity Stones 226
Infinity War 201, 204, 224, 226–227
inflation 94, 98, 99
internet 9, 81, 86, 104, 138, 140, 143–144, 146, 147, 151, 157, 161, 162, 165, 191, 198, 207, 213
The Invaders 107, 124
iPhone 144, 197–198; *see also* cellular telephones
Iran-Contra Affair 118–119
Iran Hostage Crisis 113, 116
Iron Curtain 48, 50, 123
Iron Man 2, 15, 18, 67, 78, 80, 86, 107, 160, 179, 180, 186–187, 189, 205–206, 2018, 225–227, 229; comic book 81, 156, 188,

228; film 12, 153, 165, 175, 186, 191, 201, 221, 223 see also Downey, Robert Jr.; Stark, Tony

Jackson, Michael 115, 122
Jackson, Samuel L. 178, 223, 224
JFK see Kennedy, John F.
Jihad 117, 144–145, 166, 184
Johnson, Lyndon B. 71, 74, 75–76, 92, 113
Johnston, Joe 222
Jurgens, Dan 149
Justice League of America 66, 77, 201

Kennedy, John F. 71, 75–76, 81, 91, 145
Kennedy, Robert F. 75–76, 91
King, Martin Luther, Jr. 71–72, 75–76, 91
Kirby, Jack 7, 27, 28, 35, 36, 37, 39, 42, 43, 44, 58, 61–62, 66, 70, 77–80, 81, 82, 83, 87, 88, 102, 108, 219, 222

laissez-faire 22, 120
Latchkey Kid 97, 100, 145
LBJ see Johnson, Lyndon B.
Leave It to Beaver 76, 90, 97
Lee, Stan 35, 39, 43, 57, 58, 62–63, 66, 69, 77, 79, 80, 82, 85, 101, 102, 105, 111, 161, 233
letters 85–86, 62, 79, 85; letters page and letters to editor 10, 79, 85
LGBTQ+ 33, 46, 52, 68, 73, 88, 90, 95, 96, 97, 100, 113, 118, 126, 131, 142, 146, 159, 161, 162, 231
liberalism 6, 47, 129, 181
Lincoln, Abraham 192
Little Rock Nine 68
Long Telegram 53
Lumbly, Carl 236–237

Mackie, Anthony 14, 149, 214, 224, 230, 231, 235, 237, 241
MAD see Mutually Assured Destruction
MAGA 197
Malaise Speech 94, 129
Malcolm X 75
Marvel Cinematic Universe 9–10, 12–14, 17, 21, 34, 81, 84, 88, 132, 155, 157, 175, 178–179, 182, 184, 186, 191, 204, 207, 209, 211, 213, 215, 217, 219–232, 235–238
Marvel Comics 1, 6, 13, 17, 18, 25, 39, 43, 50, 62, 67, 69, 77, 78, 79, 80, 87, 106, 108, 136, 141, 147, 150, 151, 156, 165, 175, 178–179, 182, 186, 188, 191, 205, 206, 209, 211, 213, 216, 219, 225, 233
Marvel Studios 2, 12, 14, 175, 191, 200–201, 221, 227, 229, 231
The Marvel Superheroes 217–219

Marvel's The Avengers see *The Avengers*, films
M*A*S*H 100, 123
Master of the Mystic Arts see Doctor Strange
McAuliffe, Christa 119
McCarthy, Joe 45, 47, 49, 61
McCarthyism 14, 47, 49, 61, 63
MCU see Marvel Cinematic Universe
Men's Adventures 57, 59
Mitchell, George 72
MLK see King, Martin Luther, Jr.
moderate 9–11, 13, 91, 142, 210, 215
MODOK 83, 109, 157
Morales, Robert 16, 178, 234
MTV 115, 122
Mueller Report 196
Mutually Assured Destruction 47, 66, 74

NAACP 68, 71
Namor 80, 218; see also Sub-Mariner
NASA 67
National Force 108–109
National Organization for Women 73, 95
nationalism 6, 17, 21, 31–35, 40, 110, 131, 183, 192
Nazi 6–8, 25–28, 33, 36, 37, 38, 43, 48, 57, 61, 64, 65, 70, 81–83, 87, 107–109, 130, 138, 154, 156, 161, 189–190, 206, 209, 229, 234
Nick Fury 15, 78, 80, 82, 84, 109, 157, 158, 176, 177, 178, 223, 229, 230
9/11 1, 2, 16–18, 33, 40, 146, 152–153, 157, 159, 162, 164–165, 166–168, 172–185, 189, 190, 194, 197, 203, 204, 229, 234, 241
1940 World's Fair 30
1968 91; American Indian Movement 72; Movement AGAINST the Vietnam War 75; presidential election 76
1972 63, 101, 102, 104, 116, 234; see also Equal Rights Amendment
Nixon, Richard 49, 61, 91–93, 98, 99, 105–106, 111–13, 116, 141, 209, 240
Nomad 112
North Korea 15, 50, 51, 60, 140, 168
NOW see National Organization for Women
nuclear war 45, 53, 74, 159
nuclear weapons 91, 116

Obama, Barack 153, 170–171, 180, 186, 190, 192, 193–195, 197–199, 202–204, 208, 212, 231, 233
Obamacare see Affordable Care Act
Onslaught 156, 162
OPEC 98
Operation Desert Shield 141, 144

Index

Operation Rebirth 81
Organization of Petroleum Exporting Countries *see* OPEC

Parker, Peter *see* Spider-Man
patriotism 6, 17, 21, 32–34, 38, 42, 94, 111, 115, 138, 186, 228, 240
Pearl Harbor 7, 15, 21, 29, 30, 35, 37, 38, 70, 76, 116, 145, 240
Peggy Carter *see* Carter, Peggy
Port Huron Statement 72
Presley, Elvis 54, 69
presidential election: 1972 92; 1976 94; 1980 17, 94, 95, 115, 116, 129; 1984 118, 171; 2000 164, 172; 2008 170; 2016 209
Pride Day 73
progressivism 109–110
Punisher 9, 126–128, 132, 134, 135, 150, 155, 206
Purcell, Dick 12, 218

Quicksilver 80, 150, 224

racism 27, 30, 39–40, 43, 44–45, 46, 53, 70–72, 103, 108–109, 193, 231, 232–233, 235, 236
Randolph, A. Philip 30, 43, 71
Reagan, Ronald 17, 94, 99, 113–114, 115–120, 123, 126–132, 134–138, 140, 203
Reaganomics 120
Red Skull 16, 37–38, 42, 58, 80, 82–84, 103, 112, 130, 134, 138, 153–155, 157–158, 182, 206, 208–209, 219–220, 222
Republican Party 48, 118, 167, 171, 193, 204
Rieber, John Ney 176, 184
Roe v. Wade 95–96
Rogers, Steve 2, 7–8, 15, 17–19, 35–36, 41, 43–44, 80–81, 87, 108, 111, 113, 132–135, 137–138, 155–156, 185–186, 190, 202, 203, 205, 209–211, 212–215, 222, 230, 240; death 17, 58–59, 158–162, 164–191, 228–229; fascism 17, 59; film 13–14, 224–225; live action 12–13; love *see* Carter, Peggy and Carter, Sharon; 9/11 176–178; Nomad 226–227; powers 8–9; race 63, 103–107, 237–238; shield 9; *see also* Bucky; Walker, John; Wilson, Sam
Roosevelt, Franklin D. 22, 23, 27–31, 35, 42, 44
Ross, Betsy *see* Golden Girl
Roth, Arnie 34, 130
Russo brothers 224

Salinger, Matt 13, 220
San Diego Comic-Con *see* SDCC
Scarlet Witch 15, 80, 205, 223–226

science fiction 25, 47, 66, 76–77, 138, 239
SCLC 68, 71
SDCC 200
SDI *see* Strategic Defense Initiative
SDS 72
Secret Avengers 182, 187, 204
Secret Empire 82, 109, 111, 113, 240
Secret Empire 105–107, 111–112, 209, 210–213
Seduction of the Innocent 57; *see also* Wertham, Fredric
Seinfeld 145
Sentinels of Liberty 37
September 11 *see* 9/11
Sesame Street 100, 145
Shazam *see* Captain Marvel
She-Hulk 15, 102, 201
S.H.I.E.L.D. 105, 107, 109–111, 157, 176, 180, 181, 204, 207, 208, 223, 224, 229, 230, 235
The Shield 35–36
Shore, Syd 35
Simon, Joe 7, 27–28, 35–36, 39, 42, 44, 58, 61–62, 222
Sin 206
16th Street Baptist Church 71
slavery 70–72, 100, 181, 233
Smith, Kevin 146
social relevance 99–102, 126
socialism 51–52, 208
Southern Christian Leadership Conference *see* SCLC
Soviet Union 15, 28, 41, 47–48, 50, 51, 61, 67, 69, 73, 75, 77, 81, 91, 116–117, 140, 153, 154, 158, 159, 179, 189, 199, 215
Spider-Man 2, 8, 9, 13, 14, 18, 36, 60, 67, 78, 79, 101–103, 105, 125, 127, 148, 150, 151, 153, 156, 165, 175, 178–178, 181, 209, 217, 219, 221, 225, 226
Sputnik 67
stagflation 97–99
Stan, Sebastian 179, 224, 235
Star Trek 34, 76, 123, 146, 153, 192, 200, 205
Star Wars 2, 24, 101, 123, 124, 125, 192, 199–202, 205, 222
Star Wars *see* Strategic Defense Initiative
Stark, Tony 78, 80, 81, 186, 187, 205, 224; *see also* Downey, Robert, Jr.; Iron Man
Steve Rogers: Super Soldier 204
Stevens, Richard, J. 42, 64, 87, 88, 110, 111, 113, 136, 137, 159–160, 186, 212–213, 228–229, 230
Stonewall Riots 73, 98
Strategic Defense Initiative 117
Students for a Democratic Society *see* SDS

Sub-Mariner 15, 25, 58, 65, 80, 107, 218; *see also* Namor
Super-Soldier 33, 150
Super Soldier Serum 237–238; *see also* Doctor Reinstein
Superman 2, 5, 6, 7, 8, 11, 18, 21, 24, 29, 36–37, 40, 47, 52, 55, 57, 58, 65, 66–67, 79–81, 88, 101, 103, 105, 124, 125, 141, 149, 150, 153, 173, 175, 181, 182, 200, 201, 209, 216, 217, 220, 223, 226

Tales of Suspense 80–83, 85, 86
Tarantino, Quentin 146
Tea Party 171, 193, 203–204, 213
television 5, 11, 13, 47, 49, 53, 57, 58, 60–61, 64–66, 68, 69, 71, 76, 81, 90, 95, 97, 99, 101, 105, 108, 115, 117, 121–123, 126, 141, 143, 145–147, 150, 158, 160, 165, 173–174, 193, 198, 200, 216–220, 228, 240
terrorism 17, 109, 145, 167–168, 173, 184, 189, 241
Tet Offensive 92
Thanos 226
THEM 53, 82
Thor 67, 78, 107, 157, 201, 205, 218, 221, 223, 226, 229
332nd Fighter Group 29, 137
Till, Emmett 68
Timely Comics 25, 27, 35, 38, 39, 57, 107, 218
Titanic 146, 174
Title IX 95–96
Tonkin Resolution 74
ToyBiz 150
Trickle-down Economics *see* Reaganomics
Truman, Harry 29, 31, 48, 53
Trump, Donald 120–121, 129, 135, 174, 190, 192, 195–197, 198, 200, 208, 209, 214–215, 226
Truth: Red, White, and Black 16, 18, 47, 68, 178, 232–238
Tuskegee Experiments 16, 29, 178, 234, 235
TV *see* television
20th Century Fox 13, 14, 150, 172, 201, 202, 221, 225
Twitter 191, 193, 198, 199
"Two Americas" 17, 192–215
2008 Economic Crisis *see* bankruptcy

The Ultimates 177
Ultron 201, 224–226
The Uncanny X-Men 2, 8, 125, 127, 151
The United States of Captain America 213
U.S. Agent 135, 138, 155, 206; *see also* Walker, John

USA PATRIOT Act 167
USSR *see* Soviet Union

video games 101, 124, 199–200
Vietnam 15, 29, 41, 59–60, 69, 71–75, 81, 85, 91–94, 98, 105, 111, 123, 127, 170
violence 55–57, 64, 71, 75, 103, 105, 108, 111, 157, 167, 173, 176, 183, 184, 186, 189, 192, 212, 233, 241
Viper 134
Vision 15, 80, 193, 226
Voting Rights Act 71

Waid, Mark 155
Wakanda 214, 226
Walker, Jonh 7, 10, 132–135, 138, 155, 202, 206, 233, 236–238; *see also* Bucky; Captain America; Rogers, Steve; U.S. Agent; Walker, John; Wilson, Sam
Wall Street 22, 115, 119, 120, 121, 123, 135, 138, 169, 190
War on Terror 33, 141, 167, 172, 177, 181, 184, 186, 189, 194
Warner Brothers 101, 147, 150, 201
Watchdogs 16, 133, 202–204, 233
Watchmen 115, 124–125, 148
Watergate 17, 91–93, 98, 105–107, 113, 118, 121, 133, 197, 240
websites: Amazon 143, 193, 198; Google 143, 198; YouTube 191, 193, 198, 219, 227
Wertham, Fredric 55–57, 58; *see also Seduction of the Innocent*
What If...? 37, 231
Whedon, Joss 147, 201, 223, 224
Whip Inflation Now *see* WIN
Whitewash Jones 40
Will & Grace 146, 160
William Burnside 202–203
Wilson, Sam 7, 14, 16–17, 18, 34, 63, 84, 103, 129, 130, 131, 157, 182, 191, 193, 205–208, 211, 212–215, 224, 230–231, 235–238, 241; *see also* Bucky; Captain America; Falcon; Rogers, Steve; Walker, John
WIN 99
Winter Soldier *see* Bucky
Wonder Woman 13, 18, 35, 40, 47, 65–66, 80, 88, 103, 201, 216, 220
World War I 6, 21, 25–26, 29, 44, 48, 50, 52, 235
World War II 1–3, 6–8, 11, 12, 14–18, 21, 29, 32–33, 34–35, 37, 39, 41–43, 45, 46, 48, 49–50, 51, 52, 53–54, 56, 57, 59, 61–68, 70, 72, 74–75, 79–88, 90, 91, 97–98, 100, 102–103, 107, 110, 111, 119, 124, 127, 131, 133, 139, 141, 152, 155, 156, 159–160, 168, 175, 177–178, 181–182, 184–185, 189–190,

193, 203, 208, 219, 220, 222, 224, 227, 229–230, 233, 234
WWF 132

X-Men 2, 8, 13, 18, 67, 78–79, 102, 106, 125–127, 148, 150, 151, 156, 165, 175, 177, 201, 204, 206, 221, 225
X-Men: God Loves, Man Kills 126

Yalta Conference 48
Young Allies 40, 232–233
Young Men 21, 22, 27, 44, 57–59, 71, 89, 103, 200
YouTube *see* websites

Zemo 130, 157, 206, 225

www.ingramcontent.com/pod-product-compliance
Lightning Source LLC
Chambersburg PA
CBHW032034300426
44117CB00009B/1054